CRIMINAL JUSTICE HISTORY

CRIMINAL JUSTICE HISTORY is an international forum for the history and analysis of crime and criminal justice. It annually publishes research and historiographical articles, comparative and interpretive essays, conference assessments, research notes, book review essays, and reviews. The annual encourages submissions from authors in any part of the world in disciplines such as history, law, anthropology, sociology, political science, and the criminal justice sciences that relate specifically to the history of crime and criminal justice and to its broader social, historical, legal, and institutional contexts in any geographical area or period.

Board of Editors

CRIMINAL JUSTICE HISTORY

AN INTERNATIONAL ANNUAL

Volume 12
1991

Greenwood Press
Westport, Connecticut • London

ISBN: 0–313–28318–4
ISSN: 0194–0953

First published in 1993

Greenwood Press, 88 Post Road West, Westport, CT 06881
An imprint of Greenwood Publishing Group, Inc.

Printed in the United States of America

The paper used in this book complies with the Permanent Paper Standard issued by the National Information Standards Organization (Z39.48–1984).

10 9 8 7 6 5 4 3 2 1

Contents

Preface

Reviewing the peregrinations of this Annual from its inception in 1980 to the present, there have been some major shifts in the scholarly literature which have been represented on its pages. The first two volumes reflected that literature in the study of the national areas of Britain, France and the United States, and of the topics of crime, criminality and law enforcement. The volumes for 1982–90 continued this focus on the national areas of the Atlantic world, but with more contributions on the topics of prisons and punishments—reflecting the growth of literature in the field of corrections. A subtle change in subject matter, however, can be seen in the volumes for 1988–90. Here there was more emphasis on social crime and the human dimension, on issues such as class, social perceptions, and ideology.

This volume, and the one which will follow, reflect some of the broader work of the discipline. In addition, the book review section is being expanded to reflect the increasing number of prominent works which are being published. While the Atlantic world is still paramount in our pages, there are now chapters on Asia, the South Pacific, and the republics of the Soviet Union. While crime and Criminality are still at the forefront, there are more chapters on policing, penology, and economic and jurisprudential issues. This volume reflects these research interests as follows.

The fast-growing literature on the history of policing has been overwhelming in the current scholarly environment. David Taylor, exploring the police role in an English industrial city in the mid-nineteenth century, reveals how the police force became an alternative form of employment for the Victorian working class. By examining the local police records, he has been able to form conclusions on their social and demographic origins, their standard of living, and their work regimes and careers within the context of other trades in an industrial region.

Haia Shpayer-Makov provides a contrasting view of the London Metropolitan Police at the end of the century. Using the rich records which survive for one of the largest police forces in the world at that time, he is able to form conclusions on their roles in regulating public order, providing municipal and welfare services, enforcing social norms, and arbitrating moral behavior. Rather than being despised, the police were seen by the working class as agents for the transmission of consensual values.

A similar portrait of a local police force is attained by John Weaver in his study of the police force of Hamilton, Ontario, Canada, in the second quarter of the twentieth century. Using a rich collection of archival materials,Weaver is also able to show the multivarious duties which engaged the service of these men from not only tasks such as those noted in the studies above, but also tasks such as subduing domestic disputes, tending to lost children, sheltering the homeless, and maintaining the ambulance service. The great detail in his records base enables him to make quantitative conclusions on recorded arrests, prosecutions and sentences, and the social and economic status of culprits and victims, as well as relating by example the world of petty crime on the streets of the city.

Recorded crime results in punishment, and the works of John Howard have long been widely read. Robert G. Waite explores the history of the reform movement of penitentiaries in the nineteenth century from experiments in Britain to New South Wales, Ireland, and the United States. Examining the Shift from incarceration to rehabilitation, he illuminates the roles of Alexander Maconochie, Walter Crofton, and Zebulon Brockway at the prisons in Norfolk Island, Dublin, Elmira, and Cherry Hill, as well as the issues and problems which had to be overcome.

The issues of what constitutes "correction" in the nineteenth century are at the heart of Russell C. Smandych's study of the origins and role of Canada's first penitentiary at Kingston, Ontario. Smandych examines the thoughts and ideology of the rulers of the colony, and provides a re-examination of the penitentiary as an instrument of social control, as well as the vested interests which ensured its construction.

While prisons became prominent in the nineteenth century, corporal and capital publishment date from earlier centuries. Douglas M. Peers examines how Britain, and the East India Company, used the institution of torture to assist in the establishment of a police state in the Madras presidency of India in the first half of the nineteenth century. His study reaches a number of chilling conclusions on how the police can use a very broadly defined criminal code to advance their own personal interests, as well as those of the stae; and how a state can deny the use of a system (such as torture) on the one hand, and use it systematically on the other.

Capital punishment has not been unique to "western" society. In a sweeping survey of socialist countries, Andrew Scobell provides a history of its use in China, Cuba, the German Democratic Republic, and the former Soviet

Union since 1917. Taking the reader through the four stages of state development in each of these countries, he is able to conclude how, and why, capital punishment was used in some socialist countries and not in others. His study, moreover, places the role of capital punishment in their criminal justice systems, and looks at the view from below (the people) as well as that from above (the state).

The crime problem in socialist countries is not unlike that of capital, or consuming ones, especially as these distinctions have become blurred with the technological revolution of the late twentieth century. Whether or not high crime rates accompany industrialization is the problem which Eric A. Johnson addresses in his reassessment of crime and industrialization in nineteenth-and twentieth-century Europe. Surveying the quatitative school, and authors such as Dirk Blasius and Howard Zehr, Johnson comes to several conclusions on crime rates and long-term change, and places recorded crime in the United States within this European context. As David Englander suggests in his review essay of two recent works which address quantitative crime, the perceived great disparity between real and recorded crime is a subject which is still in need of both theoretical and quantitative work.

Criminal activity begets prosecution, and the suspect, police, the prosecutor, and the judge form a network leading to a judgment which is often called the criminal justice system, but which at its core can be seen as a situationally negotiated transaction. Joseph L. Tropea takes us into the land of criminal jurisprudence in the Anglo-Saxon, or common law world, to explore the informal relations that existed behind the formal institutions. Beginning with the pre-Norman Conquest frankish jury, and perambulating through manorial, feudal, pre-modern and modern courts, Tropea is able to identity these relations and their assuptions, principles, and expectations. The story of how popular justice was transformed into state rule is not only informative for itself, but it also provides us with clues for dealing with the reform of those institutions which have come down to us.

Situationally Negotiated Transactions and Domination: From Tribe to Rational-Legal Order in the Anglo-American Legal Tradition

Joseph L. Tropea
George Washington University

Introduction

Modern state domination is made up of bureaucratic, legal, techno-scientific, and professional rule regimes, including procedures for apprehending, judging, and sanctioning persons. Yet authorities negotiate as well as follow official rules, which challenges the state's organizing principles. As a result, situationally negotiated transactions are not treated as a deep-seated part of the state's administration.[1] Indeed, they are explained by contingencies—resource shortages, policy problems, organizational subcultures, an ahistorical decision-making mode of "discretion," even personality.[2] The problem of reconciling situationally negotiated transactions with modern state authority is related to overdrawn distinctions between rational-legal domination and older forms of popular justice.

The distinction between modern and traditional authority is shaped by ideals of bureaucracy and deductive law. For example, Max Weber viewed bureaucracy as the "most rational form of organization" and saw in the pandectist codes the best approximation of a deductive legal system, contrasted with England's inductive law.[3] Rational-legal authority is understood to derive from a coherent system of organizing principles or rules, not a loose collection of moral or ethical exhortations. Its agents are rule-governed and methodical. They apply systematic knowledge, technical as well as legal, within a hierarchy of impersonal roles. Principled distinctions are made between legal and extra-legal norms and factors. Conversely, state authority, whose actions are not derivable from a coherent system of formal rules and principles, and which negotiates outcomes to fit concrete situations, is by definition and precept not modern or rational, thus making such transactions problematic.[4]

The development of the state is also associated with the destruction of blood feuds and "primitive" conciliatory proceedings.[5] This view and the use of ideal paradigms to characterize rational-legal order combine to obscure negotiation's place in the making of modern state order. This is nowhere more apparent than in the development of the English common law regime which, unlike the pandectist codes, was coterminous with centuries-old trial-and-error processes of transforming popular justice into national rule. This chapter views situationally negotiated transactions as part of the historical process. They are treated as a deep-seated organizing mode, from tribal society through incipient state formation to modern rule.

Governing Dilemma and Rationale

While the premodern significance of situationally negotiated transactions is well recognized, their place in state rule is not so well established. This place is founded in a core dilemma in governing. This dilemma is constituted by the imperative of rules and the prerogative of coercion, when the exercise of either makes authority problematic. This dilemma is moderated in concrete situations by negotiating the application of state rules and coercion—which become institutionalized actions. This dilemma and process are illustrated in historical cases that have been selected to show clearly how negotiated transactions became deep-seated and institutionalized in the making of modern order.

The place of negotiated transactions in tribal practices and in premodern edicts is briefly discussed in the following section, as is the inability of such practices or edicts to foster modern law. Then, structural bases for the eleventh century's seminal significance in the transition to the modern era are reviewed—bases which suggest little place for situationally negotiated transactions in state rule. Following sections illustrate this place through six institutions in the history of Anglo-American justice: the Frankish jury subsequent to the Norman Conquest, the manoral court during the feudal period, the justice of the peace emergent during feudalism's breakup, criminal sanctioning in early capitalism's development, nineteenth-century urban American policing, and modern court reforms.

Negotiated transactions were integral to practices in these institutions. They moderated the dilemma of governing, framed by the imperative of rules and the prerogative of coercion, and in the process laid foundations for the making of the modern state. The chronology and historical contexts in which these practices developed and their significance in building state rule are briefly summarized as follows.

The Normans, by incorporating Anglo-Saxon practices in their rule, interrelated central institutions and customary actions, which aided their domination and incipient state formation. The Frankish jury and its negotiated transactions show this process. The authority of feudal lords was enabled or limited by contingencies facing the Crown; from below, it oscillated between license and fealty obligations. The manorial court shows how negotiated outcomes moderated the problematics of feudal order and nurtured rights that matured in modern law. With the devolution of feudal order, the justice of the peace became an institution whose negotiated order helped shape the Crown's influence and central-local linkages. Early capitalism needed state coercion to protect it, and the socialization of persons into accepting such exercise of power. The negotiable exercise of criminal sanctioning abetted both the power and pedagogy of state rule. Changes in production, economic transactions, and migration made industrial social order difficult. Nineteenth-century American police practices show how negotiated transactions aided state authority in this tumultuous period. Finally, progressive-era reforms in the United States challenged negotiated transactions in many areas of state rule. Their surreptitious persistence in criminal justice, and as elements of official reforms, shows their place in modern administration.

Tribal Justice

Negotiated transactions are often identified with tribal justice. There, in dispute-settlement forums, negotiated outcomes provided situationally specific justice which entwined governance and normative order. Such practices were codified in the sixth and seventh centuries. Edicts or "laws" of the barbarians (*leges barbarorum*) provided forums for the negotiated settlement of disputes and alternatives to the blood feud.[6] Other pre-millennium examples show similar practices, such as a sixth-century bishop from Tourain who used his position to mediate between the law and parties in dispute. Such practices and edicts, however, did not foster modern law. Indeed, they are understood in lieu of law, exercised in a world of obstacles, not pathways, to legal development. Dispute-settlement assemblies were not independent bodies of professional jurists; decisions were made by community consensus, edicts had no conceptual unity or capacity for organic growth, and the "ability to buy off the spear or bear it" marginalized judgment and enforcement.[7] Many efforts such as that of the sixth-century bishop's were aborted or enfeebled for want of a structure within which they could be nurtured.[8]

The world of the sixth and seventh centuries changed in the eleventh with the centralization of ecclesiastical and secular authority that reached down through delegated officials to create institutional structures in which practices of governing were responsible to a "center." The center's actors, by codifying general rules and exercising "higher judgments," produced a corpus of law that was liberated from context. The importance of these structural changes in the making of modern law and the state is well established.[9] Yet, little place is found for negotiated transactions in this historical process.

Negotiated Order—The Jury

The Normans were brutal in conquest but effective in ruling. After the rebellions of 1067–71, only 2,000 foreign knights and 250 "incomers" remained to control the land and a population of about 1.5 million. Under such conditions, destroying Anglo-Saxon structures would have been unwise for Norman rule. Not surprisingly, William the Conqueror kept the local Anglo-Saxon courts, and Henry I incorporated their reanimation in his judicial restructuring. In the meantime, Norman rule depended on the organization of shires and hundreds and the habit of settling property disputes at county court meetings. These developments facilitated state formation by linking local and central institutions. Thus, the Frankish jury shows how negotiated order aided the process of state formation.[10]

The Frankish jury, a prerogative right of kings, came to England by the Conquest. It was used for administrative as well as judicial purposes, for accusation and trial; it found "false officials" as well as criminals, not so much in making justice (*judicia facere*) as in ascertaining the truth (*recognoscere veritatem*).[11] Royal authority was exercised in calling forth a jury of the district's "most responsible persons in the neighborhood."[12] Yet, the jury worked like a community meeting where the rule of law was negotiated and learned, not just a forum where rules were imposed. "Jury nullification" (discretion in favor of a defendant whom the jury nonetheless believed to have committed the action with which he was charged) was part of this system, as was asking an accused whether he would submit to a trial by a second jury chosen from neighbors present—a practice that lasted until 1772. This jury welded local interests and incipient state rule in governance. Its negotiable enforcement of the king's law was a small price for the king to pay if it enhanced his rule, which was also imposed on local lords through formal regulations of the assizes.[13]

Within a century of the Conquest, the jury was established throughout the realm. Henry II's administration depended on it to identify criminals and decide property cases. Questions of land holdings, including the church's, were put to its verdict: "the king himself will protect by royal writ and inquest of neighbours every seisin (possession) of a free tenant."[14] The Magna Carta enshrined these practices as principles. Jury-based discretion and negotiated outcomes, in adapting general rules to situations, influenced other institutions and practices. These included bailiffs' negotiable enforcement of fines and the king's ignoring statutory price regulations.[15]

The jury linked communal, feudal, and royal authority, enabling a small elite to rule. Like a tribal forum fitted to monarchy, it entwined negotiation and governing in adapting the king's rule to the locale. It provided information on the misconduct of royal officers as well as moderated conflict by providing an alternative to ordeal or battle. From problem determination to disclosure and verdict, the jury served governance by dealing with crimes that threatened the peace through negotiation among "neighbours."

Negotiated Obligations—The Manorial Court

The problematics of feudal authority are shown by the passage of entire hundreds into private hands, loss of jurisdictional and fiscal control to holders of franchises, the break-up of popular courts, overlapping territorial jurisdictions, and conflicting prerogatives among different levels in the social hierarchy. The manor's governance was made difficult by an open-field system of production in which strips of land were scattered among peasant families. This system produced conflict over common rights, arable meadow and pasture, movement and use of animals in plowing, and coordination of sowing and harvesting. Many problems were associated with power, obligation, and dependence in the feudal hierarchy—a hierarchy on which rested defense of the manor, economy, and community, as well as royal authority. The problem occurred between king and lord as well as between lord and villein. Roman law was even tried in the absence of custom to resolve these problems.[16]

Custom imposed few limits on the lords vis-à-vis serfs and peasants. The lords could make "the lives of their unfree tenants miserable by using every advantage that law and custom gave them."[17] Still, manorial estates depended on the villeins. This unstable relationship between coercion and dependence, from above and below the local lord in the feudal hierarchy, produced conflicts that were moderated by both the development of general rules and the manorial court's adaptations. Post-eleventh century obligations between lord and serf were subjected to the law's more precise regulation, which limited the services a lord could require. Still, applying general rules in a community with personal obligations and traditional rights was difficult.[18]

The manorial court's negotiated order moderated conflicts among law, common rights and obligations, and local rule making and administration, while adapting to lord-specific domination. Although lords' interests were omnipresent, records show that the court—whose members included serfs—did not always protect them. This court was "an assembly of cultivators" with "participatory adjudication" that handled matters, now distinguished as criminal and civil, through "deliberation and discovery."[19] It abetted governance and the rule of law between peasant and lord, created manorial law, and, through its autonomy and notions of rights, nurtured principles of modern law. In fact, "by the twelfth century all peasants in Western Christiandom, including serfs, had legally protected rights."[20] The demise of feudal society undercut the manor's significance, but not the importance of negotiated order.

Negotiated Administration—The Justice of the Peace

Changes in fealty, commerce, trade, law, labor law offenses, criminal trespasses, forceable entries, and riots accompanied the demise of feudal society. The English gentry ascended in the late medieval period as landowners, employers, and—unlike its Continental counterpart—as resident rulers. A fifteenth-century statute mandated "that justices of the peace be possessed of lands yielding £20 per annum." It was in this capacity that they administered public order in this and later centuries.[21]

The role of justice of the peace was only part of the gentry's local domination. As landowners, they were involved in many other ways in the lives of those over whom they had official authority.[22] Although local and paternal rulers, the justices were appointed by the lord chancellor. In this sense, their position was also "national":

> It is the English Constitution alone that the Security of the peace is committed by the Prince of Men of Ample Fortunes in the respective Neighbourhoods; not to venal Magistrates, but to Gentlemen who serve their country most commonly at their own Charges; not to strangers, who can ill distinguish between the Oath of the Honest Man and the Knave, but to such whose knowledge of their neighbours enables them to make a proper Judgment of the Testimony produced before them.[23]

Knowledge of "neighbourhoods," status, and "Ample Fortunes" were important in order to administer law. "As the patriarchal voice" of the community, as "mediator of his neighbourhood," the justice was advised to settle disputes "without recourse to formal legal proceedings," that is, to negotiate order.[24]

This system produced dilemmas. Although justices' interests were local, they represented central power. They maintained common law and traditions of the ancient order, but were also an emergent social and political class. They governed persons with whom they were familiar and otherwise engaged, which gave problems to royal authority: The king's law was not always applied. Yet, their local knowledge, involvement, and negotiated justice was a basis for royal rule. Still, the Crown was compromised by dependence on justices so engaged in local affairs, a problem that was addressed in part by legislation enacted in 1349. The law gave justices the authority to use truncated procedures and summary justice, which diminished a reliance on jurors, who were often even more unwilling to enforce the law.[25]

Justices adapted law for many reasons. Their origins were in the House of Commons and they, not central government, built petty sessions. They were well represented in Parliament vis-à-vis the Crown with a limited administration. There was no public prosecutor, and the criminal law depended on the victim's initiative and the subjects' cooperation. Justices were voluntary, unpaid officers, and their negotiated justice was a resource as well as a bane for the king: It enabled bargaining with hostile peasants, enhanced civil liberties, and, compared to the Continent, moderated England's reliance on torture.[26]

The justice of the peace was an institution of "joint enterprise" between central and local powers, one in which both the king and the people submitted to political discipline, and one in which "respect for custom implied the duties of self-restraint no less than the right to assert privilege."[27] It was not easily replaced by "objective" law. (A stipendiary magistry was not established until 1792.) The judges of the central courts, who lacked a community-based position of power, admired the justices' ability to use their local position and serve as "autonomous rulers," "resident representatives," and "ideal governors."[28] Judges' power, unlike that of justices', rested more narrowly on criminal sanctioning, which was made effective through its negotiable exercise.

Negotiated Sanctions—Criminal Law and State Rule

Transformation to a mercantile economy increased property movement as well as crime, which challenged the protection of wealth. The *Carriers* case, resolved in 1473, showed the inadequacies of traditional trespass laws vis-à-vis movable property offenses.[29] Two centuries later, the development and rationalization of wealth produced vigorous measures to protect property; capital offense statutes increased fourfold between 1688 and 1820. Yet, the sanctioning power these laws allowed underscored a dilemma: Its rigorous exercise might produce political and social conflict, while the failure not to exercise it could deny men the interests of property.[30]

The gentry were as much concerned with civil authority as with protecting property. Punishment might produce terror and undermine their rule: "Let civil governors . . . be admonished that the physical strength resides in the governed."[31] When a chief justice ordered a Cornish rioter's body to hang in chains, the local gentry warned him:

> In the present circumstances of affairs it would be more advisable not to do it, for tho' his crimes, as your Lordship says, demand the most terrifying Example yet there must be the greatest regard had for the Peace of our Country, which we were apprehensive might be again disturbed if that measure was pursued.[32]

Sanctioning power was critical but precarious. Its negotiable exercise, however, aided magistrates in managing public order "with delicacy and circumspection" and force. This increased the effectiveness of terror and mercy. Judges could invoke the law or grant mercy: "To punish or forgive worked in the same way to maintain the fabric of obedience, gratitude and deference."[33] They could also "terrorize the petty thief and then command his gratitude."[34]

When elite control administering the law increased in the seventeenth and eighteenth centuries, negotiable sanctioning was particularly important. It enabled magistrates to mediate between traditional doctrines of the rights of the poor and ascendant property interests. Magistrates might sanction property offenses when the poor were victims, and thereby demonstrate concern for them and the "universality" of property laws. They might be harsh when gentlemen suffered losses to show state power and wealth's importance. They might take no action, or act through the pardon or reprieve, to exhibit mercy: Only half of those condemned to death in the eighteenth century went to the gallows.[35] The "erratic and capricious" use of exemplary hangings, pardons, and reprieves contributed to public order and deference. Such actions might not derive from the principles of the modern law, but they had a place in its making.[36]

The presence of yeomen, husbandmen, men of "middling status," and gentry as victims and participants in prosecuting complaints, challenged the institution of justice in responding to many interests, including those of the legal elite. Defendants were mostly locals, seeking in crime a "modest redistribution of income."[37] Court proceedings were "both national and local, coercive and responsive, elitist and participatory,"[38] showing compromise as well as force in law's application. Seventeenth-century assizes and quarter sessions, "parliaments of the shires," were as much a part of local life as a structure imposed from above.[39]

Negotiated sanctioning was evident in many parishes, which aided elite interests. Houses were repaired in return for forgiveness; bonds were posted to not offend again; choices were given to leave the neighborhood; prosecutions were threatened only to ensure future good behavior; compensations were made for crimes; appeals for mercy were accepted; and prosecutions were dropped for fear of reprisal as well as compassion.[40]

Negotiated sanctioning, rather than its uncritical exercise, aided state legitimation and helped socialize the English people into accepting, even respecting, law. This, in turn, shaped a culture that encouraged the rule of law, something that was lacking in the colonies. There, various peoples, states, and regions made governing problematic. The refuge for negotiated justice in law's administration—which justice became an American characteristic—became no more apparent or notorious than in its nineteenth-century city.[41]

The Negotiated Municipality—The Metropolitan Police

Municipal government in America remained a "conspicuous failure" a century after France had a relatively efficient system of public administration. Post-Civil War industrialization, urban growth, and immigration exacerbated problems of governing, as did crime. While many charges brought in the eighteenth century involved attacks on officers of the law, by 1860 about ten percent of New York City's population had a criminal record. Then, old elites were ineffective in imposing law on newcomers. Brokers exchanged votes for jobs, goods, and contracts. Public officials' patronage foiled market development. Business transactions, too, were guided as much by obligation as by contract.[42] Personal transactions among "family, church, school, ethnic societies, labor unions, even political clubs, and the ward and precinct ... kept society from going to pieces in the big cities."[43] Negotiated transactions permeated city administration, commerce, and party structures, and framed the environment in which the American metropolitan police developed.[44]

Although modeled after the London Metropolitan Police Department, which was created by an act of Parliament in 1829 and continued under that body's scrutiny, nineteenth-century American metropolitan police administration was difficult, in some cases oscillating between state and local control. Ward politics encapsulated its command structure. Patrolmen were politically appointed residents of the areas in which they worked, their positions often dependent on election results. Superiors warned patrolmen to "learn the people residing or doing business on your beat.... You may need their aid, and their favor will add much to your power."[45] Indeed, an arrest could involve dragging a person blocks to the precinct, an act difficult without community "favor."[46]

Sentiments varied, often by neighborhood, and there were problems when they were not taken into account. Closing the saloons on Sunday in New York's "little Germany," for example, produced three days of rioting.[47] Pluralism in the city also affirmed local and negotiable justice:

> In some districts where foreign-born abound, a trusted inspector or captain makes the difference to whole neighborhoods between happiness and despair.... He is wise and patient, settling out of court, without arrests, without cost or any loss of self-respect to the people, many a case that comes to him, in which a less humane officer would mechanically make an arrest.[48]

Superiors often cautioned patrolmen on the side of prudence:

> If you find yourself in a position not knowing exactly what to do, better do too little than too much; it is easier to excuse a moderate course than an overt act.[49]

Some patrolmen were so effective in securing community support that citizens warned them of their supervisors: "Friendly citizens who take note of the uniformed roundsman can warn the patrolman of his approach ... can sound the warning word if there is any danger to a patrolman who is off his post, conversing, or probably in-doors."[50] Negotiated justice, however, was not always well received. Philadelphia policemen, for example, "drew criticism from the press when they separated two combatants, 'mildly asking them to desist,' instead of immediately arresting them."[51] The dilemma, framed by law and coercion, was pronounced on the patrolman's "beat" but moderated by situationally negotiated transactions.

Patrolmen were like English justices. Responsive to local interests, they used law as a resource in negotiating transactions, moderated sanctions vis-à-vis local people while they punished vagrants, and showed mercy, wrath, and capriciousness. Yet, the behavior of patrolmen is overly identified with corruption and violence. Nineteenth-century police are considered the "most pronounced failure in our unhappy municipal history," a form of "delegated vigilantism."[52] Such a normative and limited focus on American police obscures both the long-term role of situationally negotiated transactions in pre-modern England and their pervasiveness in the organization of the nineteenth-century American city. It also obscures their place in modern society and the challenge they pose to it.

Such transactions pose a strategic problem for modern society: They encumber its economy. Trans-local markets require procedures and rules for transaction predictability in varied contexts. Building infrastructures, implementing technology, investing, and planning are thwarted within a welter of locally negotiated transactions. Consequently, "doing business" was unpredictable in the nineteenth-century city, a problem that was ameliorated only through major restructuring. Contract law enhanced transaction predictability in commerce, "home rule" reduced state legislatures' deleterious interventions in municipal affairs, and city-wide representation and the reduction of city council and school board members moderated ward politics.

These changes aided municipal administration and civil service reform, made a place for the expert, shaped rational-legal order, and limited the role of negotiation in many areas—including that of criminal justice. Still, creating and enforcing rule regimes are two different things. Official rule regimes do not guarantee situational domination; the core dilemma remains, even exacerbated by modern rules and procedures.[53]

Negotiated Order—Rational-Legal Administration

The Frankish jury, manorial court, justice of the peace, criminal sanctioning, and nineteenth-century policing show situational domination to be difficult without negotiation. Older law was authoritative but its implementation was didactic; principle did not prohibit its situational adaptation. Rational-legal order is different. Bureaucratic and legal authority, staff and technical experts, make and direct rules from an institutional apex. Subordinate agents and citizens negotiating such directives are not part of its logic: The control of rational-legal order is imperative.[54]

Expert control challenges social meanings that shaped local transactions in premodern society. It limits discourse between state agents and citizens. This exclusivity of rational-legal order and its supportive culture censure the negotiation of law's meaning and application among subordinate agents and citizens; indeed, the state's protection of individual rights rests on this. Yet, the dilemma of state authority, framed by the imperative of rules and the prerogative of coercion, remains in day-to-day encounters. Rational-legal order, by limiting the public and discursive character of enforcement, encourages a more surreptitious moderation of this dilemma.[55]

From the nineteenth century, at least, American police have exercised two major options in moderating this dilemma. First, they avoid situations where enforcement would produce problems: "A policeman is therefore apt to be cautious and to refrain from taking action if there is doubt."[56] This is limited as an official strategy. Second, "discretion" moderates rule enforcement, although it, too, is limited as an official strategy. It strikes at the core of rational-legal order by suggesting idiosyncrasy rather than rules guides criminal justice administration. Because avoidance and discretion may abort rather than affirm the rule of law, they are problematic as official parts of even local domination.[57]

As in the historical cases of the Anglo-American tradition, modern state agents negotiate situationally specific rules and procedures. Unlike the past, however, rational-legal order prohibits these transactions and rules as authoritative and didactic exercises in adjusting law to the situation. Consequently, such transactions and rules, although reproduced over decades, may be kept "backstage." An example was plea bargaining, a process for negotiating outcomes by a police-criminal-prosecutor-judge network, rather than following the criminal courts' formal rules and procedures, particularly the jury trial. Plea bargaining has become so much a part of state administration, however, that it is "front stage" and not proscribed by the Supreme Court.[58]

Situationally negotiated transactions are not confined to modern state agents and criminals. They are constructed, as in the nineteenth-century city, by police and community actors:

> When the rookie officer first walks or drives his beat, he often forgets that a long history of police-citizen interaction precedes him. He is heir to a set of mutual expectations and assumptions about his role that he may not even be aware of.[59]

Such "police-citizen interactions" adapt official rules and procedures. This is a common situation in dealing with juveniles; in many middle class areas, for example, "mutual expectations and assumptions" commonly circumscribe the referral of their young people to the juvenile court.[60]

While both interactions between the police and citizens and bargains among state agents and criminals adapt official rules and procedures, their adaptations of law's administration have no official role in governing and thus do not directly challenge central authorities or principle. Indeed, such transactions become tacit or "backstage" parts of state authority. Modern criminal justice authorities depend on consequences associated with these transactions, especially reductions in administrative costs and time. In this way, situationally negotiated transactions aid modern state rule while not overtly challenging its rational-legal character—a situation different from their incorporation into official reforms.[61]

Mediation, negotiation, and dispute-resolution show the incorporation of negotiated transactions in juvenile and criminal justice, as well as in domestic, health-care, social service, civil rights, landlord-tenant, neighborhood, educational, and environmental disputes.[62] This suggests, if not legal pluralism in administration, something contrary to legal centralism. Reforms such as the courts' adoption of dispute-resolution programs not only aid state domination but also challenge its logic.

A "tension" exists between the jurisprudential character of the courts and negotiated transactions, and between some programs and statutory authority. For example, "there has not been a statutory authorization other than through the appropriation process" or there is "no current statutory authority for proceeding."[63] This is troubling: "I don't know that the judge should be deciding this at all.... You ought to tell the legislatures that it's their responsibility if they want to change the system of justice."[64] Legal theorists have problems in justifying some programs, which is not the case for administrators.[65]

The success of court-administered arbitration is measured by the reduction in trial cases. In civil cases, arbitration is often determined by monetary value, where cost disincentives discourage appeals. Coercion as well as negotiation expedite non-trial action. This has led some to suggest that support for court-administered arbitration comes from judges "who don't like little cases," or that there is a class aspect to "informal justice."[66] Also, arbitration is discontinued if it is not administratively efficient.[67]

Law and bureaucracy shape the court. Yet, using negotiated transactions to resolve dilemmas of its rational-legal order contradicts its theoretical underpinnings. While "innovative" programs affirm the long-term and deep-seated role of negotiated transactions, unprincipled mixing of "primitive conciliation" and contract in a system of imperative control suggests problems in the administration of law. Yet, administrators, long ago, "learned that when a legal system does not exist it may be necessary to invent one," and "what is left is law, however we write it and wherever we find it."[68] "It" will likely include negotiated transactions, in official or tacit forms.

Conclusion

Negotiated transactions, it has been argued, moderate the dilemma between rule-governed and coercive domination. This was illustrated in the institutional development of Anglo-American law and state administration. Because of this, the comparative approach was limited. Also, although a consequence of providing a long-term view, the treatment of cases was brief. Still, conceptually linking situationally negotiated transactions, surreptitious and official, to a dilemma of state domination is important. It offers a critical perspective vis-à-vis understandings built on cognitive "discretion" or organizational contingencies, and suggests a more responsible research agenda—historically, comparatively, and institutionally.

Situationally negotiated transactions must in the end be derived from principles. A search for such principles may well lead to the juggernaut of legal and bureaucratic imperatives. On the other hand, historical research may help identify incipient principles in these transactions, such as their public and pedagogical character, which did not mature in modern society. Indeed, in the development of law and bureaucracy, negotiation's public character was transformed into a furtive one. Understanding this transformation may aid in discovering or rediscovering principles from which situationally negotiated transactions may be derived or through which the juggernaut of legal and bureaucratic imperatives may be moderated.

Notes

An earlier version of this chapter was presented at the annual meeting of the American Sociological Association, Annual Meeting, San Francisco, 12 Aug. 1989.

1. Many negotiation systems are institutionalized in the modern state. They may be directly enabled by statute or established by administrative authority with fiscal support. Their purposes, forums, participants, procedures, and transaction rules are specified, and their practices are liable to principled review. In these ways, negotiated transactions are linked to the state and are "legal." Situationally negotiated transactions addressed in this chapter suffered from arbitrary rule, lacked systematic linkages to a center, and were not ensconced in principle. In these senses, they may be considered "extralegal" but not "legal" or "illegal"—distinctions that matured subsequent to most of the institutions and processes herein addressed.

2. *Max Weber on Law in Economy and Society*, Max Rheinstein (New York, 1954), 224; Randall Collins, "Rationalization: The Master Trend of History," in *Max Weber: A Skeleton Key* (Beverly Hills, Calif., 1986), 22–23, 61–79; Anthony T. Kronman, *Max Weber* (Stanford, 1983), 75–77, 80, 88–96; H. W. Arthurs, *Without the Law: Administrative Justice and Legal Pluralism in Nineteenth-Century England* (Toronto, 1985), 194, 206; President's Commission on Crime in the District of Columbia, *Report of the President's Commission on Crime in the District of Columbia* (Washington, D.C., 1966); President's Commission on Law Enforcement and Administration of Justice, *The Courts* (Washington, D.C., 1967); Elizabeth Reuss-Ianni, *Two Cultures of Policing: Street Cops and Management Cops* (New Brunswick, N.J., 1983); John F. Padgett, "Plea Bargaining in the Federal Courts: 1908–1934," paper presented at the annual meeting of the American Sociological Association, Atlanta, Georgia, Aug. 1988; Tom R. Burns and Helena Flam, *The*

Shaping of Social Organization: Social Rule System Theory with Applications (London, 1987), 213–40; Joseph L. Tropea and Henryk Sterniczuk, "Rule Regimes and Backstage Processes: Organizing Production and Justice," *Human Systems Management* 7 (1988): 243–51.

3. Kronman, *Max Weber*, 88.

4. Collins, "Rationalization," 22–23; Kronman, *Max Weber*, 75–77, 80, 89–96; Burns and Flam, *Shaping of Social Organization*, 217; Arthurs, *Without the Law*, 194, 206.

5. Rheinstein, *Max Weber*, 224.

6. Harold J. Berman, *Law and Revolution: The Formation of the Western Legal Tradition* (Cambridge, Mass., 1983), 53–54.

7. Ibid., 54.

8. Laura Nader and Harry F. Todd, Jr., eds., *The Disputing Process: Law in Ten Societies* (New York, 1978); Edward James, " 'Beati pacifici': Bishops and the Law, in Sixth Century Gaul," in *Disputes and Settlements: Law and Human Relations in the West*, ed. John Bossy (Cambridge, 1983), 26; Randall Collins, *Weberian Sociological Theory* (Cambridge, 1986), 85.

9. Marc Bloch, *Feudal Society: Social Classes and Political Organization*, trans. L. A. Manyon (Chicago, 1961), 2: 429; Berman, *Law and Revolution*, 86; Collins, *Weberian Sociological Theory*; Doris M. Stenton, *English Justice Between the Norman Conquest and the Great Charter, 1066–1215* (Philadelphia, 1964), 65.

10. S. F. C. Milsom, *The Legal Framework of English Feudalism* (London, 1966), 151; M. T. Clanchy, *England and Its Rulers: Foreign Lordship and National Identity* (Totowa, N.J., 1983), 62–65; Maurice Powicke, *Medieval England, 1066–1485* (London, 1950), 208; Bloch, *Feudal Society*, 429–30.

11. G. G. Coulton, *Medieval Panorama: The English Scene from Conquest to Reformation* (Cambridge, 1939), 367; Sir Frederick Pollock and Frederic William Maitland, *The History of English Law: Before the Time of Edward I* (Cambridge, 1968; orig. ed. 1895), 1: 139–40.

12. Edward Jenks, *A Short History of English Law: From the Earliest Times to the End of the Year 1919* (Boston, 1922), 47.

13. Pollock and Maitland, *History of English Law*, 1: 139–40; Clanchy, *England and Its Rulers*, 147–57; Milsom, *Legal Framework*, 36; Jenks, *Short History*, 23, 47, 51.

14. Pollock and Maitland, *History of English Law*, 1: 146.

15. Dorothy Whitelock et al., *The Norman Conquest: Its Setting and Impact* (New York, 1966), 150–52; Clanchy, *England and Its Rulers*, 64–65, 146–47; Thomas Andrew Green, *Verdict According to Conscience: Perspectives on the English Criminal Trial Jury, 1200–1800* (Chicago, 1985), xiii, xvi; Coulton, *Medieval Panorama*, 369–70; Rodney Hilton, *Class Conflict and the Crisis of Feudalism* (London, 1985), 136–37.

16. Paul Vinogradoff, *English Society in the Eleventh Century* (Oxford, 1908), 108–15, 126, 138–39; Joan Thirsk, "The Common Fields," in *Peasants, Knights and Heretics: Studies in Medieval English Social History*, ed. R. H. Hilton (Cambridge, 1976), 11; Urban Tiger Holmes, Jr., *Daily Living in the Twelfth Century: Based on the Observations of Alexander Neckam in London and Paris* (Madison, 1952), 251.

17. J. D. Griffith Davies and F. R. Worts, *England in the Middle Ages: Its Problems and Legacies* (Port Washington, N.Y., 1971; orig. ed. 1928), 68.

18. Hilton, *Class Conflict*; Robert C. Palmer, *The Whilton Dispute, 1264–1380: A Social-Legal Study of Dispute Settlement in Medieval England* (Princeton, 1984), 24, 139–40; Berman, *Law and Revolution*, 321–22; Thirsk, "Common Fields," 14; Jenks, *Short History*, 72–73.

19. Berman, *Law and Revolution*, 325.

20. Davies and Worts, *England in the Middle Ages*, 67; W. O. Ault, *Open-Field Farming in Medieval England: A Study of Village By-Laws* (London, 1972); Thirsk, "Common Fields," 10; Berman, *Law and Revolution*, 322–24; Hilton, *Class Conflict*, 238; Jenks, *Short History*, 72–73.

21. Powicke, *Medieval England*, 211; Norma Landau, *The Justices of the Peace, 1679–1760* (Berkeley, 1984), 335.

22. Ibid., 2.

23. T. Barlow, *The Justice of the Peace: A Treatise Containing the Power and Duty of that Magistrate* (London, 1745), vii–viii.

24. Landau, *Justices*, 342.

25. Powicke, *Medieval England*, 212; J. M. Beattie, *Crime and the Courts in England, 1660–1800* (Princeton, 1986), 59–65; Landau, *Justices*, 9; John G. Bellamy, *Criminal Law and Society in Late Medieval and Tudor England* (New York, 1984), 4–5.

26. Green, *Verdict*, 359; Bellamy, *Criminal Law*, 31, 111; Landau, *Justices*, 9, 344; Bertha Haven Putnam, "The Transformation of the Keepers of the Peace into the Justices of the Peace, 1327–1380," in *Transactions of the Royal Historical Society* (London, 1929), 48; John H. Langbein, *Torture and the Law of Proof: Europe and England in the Ancient Regime* (Chicago, 1977); James Heath, *Torture and English Law: An Administrative and Legal History from the Plantagenets to the Stuarts* (Westport, 1982), 9; Paul R. Hyams, "Trial by Ordeal: The Key to Proof in the Early Common Law," in *On the Laws and Customs of England: Essays in Honor of Samuel E. Thorne*, ed. Morris S. Arnold et al. (Chapel Hill, 1981), 126; Coulton, *Medieval Panorama*, 374, 379, 382.

27. Powicke, *Medieval England*, 217.

28. Lionel K. J. Glassey, *Politics and the Appointment of Justices of the Peace, 1675–1720* (Oxford, 1979), 31; Landau, *Justices*, 362, 348.

29. Raymond J. Michalowski, *Order, Law, and Crime* (New York, 1985), 86.

30. Ibid., 85–86; David Jones, *Crime, Protest, Community and Police in Nineteenth-Century Britain* (London, 1982), 11; Cynthia B. Herrup, *The Common Peace: Participation and the Criminal Law in Seventeenth-century England* (London, 1987), 5.

31. Paley, quoted in Douglas Hay, "Property, Authority, and Criminal Law," in *Albions Fatal Tree: Crime and Society in Eighteenth-Century England*, ed. Douglas Hay et al. (New York, 1975), 26.

32. Ibid., 50.

33. Beattie, *Crime and the Courts*, 430–36.

34. Hay, "Property," 26, 48–49.

35. Douglas Hay, "Property, Authority, and the Criminal Law," in *Marxism and Law*, ed. Piers Beirne and Richard Quinney (New York, 1982), 118.

36. Beattie, *Crime and the Courts*; Green, *Verdict*; Douglas Hay, "Property,

Authority, and Criminal Law," in *Albions Fatal Tree: Crime and Society in Eighteenth-Century England*, ed. Douglas Hay et al. (New York, 1975).

37. Herrup, *Common Peace*, 10.

38. Ibid., 7.

39. Ibid., 2, 6.

40. Hay, "Property," 57–58, 43; *The Paston Letters*, ed. John Warrington (London, 1975), 19–20.

41. Hay, "Property," 53; Bradley Chapin, *Criminal Justice in Colonial America, 1606–1660* (Athens, Ga., 1983), 7–10.

42. Ernest S. Griffith, *A History of American City Government: The Conspicuous Failure, 1870–1900* (New York, 1974), 68; Jon C. Teaford, *The Unheralded Triumph: City Government in America, 1870–1900* (Baltimore, 1984), 1; Kenneth Fox, *Better City Government: Innovation in American Urban Politics* (Philadelphia, 1977), 4; Douglas Greenberg, *Crime and Law Enforcement in the Colony of New York, 1691–1776* (Ithaca, N.Y., 1976), 150; Gerald Astor, *The New York Cops: An Informal History* (New York, 1971), 7.

43. Ernest S. Griffith, *A History of American City Government: The Progressive Years and Their Aftermath, 1900–1920* (Washington, D.C., 1983), 214.

44. Maurice Punch, *Conduct Unbecoming: The Social Construction of Police Deviance and Control* (London, 1985), 29; Joseph L. Tropea, "Rational Capitalism and Municipal Government: The Progressive Era," *Social Science History* 13 (2) (1989): 137–58.

45. Edward H. Savage, *A Chronological History of the Boston Watch and Police, from 1631 to 1865* (Boston, 1865), 342.

46. Roger Lane, *Policing a Great City, 1822–1885* (Cambridge, Mass. 1967), 68; James F. Richardson, *Urban Police in the United States* (Port Washington, N.Y., 1974), 38, 64; Wilbur R. Miller, *Cops and Bobbies: Police Authority in New York and London, 1830–1870* (Chicago, 1977); Frederick C. Mather, *Public Order in the Age of the Chartists* (New York, 1967), 31, 33; David R. Johnson, *Policing the Urban Underworld: The Impact of Crime on the Development of the American Police* (Philadelphia, 1979), 145, 140; Victor Bailey, "Introduction," in *Policing and Punishment in Nineteenth Century England,* ed. Victor Bailey (New Brunswick, N.J., 1981), 14.

47. Richardson, *Urban Police*, 31.

48. Arthur Woods, *Policeman and Public* (New Haven, 1919), 43.

49. Savage, *Chronological History*, 343.

50. William McAdoo, *Guarding a Great City* (New York, 1906), 26.

51. Johnson, *Policing*, 135, 143.

52. Landau, *Justices*, 9; Miller, *Cops and Bobbies*, 20, 27–28, 30–32; Richardson, *Urban Police*, 19–34, 55–61; Johnson, *Policing* 127, 131; James Q. Wilson, "Police Morale, Reform, and Citizen Respect: The Chicago Case," in *The Police: Six Sociological Essays*, ed. David J. Bordua (New York, 1967), 138; Jones, *Crime, Protest*, 19; Punch, *Conduct Unbecoming*, 29; Peter K. Manning and John Van Maanen, "Background to Policing," in *Policing: A View from the Street*, ed. Peter K. Manning and John Van Maanen (Santa Monica, Calif., 1978), 4–5; Savage, *Chronological History*; A. A. Putnam ["Judge Wiglittle," pseud.], *Ten Years a Police Court Judge* (New York, 1884); George W. Walling, *Recollections of a New York Chief of Police* (New York, 1887); William E. S. Fales, *Brooklyn's Guardians*

(Brooklyn, 1887); McAdoo, *Guarding*; Cornelius Willesme, *A Cop Remembers* (New York, 1933); Lane, *Policing a Great City*; Jonathan Rubinstein, *City Police* (New York, 1973); Griffith, *History*, 204, 329.

53. William J. Reese, *Power and Promise of School Reform: Grass-roots Movements during the Progressive Era* (Boston, 1986), 113–47; Sidney L. Harring, *Policing a Class Society: The Experience of American Cities, 1865–1915* (New Brunswick, N.J., 1983), 248–49; Samuel Walker, *A Critical History of Police Reform: The Emergence of Professionalism* (Lexington, Mass., 1977); Tropea, "Rational Capitalism"; Albert W. Alschuler, "Plea Bargaining and Its History," *Law & Society Review* 13 (1979): 211–46.

54. Anselm Strauss, *Negotiations: Varieties, Contexts, Processes, and Social Order* (San Francisco, 1978), ix; Herrup, *Common Peace*, 193; Arthurs, *Without the Law*, 194–95, 209; P. H. Gulliver, *Disputes and Negotiations: A Cross-Cultural Perspective* (New York, 1979), 5.

55. Burns and Allen, *The Shaping of Social Organization*, 213–40; Arthurs, *Without the Law*, 190; Woods, *Policeman and Public*, 28.

56. Woods, *Policeman and Public*, 29.

57. Savage, *Chronological History*, 343; William Ker Muir, *Police: Streetcorner Politicians* (Chicago, 1976), 86–87; Michael K. Brown, *Working the Street: Police Discretion and the Dilemmas of Reform* (New York, 1981), 287; Burton Atkins and Mark Pogrebin, "Introduction: Discretionary Decision-Making in the Administration of Justice," in *The Invisible Justice System: Discretion and the Law*, ed. Burton Atkins and Mark Pogrebin (Cincinnati, 1978), 1.

58. Muir, *Police*, 145; Milton Heumann, *Plea Bargaining: The Experience of Prosecutors, Judges, and Defense Attorneys* (Chicago, 1978); Malcolm M. Feeley, "Perspectives on Plea Bargaining," *Law & Society Review* 13 (1979): 199–210; Arthurs, *Without the Law*, 188–214; Tropea and Sterniczuk, "Rule Regimes"; *Santobello* v. *New York*, 404 U.S. 257, 92 S.Ct. 495 (1971); Padgett, *Plea Bargaining*, 1988.

59. Adrian Kinnane, *Policing* (Chicago, 1979), 29.

60. Michael P. Roche, *Rural Police and Rural Youth* (Charlottesville, 1985), 21, 57–58; Rubinstein, *City Police*, 324; Tropea, "Rational Capitalism," 247–48.

61. Steven Spitzer, "The Dialectics of Formal and Informal Control," in *The Politics of Informal Justice: The American Experience*, ed. Richard Abel (New York, 1982), 169–78.

62. The range of application can be noted in National Institute for Dispute Resolution, *Reports*, Nos. 1–4 (Washington, D.C., n.d.) or in the programs of the annual meetings of Society of Professionals in Dispute Resolution.

63. Hon. Robert Peckham and Rep. Robert W. Kastenmeier, statements in U.S. Congress, House Committee on the Judiciary, in *Court-Annexed Arbitration and Experimentation: Hearings before the Subcommittee on Courts, Civil Liberties, and the Administration of Justice*, 99th Cong., 2d sess. (Washington, D.C., 1986), 18, 19.

64. Alan B. Morrison, cited in "Debating Court-Ordered Arbitration," *Dispute Resolution Forum* (Aug. 1985): 7.

65. Philip J. Harter, "Regulatory Negotiation: An Overview," *Dispute Resolution Forum* (Jan. 1986): 3–4, 11–14; Arthurs, *Without the Law*, 188, 192–93; Abel, *Politics of Informal Justice*, 268–69, 300; Deborah R. Hensler, "What We Know

and Don't Know about Court-Administered Arbitration," *Judicature* 69 (5) (1986): 1–8.

66. Morrison, "Debating," 7.

67. Hensler, "What We Know," 1–4; Arthurs, *Without the Law*, 192, 200, 202–3; Abel, *Politics*, 1982; Lawrence M. Friedman and Robert V. Percival, *The Roots of Justice: Crime and Punishment in Alameda County, California, 1879–1910* (Chapel Hill, 1981), 316.

68. Arthurs, *Without the Law*, 192, 208, 11–12.

Crime and the Industrial Revolution: The German Case

Eric A. Johnson
Central Michigan University

When one thinks of the industrial revolution, Dickensian images of swollen urban populations, stinking sewage, infernal machinery, impoverished workers, sad-eyed children, and soaring crime rates come quickly to mind. Novelists, politicians, publicists, historians, and sociologists have all added their share to this by now nearly universally accepted portrait. But is it correct? Should one blithely indict the city and the mere processes of urban and industrial growth for causing violence, lawlessness, and the whole gamut of other social ills? And should scholars lend credence to the current American folk wisdom that our currently embattled cities are inexorably condemned to rot and ruin?

Whereas many North American cities today are undeniably unhappy, dangerous places, and the hardships endured during the industrial revolution in much of urban America and Europe are undeniable, my own research on Germany and France in the nineteenth and twentieth centuries, and the recent research of other scholars on the history of criminality in America, Germany, France, Great Britain, Holland, Sweden, and elsewhere have pointed to some different, perhaps surprising, conclusions about the causes of crime.[1] Over the long haul, from the Middle Ages to the present, it appears that violent crime in most of these societies has significantly decreased. Moreover, during the industrial revolution itself, there was no solid link between high crime rates and city living or city growth in several societies that have been recently studied. This chapter summarizes quantitative and qualitative findings on this subject for Germany—which, even if not always neatly overlapping, together help dispel some widely shared myths.

It is clear that no marked upsurge in criminality accompanied the economic and social changes and unsettling dislocations associated with the industrial revolution in Germany. Moreover, the size of communities, their rates of demographic and economic growth, and their predominant type of economic activity did not seriously affect criminal behavior. These findings refute the classic theories of Durkheim, Toennies, and Simmels and the warnings of various conservative political, religious, and civic leaders that urban and industrial life caused crime by means of anomie, alienation, crowding of population, and a break with church, family, and tradition. Once convincingly replicated elsewhere, such findings have both theoretical and policy implications. Politicians and citizens should eventually realize that if cities have clean streets, job opportunities, and well-housed and happy citizens, then they are likely not to have any more criminality than other types of communities.

An investigation of literary sources such as German novels, plays, short stories, and newspaper accounts serves to support and provide flesh and blood to the faceless numbers. Although the popular genre of criminal literature was less developed in Germany than in many countries, several important writers like Theodor Fontane, Gerhard Hauptmann, Wilhelm Rabbe, and Karl May wrote about crime and justice in this period.[2] An analysis of their and others' works on criminality suggests that most Germans themselves did not believe that crime was associated with urbanization or industrial change per se. Rather, the literary record shows that crime in German popular culture was most often associated with poverty, foreigners, and ethnic minorities (usually Poles or Lithuanians). The analysis of several leading newspapers from this period also shows that although crime was not usually portrayed in a prurient or even detailed fashion, most newspaper writers attributed criminality to the actions of their political enemies and to human weakness, as opposed to urban and industrial change.[3]

The Quantitative Evidence

To assess quantitatively the impact of urban and industrial change on criminal behavior it is necessary to analyze both long-term trends of national and subnational crime figures and data cutting across the entire society (or as much of the society as possible) at different points in time. It is, of course, of paramount importance to have a clear understanding of what kinds of data are being used (i.e., whether the crime figures represent conviction records, arrests, police reports, etc.), and it is always necessary to have a healthy skepticism about the accuracy of whatever data are employed. It is also widely recognized that the so-called "dark figure" in criminal data makes all findings tentative and suspect—and many have argued that criminal data reveal the actions of criminal justice officials rather than the actual amount of criminal wrongdoing. Nonetheless, all social data, not just criminal justice data, have "dark figures" which must be considered. But taking all of this into account, the German criminal justice data are perhaps exemplary in comparison with comparable data in other societies.[4] So, if the data are treated cautiously, if a variety of measures of "crime" are employed and analyzed with various and appropriate techniques, and if the results consistently point toward the same conclusions, then it is possible to make some assertions with at least a measure of validity. Furthermore, the validity of the quantitative results is strengthened if serious analysis of appropriate qualitative data points toward the same conclusions.

As early as the late nineteenth century, several German sociologists and criminologists, including Georg von Mayr, Wilhelm Starke, and Gustav Aschaffenburg, made serious headway in analyzing primarily time-series and tabular data.[5] More recently their findings have been reexamined, added to, and treated with modern statistical techniques by several historians, including German scholars like Dirk Blasius and American scholars like Howard Zehr and myself.[6] Piecing together the results of all of these works, it is possible to state with considerable assurance that the rates of most major types of criminal behavior such as theft, assault and battery, and homicide did not change much over the whole of the nineteenth century and well into the twentieth century. To be sure, there were some important fluctuations of short-term duration; property offenses, for example, rose considerably during periods of marked economic hardship like the 1840s. But many commentators agree that neither most types of either property or personal crime became measurably more frequent or infrequent over the entire time period. This means that the rates of these offenses were roughly the same before, during, and after Germany's greatest industrial advances (usually considered to be some time between 1848 and 1914). Thus the ever more urbanized and industrialized German society did not have more criminality.[7] The only significant changes in criminal behavior in fact were results of the decriminalization of some behaviors like wood theft, which prior to the middle of the century had been the most frequent of all offenses,[8] and to the creation of various new laws, mainly of a sociopolitical nature, in the late Imperial period.[9] Actually, the only serious divergence of opinion among scholars of long-term German crime trends is between Howard Zehr and myself over the issue of whether or not there was an upsurge in most forms of violent criminality at the end of the nineteenth and the beginning of the twentieth century. Zehr argues that there was an increase in assault and battery, but not for more serious offenses such as murder and manslaughter. I have argued that the reason for the apparent decline in homicide was due to more lenient sentencing practices, which are easily documented.[10] Had Zehr used measures other than mere conviction rates, such as coroners' records, he would have found that there was indeed a considerable increase in homicide. But this increase was only temporary. Homicide rates and other crime rates returned to pattern once relative normalcy was reestablished, if only briefly, during the mid-1920s. Despite the ebb and flow of the time-series rates, it is clear that urbanization, city living, industrialization, and anomie did not occasion any marked or sustained increase in crime rates when viewed over a long-term perspective.

Although time-series analysis does provide some assurance that the industrial revolution did not occasion higher levels of crime and violence, cross-sectional analyses are needed at different points in time to strengthen this argument, to test a variety of hypotheses about the impact of urbanization and industrialization on criminal behavior, and to describe the changes in criminal patterns that occurred during Germany's industrial revolution. In my first published papers on this subject, written in the mid- and late 1970s, I attempted to do this by amassing a data set that was full of socioeconomic variables. These variables, however, were limited to dependent variables (i.e., the crime variables) and taken from a level of analysis that was highly aggregated (mainly the *Regierungsbezirke* of Prussia, which are similar to the departments of France used earlier in a similar study of French criminality by Charles Tilly and his associates).[11]

This data set was then analyzed by factor, path, multiple regression, and multiple and partial correlation analyses. Results demonstrated that there was no valid statistical association between the level of urbanization/industrialization or rate of change in urban or industrial growth and any major type of criminal behavior (measured then only by court data). What did correlate with criminality of various types were measures of poverty, particularly measures of ethnicity and literacy. Furthermore, although there was considerable stability in the geographical patterns of criminality across Germany, there was a marked growth in crime rates in the Rhine-Ruhr region around the turn of the century. And this growth seemed to run parallel with the *Landflucht* (migration) of many Germans seeking work from the northeastern, primarily agricultural border districts of Prussia (now mostly in Poland and the Soviet Union) to the more industrialized and growing western regions. Since computer analyses showed no valid statistical relationship between any measure of crime and either the process, rate, or level of urban and industrial development, I concluded that anomie, Gemeinschaft to Gesellschaft, modernization, or any other theories linking the causation of crime to urban and industrial growth and change held no water. Crime in Imperial Germany was engendered primarily by poverty, geocultural traditions, and ethnic diversity.

These findings and conclusions soon seemed extremely tentative for several reasons. They did not explain why there was no correlation between urban and industrial growth and crime. There was also a marked migration of crime from the rural northeast (although levels remained quite high there throughout the period) to the more developed west. This could be explained partially by suggesting that people may have transported their cultural patterns with them, and that many of the people who moved westward were of poor, racially despised ethnic groups like Poles and Lithuanians. A larger problem was that my cross-sectional data were of limited utility for a host of reasons: The dependent variables were lumped into broad categories such as "all crimes against the person" and "all crimes against property," which lacked any real specificity;[12] my statistical analysis was so sophisticated and esoteric that few historians could understand it, and eventually I was not certain that I trusted it; and, most important, my units of analysis were so few in number, and so large, that while my analysis might have statistical validity, that validity might still have been rather spurious to more cautious historical professionals, if not to mathematically minded social scientists.

Hence I embarked on an ambitious project by which I laboriously amassed a huge data set that consisted of cross-sectional data from over 1,000 different communities of Prussia and the rest of Germany (mainly *Kreise*). This study included more specific measures of criminality such as simple and serious theft, murder, manslaughter, simple and aggravated assault and battery, and other types of criminal behavior that are commonly accepted as measures of unlawful activity in all lands. Furthermore, when possible, I gathered measures of criminal activity from sources other than court records, such as coroners' figures for homicide offenses, to add to the court records and provide a further test of their validity. The statistics used were far simpler and more readily understandable to all scholars (mainly cross-tabulations, percentages, and simple bivariate correlations). Some of my results were published in article form and others are to appear in a forthcoming book.[13] Although my findings generally supported my earlier investigations in that ethnicity and economic hardship proved to be even more highly related to criminal trends, and no measures of urban and industrial change correlated significantly with the crime variables, my view of crime causation was modified in one very significant way. The causation of some property offenses (although never any personal offenses) seemed to be partially explained by a kind of structural theory that links the urban environment, but not the rate of urbanization, to property crime. This theory was argued by Charles Tilly in his study of French criminality, and although I found it to be of some utility in my own limited work on France,[14] it has never been satisfactorily articulated and rests on much speculation. Why cities on average have higher rates of theft than towns and villages is unknown. Tilly thinks it may be because of different types of police activity, or because of a more materialistic urban ethos, but he has never been able to prove it.[15] It is still a mystery to me. Perhaps had I done a better job of controlling for possible intervening variables such as ethnicity, age, and literacy, then the theory may be shown to be totally spurious. But that awaits more work.

Clearly the quantitative evidence is powerful, but it has its weaknesses just like other types of evidence. Hence, historians and social scientists must continually make prudent judgments, always mindful of the limitations of their data and the validity of their techniques no matter if they are working with quantitative or more traditional qualitative information. Also, the more one knows about the ways in which data are generated and the workings of the society that produces the social data used by the quantifier, the more one can trust findings and the more confidently posit conclusions. Good quantitative history must be buttressed by solid qualitative evidence.[16]

The Qualitative Evidence and Conclusions

In work that I have yet to publish, I have made a serious investigation of the German criminal justice system and the popular and elite attitudes of German citizens toward crime, criminals, and criminal justice during this period. I have examined in detail the literary record left by novelists, playwrights, and short story writers;[17] I have read the comments by police officials, lawyers, judges, and other criminal justice officials; and I have read and analyzed crime news in numerous German newspapers. Not all of the evidence points sharply in the same direction, and it cannot be reduced to mathematical equations. But certain commonalities are discernible. Generally, the qualitative evidence supports the quantitative findings. Although crime was a subject of intense debate and many writers and newspaper editors used crime news to support their ideological predispositions, there was constant mention of the ways in which ethnic issues, foreignness, and economic matters prompted criminal misdeeds. Furthermore, there was nothing to suggest that urbanization or industrialization caused crime except in the tirades of some conservative writers against their ideological enemies (Jews, socialists, foreigners) who often lived in cities.

In comparison with crime rates in the United States, Germany has always had very low rates of recorded crime, especially crimes of violence. A recent *New York Times* article (27 June 1990) comparing figures for homicide deaths among young men aged fifteen through twenty-four in 1986 and 1987 showed that the homicide rate per 100,000 per year in the United States was more than twenty times that of West Germany (21.9 to 1.0). Due to a lack of uniform data for the United States it is harder to say what the rate was one hundred years ago in America. Figures provided by Roger Lane for Philadelphia show that the American rate was certainly much higher than that of Germany (which, with an overall annual homicide rate of 1.7 for Prussia, and 1.4 for Berlin, had a homicide rate very close to what it has today).[18] Lest one conclude that it was Germany that was and is the aberration and not the United States, the recent article in the *New York Times* also showed that the American rate exceeds that of every other "advanced" nation in the world by more than five times, while the German rate is nearly identical to that of Japan, Denmark, Portugal, England, Poland, Ireland, Greece, France, Switzerland, The Netherlands, Belgium, and most every other country, including Canada, just as it was a century ago.[19]

Notes

This chapter is a revised and expanded version of a paper read at the Cologne Computer Conference in Sept. 1988, and originally published as "The Industrial Revolution and Crime in Germany: Quantitative and Qualitative Observations," *Historical Social Research/Historische Sozialforschung* 15(1990): 41–50.

1. For discussions of recent research in several countries, see Lawrence Stone, "Homicide and Violence," in his *The Past and the Present Revisited* (London, 1987), 295–310; Jim Sharpe, "Quantification and the History of Crime in Early Modern England: Problems and Results," in *Quantification and Criminal Justice History in International Perspective*, special volume of *Historical Social Research/Historische Sozialforschung* 15, ed. Eric A. Johnson (Cologne, 1990), 17–32; Eric A. Johnson, "Quantification and Criminal Justice History in the Nineties," in ibid., 4–16; Jan Sundin, "Current Trends in the History of Crime and Criminal Justice: Some Conclusions, with Special Reference to the Swedish Experience," in ibid., 184–96; and Eric A. Johnson and Eric H. Monkkonen, eds., *The History of Violent Crime in Town and Country Since the Middle Ages* (forthcoming). For earlier, although still useful summaries, see Ted Robert Gurr, "Historical Trends in Violent Crime: A Critical Review of the Evidence," *Crime and Justice: An Annual Review of Research* 3(1981): 295–343; Dirk Blasius, "Kriminologie und Geschichtswissenschaft: Bilanz und Perspektiven Interdisciplinärer Forschung," *Geschichte und Gesellschaft* 14(1988): 136–49; James A. Inciardi and Charles E. Faupel, eds., *History and Crime Implications for Criminal Justice Policy* (Beverly Hills, 1980), especially the essays by Eric H. Monkkonen, Ted Robert Gurr, and Roger Lane; Richard J. Evans, "In Pursuit of the *Untertanengeist*: Crime, Law and Social Order in German History," in *Rethinking German History*, ed. Richard J. Evans (London, 1987), chap. 5; Pieter Spierenburg, "Deviance and Repression in the Netherlands: Historical Evidence and Contemporary Problems," *Historical Social Research/Historische Sozialforschung* 37(1986): 4–16; and Eva Österberg, "Criminality, Social Control, and the State: Evidence and Interpretations in Scandinavian Historiography," paper presented at the Triannual Convention of the International Association for the History of Crime and Criminal Justice, Waxholm, Sweden, July 1990.

2. For bibliography and commentary, see Rudolf Schenda, *Volk ohne Buch: Studien zur Sozialgeschichte der populären Lesestoffe 1770–1910* (Frankfurt am Main, 1970); and Rolf Engelsing, *Analphabetentum und Lektüre: Zur Sozialgeschichte des Lesens in Deutschland zwischen feudaler und industrieller Gesellschaft* (Stuttgart, 1973). One of the reasons so few German authors treated such themes was that few Germans bought their crime novels. This, however, was much more the case for serious authors such as Theodor Fontane, whose crime novels *Quitt* and *Unterm Birnbaum* failed to sell more than 500 copies each, than it was for authors of trivial literature such as Karl May, whose stories of "Old Shatterhand" in the American Wild West sold hundreds of thousands of copies.

3. See Eric A. Johnson, "Crime and Popular Opinion: Newspapers and Popular Magazines," chap. 3 in *Urbanization and Crime: Germany 1871–1914*, ed. Eric A. Johnson (forthcoming). Most German newspapers were tied to political parties representing specific ideological interests. The newspapers analyzed in greatest detail are major Berlin dailies such as the *Kreuzzeitung* (Conservative party), *Germania*

(Center party), *Vossische Zeitung* and *Berliner Tageblatt* (Liberal and Progressive parties—although both newspapers were officially "independent"), and *Vorwärts* (Social Democratic party). Newspapers from various other localities were also analyzed to ensure that the Berlin newspapers were representative of more than just the attitudes of Berliners.

4. For a discussion of the availability, strengths, and weaknesses of German criminal statistics, see Herbert Reinke, "Statistics, Administration, and Concepts of Crime: Remarks on the Development of Criminal Statistics in Nineteenth-Century Germany," *Historical Social Research/Historische Sozialforschung* 11(1986): 39–49; and Helmut Graff, *Die Deutsche Kriminalstatistik: Geschichte und Gegenwart* (Stuttgart, 1975).

5. Georg von Mayr, *Statistik der Gerichtlichen Polizei im Königreiche Bayern und in einigen anderen Länder* (Munich, 1867); Wilhelm Starke, *Verbrechen und Verbrecher in Preussen 1854–1878: Eine Kulturgeschichtliche Studie* (Berlin, 1884); Gustav Aschaffenburg, *Crime and Its Repression*, trans. Adalbert Albrecht (Montclair, 1968).

6. Dirk Blasius, *Kriminalität und Alltag: Zur Konfliktgeschichte des Alltagslebens im 19. Jahrhundert* (Göttingen, 1978); Eric A. Johnson, "The Crime Rate: Longitudinal and Periodic Trends in Nineteenth- and Twentieth-Century German Criminality, from *Vormärz* to Late Weimar," in *The German Underworld: Outcasts and Deviants in German History*, ed. Eric A. Johnson (London, 1988), 159–88.

7. For figures and a detailed discussion, see Johnson, "Crime Rate."

8. Blasius discusses this in detail in *Kriminalität und Alltag*.

9. Mostly these were new laws for worker protection and worker insurance. Even the German officials called these laws "sociopolitical in character," and discussed their importance in explaining the apparent rise of the overall crime rate in Wilhelmian Germany. See "Die Entwicklung der Kriminalität im Deutschen Reich seit 1882," in *Kriminalstatistik für das Jahr 1927*, vol. 370 of the German governmental series *Statistik des Deutschen Reichs* (Berlin, 1930), 32. Many arrests and convictions were of socialist newspaper editors for libel. In the first six months of 1913 alone, 104 Social Democratic party journalists were convicted of libel, resulting in forty years of imprisonment and 11,000 marks in fines. See Alex Hall, *Scandal, Sensation and Social Democracy: The SPD Press and Wilhelmine Germany 1890–1914* (Cambridge, 1977).

10. Rupert Rabl, *Strafzumessungspraxis und Kriminalitätsbewegung* (Leipzig, 1936); Franz Exner, *Studien über die Strafzumessungspraxis der Deutschen Gerichte* (Leipzig, 1931).

11. Abdul Quiyum Lodhi and Charles Tilly, "Urbanization, Crime and Collective Violence in Nineteenth-Century France," *American Journal of Sociology* 59 (1973): 196–218; Vincent E. McHale and Eric A. Johnson, "Urbanization, Industrialization and Crime in Imperial Germany: Parts I and II," *Social Science History* 1 (1976–77): 45–78, 210–47.

12. In partial defense of this lumping together of criminal offenses into such broad categories, my study was originally conceived as a German replication of Tilly's work on France, and he used these exact same categories.

13. Eric A. Johnson, "The Roots of Crime in Imperial Germany," *Central European History* 15 (1982): 351–76.

14. David Cohen and Eric A. Johnson, "French Criminality: Urban-Rural Dif-

ferences in the Nineteenth Century," *Journal of Interdisciplinary History* 12 (1982): 477–501. Our study replicated and added to Tilly's work by using data from both assize and correctional courts for the late nineteenth century. Tilly only used data from the assize courts for the middle of the century.

15. Tilly and his associates attempted—"unsuccessfully" by their own admission—to test the police's role in recorded urban crime rates in several societies. See Tilly et al., "How Policing Affected the Visibility of Crime in Nineteenth-Century Europe and America," working paper of the Institute for Social Research of the University of Michigan (1981).

16. This argument is made strongly in the beginning and final chapters of a recent work on the application of statistical methods to historical research by Konrad H. Jarausch, Gerhard Arminger, and Manfred Thaller, *Quantitative Methoden in der Geschichtswissenschaft: Eine Einführung in der Forschung, Datenverarbeitung und Statistik* (Darmstadt, 1985).

17. Johnson, *Urbanization and Crime*. This book follows in the tradition of the work of J. J. Tobias, *Urban Crime in Victorian England* (New York, 1972); and Louis Chevalier, *Laboring and Dangerous Classes in Paris During the First Half of the Nineteenth Century* (New York, 1973).

18. For a fuller discussion, see chap. 7 in Johnson, *Urbanization and Crime*; and Roger Lane, *Violent Death in the City: Suicide, Accident and Murder in Nineteenth Century Philadelphia* (Cambridge, 1979).

19. Emile Durkheim, *Suicide: A Study in Sociology* (London, 1952), 353.

Torture, the Police, and the Colonial State in the Madras Presidency, 1816–55

Douglas M. Peers
University of Calgary

In 1806, with much fanfare and celebration, the newly arrived British government of the Cape of Good Hope destroyed in public the instruments of torture left behind by the Dutch government. This was a symbolic act, intended to establish that a new era had begun, an era in which the rule of law would take precedence over the rule of force and superstition. Likewise, a demonstration took place in the following decade when Lord Minto ordered that similar instruments in Java be publicly consigned to oblivion.[1] These demonstrations, designed to assert the moral ascendancy of the British, conveniently overlooked two salient facts: Torture had not taken place in Dutch territories for some time; and torture continued to take place in British-administered India, often with the connivance of local officials. The practice of torture in India became public knowledge in 1854, following embarrassing allegations made in the British Parliament about the prevalence of torture within the Madras presidency.[2] Soon after, the administration of British India ordered an investigation by a committee of enquiry into these charges. Through the deliberations of this committee—which will be the focus of this chapter—we can discern the matrices of law and policing that linked communities under the colonial state.[3]

The police were crucial to the Raj, and, to some observers at least, helped establish the foundations of a police state. Rabindranath Tagore wrote of this police state: "In other words when the noose hangs round one's neck no other aid except the advice to chant one's goddess's name—it is then that in this measureless incongruity one comes to see the constable as the messenger-incarnate of the God of Death."[4] A similar sentiment was echoed by another Indian who pointed out to William Sleeman, the famous prosecutor of North Indian thugs, the "Mughals had built mosques and tombs—

the British built jails and barracks."[5] Parallels can be established with other areas of the evolving colonial world. As noted in one study on law and society in Africa, the prison was often the first type of colonial architecture produced.[6] Moreover, there is an important element of continuity that such a study reveals. Just as the police in early nineteenth-century Madras were a British modification of indigenous systems, the police of postindependence India—who have also been charged by Amnesty International with practicing torture—are a relic of the imperial past.[7]

The public debates generated by the torture revelations are also useful in defining the contours of the judicial system imposed by the British. The ideology that surrounded criminal justice most clearly formulated the new notions of sovereignty that the East India Company's officials were trying to introduce. The opening lines of Bernard Cohn's seminal article on justice in India lay out in precise terms the significance of the judiciary system to colonial rule:

> One of the first problems confronting a colonial power after establishing *de facto* or *de jure* sovereignty over a new territory is to set up procedures for settling disputes arising within the dominated society, and to establish a whole range of rights in relation to property and obligations of individuals and groups to one another and to the state.[8]

Through its donning of judicial duties, the East India Company sought to neutralize all other claims to the legitimate use of force and, hence, establish itself as the legitimate sovereign power within its territories. Such a claim did not, however, imply that all traditional modes and idioms of authority were overturned. The East India Company lacked the resources and abilities for a complete revolution in judicial procedures and principles and was therefore forced to conclude alliances with some traditional institutions. The police were one such compromise. Although they were intended to serve the colonial state, their personnel remained very much part of local society, and they used their authority and powers in local disputes over power, status, and wealth.

The use of torture and coercion in Indian society was not a novel introduction brought about by British rule. It had a long history with individuals such as Murshid Ali Khan, Nawab of Bengal, reputedly dressing his opponents in specially designed trousers into which live cats were placed.[9] Historically, it is also true that torture and physical threats frequently accompanied revenue collection, while flogging was a punishment used in both precolonial and colonial India.[10] Peasant folklore is full of comments on the abuses of the police. Popular dramas in Madras often portrayed the police as brutally torturing peasants to provide not only the revenue demanded by the state, but also protection money to the police.[11] A popular Bengali proverb reads: "Who believes that a goat does not feed on grass and a policeman does not take a bribe."[12] Astonishingly, one policeman in Bengal was found to be issuing receipts for the bribes he took in.[13] What does change with the advent of colonial rule is the surprising degree to which torture is unofficially, yet tacitly, incorporated into revenue and judicial systems. This led one circuit court judge to remark in 1840 that "the practice of torture, within the territories of the Madras government, is universal, systematic and habitual."[14]

Police corruption and abuse of authority, with all its ill effects on the Indian people such as forced migrations for those who fled from British territories into the still-independent princely states or the tea plantations of Sri Lanka, thrived not simply because of the self-interest of the police but also because police corruption did not necessarily come into conflict with the interests of the Indian state.[15] As long as torture did not directly undermine their position, the British could afford to overlook it. Only when abuses became public, and revealed the extent to which nominal subordinates were operating independent of British authority, was action demanded. From this perspective, the reforms introduced in the 1860s into the criminal law and policing systems in India can be seen to have originated in part from what transpired in Madras in the 1850s.

The Police and the Colonial State

As the police in India evolved through the nineteenth century, they resembled, just like the legal system they were meant to enforce, a curious hybrid of European and Indian institutions. They were anchored in the twilight between these two cultures. Ultimately, any explanation for the prevalence of torture must take into account the unique position occupied by the police between Indian society and the imperial state. Indian police were employed because they were cheap, convenient, and thought best able to mediate with Indian society. The *tahsildars* of Madras and the *daroghas* in Bengal were drawn from local inhabitants and bore some resemblance to traditional institutions. Yet, seen from another perspective, the police were responsible for implementing the rules of an alien regime whose definitions of criminality became one of the chief means of sustaining colonial hegemony.[16] The police were not only the agents of colonialism with the most direct and sustained contact with the peasantry—responsible for both the preservation of law and order and the efficient collection of revenues—but they also possessed a great deal of delegated power. British objectives of using allegedly familiar local institutions to mediate between them and the people was, however, largely defeated for the *tahsildars* in Madras, and the *daroghas* in Bengal could not operate as an indigenous constabulary. Instead, they were the local revenue collectors on whom the British added, almost as an afterthought, responsibilities for law and order. British definitions of property and of law and order—with the state placing a premium on order—were

Police Peon and his wife, c. 1805, artist unknown. Reprinted with permission of the British Library.

helping erode traditional reference points. The Mughals, together with other precolonial regimes, were content to leave petty crimes to local officials and concerned themselves only with matters of direct concern to the state. The British, seeking to penetrate farther down into society in order to secure their rule, introduced a much more comprehensive definition of crime and looked to the Indian police to provide the necessary enforcement and surveillance.[17] It is wrong, however, to assume that precolonial legal systems and principles disappeared abruptly with the onset of colonial rule. Legally speaking, British India resembled an imperfect assimilation of British, Islamic, and Hindu legal systems. Hence, the police can be rightly seen to be alien imports forcibly integrating alien rules into a country undergoing profound changes.

At the same time, the privileged status in Indian society enjoyed by the Indian police, a status that often allowed them personal advancement, depended on their ability to meet the claims made on them by their colonial overlords. The most persistent of these demands were for efficient revenue collection and the administration of criminal justice. Torture was often turned to in lieu of legal methods in order to satisfy either of these demands, for torture was just as effective in squeezing "ten rupees out of a man who had only eight" as it was in extorting a confession from a possibly innocent man.[18] The potential for the use of torture increased when one considers how poorly paid the police were, especially in light of their responsibilities and authority. *Tahsildars* received on average only 70 to 100 rupees a month, with their assistants often not being paid at all save for grants of clothing and grain.[19] Even as late as 1859 the lowest constable's pay was fixed to that of the average unskilled laborer.[20] Moreover, to become an assistant—commonly termed a peon by contemporaries—often took an initial investment of a bribe to the local village headman.[21] Little wonder then that for many observers the corruption and torture that flourished were linked directly to the lack of adequate remunerations for the police. "The great difficulty with regards to the police was, that they were inadequately paid, and kept in a permanent state of starvation."[22]

The Instances and Uses of Torture

The public revelations in 1854 that torture was occurring in the Madras presidency was not the first time that the British had acknowledged the existence of torture. As early as 1826, the Court of Directors directed the Madras government to investigate reports of torture, which included one case in which the suspect had "a rough rope charged with powdered chillies and mustard seed, and moistened with a solution of salt . . . tightly bound round his arm."[23] In 1832, the existence of torture within British-administered India was admitted to in a Parliamentary Committee.[24] Almost simultaneously, reports were emerging of the abuses of the police force in

Bengal.[25] A great variety of forms of physical and mental abuse are to be found. One favorite in South India was the *anundal*, a form of bondage in which the victim was doubled over backwards for an extended period of time. Another popular method was the *kittee*, which consisted of an instrument that bent the fingers back and caused excruciating pain. This instrument was often erroneously referred to as a thumbscrew by Europeans. The *kittee* was also employed on other parts of the body, with thighs and women's breasts figuring prominently in the reports. *Bastinado*, or beating of the soles of the feet with clubs, was also used together with a host of rough and ready techniques such as pulling out of mustaches and twisting of ears.[26] European observers took a gruesome interest in another common technique, "placing the carpenter beetle, or other gnawing insect, or some stinging reptile, confined in a cocoa-nut shell, in the navel or a more sensitive part of the body."[27] For many European observers, the variety of torments uncovered in India reinforced many of their stereotypes of the Indian's inherently cruel nature: "Some of them exhibit an amount of diabolical ingenuity on the part of the torturer, and a degree of abasement and degradation in their victims, of which we can hardly form a conception."[28]

The Madras government, however, responded to the 1826 allegations by insisting that reports of torture were greatly exaggerated and that the situation was improving.[29] The governor of Madras at that time, Thomas Munro, went so far as to claim that judicial affairs were well in order and that only the revenue department required improvement.[30] Underlying such glowing testimonies was an element of concern. Local governments did not always dismiss criticisms in an offhand way. Between 1806 and 1855, the superior criminal court in Madras, the *Faujdari Adalat*, issued no less than ten circulars designed to check the use of torture and other questionable practices within the police force.[31]

The year 1854, however, was the watershed. Following embarrassing revelations in the House of Commons about torture in Madras—referred to in *The Times* as "the Indian Inquisition" and the subject of a satirical advertisement in *Punch*—the East India Company instructed its officials in India to undertake an investigation.[32] Parliamentary suspicions were further raised by reports emanating out of Bengal that indicated that the problem was more widespread than previously thought.[33] In Madras, the original intention was only to examine police torture with respect to coercion employed to collect revenue payments. But when their initial enquiries revealed the extent of the abuses, the committee's mandate was extended to include all acts of torture and abuses of authority including those involved in criminal investigations. One hundred and fifty English notices were circulated while there were 10,000 in Tamil, 10,000 in Telugu, 10,000 in Kanarese, 5,000 in Malayalam, and 5,000 in Hindustani distributed and posted on all *cutcherries* (local court houses).[34]

The committee was surprised at the number of responses they handled in their seven months, which they took as indicative of the seriousness of the situation. Some 519 persons personally appeared before the committee, some of whom traveled upwards of 500 miles. One witness reportedly traveled a total distance of 1,000 miles, and a further 1,440 letters were received as evidence.[35] Some attempts were made to dismiss these findings as originating either in the congenital lying of the Indian people, or in some conspiracy directed against the British. These efforts came to naught, for the committee also canvassed its British-born officials. Of 109 officials queried, seventy-nine responded that torture was occurring and thirty were noncommittal; most important, none explicitly denied the charges.[36] Fortunately, many of the letters and petitions from the Indian peasants have been preserved, offering us a unique window into rural impressions of the police. Unfortunately, owing to the incompleteness of the sample group and the direct relationship between the number of respondents and their proximity to the committee, it is nearly impossible to use these findings in any way that is statistically meaningful. From North Arcot, for example, located only 100 miles from Madras, some 240 complaints were received, whereas from Ganjam—an area reputed for its police brutality but some 673 miles away—there were only twenty-eight submissions.[37] Furthermore, many of those who suffered torture were serving on the roads in hard labor battalions and hence could not present memorials. Therefore, recognizable, impressionistic patterns can be deduced from these testimonials rather than quantifiable, statistically valid evidence.[38]

Torture was employed principally to serve three objectives: the collection of revenue, the prosecution of criminals through the securing of confessions or evidence, and the pursuit of private gain or revenge. The conditions that gave rise to the use of torture arose in part from the coupling of revenue and policing duties that took place in Madras under the settlement of 1816.[39] This amalgamation of the offices of magistrate and collector was part of a process of land settlement commonly referred to as *ryotwari*.[40] A simplified definition of *ryotwari* was a revenue settlement that was made directly between the cultivator (*ryot*) and the state, and in which the terms could be adjusted by the collector. Hence, the government acted as landlord with no intermediaries as existed in the *zamindari* settlement of Bengal. In practice, however, such a system never came completely into being as a variety of settlement forms existed in Madras, and the government there proved to be not as hostile to intermediaries as *ryotwari* might have otherwise implied. Interestingly, one early proponent of *ryotwari*, William Thackeray, later came to criticize it. Although he admired its theoretical elegance, he recognized that it was more prone to abuse.[41]

The blending of revenue and policing duties applied to both European officials and their Indian subordinates, namely, the *tahsildars* and the peons who assisted them. *Tahsildars* had been employed in some districts to administer policing and collect the revenue before 1816. In Tanjore, for ex-

WHAT HAPPENED TO SMITH AFTER SENDING HIS WET UMBRELLA TO BE AIRED IN THE KITCHEN.

BISHOP BERKELEY v. DRUMMOND.

MR. PUNCH presents his compliments to LORD PANMURE, and begs to suggest that he should restore to BISHOP BERKELEY, author of *The Minute Philosopher*, his rightful property, unceremoniously handed over by his Lordship to MR. DRUMMOND. We mean the property in the

THE QUESTION AS TOUCHING INDIA!

(ADVERTISEMENT.)

THE Indian Question is twofold, ordinary and extraordinary, at least the latter is stated by that talented journal, the *Press*, to be practised, as a means of judicial investigation, in a portion of our Indian possessions, by the officials of the East India Company. One branch of the ordinary Indian Question is the inquiry respectfully addressed to the

HONOURABLE BOARD OF DIRECTORS

BY MESSRS. WRENCH AND GYVES,

SHEFFIELD, CUTLERS,

Manufacturers of Engines and Instruments in Hardware, &c.

Whether that statement of the *Press* can be relied on as authentic? Because, if so, MESSRS. W. AND G. confidently invite the attention of the Honourable Board to their new and extensive Stock of

Instruments of Torture,

warranted to defy Competition, and exhibiting a great superiority to the Apparatus in use during the

GOOD OLD TIMES.

In particular, they would recommend an early inspection of their

PATENT EXTRA-EXCRUCIATING THUMB-SCREWS!

on a new and improved principle; warranted to extract the truth, or its equivalent, in five minutes, with a degree of pain infinitely exceeding that produced by the complicated proceeding of binding the fingers and toes with twine, and driving pegs between them, at present resorted to by the Company's servants. W. and G. beg to submit to the notice of the Directors a large assortment of

SELF-ACTING SYNCLASCELES FERRO-CALEFACIENT BOOTS!

in which the Leg is crushed by Machinery, and at the same time subjected to the action of a high degree of Heat: thus possessing important advantages over the old Iron Boot unsuccessfully employed for the subjugation of the Scottish Covenanters. May be had of all sizes. This invention will procure, in a few hours, results, which by the Indian Stocks, with sharp-edged holes and ankle-pegs, are sometimes with difficulty obtained in as many weeks. An ancient invention for the figure of square men in the round holes, and round men in square. Nothing, it was alleged, could go well with us until we had the right men in the right places—

"Or, my Lords, to use the quaint expression of my friend, Mr. Drummond, until the square men shall be put into the square holes, and the round men into the round holes." (*Laughter.*)

Mr. Drummond, of course, never reads the *Times;* otherwise he would, doubtless, have immediately written, disavowing all property in the "quaint expression," too liberally given to him. "The world seems to me," says the original author, "to be like a board pierced with square holes and round holes; with the round pegs in the square, and the square in the round." Now let not a Cabinet Minister despoil of his own, even a Bishop. Mr. Drummond may be a great wit, but he is not yet up to Bishop Berkeley; hardly up to the Bishop's beadle.

DOWN WITH THE LADIES.

We never heard anything so ungallant as the remarks made by Lord Redesdale on the presence of Ladies at the debate on the motion of Lord Ellenborough. The former Nobleman declared that the presence of the fair sex depressed the eloquence of the best speakers among the Peers, who were prevented from reaching the sublime by the counteracting effects of the beautiful. It is strange that a sex so remarkable for garrulity in itself should be the cause of the taciturnity of others. We presume, of course, that all the Ladies present on the occasion alluded to were beautiful, and it would have been more polite of Lord Redesdale to have complimented them on this head at least, by saying that "the power of speech of the Peerage was taken away, by seeing so many regular stunners in the way of female loveliness."

Not a Magic Minstrel.

Herr Wagner, Professor of the "Music of the Future," appears, in conducting at the Philharmonic, to have made strange work with the music of all time. He alters Mozart, it appears, if not exactly as a parish clerk once said that he had altered Haydn for the singing gallery, yet in a manner nearly as audacious, altering "*allegro*" to "*moderato;*" "*andante*" to "*adagio;*" "*allegretto*" to "*andante;*" and "*allegro*" again to "*prestissimo.*" Wagner would seem strongly to resemble his namesake in *Faust*, in the particular wherein that *Wagner* differs from his master—that is, in the circumstance of being no conjuror.

infliction of suffering has been modified by W. and G., and is submitted by them for approval to the Leadenhall Street authorities under the appellation of

THE SCAVENGER'S YOUNGER DAUGHTER!!!

Through the judicious application of the lever, and other mechanical principles, this instrument is capable of being worked by a child; consequently saving the executioner an amount of muscular exertion unduly fatiguing in a warm climate. Whilst bending the body into an orbicular form it also, by means of a spring affixed to its lower end, applies the bastinado to the soles of the feet. The trouble of hauling a prisoner up to a tree by the arms tied behind him, and beating him at the same time with sticks on the shins, may thus be dispensed with, by an operation which is as easy to the official as it is intolerable to the native. Polished Metal Reflectors, for intensifying the effect of Exposure in a state of nudity to the Rays of the Sun; also Cayenne-Pepper Inhalers, for causing suspected individuals to breathe the fumes of Cayenne-pepper, volatilised by burning charcoal, which will be found much more convenient than the nosebag now employed, have also been manufactured by W. and G. in great numbers; but perhaps their most perfect agonific apparatus will be pronounced to be their

STEAM RACK!!!!

which, by the exquisite suffering which it is adapted to inflict, extorting any confession that can possibly be required, will altogether supersede all the other modes of torture described by the *Press*, as well as those which that journal refrains from mentioning. Wheels, with Iron Bar, &c., complete. Pincers, Branding Irons, &c. &c.

☞ N.B. Wrench and Gyves, Sheffield, Makers to His Majesty the King of Naples.

A Poet's Prayer Granted.

Recollecting, as *Mr. Punch* sat with his toes on the fender, last Friday week, that this was the merry month of roses, he felt inspired, and began an ode. He had, however, only got as far as "Hail, May!" when *didn't* it?

"A QUIVER FULL OF DAUGHTERS."

Happy is he who—according to Lord Granville's new version—has a quiver full of daughters; and happier still, if all that are in the quiver meet with the proper bow.

Advertisement in *Punch* (28 [19 May 1855]: 204).

ample, regulations of 1802 granted them the power to deal with petty cases and to administer corporal punishments, provided that whippings were done with tamarind branches and not with rattans.[42] The regulations of 1816 were an attempt to systematize and consolidate the use of *tahsildars* and introduce them throughout the presidency. Policing was viewed by the state as a secondary function, with the emphasis being placed by the authorities on efficient revenue collection. The sustained opposition in Bengal to the introduction of *ryotwari* was due in part to the open acknowledgment of what Bengal officials saw as the chief "deficiency"—namely, the subordination of police work to revenue collection.[43] Even the choice of the term *tahsildar* to designate police officials reflects this bias, for it is a word of Mughal origin meaning "revenue collector."

The system imposed on the Madras presidency in 1816 disclosed an attempt to merge the pragmatic demands of the colonial state with what many considered to be the principal building block of Indian society—the idealized village republic. Charles Metcalfe produced what has since become the most famous statement concerning the village republic: "The village communities are little republics, having nearly everything they want within themselves, and almost independent of any foreign relations. They seem to last where nothing else lasts."[44] States and empires may come and go; the village, however, remained self-contained and timeless. Such a depiction of Indian society did not, however, square with reality, for the villages were neither as isolated, nor as static, as the British wished to believe.[45] Nonetheless, this idea of the village republic continued to inform British actions and policies, largely because of its usefulness in legitimating policies that initially rested on pragmatic responses. A localized structuring of police and revenue authority was attractive both because of its cheapness and because it provided a direct channel between the state and the local population. Cost is a factor colonial administrators always had to bear in mind; hence, even the continued use of whipping as a punishment can be partially explained by it being the cheapest punishment to inflict. Therefore, the end result in Madras was a system designed to rest on strictly delineated hierarchical controls, as compared with that in Bengal with its use of elaborate checks and balances.[46]

After surveying the systems in use throughout all the districts of Madras, the *tahsildar* was considered to be the ideal person in whom the management of local affairs could be entrusted.[47] Instrumental in this decision was Thomas Munro, governor of Madras between 1819 and 1827, who was intellectually predisposed to a system which—by virtue of its structured hierarchies—was more akin to a military organization, employing whenever possible Indians who were calculated to be better equipped at reading local conditions.[48] The *tahsildar*, however, was not the traditional locus of authority in rural Madras. Instead, in most areas it was the militarized nobility, the *poligars* and *kavilgars*, who had served as both the effective and popularly accepted authority. The British, however, were loath to entrust authority to those who had so recently resisted them. Hence, the *poligars* and *kavilgars*, like their equivalents elsewhere in India such as the *zamindars* and *taluqdars* of the north, were demilitarized and quickly written off as petty tyrants.[49] Ironically, many of these dispossessed magnates were later frequently implicated in cases of *dacoity* or gang robbery.[50]

Not only were the individuals chosen to act as the police determined by a misunderstanding of local society, but Munro's vision of an integrated police apparatus that would link the village with the metropole was unattainable from the beginning. Such a system would have required a much greater degree of British commitment in money and men to coordinate it than the state was willing to provide. British pretenses to omnipotency and omnicompetency were continually being undermined by what one historian has aptly termed "dynamic immobility."[51] Through the conjunction of unwillingness and incapacity, the ideal of a strictly subordinated police system soon gave way to a decentralized system in which an unintended amount of discretionary power was vested at the local level. In one case, a district magistrate was forced to turn to existing local power networks and employ private protection from the *Maravas*, a South Indian community that has historic ties with the occupation of soldiers and guardsmen.[52] Moreover, the *tahsildars* accumulated even more powers as the 1820s wore on. Of crucial importance was when the *tahsildars* and their subordinates at the village level were given the authority to try and punish individuals for petty crimes. Such crimes included petty assault, petty theft, and idleness, while the punishments they were able to apply on their own initiative included flogging, fines of no more than three rupees, confinement for no more than twenty-four hours, or any combination of the above.

Legal proceedings at this level largely escaped colonial notice. Although tables were kept of the numbers charged and convicted, no records were maintained to show how guilt was established or how sentences were arrived at.[53] Occasionally, hints of abuses would percolate upwards into the highest reaches of the colonial state, as illustrated by the discovery in 1825 of a *tahsildar* in southern Madras who arrested, convicted, and flogged 217 people in a single year without acquitting anyone.[54] In effect, the decision to grant more powers to the local and village police removed one of the few checks that had been left by the regulations of 1816–the local collector. The statistics we do have access to illustrate the extent to which local police were administering local affairs. In the period 1 July 1839 to 30 June 1840, village police prosecuted a total of 5,700 cases and the *tahsildars* dealt with a further 109,083. In contrast, magistrates attended to only 2,695 cases and criminal courts a further 7,752, while the two highest levels of judicial authority—the circuit courts and the *Faujdari Adalat*—decided on 2,093 and 210, respectively.[55] These extensive powers in local hands imply that the colonial state had concluded that revenues could be gathered effectively only when the collectors and their assistants had instant access to legal means of coercion. This is an interesting illumination of colonial psychology. It is apparent that in many cases, however, these legal means soon proved inadequate for the tasks expected of the police, and that they were often supplemented by extralegal methods.

Torture appears to have been used primarily in revenue collection. Some 488 of the complaints referred to revenue as its cause compared to 173 for criminal investigation.[56] This is not surprising, given the British dependency on land revenues in a country of small farmers. Land revenues were the principal means of funding the colonial state, and, unlike contemporary Britain in which a reasonably sophisticated and progressive revenue system had been imposed, revenue administration in India was marked by rapacity and heavy-handedness.[57] Not surprisingly, the peasants employed many strategies for evading the demands of tax collectors. The police in turn fully realized that their chances of promotion were directly linked to their ability to collect all that was expected. Conflict between the colonial state and the peasantry was inevitable, and the police were caught in the cross-fire between these two communities. The reluctance of the peasants to concede without struggle to the government's demands is easily understood. It is, therefore, not surprising that a recent study of criminality in Madras has established the close correlation between famine and outbreaks of *dacoity*.[58]

British rule was distinguished from its predecessors by its more ambitious appetite. British revenue expectations were upwards of fifty percent of the gross produce of the land as compared to approximately thirty percent in the case of previous regimes.[59] Moreover, the British were not as flexible as their predecessors, failing to allow, for example, in times of famine a relief on the amount of taxes demanded. This situation was made even worse for the *ryot*, whose capacity to pay steadily diminished as the first half of the nineteenth century wore on. Prices were constantly declining, reaching their nadir in 1843–44, when they were only fifty percent of what they had been in the period between 1816 and 1825.[60] Consequently, a survey undertaken in 1850 revealed that only seventeen percent of the peasantry could meet their revenue demands without having to seek assistance from moneylenders.[61] The police became trapped between the resistance of the peasant and the acquisitiveness of the Raj, and torture became one method of squaring this circle. One *sheristidar* (officer of a court) brought before the committee admitted that "in all cases where a *tahsildar* as Revenue Officer found it difficult to induce the ryots to come to a settlement, he used to trouble them by exercising and abusing the powers vested in him as a police officer."[62] The sums the collectors were pursuing were often insignificant—in some cases as low as one rupee, four annas (2s 6d).[63] Hence, it was generally the most marginalized members of the peasantry who experienced torture. Wealthier members were more likely to possess sufficient influence to limit the depredations of the police.

Viewing the Madras presidency in its entirety, some regional discrepancies in the use of torture emerge. Districts such as Rajahmundry, Canara, and Cuddapah show in real terms a greater number of complaints directed at criminal investigation than at revenue collection. One circuit court judge in Cuddapah explained the situation in that province by the many wealthy individuals in the area, together with its proximity to independent states. These factors encouraged the police to join in, and even lead, the bands of *dacoits* operating across the frontiers.[64] In some districts the ratio that results from setting the number of police complaints against revenue complaints is much higher than the average. Given the inherent weaknesses in our sample, one cannot come to any precise explanations. The distinctions might simply be the result of comparing two different samples. There are several possible explanations, however, which might in part resolve these differences. Revenue assessments were not uniform across southern India, and there were marked differences in the enthusiasm with which the government's demand was pursued. Ecology also comes into play, for in places such as Malabar and Canara not only were revenue demands lower, but the likelihood that the rains would fail was much less than on the eastern coast, and hence the peasants were not under the same pressures. In the district of Bellary, the large numbers of *brinjaries* (a historic community of grain merchants who roamed across India and who in wartime provided armies with logistical support) which operated from this region appear to have been heavily involved in fracases with the police.[65] Interestingly, the *brinjaries* would later become one of the communities which were singled out by the British as a "criminal tribe."

Torture for revenue purposes can be distinguished from that used in criminal investigation in that the tortures employed were generally less painful and less likely to result in permanent injury. An explanation for this might be the wish not to remove the peasant from the area's agricultural production. As one observer reported: "Cases in which death or wounds or injury to limbs occur must be looked upon as highly exceptional; ordinarily the violence is of a petty kind, although causing acute momentary pain."[66] Favored techniques in coercing revenues from peasants included whippings, beatings, or the use of the *anundal*. Especially widespread was the use of the *kittee*. Appanda Nynar's evidence that it was used throughout Madras to force cultivators to pay their assessments was supported by an anonymous *sheristadar* who admitted that *kittees* could be found in most police stations, and when they could not, local carpenters would provide them without question.[67] For criminal cases, when torture was used to secure confessions or extract evidence, a much greater degree of ingenuity and pain was evinced. A rope soaked in hot chillies, mustard seeds, and salt, and then tightly bound around the arm, was a popular method. So too was the introduction of hot chillies or scratching insects into sensitive parts of the body, such as the eyes or genitalia.

The frequency with which recorded incidents of torture manifested themselves was partly determined by geography. The farther removed from the central control of the government an area was, the greater the likelihood of torture occurring.[68] The city of Madras, for example, had no recorded instances of torture, although complaints of police corruption flourished. The police in Malabar and Canara, areas far removed from the scrutiny of the government, were notorious for their use of torture.[69] In these two districts, however, the normal motive behind torture—the securing of revenue payments—is not much in evidence. Instead, because the level of assessment was much lower in these areas, torture was almost exclusively used for criminal investigations. Malabar was widely viewed as one of the most lawless areas of India, largely on account of the communal tensions between the *mappilas*, or Malabar Muslims, and their Hindu and Christian neighbours.[70] Hence, and not surprisingly, the use of torture in revenue collection was largely determined by the level of taxation imposed on the peasantry. Of course, the absence of complaints does not necessarily indicate that torture was not taking place, for the police had many means at their disposal to mask their actions. One apparently popular method was not to hand over to the jails those who were tortured until the marks had disappeared. In cloaking their actions, the police found an unwitting ally in the criminal procedure, which moved so slowly that, in the words of the Committee, "marks even of severe torture would be obliterated or very indistinct at the time of the trial."[71]

Geographical differences in the extent to which the police abused their powers also occurred due to localized shifts in the distribution of wealth and status. As has been shown for the area of Tirunelveli in the southernmost part of Madras, economic development under British rule profoundly upset traditional relations between communities. In this district, a previously low-status and low-wealth community of *Shanars*, which historically had undertaken the cultivation of palm trees, took advantage of changing economic circumstances to challenge the previously dominant community of *Maravas* who had historic claims to warrior status.[72] The *Marava* community struck back at these upstarts in a number of ways, one of which was through the increasing presence of *Maravas* in the police. For such declining communities as the *Maravas*, the police offered not only a lucrative means of employment, but also held out the chances of reasserting local dominance.

In choosing a method of torture, the police appear to have been influenced less by gender than by caste. Women were commonly tortured, as evidenced in the testimony of Runjiah Chitty, a weaver of Chingleput, not so much for the crimes they may have done but rather to coerce their families into confessing.[73] From Bengal, an Indian court orderly confessed to having helped place a woman in a sack filled with dried chillies to force her to reveal some information.[74] In another recorded instance, an elderly woman was suspended from a roof beam and flogged with nettle branches until she confessed to an alleged theft.[75] Physical pain appears to have been rarely directed at the highest castes, revealing that methods were tailored to the status of the victim. Appanda Nynar reported that throughout the Madras Presidency whips were often employed on *sudras* (a lower caste often found as cultivators) but never on Brahmans.[76] Instead, the torturers tried to humiliate Brahmans, forcing them to carry outcastes on their backs or wear necklaces of polluting materials around their necks.

The use of torture in criminal proceedings by the *tahsildars* and their peons needs to be understood within the framework established by the British legal system. They were supposed to maintain law and order and block threats to colonial rule—all of this at a time when rural order was disintegrating under the weight of foreign rule and impositions. New forms of property rights, and the weight of the revenue assessment, unleashed noticeable increases in rural unrest. Much of this unrest was led and orchestrated by the traditional elites, who had been stripped of their economic and political status. *Zamindars* in Bengal, and *poligars* in Madras, were often at the center of the so-called crimes. The *tahsildars*, therefore, were forced into conflict with their previous superiors who often had more public support than the police.

To compound these difficulties, the police were expected to enforce an alien legal system. The British were ordering an Indian institution to enforce new and more rigorous forms of social control and state authority over daily life than had hitherto been the case. This was largely the result of a hasty and rather ill-conceived marriage of Islamic law and British regulations that made up criminal law as it was applied in British-administered India. In the words of one member of the Indian Law Commission, Islamic law was "dis-stated to such an extent as to deprive it of all title to the religious veneration of Mohammedans, yet retaining enough of its original peculiarities to perplex and encumber the administration of justice."[77] British regulations, as appended to existing Islamic laws, reveal the growing intrusiveness of the state. Crimes against the person and property were joined by a series of crimes best described as moral in nature. Behavior that offended the moral sensibilities of the new rulers was eagerly monitored by the state and measures were designed to eradicate it. Such "crimes" included those of "wantonly destroying trees," disobedience of orders (a variant of the master-servant laws in Britain), "pretending to witchcraft," "bartering spirits for grain," and refusing to pay a promised dowry.[78] The list goes on to include "riding or driving furiously," for which the penalty was often flogging, begging, gambling, selling obscene books, and "exciting charity by exhibiting bodily deformities."[79] *Tahsildars* were also expected to punish vagrancy and to monitor the activities of "idle" people.[80] Quite clearly the state was setting out to monitor and discipline the actions of people in ways hitherto not experienced in India.

The Colonial State and the Persistence of Torture

The Indian police failed to meet the expectations placed on them by their colonial employers. Throughout the nineteenth century, conviction rates for criminal acts were very low in spite of what were considered to be very high levels of criminal activity. Once again, we lack statistically precise figures on the extent to which crime was occurring. Some scattered collections of figures comparing arrests with convictions do exist. One such series, from 1 July 1839 to 30 June 1840, exposes the very low rates of conviction. Of a total of 132,620 people brought before the various levels of courts in Madras, 90,588 were either discharged or acquitted.[81] The situation in Madras in 1829 was broadly similar, with a total of 121,622 arrests and only 41,127 convictions.[82] Successful prosecutions for *dacoity* were especially rare. Between 1819 and 1828, only twenty of the more than two hundred reported incidents in the district of Canara were brought to trial.[83] This situation was not to the liking of East India Company officials in London, and their displeasure with the government of Madras was made manifest on several occasions.

> Heinous crimes appear to be very prevalent, and many were reported to have been committed, the perpetrators of which were not discovered; the number of persons apprehended for the more serious crimes was very small in proportion to the supposed number of criminals; the persons apprehended for petty offences, (especially assaults) and the persons acquitted in proportion to those apprehended, were very numerous, and there were many false and malicious complaints.[84]

Much evidence suggests that torture often resulted out of a sense of exasperation with the foreign procedures of the British-administered court system, since these courts often demanded types of evidence that a weak and poorly paid force could not provide. The structure and nature of the judicial system in use in Madras are largely accountable for this. As already noted, much justice was administered in an ad hoc way by the village police and the *tahsildars*. Above them in the judicial hierarchy in ascending order of importance were their superiors, the district magistrates, and then in a different administrative line the criminal courts, the circuit courts, and the supreme criminal court or *Faujdari Adalat*. Presided over by civil servants brought from England, it is quite apparent that such officials lacked not only the training, but also well-designed judicial procedures to handle the cases they confronted. The judiciary was not considered by the East India Company as a distinct and different operation of its civil service; personnel not only received the same broad training no matter what their occupation

Prisoner before a court, c. 1850, artist unknown. Reprinted with permission of the British Library.

in India, but they were also subject to reassignment from revenue to judicial functions and vice versa. At the East India Company's training college at Haileybury, England, a common syllabus was offered to the students in which the most legal training they could normally expect to receive was ninety hours spread over the two-year course.[85] One exception to this was those students who undertook training in Sanskrit; one of the texts which figured in their training was the *Laws of Manu*.[86] This introduction to Hindu legal thought would, however, be of little service in criminal procedure, for the use of Hindu legal practices was confined to civil actions. Noticeably, translated Islamic legal works did not figure in the rubric. The lack of adequate training in what amounted to an imperfectly joined dual legal system forced the courts to rely on the advice provided by the *muftis*, advisors on Muslim law who were expected to inform the judge whether an action was considered to be a crime under Islamic law. In many instances, it was the *muftis* who determined guilt; the European judge's participation was limited to the sentencing of the individual. Another blow to efficient legal procedure was struck when the best students at Haileybury, and those company officials who most impressed their supervisors, were directed into revenue administration, leaving second-rate officials to administer justice.

The lack of a sound foundation in legal practices, when coupled with a flawed judicial system, can hardly be expected to provide the consistent and methodical application of the rule of law so eagerly sought—and so often claimed—by the British. Those who claimed that these deficiencies could be compensated by training in the field were perhaps the most wishful thinkers of all. Persons who arrived in India to practice law were almost unanimous in condemning the existing arrangements. J. B. Norton, a barrister at the supreme court in Madras and an active publicist on the need for judicial reform, claimed that "throughout the length and breadth of this Presidency, those who occupy the judicial benches are totally incompetent to the decent fulfillment of their duties."[87] Even allowing for Norton's hyperbole, the evidence he presents is very unflattering to the Madras judicial system. In one instance, the *Faujdari Adalat* convicted and sentenced to death a person for murder even though in the course of the trial no evidence was recorded to establish the identity of the corpse.[88] Norton also raised the important issue of the independence of the judiciary. In his opinion, all judicial officials lived in fear of the government's censure, or in the parlance of the time, "a whigging."[89] This lack of independence was clearly the result of the subordination of the judicial function to revenue needs as well as the government's ability to reassign its servants at will.

Within this flawed legal system, the use of torture should be understood as a cheap and effective means to secure a confession, which most police understood to be the proof their superiors wanted. The *Faujdari Adalat* warned that it was common for "confessions to be extorted and evidence concocted to save themselves from the stigma, and consequences of failure in the detection of crime."[90] One circuit court judge reported that "there is a general distrust of police proceedings in Cuddapah; of this the police are so sensible that they endeavour to remedy the defect by false evidence."[91] Even defenders of the existing system were forced to admit the degree to which confessions and evidence were manufactured, with one writing that "the very best of them [police] will not hesitate at strengthening a case by a little perjury."[92] It is here that we find an amazing paradox that reconciles the low rate of convictions with the frequent use of torture.

Confession has been termed by one recent writer the Queen of Proof, and confessions served as the basis of most convictions in India.[93] Confessions, and other forms of oral testimony, were the most frequent types of evidence produced. In the words of one circuit court judge: "The great number of witnesses called for the prosecution, as well as for the defence . . . amply attest the values of oral testimony, on which most criminal prosecutions depend."[94] Yet, British judges were allegedly predisposed to treat as suspicious any confession given before a police officer because they generally suspected that it had been secured through torture. The problem, however, arose in the way in which evidence was accumulated and then presented in court. Evidence accumulated by the police was, for institutional reasons, treated as already proven. In cases where the trial was conducted by European criminal court judges, acquittals or convictions depended entirely on the evidence collected by *tahsildars* and their assistants.[95] Criminal court judges, because they lacked any authority over the police, had to take a very circuitous route through the magistrate-collector if they wanted more information. Frequently, they were too late. Because of this, one committee appointed to investigate criminal procedure found that "although it most often happens that further investigation is required, or the presence of other parties than those who have been forwarded by the police officers, the criminal judge has no alternative; the Regulations which declare that 'no other communication shall be necessary [to the police]' puts an end to the proceeding."[96] This failing was only addressed much later in the Code of Criminal Procedure introduced in 1861.[97]

Forced by the judicial system to rely almost exclusively on the probity of the police, judges were bounded in reaching their decisions by the limited extent of evidence presented by the police. Hence, a confession was often the only evidence presented to the judge. The aforementioned committee also found that "where there is a confession, or pretended confession, almost always the examination before the police officer contains little direct or circumstantial evidence."[98] Bearing in mind the widespread suspicions entertained by European judges of the truthfulness of most confessions and the lawfulness by which they were secured, it is no wonder that so many individuals were acquitted. A further inducement to discount testimonies and confessions was based on racist appreciations of the Indian people, which argued that Indians had, in the words of one English jurist, a "habitual disregard for the truth."[99] Such stereotyping was also extended to the police: "As might be expected, native inaccuracy of mind is equally conspicuous in Police Officers."[100] As early as 1815, the *Faujdari Adalat* instructed circuit court judges to treat cautiously any confession given to a police officer.[101] In spite of these reservations, confession continued to be the basis for most convictions. One contemporary source estimated that only 4 in every 100 convictions in Britain arose from confession as compared to 70 out of 100 in India.[102] Confessions were the means to bring alleged criminals to court and were instrumental in securing the conviction of those found guilty, yet simultaneously ensured that most crimes went unpunished. This contradiction, which lay at the heart of many claims of torture, did not pass unnoticed. "The smallest discrepancies in the evidence are held to invalidate truth, but when the witnesses agree in any particular point, this agreement is also looked to be the surest proof of their falsehood."[103]

Any *ryot* unfortunate enough to be tortured had little hope of redress. The torture committee pointedly noted that "in the course of this investigation there is one thing which has impressed us even more than the conviction that torture exists; it is the difficulty of obtaining redress."[104] Once again, this should not be seen as a revelation, for similar sentiments had been voiced twenty years before. At that time, a parliamentary committee expressed "our astonishment at your supineness and indifference on this important subject."[105] This failure to address individual complaints arose in part from the nature of the judicial system. But it also arose through the blind eye that many British officials willfully turned toward this practice. Institutionally, the possibilities of submitting a grievance against the police were very restricted. At the local level, the investigating officer was most likely either an accomplice, or the superior of the peon or *tahsildar* who inflicted the torture. Appeals further up the hierarchy were similarly doomed to failure. It was a well known practice of *tahsildars*, and for that matter their equivalents in Bengal the *daroghas*, to employ spies to observe their superiors and warn them of any enquiries being directed at their actions.[106] Should they not be forewarned, any investigations from above would be based on little evidence, for as previously noted, digests of local police activity were not commonly kept. Moreover, the most likely person to uncover evidence of torture, the criminal court judge, lacked the authority to undertake either an investigation or the prosecution of the offender.[107]

Once again we find the curious subordination of judicial to revenue functions at work, for the police were answerable only to the collector-magistrate. Hence, they were not linked to the judicial system. "The judicial officers are not allowed to interfere with them, nor even with the magistrate, except in a very limited number of cases."[108] Torture, or any other form of official abuse of authority, did not constitute one of these limited number of cases. This left the victim to try and seek redress through the civil court apparatus, a procedure that was costly, slow, and uncertain. Even if allegations of torture were successfully introduced into a court, and the alleged perpetrators brought to trial, an astounding number of accused were released. Records from the court in North Arcot show that of ninety-three charged, only seven were convicted. Interestingly, however, the verdict for the remainder was not "not guilty," but "dismissed as not proved." This decision, reminiscent of the Scottish "not proven" verdict, suggests that although there were often good grounds for suspicion, it was very difficult to establish beyond reasonable doubt that torture had actually taken place. Fake death certificates were apparently easily obtained and, as already noted, the police were careful not to release prisoners into the custody of the jails until torture marks had disappeared.

When police officers were found guilty of torture (and a surprising number were given the judicial handicaps outlined above), the punishments meted out to them were farcical in their leniency. In most cases (twenty-six out of twenty-seven in 1829), a fine was all that was imposed.[109] The same was true in 1859, when 1,351 of 1,413 cases brought against the police resulted in fines.[110] They were rarely docked more than a few rupees, with most fines falling between three and seven rupees—less than a month's wage.[111] Dismissal appears to have been the most severe punishment normally awarded, and as one witness to the committee confided, dismissal was counterproductive because it encouraged torture and extortion; simply, many police wanted to make their fortunes while they had time to do so.[112]

Ultimately, the persistence of police torture depended on the degree to which the colonial state was willing to tolerate its existence. As one circuit court judge insisted in the 1820s, "I see no other way of accounting for it than in the leniency with which such aberrations are noticed by their immediate superiors."[113] In the case already noted of the elderly woman being flogged with nettle branches, the perpetrators were never punished even though a civil surgeon was called to treat the woman's wounds.[114] Even more revealing are the testimonies of the witnesses to the committee, testimonies to which, unsurprisingly, the committee took little notice. Kistna Pallay of Tanjore stated that after being tortured, "I did not complain to the Collector; what is the use of a poor man like me complaining."[115] Further indictments of the system emerged from other witnesses. Chenchoo Raumoodoo reported that when he complained to the magistrate in Nellore, "he got angry and told us to go away."[116] Nullandy Naik of Chingleput told the committee that he had been falsely accused of participating in a robbery. When he refused to confess, first his wife was tortured, which resulted in her death, and then his son was tortured to such an extent that he gave false evidence against his father. At the trial, Nullandy protested his innocence and his son retracted his statement, claiming it had been extracted by torture; but the British judge took no notice of it.[117] One of the most blatant episodes of a British magistrate covering up for his subordinates occurred when a Shaivite Brahman named Sundarapa Iyer delivered a written complaint to the magistrate, a complaint supported by a testimonial from the prison surgeon about the beatings he had sustained while in police custody. Moreover, his injuries were still visible. On this occasion the collector tore up the complaint, and as Sundarapa noted, it was because of the close relationship he had with the *tahsildar*.[118]

In the climate of the time, few pressed for an investigation of British complicity. The committee chose not to pursue it, while others were content to criticize the judicial system for not controlling its subordinates, thereby transferring direct responsibility to the Indian police. No one wanted to raise the possibility that some British officials deliberately overlooked obvious instances of torture taking place in their districts. To have done so would have meant questioning the fundamental assumptions regarding the efficacy and morality of British rule. One of the few exceptions to this conscious act of self-delusion can be found in the *Edinburgh Review*.[119] This article, while maintaining that the source of torture in India ultimately derived from the characteristics of the people, does explicitly charge the British administration with a degree of conscious complicity in the persistence of torture.

Conclusion

That torture was so long tolerated in India can be explained in two ways: It did not interfere directly with the administration of the Raj, and it was believed to be inherent in Indian society. Regarding the first of these, it was argued that the loyalty of the people in the Madras Presidency, as evidenced by their quiescence during the mutiny, proved that torture in itself was not undermining British rule.[120] Furthermore, to rid India of torture would require a profound feat of social engineering because many saw torture as deeply embedded in the nature of the Asiatic character. Mere legislative enactment could not do away with it. In contesting the outcry raised in Parliament over allegations of torture in Madras, the *Calcutta Review* observed: "Torture in its real sense has always been resorted to in oriental countries, to obtain proof of guilt, or recover stolen property."[121] This assumption that torture was culturally rooted in India offered for many a convenient escape because it meant that any type of remedial action, short of replacing all Indian police with British-born ones, was predictably bound to fail. An interesting twist on this racist explanation was offered by *The Times*: "It is not the torture of the high European sort... Indian torture is ready, impromptu, ingenious, cheap, annoying, disgusting, revolting and petty in the extreme... It is the torture of very wicked children."[122]

When action was taken against these abuses—action whose efficacy is dubious given that torture continued right through until independence—it was owing less to Victorian sensibilities and attachments to due process of law than to the realization that the publicity attached to the committee of

1855 revealed in stark detail that the claims to moral ascendancy and political omnipotency were being made a mockery. That this was the case is revealed in a key passage from the Court of Directors, who complained that action must now be taken because of the public outcry "rather than the earlier reports of our own servants."[123] As one critic of the Company put it, "cases of torture by the police are notoriously of frequent occurrence ... but as no political object can be served by taking notice of them, they are looked upon with perfect placidity by the government."[124]

Events in 1854–55 suddenly made torture a politically sensitive topic, seriously embarrassing the East India Company and exposing its occupancy of the moral high ground as a charade at a time when its charter was becoming ever more threatened in Britain. Action, or at least the appearance of action, was required. Even then, and in spite of the committee's efforts and such subsequent reforms as reorganizing the Indian police and codifying criminal law, torture persisted. In a regime in which subordination was more successful than legitimation, and in which subordination rested ultimately on coercion, the use of torture by the police can only be understood within the context in which the police operated. They too lacked legitimacy, and in their efforts to improve their position, and satisfy the demands imposed on them, torture was the outcome. This study of police and torture in India bears out the observation made by Ranajit Guha on what he saw as the fundamental paradox in colonial rule,

> the paradox that law, intended to serve as a basic defining principle of colonial rule, indeed as a primary signifier of British dominance in the subcontinent corresponding in function and structure to the hegemonic signifier of Rule of Law in metropolitan Britain, became itself an instrument of misunderstanding about the very nature of that dominance.[125]

Notes

An earlier version of this chapter was presented in May 1990 at the Canadian Historical Society's annual conference in Victoria, Canada. I have been most fortunate when redrafting this chapter to have been able to draw on the talents of a diverse body of scholars. The conclusions, however, are mine alone. My sincere thanks to L. Knafla, S. Ambirajan, J. R. Ferris, M. Konnert, E. Moulton, and E. Ingram for their contributions. P. Kattenhorn of the India Office Library and Records rendered invaluable assistance in tracking down contemporary prints and drawings of the police in Madras.

1. C. A. Bayly, *The Imperial Meridian: The British Empire and the World, 1780–1830* (London, 1989), 153. I am grateful to P. J. Marshall for references to Minto's activities in Java.
2. Presidency of Madras, *Report of the Commissioners for the Investigation of*

Alleged Cases of Torture in the Madras Presidency (Madras, 1855); Debates of the House of Commons, 11 July 1854, *Hansard*, 3d ser., 135 (1854): 59–90.

3. The Madras committee's report has been featured in several other works, most notably Malaise Ruthven, *Torture: The Grand Conspiracy* (London, 1978); and Edward Peters, *Torture* (Oxford, 1985). In these works, however, torture itself is the focal point, and what happened in Madras is merely illustrative material, rather than the case here, where torture is examined to shed light on the operations of the police.

4. Peter D. Fraser, "Observing the Empire: Gandhi, Malabari, Tagore and Edun, 1888–1928," *Indo-British Review* 16 (1989): 9–10.

5. Bayly, *Imperial Meridian*, 129.

6. D. Killingray, "Punishment to Fit the 'Crime'?: Penal Policy and Practice in British Colonial Africa," unpublished seminar paper delivered at the School of Oriental and African Studies, University of London, May 1985.

7. Amnesty International, *Amnesty International Report for 1988* (London, 1988), 158–60.

8. Bernard S. Cohn, "From Indian Status to British Contract," *An Anthropologist among the Historians and Other Essays* (Delhi, 1987), 463.

9. [C. W. Russells and Maj. Smith], "The Use of Torture in India," *Edinburgh Review* 103 (1856): 178.

10. Cohn argues that the three traditional dispute-settling devices in India on the advent of British rule were "supernatural intervention, the naked use of force and the rhetoric of compromise" ("From Indian Status to British Contract," 465).

11. *Report*, 50. I am grateful to S. Ambirajan for drawing my attention to the richness of local folklore.

12. Ranjan Chakrabarti, "Pax Britannica and the Nature of Police Control in Bengal Rural Society, c. 1800–1860," *Bengal Past and Present* 105 (1986): 92.

13. Basudev Chatterji, "The Darogah and the Countryside: The Imposition of Police Control in Bengal and Its Impact (1793–1837)," *Indian Economic and Social History Review* 18 (1981): 28.

14. Malcolm Lewin, *Torture in Madras* (London, 1857), 8.

15. *Report*, app., clxii.

16. The most comprehensive and stimulating discussion of law and policing in India is David Arnold, *Police Power and Colonial Rule; Madras, 1859–1947* (Delhi, 1986). See also the various essays in *Crime and Criminality in British India*, ed. Anand Yang (Tucson, 1985).

17. Sandria Freitag, "Collective Crime and Authority in North India," in Yang, *Crime and Criminality*. For a provocative reassessment of the role of law in colonial society, see D. A. Washbrook, "Law, State and Agrarian Society in Colonial India," *Modern Asian Studies* 15 (1981): 649–721.

18. Speech of Danby Seymour, 11 July 1854, *Hansard*, 3d ser., 135 (1854): 61.

19. F. J. Halliday, *Minute on the State of the Police* (Calcutta, 1857), 14–17.

20. Inspector General of Police, *History of the Madras Police* (Madras, 1959), 288–89.

21. [A Native Revenue Official], *On Bribery as Practiced in the Revenue Administration of the Madras Presidency* (Madras, 1858), 22.

22. House of Commons Debates, 11 June 1857, *Hansard*, 3d ser., 145 (1857): 1524.

23. India Office Library and Records (IOLR), Judicial Letter to Madras, 11 Apr. 1826, L/P&J/3/1386.

24. Evidence of Alexander Campbell, *Select Committee on East India Company Affairs*, Parliamentary Papers 12 (1832): 114.

25. IOLR, Judicial Letter from Bengal, 15 June 1830, E/4/131.

26. Lewin, *Torture in Madras*, 21; *Report*, app., xxvii.

27. George Thomas Kepple, Earl of Albermarle, *Speech of the Earl of Albermarle on Torture in the Madras Presidency* (London, 1856), 1.

28. "Torture in India," *Edinburgh Review*, 160.

29. IOLR, Judicial Dispatch to Madras, 11 Apr. 1826, L/P&J/3/1386; Thomas Munro, Minute of 30 Jan. 1827, Eur MS F151/104.

30. Thomas Munro, "Minute Reviewing the Condition of the Country and the People," 31 Dec. 1824; G. R. Gleig, *The Life of Major General Sir Thomas Munro* (London, 1830), 3: 319.

31. *Report*, 8.

32. House of Commons Debates, 11 July 1854, *Hansard*, 3d ser., 135 (1854): 59–90; *The Times*, 3 Sept. 1855, 6; *Punch* 28 (19 May 1855): 204; IOLR, Revenue Dispatch to Madras, 26 July 1854, E/4/980.

33. Anon., *Police Torture and Murder in Bengal* (Calcutta, 1861).

34. *Report*, 2.

35. Ibid.

36. Ibid., *passim*.

37. Ibid., 72.

38. Further difficulties in trying to use these testimonials in a statistical way are presented by the nature of the testimonials themselves. There was no common format used in them, and hence there is considerable variety in the amount and type of information each presents. Some provide a very complete narrative of the events, while others give only the sketchiest information.

39. "The police establishment which may be transferred to the Collector as Magistrate, shall not be considered as distinct from the revenue establishment, but shall be equally employed in police and revenue duties" (Regulation 11 [1816]).

40. For the evolution of this system, an excellent discussion is offered in Burton Stein, *Thomas Munro* (Delhi, 1989).

41. Ibid., 167.

42. Ibid., 35–36.

43. Bengal Judicial Letter, 15 June 1830, *S.C. on East India Affairs* 12 (1832): 281.

44. Minute of Charles Metcalfe, 7 Nov. 1830, ibid., 331.

45. The misunderstandings that sustain the myth of the village republic, and the consequences that followed, have become the subject of several excellent studies: Clive Dewey, "Images of the Village Community," *Modern Asian Studies* 6 (1972): 291–328; and David Ludden, *Peasant History in South India* (Delhi, 1989). In Ludden's words, "Research has relegated nineteenth-century ideas about isolated village republics in changeless rural India to the status of quaint historical fiction" (pp. 6–7).

46. Eugene Irschick offers one of the most recent summaries of historical explorations in this area. See "Order and Disorder in Colonial South India," *Modern Asian Studies* 23 (1989): 459–92.

47. For a fuller treatment of this, see the discussions of the committee appointed to restructure police and revenue arrangements in 1814 (IOLR, Madras Police Proceedings, Jan. 1814, P/328/56–57).

48. Stein, *Sir Thomas Munro*, 176 ff.

49. IOLR, Evidence of William Garrow, Collector at Coimbatoire, Madras Police Proceedings, Jan. 1814, P/328/56, 510. See also Arnold, *Police Power and Colonial Rule*, 1–35.

50. John R. McLane, "Bengali Bandits, Police and Landlords after the Permanent Settlement," and David Arnold, "Crime and Crime Control in Madras, 1858–1947," in Yang, *Crime and Criminality in British India*. See also Chatterji and Chakraborti.

51. Washbrook, "Law, State and Agrarian Society," 714.

52. Ludden, *Peasant History*, 128.

53. Madras to Bengal, 26 Aug. 1828, *S.C. on East India Company Affairs* 12 (1832): 293.

54. Ibid.

55. W. H. Sykes, "Statistics of Civil and Criminal Justice in British India, chiefly from the year 1836 to 1840 Inclusive," *Journal of the Statistical Society of London* 6 (1843): 112–14.

56. Ibid.

57. Patrick O'Brien, "The Political Economy of British Taxation, 1660–1815," *Economic History Review* 41 (1988): 1–27; John Brewer, *The Sinews of Power: War, Money and the English State, 1688–1673* (London, 1989); Douglas M. Peers, "War and Public Finance in Nineteenth Century British India: The First Burma War," *International History Review* 11 (1989): 628–47.

58. David Arnold, "Dacoity and Rural Crime in Madras, 1860–1940," *Journal of Peasant Studies* 6 (1979): 140–68.

59. A. Sarada Raju, *Economic Conditions in the Madras Presidency, 1800–1850* (Madras, 1941), 50. See also Dharma Kumar, "Agrarian Relations in South India," *The Cambridge Economic History of India*, ed. Dharma Kumar (Cambridge, 1983), 2:219.

60. Dharma Kumar, "Regional Economy—South India," *Cambridge Economic History of India*, 2:361.

61. A. Sarada Raju, *Economic Conditions in the Madras Presidency*, 241.

62. *Report*, 61.

63. Ibid., app., cxxx.

64. Lewin, *Torture in Madras*, 11.

65. Ibid., 10.

66. IOLR, Quoted in Revenue Dispatch to Madras, 12 Sept. 1855, E/4/983.

67. *Report*, 50, app., xlvii.

68. Evidence of James Oldham, Circuit Judge of Bareilly, 1832, *S.C. on East India Affairs* 12 (1832): 53.

69. *Report*, 49.

70. Stephen Frederic Dale, *Islamic Society on the South Asian Frontier: The Mappilas of Malabar, 1498–1922* (Oxford, 1980).

71. *Report*, 50.

72. Ludden, *Peasant History*, 188–96.

73. *Report*, 24.

74. Panchkouree Khan, *Confessions of an Orderly* (London, 1849), 11.

75. *Police Torture in Bengal*, 3.
76. *Report*, app., xlvii.
77. Eric Stokes, *The English Utilitarians and India* (Delhi, 1989), 225.
78. *S.C. on East India Affairs* 12 (1832): 616.
79. Government of India, *General Report for the Year 1859* (Calcutta, 1860), 2: app., 4.
80. *History of the Madras Police*, 111.
81. W. H. Sykes, "Statistics of Civil and Criminal Justice in British India, chiefly from the year 1836 to 1840 Inclusive," *Journal of the Statistical Society of London* 6 (1843): 112–14.
82. Judicial Letter to Madras, 12 Oct. 1831, *S.C. on East India Affairs* 12 (1832): 216.
83. Ibid., 217.
84. Ibid., 215.
85. Evidence of William Empson, professor of law at Haileybury, *S.C. on East India Affairs* 12 (1832): 129.
86. Evidence of Richard Clarke, *S.C. on East India Affairs* 12 (1832): 2.
87. J. B. Norton, *The Administration of Justice in Southern India* (Madras, 1853), 4.
88. Ibid., 46.
89. Ibid., 74.
90. Presidency of Madras, *Papers connected with the Reorganization of the Police Department* (Madras, 1859), 4.
91. Lewin, *Torture in Madras*, 13.
92. William Holloway, *Notes on Madras Judicial Administration* (Madras, 1853), 22. This pamphlet was written as a counterattack to the allegations raised by Norton.
93. Peters, *Torture*, 41.
94. Lewin, *Torture in Madras*, 10.
95. *S.C. on East India Affairs* 12 (1832): 219.
96. Ibid.
97. Stokes, *English Utilitarians*, 262–63.
98. Madras Judicial Letter to Bengal, 26 Aug. 1828, *S.C. on East India Affairs* 12 (1832): 292.
99. W. B. Bayley, *S.C. on East India Affairs* 12 (1832): 88.
100. Holloway, *Notes on Madras Judicial Administration*, 22.
101. *Report*, app., xxii–xxiii.
102. *Calcutta Review* 6 (1846): 35–89.
103. *Report*, 40.
104. Ibid., 51.
105. *S.C. on East India Affairs* 12 (1832): 221.
106. Chatterji, "Darogah and the Countryside," 36–37.
107. *S.C. on East India Affairs* 12 (1832): 220.
108. Ibid., 219.
109. Ibid., 615.
110. *General Report of 1859*, 2: app, 9.
111. *Report*, 41.
112. Evidence of A. Nulla Moothu, *Report*, app., clvi.
113. IOLR, *Judicial Dispatch to Madras*, 11 Apr. 1826, L/P&J/3/1386.

114. *Police Torture and Murder in Bengal*, 6.
115. *Report*, 26.
116. Ibid., app., xlvi–xlvii.
117. Ibid., app., xlix.
118. Ibid., app., lxxi.
119. "Torture in India," *Edinburgh Review*, 171–72.
120. "Torture in Madras," *Calcutta Review* 29 (1857): 441.
121. Ibid., 460.
122. *The Times*, 3 Sept. 1855, 6.
123. IOLR, Revenue Dispatch to Madras, 26 July 1854, E/4/980.
124. *Police Torture and Murder in Bengal*, 2.
125. Ranajit Guha, Introduction to Cohn, *Anthropologist among the Historians*, xix.

Tory Paternalism and the Politics of Penal Reform in Upper Canada, 1830–34: A "Neo-revisionist" Account of the Kingston Penitentiary

Russell C. Smandych
University of Manitoba

Over the years historians have made several attempts to unravel the reasons for the emergence of the penitentiary in nineteenth-century Ontario.[1] The routine question addressed in these studies is that of why legislation was enacted in Upper Canada in the 1830s to provide funding for the construction of a provincial penitentiary at Kingston. While the interpretations that historians have offered of the social forces that gave rise to this discussion differ in many respects, they commonly agree that Upper Canadians living during that decade came to view crime as a serious social problem, and that the construction of an Auburn-model penitentiary was part of the solution they came up with for dealing with the problem. The other part of the solution rested in the reform of the criminal law. In the same year that the legislature of Upper Canada enacted legislation to authorize the construction of a provincial penitentiary at Kingston,[2] legislation was enacted to reduce the number of crimes punishable by capital punishment and to substitute sentences of imprisonment at hard labor for many former capital offenses.[3]

The conclusions arrived at in these earlier studies have tended to be accepted without question by more recent investigators of the Upper Canadian experience with institutional reform. For instance, while undertaking much more detailed "micro"-level research on Upper Canadian responses to crime,[4] and the factors that gave rise to specific Upper Canadian penal reform developments,[5] more recent historians have for the most part continued to draw uncritically on the accounts offered by earlier penal reform historians. At the same time, while more critical "sociologically-informed" investigators have attempted to develop more "macro"-level accounts of the development of the penitentiary alongside other "disciplinary" institutions that emerged in Upper Canada in the 1830s,[6] these authors also fail to question the common assumptions underlying the accounts offered by earlier Upper Canadian historians of the penitentiary.

In the meantime, the work of leading foreign "revisionist"[7] and "neo-revisionist"[8] historians of criminal justice reform suggests that a fundamental reexamination of all aspects of Upper Canadian correctional history is in order. Most significantly, the accounts offered by these authors raise a host of new questions about the direction taken by nineteenth-century penal reform developments that have not been addressed in the Canadian context. In his path-breaking studies of the "discovery of the asylum" in Jacksonian America and the direction taken by criminal justice, mental health, and child welfare reforms in the "Progressive era," David Rothman offers critical insights into the factors that should be taken into account in attempting to explain the emergence of new nineteenth-century state control institutions like the penitentiary, and analogous changes in the character of dominant mechanisms of social control. Most notably, his studies point out the importance of exploring data bearing on the interrelatedness of the origins of parallel state institutions of control, the effect that national and regionally-specific indigenous circumstances and ideas have in giving rise to changes in social control, and the possible sources of opposition that emerge in reaction to and affect the outcome of efforts made at bringing about specific, well-intended "humanitarian" reforms.

Like Rothman's study of American developments, Michael Ignatieff examines the rise of the penitentiary within the context of major historical shifts that affected English society between the late eighteenth and early nineteenth centuries. While concerns with the morality and effectiveness of existing punishment alternatives provided the impetus for penal reform in late eighteenth-century England, these concerns, in Ignatieff's view, do not explain how the penitentiary came to be accepted as a rational solution to the problem of crime. Instead, Ignatieff argues that in order to adequately account for the rise of the penitentiary in England, one must examine the interrelated ideological, political, and economic factors that inspired the movement toward penal reform.[9] While sharing notable similarities with the work of other leading "revisionist" historians of the penitentiary, Michel Foucault's account suggests the need for an even more encompassing historical analysis.[10] In pointing to the dispersal of "disciplinary power" throughout the entire fabric of society as a major factor involved in the birth of the prison in France and other Western European countries, he brings into serious question the extent to which the state may be viewed as a dominant vehicle for exerting "social control." Most significantly, Foucault's analysis suggests that in any attempt to explain the emergence of new nineteenth-century state coercive control institutions like the penitentiary, one must also investigate the extent to which non-governmental, and often less coercive, agencies such as the family, the church, and private charitable organizations continued to play a role in exerting control over the deviant and the dependent in the period coinciding with and following the advent of new state-supported coercive control institutions.[11]

Among more recent "neo-revisionist" investigators who have drawn critically on the writings of Rothman, Ignatieff, and Foucault, the work of David Garland is most notable. In his study of changes in the character of British "penality" between the nineteenth and twentieth centuries,[12] Garland points to the need for overcoming the tendency (reflected in the work of leading revisionist authors) to focus on explaining apparent major changes in social control, at the expense of examining elements of historical continuity in the manner in which control was exerted over the deviant and the dependent. He recognizes that the beginning of the twentieth century witnessed various elements that came together to give rise to the development of "new" strategies for coping with the criminal and the poor. Unlike earlier revisionist authors, however, Garland investigates the "fragmentary" and "incremental" nature of these changes, and the extent to which they were the product of struggle, resistance, and compromise on the part of reformers and their opponents.[13] While the emergence of these new penal and public welfare strategies marked a significant change in the character of dominant mechanisms of control, he acknowledges that the new "structure of modern penality" that emerged in Britain did not represent "some kind of total rupture in which the previous practices altogether disappeared to be replaced by an array of newly-invented institutions carrying no trace of their past."[14] On the contrary, he points out that "many of the sanctions, institutions, and practices which existed within the (nineteenth-century) Victorian system still survive and play an important role in the modern (penal-welfare) complex." In discussing the specific types of institutions and practices that played a role in exerting control over the criminal and the poor during the Victorian era,[15] Garland, unlike earlier revisionist authors, points to the interdependent co-existence of various state and non-state agencies of control.

This chapter attempts to develop a more adequate account of the factors associated with the emergence of the penitentiary in nineteenth-century Upper Canada. It does this by undertaking a historical enquiry directed at exploring data sources that bear on questions about the rise of the penitentiary raised in the work of leading "revisionist" and "neo-revisionist" historians of penal reform. Most important, the work of these investigators suggests the need for an account of the Upper Canadian experience that encompasses a closer investigation of the following: (1) the broader macro-historical context within which Upper Canadian penal reform developments were situated; (2) the extent to which penal reform developments of the 1830s reflected elements of historical continuity in the manner in which social control was exerted over the Upper Canadian population; and (3) the nature and outcome of the politics of penal reform in Upper Canada in the decade. Most significantly, this chapter is concerned with showing how knowledge of these overlooked aspects of the Upper Canadian experience can alter our understanding of the circumstances that led Upper Canadians to build an Auburn-model penitentiary.

The Historiography of the Origins of the Kingston Penitentiary

Historians provide a common description of the circumstances that led to the founding of the Kingston penitentiary. According to this accepted view, the move toward penal reform was led by H. C. Thomson, the publisher of the Kingston-based *Upper Canada Herald* and a "moderate Reform" member of the House of Assembly from 1825 until his death in 1834. Thomson introduced a motion in the House of Assembly as early as 1826, in which he called on the legislature to consider the idea of constructing a penitentiary. Although a committee was appointed to look into the matter, the idea was dropped and nothing happened until 1830, when Thomson introduced a similar motion calling for the creation of a penitentiary.[16] Upon reintroducing the matter in 1830, Thomson's views concerning why Upper Canada needed a penitentiary were formally accepted and acted on. In 1831, Thomson, who had already visited a number of penal institutions in Britain and the United States, was made chairman of a select committee appointed to enquire into "the propriety of establishing a penitentiary" in Upper Canada. The preliminary report of the select committee was issued within a month of its having been appointed. In the report, Thomson outlined the major reasons he felt that Upper Canada needed a penitentiary, and expressed his view on what he thought should be its primary objectives. In essence, Thomson reported that he endorsed the penitentiary because he felt that it would serve as a more effective deterrent to crime than either existing commonly used punishment alternatives (like fines, whipping, banishment, and imprisonment in district jails) or the often unrealized threat of the death penalty.[17]

In 1832, Thomson and John Macaulay, a well-known "ardent Tory" and member of the governing "Family Compact" at Kingston,[18] were appointed as commissioners responsible for procuring plans and estimates for building a penitentiary, and gathering information on the system of management to be adopted in the institution. In carrying out their mandate, Thomson and Macaulay visited several penal institutions in the northeastern United States. They returned from their tour convinced that the system of prison discipline employed in the penitentiary at Auburn, New York, should be adopted in the institution proposed for Upper Canada.[19] Acting on recommendations contained in their report, in 1833 the House of Assembly enacted legislation providing £12,500 over three years to meet the cost of building a penitentiary, and appointed Thomson, Macaulay, and Henry Smith as commissioners to purchase the building site and oversee its construction.

Although providing a common description of the immediate circumstances and events that led to the founding of the Kingston penitentiary, historians have offered different accounts of the social forces that gave impetus to penal reform. In his study of changing attitudes toward crime and punishment in the 1830s, J. J. Bellomo argues that the major factor underlying the move toward establishing a penitentiary in Upper Canada was the "fear of growing disorder" and the perceived threat to traditional social values posed by the "influx of criminal elements" to the province. According to Bellomo, with the massive increase in immigration to Upper Canada in the 1830s, a "collective alarm" permeated society over the unprecedented "increase in crime."[20] Drawing on reports of criminal trials that suggested an increase in the severity of punishments imposed on individuals convicted of assault in the 1830s, he claims that Upper Canadians perceived that there was a dramatic increase in violent crime, and that this increase led judges to begin imposing more severe prison sentences on convicted offenders. In turn, this led to the serious overcrowding of district jails and a growing recognition of the need for more effective methods to deter violent criminal behavior. Bellomo concludes that Upper Canadians' perceptions of the growing incidence of violent crime, combined with the overcrowding of district jails that resulted from judges imposing harsher sentences, "made the construction of a penitentiary a legislative priority."[21]

Rainer Baehre offers a somewhat different account of the circumstances that motivated Upper Canadians to undertake the construction of a penitentiary. Although recognizing that the deplorable state of the district jails was a cause of public concern in Upper Canada, he argues that this concern was not the only factor that led Upper Canadian penal reformers to move toward establishing a penitentiary. More important, he contends, the impetus toward penal reform in Upper Canada stemmed from the move that was already underway to reform the criminal law in England, and "the 'discovery' of the penitentiary in the United States." Specifically, Baehre argues that while the "ideological origins" of the penitentiary "were rooted in the reforms of English criminal law in the 1830s," the specific features of the penitentiary system that developed in Upper Canada were more importantly influenced by penal reform developments that were occurring in the United States, especially at Auburn and Philadelphia.[22] Contrary to Bellomo's argument that the penitentiary was established first and foremost as a deterrent to violent crime, Baehre contends that, from the onset, the penitentiary was intended as a vehicle for bringing about the "moral reformation" of the criminal offender. Following closely on the Auburn model, Upper Canadian penal reformers set about establishing a penitentiary system that would work to bring about the "moral reformation" of criminal offenders through requiring them to engage in "hard labour," "preserve unbroken silence," and yield "perfect obedience and submission to their keepers."[23] According to Baehre and other historians,[24] the decision that penal reformers made to opt for the Auburn model also stemmed from their optimistic view that the employment of convicts at hard labor would make the penitentiary financially self-sufficient, and possibly even a source of added revenue for the province.

John Beattie offers another view of the circumstances that gave impetus to penal reform. Unlike Bellomo, Beattie argues that although "serious offences" were uncommon in the 1830s, Upper Canadians nonetheless felt that crime was a "serious problem."[25] More specifically, he claims that to "the men who shaped and administered the laws" of Upper Canada, criminality "provided evidence of much deeper and more serious evils . . . evils that threatened the moral and social fabric of society, and that called for powerful measures of defence."[26] Moreover, he argues that for "those who controlled the criminal justice system," "serious offences" included not only crimes against the person, but also, and more significantly, a wide range of property crimes such as arson, robbery, and theft.[27] Beattie contends that, as in England, the criminal law of Upper Canada was primarily concerned with the protection of property, and that in the 1830s Upper Canadians increasingly came to believe that "a large proportion of crimes against property" were being committed by a "criminal class" made up of idle "vagrants and foreigners" who were "similarly detached from the community" and "similarly feared and distrusted." Since the essence of the criminal law was the protection of property, and the existing system of "terror by example" appeared to be failing to deter crime, Upper Canadian penal reformers began searching for an alternative solution. At the same time in the decade, "the reform of the criminal came to be seen as the key to the future stability of society." As a result of their perception of the serious problem of property crime, and the growing belief in the importance of the "moral reformation" of criminal offenders, Upper Canadians moved toward building a penitentiary. In essence, Beattie concludes that Upper Canadian penal reformers believed that the penitentiary's ability to promote "internal discipline and good work habits would succeed in protecting property from the envy of the lower orders where the horrors of the gallows failed."[28]

Although offering slightly different interpretations of the social forces that gave impetus to penal reform in Upper Canada, the accounts offered by the above noted historians share several underlying assumptions. One common feature is their assumption that the factors that led Upper Canadians to build a penitentiary and reform the criminal law can be found in events and circumstances of the early 1830s, the most important being the massive increase in immigration to the province, and the consequent growing concern with the problem of crime. Another common feature of these accounts is their assumption that the move toward penal reform in the decade was a "popular" movement that stemmed from the widespread acceptance of the view that existing methods of preventing and controlling crime were no longer effective, and that new "penal measures" were urgently needed. A third common feature of these accounts is the sparse attention they give to identifying precisely who led the move toward penal reform in Upper Canada, and who, if anyone, opposed it.

One important exception to these narrowly-framed conventional accounts can be found in the recent work of Peter Oliver.[29] In his unpublished work on the history of corrections in Upper Canada, Oliver raises serious questions about the plausibility of earlier accounts of the origins of the Kingston penitentiary. Contrary to Bellomo's claim that Upper Canadians were motivated to build a penitentiary because of the threat to social order posed by the "influx of criminal elements" to the province, Oliver argues that "there is amazingly little (evidence) to lend support to the thesis that Upper Canada was perceived to be on the brink of social disorder or that the threat posed by deviant populations required the resort to some harsh new regimen of social control." In a similar vein, Oliver questions Beattie's claim that Upper Canada's "criminal laws were designed primarily to protect property rather than persons," and that sentencing offenders to hard labor in the penitentiary was viewed by Upper Canadians as a more effective method of achieving this end. Oliver argues that, while this may have been so in England, the basis for applying this judgment to Upper Canada is unclear. Oliver also questions the suggestion, made by both Bellomo and Beattie, that "the men who shaped and administered the laws" of Upper Canada believed that crime was a "serious problem."[30]

Oliver's account of the move toward penal reform in Upper Canada departs significantly from the interpretations offered by other historians. The feature that most obviously sets his work apart is the attention he gives to the emergence of the penitentiary within the context of other coinciding developments in Upper Canadian correctional history, and the development of other state-supported segregative institutions for dealing with the deviant and the dependent. In his account of the history of the district jails of Upper Canada, Oliver points out that in the same years that Upper Canadians began to move toward building a penitentiary, significant efforts were being made to improve and reform the province's district jails. The most significant feature of Oliver's unpublished account is the mention he makes of the crucial role played in the realm of institutional reform by the leading members of Upper Canada's Tory governing elite, and the likely reasons why they decided to give their support to building institutions like the penitentiary and the insane asylum.

Far from being motivated by the fear of growing social disorder, Oliver suggests that the institutional reform efforts engaged in by Upper Canadian Tories were more likely tied to the state of crisis that existed in relation to the province's district jails, and to the traditional paternalism of the Tory governing elite. According to Oliver, by the 1830s it became obvious that the district jails of Upper Canada were in need of drastic reform. Although the district jails had for many years served, more or less adequately, as places of confinement and refuge for criminals, the poor, and the insane, the massive influx of immigrants to the province created a situation where district magistrates no longer had sufficient political power or taxing authority to deal with social welfare problems at the local level. Faced with having to deal with this crisis, Oliver maintains that leading members of the province's Tory governing elite like John Beverley Robinson[31] and John Macaulay,[32] who were also always "staunch believers in the efficacy of institutions, turned readily to the central state to provide power and authority to effect necessary reforms."[33] These reforms included making serious efforts to improve conditions in district jails, establish an asylum for the insane, and found a penitentiary for dealing with more hardened criminals. Most suggestively, Oliver claims that the governing elite's "willingness to resort to large institutions financed largely by the state (owed) more to the traditional values of eighteenth- and nineteenth-century Toryism than to incipient social disorders of the 1830s."[34]

The most distinctive feature of Oliver's account is the extent to which it rests on an understanding of the dominant conservative ideology that prevailed in Upper Canada throughout the period from the 1790s to the 1830s, and the crucial role played in all aspects of the development of the province by members of Upper Canada's powerful Tory governing elite. At a more general theoretical level, Oliver's account lends support to the view that in order to understand why "Upper Canadians" moved toward reforming the criminal law and building a penitentiary, one has to appreciate the extent to which these developments reflected elements of historical continuity in the manner in which Upper Canada's Tory governing elite thought they should rule over the province's population and approach the task of dealing with different types of deviance and dependency.

Historical Continuity in Thinking about Reform: The Importance of Traditional "Tory-Paternalist" Sensibilities

The move toward penal reform in Upper Canada in the 1830s cannot be adequately understood without knowledge of the earlier sensibilities that leading Upper Canadian Tories shared about the need for state coercive control institutions, and the wisdom of supporting "humanitarian" reforms aimed at improving the lot of the colonial population. The clearest evidence of the sensibility that members of the Tory governing elite shared about the need for institutions exists in the form of a major criminal law reform statute enacted in the province in 1800.[35] Two major reforms brought about by this Act were the substitution of the sentence of banishment for transportation and the introduction of alternatives to the punishment of "burning in the hand," which was imposed on persons convicted of a felony who pleaded benefit of clergy to avoid a harsher sentence. As an alternative to this second "often disregarded and ineffectual" punishment, the Act stated that in the future it would be lawful for the courts to impose "a moderate pecuniary fine" on the offender or sentence him or her to be "either publicly or privately whippt [*sic*]." While the legislation of 1800 authorized the use of new criminal punishments to deal with felony offenders, it also contained this qualifying provision:

> Nothing in this act contained, shall abridge or deprive any court of the powers now vested in it by law, of detaining and keeping in prison, for any time not exceeding one year, or of committing to the house of correction or public workhouse, to be kept to hard labor, for any time not less than six months, or exceeding two years, any such offender as aforesaid.

The wording of this statute reveals a great deal about the sensibility that early Upper Canadian legislators (who were invariably members of the Upper Canadian Tory governing class) shared about the need for state coercive control institutions. Most important, the wording of the act of 1800 indicates that, even as early as this date, Upper Canadian legislators recognized the need for multi-purpose institutions to be built to deal with criminals and the recalcitrant poor. Specifically, the wording of the statute reveals that legislators drew a clear distinction between "prisons," whose main purpose was that of simply detaining or "keeping" inmates, and "work-houses" and "houses of correction," which, at least when in full working operation, had the added feature of requiring inmates to engage in "hard-labor." The idea that institutions could be used to bring about the "moral reformation" of inmates through forcing them to engage in "hard labor" was not a new idea to Upper Canadians who lived in the 1830s. From the earliest years of the province's existence, Upper Canadians were prepared to turn to the state to develop coercive control institutions for dealing with more troublesome forms of deviance and dependency. Although the authors of this early criminal law reform statute recognized that the province could not yet support the establishment of separate "prisons," "work-houses," and "houses of correction," they clearly anticipated that these institutions would eventually be built.

The wisdom of giving support to "humanitarian" reforms had also long been recognized by Upper Canada's Tory leaders. As early as 1814, in his "victory sermon" commemorating the end of the Napoleonic wars, the Reverend John Strachan, who is widely recognized to have been one of the key figures of the Tory governing elite throughout the period to the end of the 1830s,[36] pointed to the need for countries to be ruled by "enlightened and humane" leaders who would work toward bringing about "wise reforms" aimed at improving the condition of the masses.[37] More specifically, in his famous "victory sermon," Strachan pointed to the need for European monarchs, whose armies had just put an end to the spread of "republican democracy" from "atheistical France," to begin introducing pragmatic reforms aimed at raising "the lot of the lower classes," removing "oppressive systems of taxation," and "revising criminal codes" to make them more just and humane. According to Strachan, the outcome of the Napoleonic wars clearly showed that "the most solid improvements in the Science of governments" were obtained by taking "peaceable and gradual steps" toward political reform, not "by revolutions."[38] John Beverley Robinson, John Macaulay, and other leading Upper Canadian Tories shared a similar view of the role that "enlightened and humane" leaders should play in giving support to reforms aimed at improving the lot of those who were subject to their rule. In light of this knowledge of the common "paternalist sensibility" about reform shared by leading members of the Upper Canadian Tory governing elite, it is not surprising to find that they were the ones who led the move toward penal reform in Upper Canada in the decade.

The Tory Impetus to Reform: The Criminal Law and the Penitentiary

Contrary to the view shared by earlier historians of the Kingston penitentiary,[39] H. C. Thomson was not the driving force behind the move toward penal reform in the 1830s. Rather, it was leading members of the Tory governing elite, and in particular Lieutenant-Governor Sir John Colborne and Chief Justice John Beverley Robinson, who led the initiative to reform the criminal law and establish a penitentiary.

The key role played by the Tory governing elite in the move toward penal reform is revealed in part in the specific timing of developments. Although Thomson first introduced the idea of constructing a penitentiary to the House of Assembly in 1826 when he was still a "moderate Reformer,"[40] it is significant that during the two years in which the Reform Party of Upper Canada led by William Lyon Mackenzie held a majority in the assembly from 1828 to 1830, no steps were taken to follow up on Thomson's motion. It was only after the election of 1830, which returned a majority of Tories to the assembly, that attention was again given to considering the need for building a penitentiary. In the meantime, Thomson, who had come to deplore Mackenzie's brand of "radical" Reform politics, shifted his political affiliation. By the opening of the eleventh parliament of Upper Canada, which lasted from 1830 to 1834, Thomson had "become a consistent supporter of the administration."[41]

The person who called on the legislature in 1830 to consider building a penitentiary was Lieutenant-Governor Colborne, not Thomson. In his address to the assembly at the opening of Parliament in January 1830, Colborne "referred specifically to the need for a penitentiary and expressed his hope that the Assembly would take steps to bring forward a bill."[42] Significantly, it was only in response to his personal recommendation and encouragement that, in the ensuing session of Parliament, Thomson introduced a motion calling on the assembly to provide funds for building a provincial penitentiary. Earlier historians have tended to accept Thomson's motion, and his subsequent report of 1831, as evidence of his having led the move toward penal reform. Had they investigated the role played by members of the Tory governing elite in the realm of penal reform more closely, however, they would have arrived at very different conclusions about the impetus underlying the move toward the reform of the criminal law and the penitentiary. Specifically, they would have seen that the move toward penal reform in Upper Canada in the 1830s was intimately connected to, and in many ways a product of, the traditional paternalism of the Tory governing elite.

The underlying conservative impetus toward penal reform is also revealed in the fact that it was leading Upper Canadian Tories, the most significant being Chief Justice John Beverley Robinson, who led in reforming the criminal law. Robinson played a central role in the legislative process that led to the enactment of legislation aimed at reducing the number of offenses punishable by capital punishment. This role included his lead in introducing the capital punishment bill in the Legislative Council, and then, after it received the council's stamp of approval, forwarding the bill to the assembly.[43] It is also very likely that it was the Chief Justice himself who drafted the legislation.[44]

In addition to spearheading the enactment of the Capital Punishment Act of 1833, Robinson played an important role in informing Upper Canadians about the new legislation. One of the clearest indications of this is the charge he gave to the Grand Jury of the Home District assizes the first time it met following the introduction of the new law.[45] In his charge, which was later published in the form of a twenty-two-page essay for distribution to the public, the recent changes that had been made to the criminal law were described at length together with the reasons why the government had decided to introduce them. Although providing support for the view that Upper Canadians' thinking about the need for criminal law reform was greatly influenced by developments that were occurring in England,[46] the account also provides evidence that the reform of the criminal law in Upper Canada was very much a product of the traditional conservative values shared by the province's Tory governing elite.

The Chief Justice noted that whereas the criminal law of Upper Canada had remained essentially the same since 1800, many changes had been made in England to mitigate the severity of punishment. He pointed out that while it was "in imitation of this humane course" that the legislature of Upper Canada proceeded to mitigate the severity of punishment, in actual fact the reformed criminal code of Upper Canada went "considerably beyond the limits which have been set to the relaxation in England."[47] One of the major reasons for this liberal "relaxation" in the severity of the criminal law of Upper Canada was the fact that the previous law had never been closely followed. As evidence of this, Robinson pointed out that although over the years there had been "a great number of capital convictions" registered for horse stealing and other crimes, in so far as he could remember "the number of cases in which the sentence of death has been actually executed, has not exceeded forty, in the forty years that (had) elapsed" since 1791. This lenient application of the criminal law was attributed, among other factors, to the wise and humane manner in which judges like himself administered the law. Indeed, it was pointed out in the course of offering his history lesson on the province's criminal law:

> While the law stood on its former footing, as to the severity of punishment which it PERMITTED, it has been so carried into effect in this Province, that our criminal law, as it has been actually administered, will be found not to have been undeserving of that character for leniency, which in this sense has been conceded to the criminal law of England, by the most enlightened men of all countries. I mean that the innocent have found here the same protection in the independence, patience and humanity of juries, and speaking of my predecessors, I trust I may add, without indelicacy—in the impartiality of the Judge—while on the other hand, the guilty have found some refuge in the merciful interposition of the Crown, and have not actually paid the dreadful forfeit of life, except for crimes which it is still deemed necessary and justifiable to punish to death.[48]

The decision to reform the criminal law was not simply a matter of making an effort to "catch up" with the changes that had been made to the criminal law of England. Rather, this decision was more a product of the traditional "paternalist sensibility" that the Tory governing elite shared in the need for the leaders of a nation to work toward bringing about wise and prudent reforms. Although undeniably greatly influenced by developments that were occurring in England, Upper Canadian penal reformers had their own reasons for wanting to reform the criminal law. Most indicatively, at the end of his discussion of why the government of Upper Canada had decided to enact the Capital Punishment Act of 1833, Robinson told the members of the grand jury that "this retrospect may appear to you neither unsatisfactory nor uninteresting at this particular time, when we are about to enter upon the administration of a system of criminal law, more lenient in the letter, and therefore more congenial to the feelings of those whose duty it is to enforce it."[49]

In the years leading up to the reforms of 1833, the Chief Justice also used his charges to grand juries to express the reasons he supported the move toward establishing a penitentiary. Whatever the other purposes it might work to fulfill, for him the penitentiary was a necessary adjunct, or corollary, to reforming the criminal law. In his charge to the Grand Jury of the Home District assizes at its sitting in May 1832, he announced:

> It is with sincere pleasure that I congratulate you on the first step being taken towards the foundation of a Penitentiary, or of such other establishment for the employment

and correction of convicts, as the information which the Legislature has taken measures of obtaining, shall shew to be most proper.

Some institution of this kind it is really necessary to provide, before much can be prudently done, for mitigating the apparent rigor of our criminal code.[50]

In his charge to the grand jury at the opening of the Home District assizes in October 1832, Robinson informed the jurors of the progress that had been made on the penitentiary since their last sitting, and outlined other reasons he felt that such an institution was needed.[51] The most important was that it promised to offer a much more "humane" way of dealing with criminal offenders than the current practice of confining them in the miserable district jails. More specifically, he informed the Grand Jury:

I have much pleasure in adverting to the prospect of the speedy accomplishment of an object of much importance to the well being of this Province; I mean the erection of a Penitentiary, or the establishment of some public institution, by whatever name it may be called, in which convicts shall be received, and disposed of in such a manner as may make their imprisonment less burthensome to the community, and at the same time, a punishment more likely to be of service to themselves; for it cannot be denied that, under the present system, imprisonment is merely productive of unmixed misery to the convict.[52]

In summing up his discussion of the reasons why Upper Canada needed a penitentiary, Robinson said:

Policy and humanity both concur to recommend the course upon which we are about to enter. We had the advantage of a long experience with this system both in England and the United States of America, to direct us; and the Province we may hope will now be found not unequal to the expenditure which the establishment must, in the first instance, unavoidably occasion.[53]

The finding that stands out most from examining the penal reforms initiated by Upper Canada's governing elite is how little they were motivated by a sense that crime was a serious problem, or that new penal measures were urgently needed in order to deal with the problem. Indeed, a common theme that runs through Upper Canadian newspaper accounts of crime and the administration of justice in the 1830s, including those given attention to by earlier historians, is how little "serious crime" there was, and how judges—in their frequently reported charges to grand juries—most often accounted for any apparent increase in crime as being simply the result of an increase in the population. Earlier historians have attempted to explain the emergence of the penitentiary by arguing that Upper Canadians nonetheless perceived that crime was on the increase,[54] or that it was nonetheless still viewed as a "serious problem."[55] Had they taken into account evidence of elements of historical continuity in the way Upper Canadians thought about the institutions that were needed to exert control over the deviant and the dependent, they would have arrived at a far different view of why they decided to move toward building a penitentiary.

At least from the point of view of the Tory governing elite, crime was not a problem that required striking new departures in penal practice in order to be brought under control. The reason they did not view crime as a serious problem was because they recognized the important role played by less-coercive "non-state" agencies in working to prevent crime and other troublesome forms of deviance and dependency from becoming a problem. Indeed, for Tory penal reformers like Robinson and Macaulay, the effort to bring about "humanitarian" reforms to the criminal law and build a penitentiary went hand in hand with efforts to improve the "moral condition" of the population through less-coercive "non-state" institutions and agencies.

The fact that Tory penal reformers held this view is most explicitly reflected in the charges they gave to grand juries in the years leading up to the reforms of 1833. In his charge to the Grand Jury of the Court of King's Bench in the Johnstown District in August 1831, Robinson praised local residents for the fact that there were "so few instances of aggravated crimes," even while "the condition of society" was still to some degree "fluctuating" and the district had such a large population. Moreover, just two years before the enactment of the Capital Punishment Act of 1833, he remarked on how well the "good example" of religious instruction, in conjunction with the wise and just administration of the criminal law, were working to maintain the security and stability of society. Indeed, informed residents of the Johnston District were told:

> There are, indeed a few, and but a few charges of a serious nature to be investigated, and we should be indulging in a very visionary expectation, if we are to imagine that the best efforts of humanity can ever succeed in preserving a large society of men altogether without offence. The prevalence of good example, the effect of moral and religious instruction, and the CERTAINTY rather than the SEVERITY of punishment (through the prompt and vigilant administration of justice), may so far repress outrages and disorder as to afford, on the whole, satisfactory security for life and property, and for whatever can be protected by law; and in this state I trust the inhabitants of this District have now the happiness to live.[56]

John Macaulay also recognized the important role that less coercive "non-state" agencies played in maintaining the security and stability of society. In his charge to the Grand Jury of the Midland District Quarter Sessions in April 1832, Macaulay made similar praiseful remarks about the relative absence of crime in the district and the evident healthy state of public morality. Like Robinson, he felt that much of this was due to the organized efforts being undertaken by local residents to improve the "moral condition" of their fellow citizens. Macaulay was particularly struck by the decline in public drunkenness in the district, which he in part attributed to the efforts being pursued by recently established temperance societies. Indeed, in the same year that he toured the northeastern United States with Thomson to compile plans and estimates for building a provincial penitentiary at Kingston, Macaulay informed the Midland District Grand Jury:

> There appear to be more cases of assault from the country parts, on the present occasion, than usual, and fewer from the town. Taking the whole together, and considering the extent and population of the district, we may fairly say that though the numbers of our population have rapidly increased, and though the class of transient residents have also increased, offences have not multiplied in the same degree. Hence it may be inferred that public morals are improving. Indeed my own personal observations, so far it goes, leads me to consider such is decidedly the fact; for I have by no means witnessed so many instances of the effects of intemperance in our streets within the last twelve months as in former times... Education, common sense, and the admonitions of Holy Writ, all conspire to produce the result; which however, promises fare to be hastened by the powerful efforts of public associations having in view that laudable end.[57]

The decision to build an Auburn-model penitentiary in Upper Canada was clearly a decision that was made by the Tory governing elite. In addition, it is clear that leading Tory penal reformers intended the penitentiary to serve as a complementary mechanism of control, rather than as an alternative to what were perceived to be earlier "outmoded" and "ineffective" ways of preventing and controlling deviance and dependency.[58] While Robinson and Macaulay only allude to this in their charges to various grand juries, there is a wealth of historical evidence pointing to the fact that throughout the period to the mid-1830s prominent Upper Canadian Tories assumed a leading role in organized efforts that were undertaken to bring about the "moral uplifting" of the population through education and religious instruction.[59] Moreover, it has also been shown that in exactly the same years that they began moving toward reforming the criminal law and building a penitentiary, the Tory governing elite also began offering financial support to "private" benevolent societies that would enable them to continue their efforts at providing for the "worthy poor" and preventing the spread of pauperism.[60] Far from their having been motivated to build a penitentiary out of a fear of growing social disorder[61] or the perceived need for striking new departures in penal practice,[62] members of the Tory governing elite simply viewed it as another mechanism that could be employed to maintain a "well-ordered" society. It is significant, however, that while prominent Upper Canadian Tories like Robinson and Macaulay felt that having a penitentiary in which convicts could be usefully employed would be good for both criminal offenders and society, there were many Upper Canadians who did not share this view.

The Politics of Penal Reform: The Outcome of Opposition to the Penitentiary

As in the case of many of the other undemocratic policy decisions made by the province's governing elite, the decision to build a penitentiary at Kingston aroused considerable public debate. Unlike many other policy decisions made by the Tory governing elite during its long reign over the province, however, the decision to build a penitentiary at Kingston was not an issue that divided Upper Canadians strictly along ideological and political lines. While some leading Reformers at least initially supported the move, some of the province's leading Tories, with the notable exception of those who resided at Kingston, were vehemently opposed.

The study of the politics of penal reform in the 1830s provides further evidence of the inadequacy of earlier accounts of the emergence of the penitentiary in Upper Canada. First, it provides further evidence of the fact that Upper Canadians did not view crime to be a serious problem, and that they did not feel that new departures in penal practice were urgently needed in order to deal with the problem. Second, it shows that Upper Canadians, including even the most enthusiastic Kingston penal reformers, were not convinced that building a penitentiary based on the Auburn model would reduce the level of crime, or that an institution built on this model would eventually be self-sufficient. Third, the study of the politics of penal reform provides added insight that can be gained through addressing the question of who opposed the move toward building the Kingston penitentiary, and what the outcome of this opposition was.

One indication of the fact that Upper Canadians were not convinced of the "urgent" need for a penitentiary is the initial opposition there was to Thomson's motion of 1830, in which he called on the assembly to pass a bill authorizing the spending of funds to begin work on a penitentiary. In February 1830, the *Colonial Advocate* reported at length on the discussion that took place in the assembly over "Mr. Thomson's motion for a penitentiary."[63] The individuals who spoke on the motion included the Speaker of the House, the Reformers William Lyon Mackenzie and Peter Perry, and Thomas Dalton, a Tory member of the assembly and editor of the *York Patriot*. In spelling out his reasons for not supporting Thomson's motion, the speaker said "he would support the bill if we had the means of carrying its provisions into execution." He also agreed that "it was very important that the sentence of the law should be carried out in this country, if we had any proper mode of punishment, for crime was increasing, and it would increase with the population." However, "he would not vote for it at present because he thought there was not (enough) money on hand to carry its provision into effect."[64]

Peter Perry, the Reform member for Lennox and Addington, also opposed the motion because he felt "there was not the means to pay for it." The assembly had already been "called upon to improve the roads and bridges for the improvement of the country," but it did not have the means to pay for these either. He further pointed out that the assembly had also recently been called on to provide "25,000 pounds for the Welland Canal and for other purposes, for which, the finances of the Country were not sufficient." Perry acknowledged that he was aware that there was a prospect that the province's revenue situation might improve "in the course of a few years" as a result of the recent promise made by "His Majesty's government" to increase operating funds to the province.[65] If that occurred, he would be prepared to vote in favor of Thomson's motion.

William Lyon Mackenzie also initially favored the idea of building a penitentiary. However, he said that he "had lived long enough to know" not to count on the "Mother Country" to come up with funds that could be used by the assembly to bring about needed changes in the province. He suggested that rather than waiting to see whether the British government would provide more operating revenue, the assembly should try to raise a "small sum" in order to enable work to begin on building both a penitentiary and a "House of Refuge." He favored the idea of building a penitentiary because he recognized that "(o)ne of the greatest safeguards of our lives, liberty, and property, is the absence of crime; and (that) the present mode of prison discipline was not calculated to prevent it." His main reason for wanting to build a "House of Refuge" was that he recognized that an alternative was needed to the current practice of using the district jails as multi-purpose institutions, and because he had heard that "(c)rime had greatly diminished since the erection of Houses of Refuge in New York and Philadelphia." Although Mackenzie felt there was not enough money presently available to support Thomson's motion, he thought that "(a) Penitentiary and (a) House of Refuge for the Province could be begun and we could spare a little yearly towards finishing them."[66]

Like the leading Reformers who spoke on the matter, Thomas Dalton said that while he also felt "well disposed towards the measure" proposed by Thomson, he could not vote in favor of granting the sum asked for under the present circumstances. Dalton agreed, however, that if it turned out that "His Majesty's government" came through with its promise of increasing the province's operating revenue, he would be willing to support Thomson's motion. In addition, he said he hoped that as soon as more money was made available that steps would be taken to develop a "national system" of "elementary and general education" along the lines of the one being developed in the United States.[67]

The initial pragmatic opposition voiced against Thomson's motion indicates that, at least in 1830, members of the assembly did not feel that the construction of a penitentiary should be made a legislative priority. While Thomson's report of 1831 was eventually acted on, the decision made to build a penitentiary at Kingston was neither the product of a widespread belief that crime was becoming a "serious problem," nor that of a widely shared view that constructing a penitentiary would solve the problem. Indeed, one of the most significant findings that stems from the study of the politics of penal reform in the 1830s is how divided Upper Canadians were over the question of whether a penitentiary was really the answer to the problem of crime.

Although both Reformers and Tories in the assembly initially favored the idea of building a penitentiary, this consensus of opinion was short-lived. By 1833, Upper Canadians were embroiled in a heated debate over the decision to build a penitentiary at Kingston. While involving a much broader segment of the population,[68] it is significant that part of this debate was fought out among prominent Upper Canadian Tories, the most aggressive contenders being the editors of the Tory press at Kingston and York. The debate fought out in the Tory press was sparked by a letter that James Buchanan, the British consul at New York, wrote to Lieutenant-Governor Colborne in March 1833. In his letter, Buchanan outlined his views on the operation of penitentiaries in the United States, and warned Colborne about what the government of Upper Canada could expect if it went ahead with its plan to build a provincial penitentiary. Buchanan also sent a copy of his letter to Dalton, who published it on the front page of the *York Patriot* on 5 April 1833.

Buchanan informed Colborne that he had written his letter out of "deep interest" in the welfare of Upper Canadians, and his serious concern about the recent appropriation that had been made by the legislature to build a "State Prison" in the province. He said that his conclusions about the operation of penitentiaries were based on fourteen years of observing how they worked in the United States, as well as on the formal investigation he carried out on American penitentiaries at the request of the British government. In light of the information he had on the type of penitentiary system that was being proposed for Upper Canada, it was his duty to warn Upper Canadians:

> The introduction of this system will prove a great evil to the Province; a continually absorbing gulf of expenditure; that the funds it will from year to year require, independent of the crime it will generate would be sufficient to carry railroads from one end of the province to the other. I beg leave thus to record my testimony against the introduction of this system, and to warn my fellow subjects and all possessors of property that they are laying an egg which will produce a monster, that will absorb the taxes which we or our children must pay.[69]

Buchanan directed numerous specific criticism at the manner in which penitentiaries operated in the United States. First, he pointed out that unless inmates were separated from each other twenty-four hours a day, penitentiaries simply became a place for criminals to learn more about crime.

Second, he remarked that penitentiaries in the United States were well known for being "Schools of Vice" that worked "to furnish inmates for the State Colleges of Crime, where villainy attains its highest degree." Another major problem with penitentiaries was the fact that they ended up being filled by inmates who worked at trades that put them in direct competition with "the honest mechanic" who had to depend "on his own labor to sustain his family." In addition, he argued that, far from "reforming" inmates, the fact of their being sentenced to imprisonment at hard labor had the effect of terribly stigmatizing individuals. Even if they happened to learn a trade, they would never be able to practice it or "be admitted among respectable mechanics" once they got out of prison. According to Buchanan, while "escaping the gallows" or having been found guilty of killing one's fellow man "may be overlooked," "having been in a state prison or penitentiary is a degree of degradation not to be purged, and clings to the third and fourth generation." Just as seriously, he warned Colborne that one had to be skeptical of the claims made by advocates of the penitentiary. They were often motivated more by their own economic interests than a sincere belief in the effectiveness of the convict labor system in "reforming" criminal offenders. Indeed, the Lieutenant-Governor was informed:

> I do not presume to say cases may not have arisen, nor do I question the persuasion which prevails in the minds of those who have stated cases of reformation (were) the effect of prison discipline; but I have not yet found a clear decided case of amendment and restoration to society, while my inquiries have been incessant among the advocates of the system. The principle holds good in both hemispheres that all advocates for, gainers by, and officers connected with an institution, cheerfully award praise where a portion is sure to be reflected on themselves, or that upholds an institution that affords patronage or gain.[70]

Of all the problems he identified, Buchanan said that his major concern was that building penitentiaries diverted attention away from efforts at preventing crime. Buchanan argued that it was a wasteful exercise spending huge amounts of money attempting to reform criminal offenders—which was rarely if ever successful—when this money could be better used to support institutions that worked to prevent crime. In particular, he pointed out how important it was to support "Sunday Schools" and other "public institutions of religion" that were concerned with "training up the rising generation in a regard for the Lord's day, and acquaintance with the Holy Scriptures." In summing up the major reason he felt obligated to warn Upper Canadians about going ahead with building a penitentiary, Buchanan stated:

> My great anxiety is to endeavour to arrest the misdirection of public funds, and exertions of the benevolent from making provision for criminals, to measures having in view the prevention of crime, and awaken sympathy on behalf of those on the

edge of the pit, instead of such liberal provision for those who have already fallen into it.[71]

The publication of Buchanan's letter added strength to the opposition that was growing over the decision to build a penitentiary at Kingston. By the fall of 1833, local Kingston mechanics, backed by both Reformers and Tories from outside Kingston, were openly campaigning to stop the penitentiary from being built.[72] In December 1833, local Kingston opponents of the penitentiary gathered over 500 signatures on a petition they sent to Lieutenant-Governor Colborne, in which they spelled out their reasons for wanting to see the project stopped. Specifically, these petitioners shared the following view:

If a Penitentiary should go into operation, under the system of manufactory, it will have a tendency to bring the labor of rogues in competition with that of honest men, and by the greater facilities in manufactory tend ultimately to drive from this Town the most valuable and industrious portion of its inhabitants: That while the population of the Province has been of late years greatly on the increase, the diminution of crime has been in like proportion affording a just criterion that the establishment of a Penitentiary is not called for; That your Petitioners are of opinion that Treadmills, adjoining to the District Jails, would amply suffice for purposes of useful correction, and could be erected for a trifling expense.[73]

In weeks following this petition, the debate over the penitentiary reached its height in the Tory press. While the editor of the *Kingston Chronicle and Gazette* took up the cause of defending "the system of manufactory" proposed for the penitentiary,[74] the editor of the *York Patriot* stood firmly behind the Kingston mechanics and their opposition to convict labor.[75] The *Patriot* published a response to the *Chronicle's* defense of the penitentiary on 24 December in which it made its views abundantly clear. Acknowledging the debt he owed to the information provided by Buchanan, the editor of the *Patriot* stated:

We consider the movement of the Mechanics of Kingston as indicative of a great advance in moral intelligence. Penitentiaries have been found in the United States "*a splendid failure*", no human effort can resuscitate their reputation, and it is nothing complimentary toward the Legislature that it has consented to put on the case of rags of the States. They will doubtless still continue for a time to be lauded in books, pamphlets and newspapers like the dogmas of drawling sectaries, because there are so many to uphold them to whom they are a source of profit; but to need besides, is American prison discipline other than an object of scorn and derision and disgust. If as the Kingston Chronicle assumes (there is) an argument in favour of Penitentiaries . . . we would ask if their source of information be any better than those of the British Consul who has resided on the spot for more than 20 years, and taken special pains to inform himself on the subject, by order and for the information of the British government.[76]

In response to the claim made in the *Chronicle* that the penitentiary would work to bring about the "moral reformation" of convicts, the *Patriot* stated further:

As for "reforming" your penitentiary gentry it is all fudge: how many have ever been reformed? and as to the punishment of criminals, what punishment can be deemed when it is notorious that many industrious mechanics commit petty crimes for the purpose of procuring a maintenance in the jail which the blighting system has prevented him from obtaining outside the prison walls.[77]

In its following issue, the *Chronicle* responded to the accusations made in the *Patriot* by criticizing it for having copied its line of argument from the *Colonial Advocate* and other "papers of an infidel character," while ignoring that "the great body of the American press and people are in favor of penitentiaries as now carried out." In a somewhat more conciliatory manner, the editor of the *Chronicle* responded that even those who supported the move toward building a penitentiary based on the Auburn model recognized that there was no guarantee that it would work to reduce crime. In an attempt to bring the debate over the penitentiary to a mutually agreeable end, he conceded as follows:

We would by no means arrogate to ourselves as the Patriot intimates, the exclusive right of treating on the affairs of Kingston, nor are we "quite so sage" as not to acknowledge that the Patriot may feel, and always feel a warm interest in the Town of Kingston, and be able to defend her interests, as he has done before, with fidelity and ability: yet we have not been prepared to admire a useless and pernicious crusade against Penitentiaries, as that they be held up as objects of "scorn, derision and disgust", before they have even had a trial, nor should we like to have any attempt made at a distance, to set our Townsmen by the ears, to no purpose and merely to serve the notions of an individual. We consider, as we have said before, the Penitentiary to be a Provincial institution, and no individual whims, hobbies, or opinions should be suffered to thwart its object. The right of a prison, of course, remains undoubted; but let us try, before we condemn.[78]

The response of the *Patriot* to this peace overture was no doubt found less compromising than the one that leading Kingston Tory advocates of the penitentiary had hoped for. On 7 February 1834, the *Patriot* published another stinging attack on the penitentiary project. Thomas Dalton ironically noted how "admirable" it was "to see the coolness with which we are told in the papers, that the Penitentiary at Kingston is to cost 56,000 (pounds) and that jailers, and turnkeys, and masons have been engaged in America at great expense to superintend the perfection of this insane conception." He concluded, however, that it was even still not too late to reverse the mistake. Specifically, he recommended:

Let our Legislature pause, ere it aim a deadly blow at civil liberty, and the prosperity of the most valuable class of our population. It is not too late to retrograde, a few pounds of Gunpowder will efface the shame of the Province, and half the money that was required for the Penitentiary, will build FIFTY CHURCHES, OR A HUNDRED SCHOOLS AND THE RESIDUE WOULD HANDSOMELY ENDOW THEM!!!![79]

Conclusion

Given the vehement opposition to building an Auburn-model penitentiary in Upper Canada, one might well ask why the Kingston project was ever completed. One most probable reason was the simple fact that the power of those who wanted to see the penitentiary built outweighed the power of the forces of opposition. In the mid-1830s, the Tory governing elite of Upper Canada still had firm control over the province. At the same time, the leading Kingston Tory advocates of the penitentiary—John Macaulay and H. C. Thomson—had an ideological and personal vested interest in seeing the project completed. Macaulay was clearly the most important figure behind the construction of the penitentiary. In his role as one of the commissioners appointed to oversee the project, he assumed the lead in working to ensure that the penitentiary was built to conform to the Auburn model.[80] The seriousness with which the commissioner took up his appointment no doubt had a great deal to do with his "profound conviction that proper institutions, whether they be constitutional, religious, or educational, could not only control conduct but transform men into persons as sober, sound, and respectable as himself."[81] For Thomson, the rewards were even more personal. One of the reasons he recommended that the provincial penitentiary be built at Kingston was his desire to be the first penitentiary warden in Upper Canada. If he had not died in 1834, it is almost certain that he would have been.[82]

While these factors undoubtedly contributed to the completion of the Kingston penitentiary, there was one other factor that made it a certainty. As Garland has shown to have been the case with changes in dominant mechanisms of control in early twentieth-century England,[83] the acceptance of the penitentiary among Upper Canadians living in the 1830s was in part the result of conflict and compromise between the advocates of reform and their opponents. Owing to the widespread opposition to establishing a penitentiary system that threatened the livelihood of "honest mechanics," Kingston Tory advocates of the penitentiary made concessions to "anti-Penitentiary" Kingston tradesmen and their supporters. By March 1834, the editor of the *Kingston Chronicle and Gazette*—writing on behalf of the penitentiary's supporters—had come to accept the view that "convict labor shall never be instituted so as to cause injury to honest mechanics." In a further effort to dampen opposition to the penitentiary, it was agreed that "in no case... should (the) products of prison labor be sold below current prices, and each section of the province should receive its appropriate share of the goods."[84] It was only after these commitments that opponents of the penitentiary ended their campaign.

Although a case could be made for the argument that a penitentiary would have been built in Upper Canada regardless of either the long-standing paternalist sensibility about reform shared by the province's Tory governing elite, or the presence or absence of the opposition, the specific direction taken by penal reform developments in the province would have been much different had it not been for these factors. Had it not been for the initiative taken by the Tory governing elite and the personal interest taken by leading Kingston Tory penal reformers, the penitentiary would not have been established when it was. On the other hand, had the forces of opposition prevailed over the advocates of the penitentiary, the subsequent history of corrections in Upper Canada and later Ontario would likely have been much different. Indeed, if this opposition had not been overcome, it would have been many years later, after the "Treadmills" had either worn out or been found insufficient for the "purposes of useful correction," that Upper Canadians would have endorsed the idea of building a penitentiary.

Notes

An earlier version of this chapter was presented at the 1989 Annual Meeting of the American Society of Criminology held at Reno, Nevada. The author would like to thank Rod Kueneman, Beverly A. Smith, and the reviewers for *Criminal Justice History* for their constructive comments and editorial advice. This research was facilitated by funding received from the Solicitor General of Canada through its contributions to the Centre of Criminology at the University of Toronto and the Criminology Research Centre at the University of Manitoba. Additional funding was received from the Social Sciences and Humanities Research Council of Canada and the Ministry of Colleges and Universities of Ontario.

1. Rainer Baehre, "Origins of the Penitentiary System in Upper Canada," *Ontario History* 69 (1977): 185–207; J. Jerald Bellomo, "Upper Canadian Attitudes Towards Crime and Punishment," *Ontario History* 64 (1972): 11–26; John Beattie, *Attitudes Toward Crime and Punishment in Upper Canada, 1830–1850: A Documentary Study* (Toronto, 1977); C. J. Taylor, "The Kingston Ontario Penitentiary and Moral Architecture," *Histoire Sociale/Social History* 12 (1979): 385–408.
2. *Statutes of Upper Canada* (1833), 3rd William IV, chap. 44.
3. *Statutes of Upper Canada* (1833), 3rd William IV, chap. 4.
4. John Weaver, "Crime, Public Order, and Repression: The Gore District in Upheaval, 1832–1851," *Ontario History* 78 (1986): 175–207.
5. John D. Blackwell, "Crime in the London District, 1828–1837: A Case Study of the Effect of the 1833 Reform in Upper Canadian Penal Law," *Queen's Law Journal* 6 (1981): 528–67.
6. Thomas Brown, "The Origins of the Asylum in Upper Canada, 1830–1839,"

Canadian Bulletin of Medical History 1 (1984): 27–58; Barry Edginton, "The Formation of the Asylum in Upper Canada" (unpublished Ph.D. diss., University of Toronto, 1981); Robert Gaucher, "Class and State in Lower and Upper Canada, 1760–1873: Groundwork for the Analysis of Criminal Justice in Pre-Confederation Canada" (unpublished Ph.D. diss., University of Sheffield, 1982); "Canadian Civil Society, the Canadian State, and Criminal Justice Institutions: Theoretical Considerations," in *State Control: Criminal Justice Politics in Canada*, ed. R. Ratner and J. McMullan (Vancouver, 1987), 167–97.

7. Michel Foucault, *Discipline and Punish: The Birth of the Prison* (New York, 1977); Michael Ignatieff, *A Just Measure of Pain: The Penitentiary in the Industrial Revolution, 1750–1850* (New York, 1978); "State, Civil Society, and Total Institutions: A Critique of Recent Social Histories of Punishment," *Crime and Justice: An Annual Review of Research*, ed. M. Tonry and N. Morris (Chicago, 1981), 3: 153–93; David Rothman, *The Discovery of the Asylum: Social Order and Disorder in the New Republic* (Boston, 1971); *Conscience and Convenience: The Asylum and Its Alternatives in Progressive America* (Boston, 1980).

8. John Beattie, *Crime and the Courts in England 1660–1800* (Princeton, 1986); Jennifer Davis, "A Poor Man's System of Justice: The London Police Courts in the Second Half of the Nineteenth Century," *The Historical Journal* 27 (1984): 309–35; Margaret DeLacy, *Prison Reform in Lancashire, 1700–1850: A Study in Local Administration* (Stanford, 1986); David Garland, *Punishment and Welfare: A History of Penal Strategies* (Aldershot, 1985).

9. Ignatieff, *Just Measure of Pain*. In a subsequent paper, "State, Civil Society, and Total Institutions," Ignatieff offers a constructive critique of the work of leading revisionist historians of the penitentiary (including his own), and provides further insight into the type of research that is needed in order to develop a more plausible account of the origins of the penitentiary.

10. Foucault, *Discipline and Punish*.

11. For more detailed discussions of the range of theoretical insights offered in the work of leading revisionist historians of the 1970s, see Stanley Cohen, *Visions of Social Control: Crime, Punishment and Classification* (Cambridge, 1985); Russell C. Smandych, "The Upper Canadian Experience with Pre-Segregative Control" (unpublished Ph.D. diss., University of Toronto, 1989); and David Garland, *Punishment and Modern Society: A Society in Social Theory* (Chicago, 1990).

12. Garland, *Punishment and Welfare*.

13. Ibid., 162.

14. Ibid., 5.

15. Ibid., 36–70.

16. Baehre, "Penitentiary System in Upper Canada," 189; Taylor, "Kingston Ontario Penitentiary," 386.

17. Beattie, *Attitudes Toward Crime and Punishment*, 80–86.

18. Baehr, "Penitentiary System in Upper Canada," 191.

19. Beattie, *Attitudes Toward Crime and Punishment*, 86–96; Taylor, "Kingston Ontario Penitentiary," 387–89.

20. Bellomo, "Upper Canadian Attitudes," 16.

21. Ibid.

22. Baehre, "Penitentiary System in Upper Canada," 189, 207.

23. Ibid., 199.

24. Beattie, *Attitudes Toward Crime and Punishment*; Taylor, "Kingston Ontario Penitentiary."

25. Beattie, *Attitudes Toward Crime and Punishment*, 1.

26. Ibid., 2.

27. Ibid., 6.

28. Ibid., 12–13.

29. Peter Oliver is a leading Ontario historian who has been engaged for several years in undertaking a major study of the history of corrections in Ontario for the province's Ministry of Correctional Services. Although Oliver's research is still in progress, he kindly allowed me to read and make notes from the early manuscript chapters of his forthcoming book on the subject, *A History of Corrections in Ontario*. The following presentation of Oliver's arguments draws on this manuscript and his published account of the history of Upper Canadian district jails, "From Jails to Penitentiary: The Demise of Community Corrections in Early Ontario," *Correctional Options* 4 (1984): 1–10.

30. Oliver, *History of Corrections in Ontario*, n.p.

31. John Beverley Robinson was born in Berthier, Lower Canada, in 1791. He was the son of a Virginia Loyalist who had come to the province with his family after the American Revolution. Although his father's death led to the impoverishment of his immediate family, Robinson was fortunate in gaining the interest and concern of prominent citizens in his education and professional future, the most notable being the Chief Justice of the province, William Dummer Powell. During his youth Robinson was a student at John Strachan's elitist Cornwall Grammar School. He subsequently went on to become a key figure in the province's Tory governing elite. While still a law student, at age twenty-one, Robinson was appointed as acting-Attorney-General for Upper Canada, and later held the positions of elected House of Assembly member, Legislative and Executive Councillor, Solicitor General, and Attorney General. In 1828 he was appointed as the Chief Justice of Upper Canada. For more detailed biographies of Robinson, see Patrick Brode, *Sir John Beverley Robinson: Bone and Sinew of the Compact* (Toronto, 1984); and R. Saunders, "Sir John Beverley Robinson," *Dictionary of Canadian Biography*, 9: 668–78.

32. In addition to being a prominent Kingston Tory office holder and merchant, John Macaulay is said to have served for many years as "the chief organ of Tory (newspaper) opinion in the province" (S. F. Wise, "John Macaulay: Tory for All Seasons," in *To Preserve and Defend: Essays on Kingston in the Nineteenth Century*, ed. G. Tulchinsky [Kingston, 1976], 190). From 1818 to 1832, Macaulay, along with two other prominent Kingston Tories, was the owner and editor of the *Kingston Chronicle*.

33. Oliver, *History of Corrections in Ontario*, n.p.

34. Ibid.

35. *Statutes of Upper Canada* (1800), 40 Geo. III, chap 1. "An Act for the further introduction of the criminal law of England in this province, and for the more effectual punishment of certain offenders."

36. See G. M. Craig, "John Strachan," *Dictionary of Canadian Biography*, 9: 751–66; G. W. Spragge, "John Strachan's Contribution to Education, 1800–1823," in *Historical Essays on Upper Canada*, ed. J. K. Johnson (Toronto, 1975), 74–85; Robert Fraser, "Like Eden in Her Summer Dress: Gentry, Economy, and Society: Upper Canada, 1812–1840" (unpublished Ph.D. diss., University of Toronto, 1979);

S. F. Wise, "Sermon Literature and Canadian Intellectual History," in *Canadian History Before Confederation*, ed. J. Bumstead (Georgetown, Ont., 1972), 253–69; "God's Peculiar Peoples," in *Studies in Canadian Social History*, ed. M. Horn and R. Sabourin (Toronto, 1974), 260–86.

37. Wise, "Sermon Literature," and "God's Peculiar Peoples." Before arriving in Upper Canada in 1799, Strachan was trained as a teacher and Anglican minister in Scotland. In 1803 he established a grammar school at Cornwall, which for many years remained the institution where most of the figures who would go on to become members of the province's governing elite received their primary education. Within a few years of arriving in the province, Strachan also became the Archdeacon of the Anglican Church in Upper Canada. For more than two decades he also served as an Executive Councillor and member of the Legislative Council, thus exerting a considerable influence over succeeding Lieutenant-Governors.

38. Cited in Wise, "God's Peculiar Peoples," 280.

39. Baehre, "Penitentiary System in Upper Canada"; Beattie, *Attitudes Toward Crime and Punishment*; Taylor, "Kingston Ontario Penitentiary."

40. H. P. Gundy, "Hugh C. Thomson: Editor, Publisher, and Politician, 1791–1834," in *To Preserve and Defend: Essays on Kingston in the Nineteenth Century*, ed. G. Tulchinsky (Montreal, 1976), 215.

41. Ibid., 203.

42. Ibid., 219; *Colonial Advocate*, 18 Feb. 1830.

43. Brode, *Sir John Beverley Robinson*, 184.

44. Blackwell, "Crime in the London District," 539–41.

45. John Beverley Robinson, "Upper Canada. Statute 3d. Wm. IV. chap. 4. RELATING TO CAPITAL OFFENCES: with an exposition of its provisions, in a charge of Chief Justice Robinson, to the Grand Jury of the Home District," York, Upper Canada, 1833. Printed by Robert Stanton.

46. Beattie, *Attitudes Toward Crime and Punishment*; Baehre, "Penitentiary System in Upper Canada."

47. Robinson, "(C)harge . . . to the Grand Jury of the Home District," 22.

48. Ibid., 36.

49. Ibid., 37.

50. *Hallowell Free Press*, 1 May 1832.

51. *Hallowell Free Press*, 6 Nov. 1832.

52. Ibid., n.p.

53. Ibid., n.p.

54. Bellomo, "Upper Canadian Attitudes."

55. Beattie, *Attitudes Toward Crime and Punishment.*

56. *Brockville Gazette*, 11 Aug. 1831.

57. *Brockville Gazette*, 25 Apr. 1832.

58. This argument is developed in more detail and substantiated on the basis of a much broader range of historical data in Smandych, "Upper Canadian Experience with Pre-Segregative Control."

59. Ibid., 303–41.

60. Ibid., 271–302.

61. Bellomo, "Upper Canadian Attitudes."

62. Beattie, *Attitudes Toward Crime and Punishment.*

63. *Colonial Advocate*, 18 Feb. 1830.

64. Ibid.
65. Ibid.
66. Ibid.
67. Ibid.
68. Bryan Palmer, "Kingston Mechanics and the Rise of the Penitentiary, 1833–1836," *Histoire Sociale/Social History* 13 (1980): 7–32.
69. *Patriot*, 5 Apr. 1833.
70. Ibid.
71. Ibid.
72. Palmer, "Kingston Mechanics."
73. Public Archives of Canada (PAC), Ottawa, Upper Canada, Provincial Secretary's Correspondence Files, RG5 B3 vol. 7, 1833.
74. *Chronicle and Gazette*, 21 Dec. 1833, 28 Dec. 1833, 4 Jan. 1834, 18 Jan. 1834.
75. *Patriot*, 24 Dec. 1833, 7 Jan. 1834, 7 Feb. 1834.
76. *Patriot*, 24 Dec. 1833.
77. Ibid.
78. *Chronicle and Gazette*, 28 Dec. 1833.
79. *Patriot*, 7 Feb. 1834.
80. Public Archives of Ontario, *Macaulay Papers*, William Powers, Deputy Keeper, State Prison Auburn, to J. A. Macaulay, 20 Feb. 1833, 11 May 1833; B. C. Smith, Chaplain, State Prison Auburn, to J. A. Macaulay, 12 Mar. 1833, 13 Mar. 1833.
81. Wise, "John Macaulay," 202.
82. PAC, Upper Canada, Provincial Secretary's Correspondence Files, RG5 C1, vol. 1; H. C. Thomson to Lt. Col. Rowan, transmitting a copy of the proposed act for the government of the penitentiary and applying for the appointment of warden of the penitentiary, Kingston, 10 Oct. 1833; Gundy, "Hugh C. Thomson," Editor, Publisher, and Politician," 219.
83. Garland, *Punishment and Welfare.*
84. *Chronicle and Gazette*, 8 Mar. 1834, 22 Mar. 1834; Palmer, "Kingston Mechanics," 13.

From Penitentiary to Reformatory: Alexander Maconochie, Walter Crofton, Zebulon Brockway, and the Road to Prison Reform—New South Wales, Ireland, and Elmira, New York, 1840–70

Robert G. Waite
Washington, D.C.

Throughout the nineteenth century, American prison reformers looked to colleagues in England for ideas and models for reform. The writings of John Howard on the conditions of British jails and prisons in the 1790s were widely read in the United States. Howard inspected prisons throughout England and Europe and described the wretched conditions in great detail. His descriptions and suggestions challenged authorities to construct more humane jails and prisons. Several English counties did build new institutions along the lines recommended by Howard. In addition, his writings were in large measure responsible for the first experiments in penal reform at the Cherry Hill Prison in Philadelphia and the New York State Prison at Auburn. Each was designed and built to serve the dual functions of prison and house of correction. In contrast to the conditions prevailing at most jails, where all offenders were housed in large rooms, these new institutions had cells where the prisoners were held in solitary confinement. English reformers visited the institutions at Philadelphia and Auburn to observe the new prison ideas in operation.[1]

The influence of British prison reformers on the prison system of the United States was particularly important in the transition from the penitentiary to the reformatory system of prison discipline. The shift from penitentiaries, with their program of incarceration where inmates contemplated their fate and did penance for their crimes, to reformatories, with their built-in emphasis on the rehabilitation and reform of the individual, was of great importance. This transition found its first and most complete development in the United States at New York State's Elmira Reformatory.[2]

Established in 1870, Elmira marked the full adoption of reform as the goal of incarceration; its entire program was aimed at reforming the prisoner.

John Howard. From James Baldwin Brown, *Memoirs of the Public and Private Life of John Howard, The Philanthropist*, 2d ed. (London, 1823).

The establishment of the Elmira Reformatory, in which American reformer Zebulon Brockway played a central role, was the culmination of work begun by two Englishmen—Captain Alexander Maconochie and Sir William Crofton. Their pioneering efforts were undertaken not in England but in Australia and Ireland, and their ideas were recognized and adopted by a group of American reformers led by Brockway.[3]

At the center of the shift from a penitentiary system of prison discipline to the reformatory system, as developed by these reformers, was the substitution of the indeterminate sentence and probation with its underlying premise that prisoners were capable of being reformed in the fixed time sentence of the penitentiary. In the penitentiary, the inmate did penance in virtual solitary confinement, which permitted him time to think of his evil deeds and to communicate with the Lord. The prisoner did his time, often in absolute isolation from other human beings and in miserable conditions; through severe discipline and corporal punishment the prisoner was expected to be punished and saved. To a large degree, such a system was intended to break the prisoner in spirit, which was believed necessary before the punishment of incarceration could work its eventual good.[4]

In a reformatory, the prisoner was largely the master of his own fate. Freedom from incarceration was secured through demonstrated good behavior, hard work, progress in schooling, and successful probation. The methods employed were less severe and brutal than those of the penitentiary; they were aimed at building the inmate's self-respect and dignity, rather than destroying them. During the final stages of internment, the prisoner worked in an environment of considerable liberty where he learned how to function in society. Prison authorities monitored his progress, and if he learned a skill and demonstrated an ability to operate outside of prison, he gained a conditional release, a so-called ticket of leave. Those reformers who developed and advocated the reformatory system firmly believed that this was the best way to combat crime and to protect society.[5]

Background

Ideas to reform the prison system in England had already emerged in the eighteenth century. The work of the utilitarians and Jeremy Bentham, their most prominent representative, focused attention on the miserable conditions of the prisons and the need to transform the nature of incarceration. But their efforts brought about little improvement.[6] Furthermore, the primary concern of Bentham and the utilitarians was not the reduction of the severity of imprisonment, but the justification for punishing criminals and the efficacy of the methods employed. In the 1790s Bentham had advocated a new system of imprisonment, one that emphasized the reforming of the inmate. Bentham's efforts went unrealized in England in part because he challenged widely accepted and well-established ideas and prison practices. In addition, Bentham's new system would have required a major shift in the official attitude toward crime and criminals.[7]

In the 1820s and 1830s, several British reformers called for more humane treatment of prisoners and identified some of the elements that later became integral to the reformatory system. Bishop Richard Whately advocated far-reaching changes in the penal system, and his writings were widely read. He was, however, motivated largely by the problems of transportation, especially the expense of moving convicted offenders to distant colonies, and advocated that the government "should try various experiments in secondary punishments." Whately's suggestions had little practical impact.[8] Opposition to transportation led prison administrator Joshua Jebb to introduce a progressive system of discipline in the late 1830s.[9]

The pioneers in the decisive shift to a reformatory system of prison discipline, those who implemented the crucial innovations, were Captain Alexander Maconochie, whose work in Australia in the 1840s was the first attempt at penal institutions to substitute good behavior, hard work, and probation for a fixed sentence,[10] and Sir Walter Crofton, who elaborated this idea in reforming Irish prisons in the 1850s.[11] Their work provided the models and the intellectual encouragement to American reformers that came to fruition at the Elmira Reformatory. The work of Zebulon Brockway at Elmira made the reformatory system known throughout the world.

Maconochie and Crofton launched their reforms outside of England largely because of a variety of domestic factors. Until the 1840s, England was spared the task of thoroughly reviewing and changing its penal system by transportation.[12] Simply loading convicts onto ships and deporting them to a distant colony proved initially to be cheaper and more convenient than incarcerating them at home. The colonies provided useful dumping grounds, and after America announced its independence in 1776, Australia became the major recipient.[13]

The structure of English prisons also worked against far-reaching reform. Little attention was given to the conditions in national prisons that held convicts sentenced to transportation, penal servitude, or death. Most convicted criminals served their time in local jails, where the conditions remained abysmal throughout most of the nineteenth century. As observers noted, the local prisons were little more than the training grounds for crime. Some attempts to reclaim criminals were made, but these remained isolated and largely without success. There was little incentive to reform these jails, and the public did not exhibit much interest in them. In fact, as the crime rate increased during the nineteenth century, public attitudes hardened, and prison administrators grew more determined in their efforts to win penitence through severe conditions, brutal treatment, and long sentences. No thought of the reformation of the prisoner was contemplated or tolerated.[14]

Alexander Maconochie and Norfolk Island

The worst of the criminal offenders—those who had committed a crime while under the sentence of transportation—were sent to Norfolk Island, New South Wales. It was here, in the worst imaginable conditions and among the most serious criminals, that Captain Alexander Maconochie launched his experiment in penal reform.[15] After having served as secretary to the governor of New South Wales, Maconochie was placed in charge of the penal colony. He arrived there on 6 March 1840. He had no professional training or experience in this field, but had published two tracts on convict management in the late 1830s that outlined his initial thinking.[16] At Norfolk Island one of his first acts was to eliminate the flat time sentence and to

Alexander Maconochie, 1836. From John Vincent Barry, *Alexander Maconochie of Norfolk Island. A Study of a Pioneer in Penal Reform* (Melbourne, 1950).

replace it with commutation through collective hard work and good behavior.[17]

Maconochie was a firm critic of the prison system, arguing that it worked against human nature, cost too much, was impractical, and did not work. "All past plans of secondary punishment have been found to make men worse," he wrote. "Our secondary punishments have thus formed a vast manufactory of wickedness, elaborately taught, at great expense, and utterly unworthy of an enlightened Christian people—the reason being, as I contend, that we make it no prisoner's *immediate* interest to improve, and, on the contrary, we give him many strong *immediate* impulses to become worse." With the fixed time sentences, Maconochie argued, the prisoner "has a direct interest in seeking to cheat in any way that he can, whether

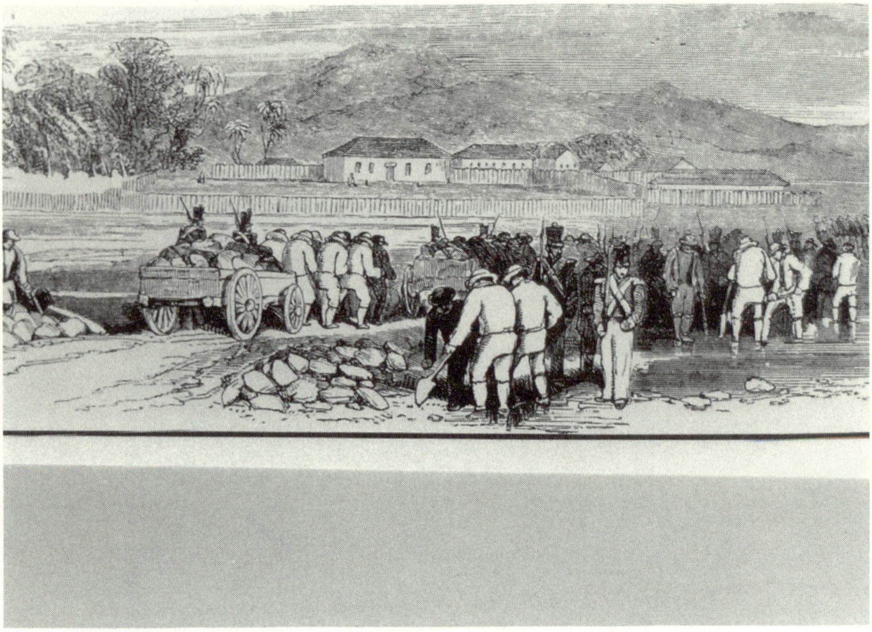

Chain gang at Norfolk Island. From *Convict Life in Australia* (Sydney, 1977).

by evasion, deception, sensual indulgence, gross act, conversation, or thought: and the stimulants by which we endeavour to check the tendencies thus by ourselves directly given, are equally of a low, deteriorating character." Such punishments "appeal only to the selfish and craven feelings of man's nature, not to its better impulses. They do not consist of advantages to be gained from good conduct, but of denunciations of punishment for bad,—and such punishments too!"[18]

Under the program developed by Maconochie with its reliance on the so-called mark system (the abolition of time sentences and their replacement by task sentences), the convict was given the opportunity to improve himself and to demonstrate that reform had taken place. Such a system of punishment conformed, Maconochie believed, with human nature, and therefore would inevitably be more effective in rehabilitating the offender and preventing further crime. The mark system had three central elements, as Maconochie explained in an 1847 publication:

1. That the duration of sentences be measured by labour and good conduct combined, with a minimum of time, but no maximum,—instead of, as now, by time only. The purpose of this is to make a man's liberation, when he is once convicted of a felony, depend on the subsequent conduct and character evinced by him, rather than on the quality of his original offense.

2. That the labour thus required be represented by marks;—a certain number of

Penal colony at Norfolk Island, c. 1835. From Barry, *Alexander Maconochie.*

these, proportioned to the original offence, being required to be earned in a penal condition before discharge. Then, according to the amount of work rendered a proportion of them should be credited day by day to the convict;—a moderate charge be made in them for all provisions and other supplies issued to him,—and should he misconduct himself a moderate fine in them be imposed on him,—only the clear surplus, after all similar deductions, to count towards his liberation. By this means it is sought to place his fate in his own hands... make him feel the burthen and obligation of his own maintenance,—and train him, while yet in bondage, in those habits of prudent tastes and impulses to ulterior advantages, which after discharge will best preserve him from again failing.

3. That to strengthen these moral checks and stimulants, when prisoners are kept together in numbers they be distributed into small parties (say) of six, with *common* interests, each man thus laboring and refraining for others as well as for himself. By this means it is hoped to implant and cultivate kindly and social feelings, instead of the intensely selfish ones which usually characterize the criminal, and especially grow up in the solitude of an unconnected crowd.[19]

In practice, the effect of the mark system on the prisoner was remarkable. As Maconochie later wrote, "I found the Island a turbulent, brutal hell, and I left it a peaceful well-ordered community."[20] According to the program he introduced at Norfolk Island, every convict was debited with a number of marks that had to be earned by labor, good conduct and habits, or schooling. The prisoner, as he advanced toward liberty, accumulated a specific number of marks. The most important and innovative feature of

Exercise of prisoners at the Pentonville Prison, c. 1858. From *Journal of Prison Discipline* 13 (1858).

Maconochie's system came during the final stages of imprisonment. At that time the convict earned a wage from his labor, and he was subject to less restrictive discipline and improved conditions which, in turn, provided more freedom. The intention of this program was to prepare him for eventual release.[21]

Maconochie was a thoughtful reformer who stressed the rehabilitation of criminals rather than vindictive punishment. But the mark system, with its built-in leniency, invited criticism. For example, when he granted prisoners a holiday in honor of the Queen's birthday in 1840, offering, as he later recalled, "a glass of rum-punch to all hands to drink the Queen's health, and had two plays acted the same evening," he was severely criticized. Maconochie's purpose for the celebration was, however, simple and important: "I had very early observed, and with great regret, in the penal colonies generally, the hatred existing in most prisoners in them towards their native country and all her institutions," he wrote. "They have for the most part known little of her, but the vicious social combinations which plunge so many of them inevitably into crime, and then the vindicative penal institutions which convert them ultimately into fiends." Through this celebration, "I wished to overcome this feeling."[22] When reports of the convicts' festivities, which were orderly and secure, reached Sydney and London, many were shocked.

British officials reacted with outrage to Maconochie's actions, and it became only a question of time before Maconochie was recalled. For these officials, imprisonment and penance had long been associated with misery, suffering, and guilt. Although Maconochie was replaced at Norfolk Island, he had done something of immense importance when he demonstrated that treating prisoners with respect and striving to rehabilitate them did not invariably lead to more disorder or an increase in crime as had often been claimed.[23]

While the mark system introduced by Maconochie received inadequate support from the officials in Australia who replaced him in 1844, it did attract the attention of a small group of reformers at home. Maconochie, bolstered by what he viewed as the demonstrated effectiveness of the mark system, returned to England with new determination to publicize its benefits. He wrote numerous pamphlets[24] and associated with other prison reformers. In 1849, Maconochie received another opportunity to test his program when he was appointed governor of the new Birmingham Borough Prison. Local justices gave him permission to introduce the mark system, but when implemented, it contradicted their notions about punishment. These reservations and Maconochie's use of questionable means of discipline prompted the justices to dismiss him. The deputy governor took over and reintroduced a system of discipline based on cruelty and terror. A royal commission investigated conditions at the prison after rumors of brutality became widespread and several inmates committed suicide. The widely accepted alternative to Maconochie's system failed in Birmingham as it had at Norfolk Island.[25]

Maconochie believed firmly that he had developed a more satisfactory way of dealing with convicted criminals. In an 1850 report to Parliament, he summed up his system and in doing so outlined what was to be at the center of Walter Crofton's work in Ireland and Zebulon Brockway's work at Elmira. As he wrote,

> I think that time sentences are the root of very nearly all the demoralization which exists in prisons. A man under a time sentence thinks only how he is to cheat that time, and while it away; he evades labor, because he has no interest in it whatever, and he has no desire to please the officers under whom he is placed, because they cannot serve him essentially; they cannot in any way promote his liberation.
>
> Now . . . these evils would be remedied by introducing the system of task sentences. . . . A man under a task sentence would strip his coat to work, he would set a proper value on time, which under a time sentence is hated, and he would exert himself in such a way that he could not but improve.[26]

Maconochie continued to publicize his ideas after his dismissal from Birmingham Borough Prison, but he was never employed in prison administration again. His ideas did become, however, part of a penal reform movement in England and the United States. A large group of reformers, led by Frederick Hill, Matthew Hill, and Mary Carpenter, advocated a prison system based on the reform of the offender; Maconochie had provided an important model. Reformers gained an opportunity to lead England to a system of graded punishment when Parliament ended transportation in 1857. Bishop Whately, George Combe, and the Hill brothers popularized the concept of the task sentence, and their efforts gained widespread attention. But the full adaptation of the system in England was thwarted by a hardening of public opinion toward criminals that grew out of a crime wave that swept the country in the 1860s.[27]

Walter Crofton and Reform of the Irish Prisons

In Great Britain, the work of Maconochie was continued by Walter Crofton who in 1853 adopted the mark system as a central element of his reorganization of the Irish prisons, and in 1855 introduced the intermediate convict system.[28] Crofton acknowledged his debt to Maconochie, and went on to do much to demonstrate the effectiveness of task sentences and probation. Crofton's work received attention from reformers in the United States, many of whom applauded his efforts and stated outright that it needed to be adapted to the American prison system. The leading journals of the day discussed Crofton's work, and he came to the United States in 1870 in order to address the National Congress on Penitentiary and Reformatory Discipline in Cincinnati.[29]

In Ireland, Crofton expanded the reform system developed by Maconochie from a three- to a four-stage process that began with a period of confinement.[30] This was followed by an indeterminate reformatory stage; then came the probationary stage, which was followed by conditional release on a ticket-of-leave. The so-called Irish or Crofton system embodied the ideas that later came to be associated with the Elmira Reformatory. The inmates were rewarded for hard work, good conduct, and the development of good habits. The goal of imprisonment was to rehabilitate the prisoners and to provide convicted criminals with the attitudes and skills they needed to become useful members of society. Their final release was dependent upon this, and as the prisoners moved toward gaining their liberty they progressed through several distinct grades.[31]

During the first stage, confinement, the prisoner was locked up at the Mountjoy Prison in Dublin. The staff at Mountjoy was, according to observers, sincerely interested in the inmates' progress.[32] The concern of the staff helped the inmates build their self-esteem, an essential part of the reformatory process. After eight months of incarceration nearly all advanced to the second stage, "progressive classification," and here, each inmate was placed in one of five classes or grades. Through hard work, much of it on public works projects, good conduct, and schooling, the prisoner earned marks or points and advanced through the grades as these points were accumulated.[33]

A central element of the Crofton system was the intermediate stage, added after the second one. It was designed to filter prisoners, to identify those who were reformed and could function in society on their own. The four prisons in Ireland where the convicts spent this stage were organized to aid in the inmates' rehabilitation, and the convicts received extensive training in situations of partial freedom, which aided them in preparing for full freedom.[34]

While working in the final two stages, the prisoners' earnings were credited to their accounts, and this made the system cheap to operate. An American observer called the Crofton system "a magnificent triumph of reason and humanity over coercion and brute force—a splendid and irrefragable testimony to the soundness of these principles of progressive classification as the corner-stone of a reformatory system of prison discipline."[35] Only after the inmate had demonstrated his rehabilitation in the third stage did he gain parole, or a ticket-of-leave (the final stage). The ticket-of-leave could, however, be revoked for poor conduct at any time during the original period of the sentence. Throughout the time spent in this final stage, the convict remained under supervision.[36] A mechanism for the rehabilitation of prisoners was built into the program, and most observers concluded that it worked. The drop in Ireland's conviction and recidivism rates further demonstrated the success of the Crofton system.

As a contemporary German penologist, Baron Franz von Holtzendorff, wrote:

> Even the most cursory glance at the general characteristics of this system will necessarily satisfy us that, instead of it having failed to accomplish its objects, during the short period of time which has elapsed since the passing of the Irish Convict Prisons' Act, it has proved itself to be more effective than any other which preceded it. The facts which have been published, and which carry particular weight from the circumscribed boundaries of Ireland, show that since 1854 [to 1860] the number of convictions for crime has progressively diminished, and that in a steady and striking manner.[37]

Stirrings of Reform in the United States

Reports on the Crofton system were circulated in America as early as the 1850s. Articles on the "intermediate system" of discipline, the central element of the Crofton system, appeared in the *Journal of Prison Discipline and Philanthropy*, an influential journal published by the Philadelphia Prison Society.[38] In 1863, Gaylord Hubbell, warden of Sing Sing Prison in New York, visited England and Ireland. He returned to the United States an enthusiastic supporter of the Crofton system. Hubbell called for the introduction of a new type of prison discipline, one modeled on the Crofton system, into the prisons of New York State.[39]

Another advocate of the Crofton system was Franklin Benjamin Sanborn, inspector of prisons in Massachusetts and one of the founders of the National Prison Association. In the mid-1860s Sanborn learned of the innovations launched by Crofton in Ireland, and urged that a similar program be developed in the United States. Sanborn was instrumental in popularizing the idea of a graded system of punishment in the United States.[40]

These reform-minded American penologists were joined by Zebulon Brockway, a prison administrator who had developed similar programs at the Albany Penitentiary and the Detroit House of Corrections. They led the movement for change in the American prison system in the 1860s, advocating the establishment of prisons in accordance with the principles of Walter Crofton and his so-called Irish system.[41]

By the late 1860s, the United States was ready for a thorough reform of its penal system. The long tradition in this field, beginning with the construction of the Philadelphia Prison at Cherry Hill, remained strong. In addition, a group of professional administrators committed to reform emerged from the Philadelphia Prison and other newly established institutions as well as from the various prison societies. At about the same time, reports of the miserable conditions of Civil War prisoner of war camps prompted widespread concern for prison conditions. With a rising crime rate came the recognition that the existing penitentiaries and the prevailing methods of prison discipline had failed.[42]

The first important expression of the widespread support for prison reform along the systems developed by Maconochie and Crofton came in 1870 at the National Prison Association meeting in Cincinnati. Enoch Wines called for the meeting that was to give reformers the opportunity to plan a model prison. Delegates to the convention adopted a Declaration of Principles, which advocated inmate rehabilitation as a major objective of incarceration. The delegates also called for the progressive classification of prisoners on the mark system, indeterminate sentences, vocational training, and education programs which would build the inmate's self-respect. The reformers were aided by Mary Carpenter and Sir Walter Crofton.[43]

The Elmira Ideal

Even before the Cincinnati meeting, advocates of the Crofton system had worked toward gaining support of the New York State legislature for the establishment of a new prison based on those principles. On 8 January 1867, reformers Enoch Wines and Louis Dwight told lawmakers in Albany:

> We have no hesitation in expressing the opinion that what is known and has become famous as the Irish system of convict prisons is, upon the whole, the best model of

> which we have any knowledge; and it has stood the test of experience in yielding the most abundant as well as the best fruits. We certainly in all its details—it may be applied, with entire effect, in our own country and in our own state.[44]

Wines and Dwight were committed to improving the American prison system, and they, along with other reformers, saw a solution in the work of Crofton. Their advocacy for the Crofton system was immediately adopted by the New York Prison Association, which proved to be an effective lobbying force. Largely as a result of its efforts, the legislature appointed a commission in 1868 to select a site for a new state prison. The act establishing the Elmira Reformatory was passed in 1869, and the first prisoners arrived in July 1876.[45]

The program at Elmira went further than the Crofton system in Ireland. The entire organization of the Elmira Reformatory was directed toward reforming the inmate, a focus that came from Zebulon Brockway, the superintendent from 1876 to 1900. Before his call to Elmira, Brockway had considerable practical experience, and he had outlined his ideas on penal reform at the 1870 convention in Cincinnati. In a paper entitled "The Ideal of a True Prison System for a State," Brockway called for a prison system that would prevent crime and rehabilitate the convict. He stated that the penitentiaries had failed to curb crime, for they stressed the punishment of the offender rather than the protection of society. Brockway also rejected the central role that religion played in the penitentiary system and the use of fixed sentences. Before taking over the Elmira Reformatory, Brockway secured from the New York State Legislature a law providing for indeterminate sentences. This was the key element of his program. The law granted Brockway and the managers of the reformatory complete control over the length of imprisonment.[46]

Brockway's most important contribution to prison reform was the establishment of a program at Elmira that effectively reformed the inmates. In practice, the Elmira system was a combination of marks, grades, and parole available under indeterminate sentencing, a program outlined in his 1870 paper. The prison staff closely watched and recorded the behavior of each inmate. The convicts were aware of this, and they knew that release depended on their personal reform.[47]

Drawing from the work of Maconochie and Crofton, the program provided for the separation of the inmates into three classes or grades. All prisoners entering the Elmira Reformatory were placed in the middle or second class, where they spent six months. With good conduct, they could advance to the first class. After six months of good behavior in this stage, convicts were eligible for parole. Prisoners who misbehaved were dropped to the third class. Corporal punishment was also available. This system of grades and advancement had been developed by Maconochie and Crofton, and its application at the Elmira, Reformatory again demonstrated its ad-

Zebulon Brockway. From Fred C. Allen, comp., *Handbook of the New York State Reformatory at Elmira* (Elmira, N.Y., 1906).

vantages over the penitentiary system. Maconochie, Crofton, and Brockway, the first superintendent or warden at Elmira, emphasized the reform of the prisoner rather than incarceration and punishment.[48]

As the program developed at Elmira, reform meant a change in the habits and character of the prisoner to the extent that he would not commit another crime. The main instruments were labor, education, vocational training, military drills, and to a lesser extent religion. Work, however, was the most important element. As reformer Frederick Wines wrote, "labor, if real and productive, is not only a means of bodily health and strength, but compels thought, thus awakening and moulding the mind, and in many ways it reacts favorably upon the moral character of the workman."[49]

Regular and hard work was supplemented by an extensive and rigorous

The Elmira Reformatory, c. 1907. From postcard.

educational program. Inmates were provided with basic schooling, and success here aided their advance through the system. An active program of physical education was also adopted. As Brockway wrote, "The intention was to invigorate by means of physical culture the entire prison population and, particularly through specific scientific physical renovation, to improve defectives and dullards in their mental and moral habitides."[50]

The success of the program developed by Brockway was considerable, and almost immediately evident—so Brockway wrote in his autobiography.

> It was my high privilege . . . to test again and again in actual practice with the thousand and more men then . . . in custody and houses of others to be afterwards received, the actual and maximum efficiency of our theory of reformation, which, to put it epigrammatically, is socialization of the anti-social by scientific training while under completest governmental control.[51]

His claims were supported by the numerous American and European penologists who visited and studied the Elmira Reformatory. In addition, the recidivism rate among those released from Elmira remained low. During a seventeen-year period following the opening of the Elmira Reformatory, 3,723 men were set free on parole. Only an estimated 18 percent were later convicted of a criminal offense.[52]

With this high success rate and a large number of prison reformers ap-

Military exercises. From Allen, *Handbook of the New York State Reformatory at Elmira*.

plauding the work of Brockway at Elmira, it is not surprising that the system was widely imitated in other states and in Europe. Elmira provided the model for prison construction and programs in the United States in the First World War. Many European penologists came to Elmira to examine the operation of the reformatory system. The reformatory at Elmira also had an immediate impact in England. Sir Evelyn Ruggles-Brise, the director of the British prisons, started the borstal system after he viewed the workings at Elmira in an 1897 visit. Other European observers came to Elmira and returned home advocates of the reformatory system. Elmira was a strong success, and the techniques developed there for handling and treating prisoners were instrumental in the development of America's prisons.[53]

Conclusion

The shift in prison practices from the penitentiary, with its emphasis on fixed time sentences, to the reformatory, which called for the reform of the inmates, evolved only gradually in the nineteenth century. As scholars have pointed out, the primary initial impetus came from Alexander Maconochie and Walter Crofton, whose efforts were applauded by other English reformers, but not supported by the authorities. Conditions in the English prisons, the inefficiency of local government, and the lack of a coherent and influential group of professional reformers meant that few long-term changes were implemented. It needs to be emphasized that the transition from the penitentiary to the reformatory system of prison discipline, however, culminated in the United States where reformers—aware of the work of Maconochie and Crofton—adopted their principles and built on early American experiments in prison reform to establish the first reformatory at Elmira, New York. The debt of the American reform movement to Maconochie and Crofton was great, for it drew directly from their experiences; the elements of the Elmira system, as articulated by its first superintendent Zebulon Brockway, came from the work of Maconochie and Crofton. For forty years after its establishment, the Elmira Reformatory was the most widely discussed and emulated prison in the world. Its success was repeatedly demonstrated by the low rate of recidivism and the large number of imitators.

Notes

1. For a summary of the life and work of John Howard, see "Howard, John," *Dictionary of National Biography* (London, 1937–38), 10: 44–48; Martin Southwood, *John Howard: Prison Reformer* (London, 1958), 66–86; D. L. Howard, *John Howard: Prison Reformer* (London, 1958), 53–59, 164–73; Max Grünhut, *Penal Reform: A Comparative Study* (Montclair, N.J., 1972; orig. ed. 1948), 43–83, 89–94; Thorsten Eriksson, *The Reformers: An Historical Survey of Pioneer Experiments in the Treatment of Criminals* (New York, 1976), 32–42; N. K. Teeters, *The Prison at Philadelphia, Cherry Hill. The Separate System of Penal Discipline: 1829–1913* (New York, 1957), 3–23, 33–50, 56–71; Walter David Lewis, *From Newgate to Dannemora: The Rise of the Penitentiary in New York, 1796–1848* (Ithaca, N.Y., 1965), 1–26, 54–70.

2. For an overview of this change and the importance of the Elmira Reformatory, see Frederick Howard Wines, *Punishment and Reformation: A Study of the Penitentiary System* (New York, 1895), 192–228.

3. For a brief account of the contributions made by Maconochie and Crofton, see E. C. Wines, *The State of Prisons and Child-Saving Institutions in the Civilized World* (Cambridge, 1880), 32–33; Grünhut, *Penal Reform*, 77–88.

4. Wines, *Prisons and Child-Saving Institutions*, 613–16.

5. The best short statement of the reform philosophy and elements of the reformatory system of prison discipline is Maconochie's pamphlet *Norfolk Island* (London, 1848).

6. On the work of Jeremy Bentham, see Coleman Phillipson, *Three Criminal Law Reformers. Beccaria/Bentham/Romilly* (Montclair, N.J., 1975, orig. ed. 1923), 109–236; Gilbert Geis, "Jeremy Bentham (1748–1832)," in *Pioneers in Criminology*, ed. Hermann Manheim (New York, 1972) 51–68. For a critical view, see the pamphlet by Captain Maconochie, *Comparison Between Mr. Bentham's Views on Punishment and Those Advocated in Connection with the Mark System* (London, n.d.), 1–8.

7. Phillipson, *Three Criminal Law Reformers*, 192–96, 210–17, 227–29; Geis, "Jeremy Bentham (1748–1832)," 59–67; Anthony Babington, *The English Bastille:*

A History of Newgate Gaol and Prison Conditions in Britain, 1188–1902 (New York, 1971), 125, 130.

8. Richard Whately, *Thoughts on Secondary Punishments, in a Letter to Earl Grey* (London, 1823), 1, 5, *passim*; "Article on Transportation from the London Review, 1829," "Remarks on Transportation, in a Second Letter to the Late Earl Grey," and "Substance of a Speech on Transportation," in *Introductory Lectures on Political-Economy* (London, 1855), 233–309. On his life, see "Whately, Richard," *Dictionary of National Biography*, 20: 1334–40; Captain Maconochie, *Crime and Punishment. The Mark System, Framed to Mix Persuasion with Punishment, and Make Their Effect Improving, Yet Their Operation Severe* (London, 1846), 41–43.

9. "Jebb, Sir Joshua," *Dictionary of National Biography*, 10: 698–99; Rev. Walter Clay, *The Prison Chaplain: A Memoir of the Rev. John Clay* (Montclair, N.J., 1969; orig. ed. 1861), 258, 282; Grünhut, *Penal Reform*, 85–88; Thorsten Sellin, "Paley on the Time Sentence," *Journal of Criminal Law and Criminology* 22(1931): 264–66.

10. *Convicts and Colonial Society, 1788–1868*, ed. Lloyd Evans and Paul Nicholls (Melbourne, 1984), 77–106.

11. Wines, *State of Prisons and Child-Saving Institutions*, 233–39.

12. Whately, *Thoughts on Secondary Punishment*, 1; A. G. L. Shaw, *Convicts and Colonies. A Study of Penal Transportation from Great Britain and Ireland to Australia and Other Parts of the British Empire* (Melbourne, 1977), 21–57; Harry Elmer Barnes, *The Story of Punishment. A Record of Man's Inhumanity to Man*, 2d ed. (Montclair, N.J., 1972), 68–88.

13. Shaw, *Convicts and Colonies*, 38–57; Captain Maconochie, *Thoughts on Convict Management, and Other Subjects Connected with the Australian Penal Colonies* (Hobart Town, 1838), 55–65.

14. On the problems of English prisons, see Sidney and Beatrice Webb, *English Prisons under Local Government* (London, 1922); Joseph Adshead, *Our Present Gaol System Deeply Depraving to the Prisoner and a Positive Evil to the Community. Some Remedies Proposed* (Manchester, 1847), 1–26; *On Juvenile Criminals, Reformatories, and the Means of Rendering the Perishing and Dangerous Classes Serviceable to the State* (Manchester, 1856), 1–17; Alex Thomson, *Punishment and Prevention* (London, 1857), 25–181.

15. On the conditions at Norfolk Island, see Clay, *Memoir of the Rev. John Clay*, 248–51; Maconochie, *Norfolk Island*, 4–5; John Vincent Barry, *Alexander Maconochie of Norfolk Island. A Study of a Pioneer in Penal Reform* (Melbourne, 1950), 111–20.

16. Maconochie, *Thoughts on Convict Management; General Views Regarding the Social System of Convict Management* (Hobart Town, 1839). See also the documents in *Convicts and Colonial Society*, 77–106.

17. Maconochie, *Norfolk Island*, 1–16. On the conditions at Norfolk Island, see Clay, *Memoir of the Rev. John Clay*, 246–47; Barry, *Alexander Maconochie*, 88–95.

18. Captain Maconochie, *On Secondary Punishment* (London, 1846), 1.

19. Captain Maconochie, *The Mark System* (London, 1847), 1–2; Barry, *Alexander Maconochie*, 69–79.

20. Maconochie, *Norfolk Island*, 13.

21. Captain Maconochie, *On Secondary Punishment*, 1–4; John Vincent Barry, "Alexander Maconochie, 1781–1860," in *Pioneers in Criminology*, 90–92; Clay, *Memoir of the Rev. John Clay*, 247–48.

22. Maconochie, *Norfolk Island*, 6–7.

23. Ibid., 17–27; Barry, "Alexander Maconochie," 96–97.

24. Maconochie wrote on virtually every aspect of his reforms. For his most comprehensive defense of the Mark System, see his book *Crime and Punishment*.

25. Ibid.; Wines, *Punishment and Reformation*, 195; Clay, *Memoir of the Rev. John Clay*, 252–55; Barry, "Alexander Maconochie," 98–99.

26. Maconochie, *Thoughts on Convict Management* and *General Views*; Webb, *English Prisons under Local Government*, 167.

27. Matthew Davenport Hill, *Suggestions for the Repression of Crime* (London, 1857), 265–74; Babington, *English Bastille*, 220; Wines, *Punishment and Reformation*, 217; Clay, *Memoir of the Rev. John Clay*, 255–59.

28. Baron Franz von Holtzendorff, *The Irish Convict System, More Especially Intermediate Prisons* (Dublin, 1860), 1, 9–13, 24–34; Captain Walter Crofton, *Immunity of "Habitual Criminals": With a Proposition for Reducing Their Number by Means of Longer Sentences of Penal Servitude; Intermediate Convict Prisons; Conditional Liberation; and Police Supervision* (London, 1861), 5–9, 22; Eriksson, *Reformers*, 89–97; Grünhut, *Penal Reform*.

29. David Dyer, *Impressions of Prison Life in Great Britain Submitted to the Inspectors and Superintendent of the Albany Penitentiary* (Albany, N.Y., 1868), 3–5, 18; Mary Carpenter, *Reformatory Prison Discipline as Developed by the Rt. Hon. Sir Walter Crofton, in the Irish Convict Prisons* (London, 1872), v–ix, xiii–xiv, 125–29; Crofton, *Habitual Criminals*, 34; Frank B. Sanborn, "The Elmira Reformatory," in *The Reformatory System in the United States*, ed. S. J. Barrows (Washington, 1900), 28–29. See Crofton's letter read before the National Prison Reform Congress in Baltimore, Maryland, on 21 Jan. 1873, "Remarks on Sundry Topics Considered in the International Penitentiary Congress of London," in E. C. Wines, *Report on the International Penitentiary Congress of London, Held July 3–13, 1872* (Washington, 1873), 354–57.

30. Wines, *Punishment and Reformation*, 196; Matthew Davenport Hill, *A Letter to C. B. Adderley, Esq., M. P., on His Review of the Charge of the Recorder of Birmingham, on the Subject of Tickets of Leave* (London, 1856), 1–20.

31. Rev. Orby Shipley, *The Purgatory of Prisoners: Or an Intermediate Stage Between the Prison and the Public* (London, 1857), vi–x, 1–19; Wines, *Prisons and Child-Saving Institutions*, 233; Clay, *Memoir of the Rev. John Clay*, 418–32; Carpenter, *Reformatory Prison Discipline*, 5–18.

32. On the administration of the Irish prisons, see *Rules and Regulations for the Government of the Irish Convict Prisons* (Dublin, 1861), 13–19, 22–23; *Observations on the Treatment of Convicts in Ireland* (London, 1862), 1–13, 20–22.

33. Clay, *Memoir of the Rev. John Clay*, 419–32; Carpenter, *Reformatory Prison Discipline*, 6–10.

34. *Defects in the Criminal Administration and Penal Legislation of Great Britain and Ireland, With Remedial Suggestions* (London, 1872), 105–16; Clay, *Memoir of the Rev. John Clay*, 425–26; Carpenter, *Reformatory Prison Discipline*, 10–22.

35. Wines, *Punishment and Reformation*, 237.

36. "Results of Observation," *Journal of Prison Discipline and Philanthropy*

(hereinafter *JPDP*) 27(1872): 73–75; Carpenter, Reformatory Prison Discipline, 45–64; *Observations on the Treatment of Convicts in Ireland* (London, 1862), 64–103. For less favorable views, see "Zur Beleuchtung der Irlandischen Gefängnisschwindelei," *Gerichtssal* (hereinafter *GS*) 16(1864): 459–67; J. Domela Nieuwenhuis, "Ueber das sog. irische System des Strafvollzugs in Vergleich zur Einzelhaft," *GS* 19(1867): 171–211.

37. Holtzendorff, *Irish Convict System*, 166.

38. See, for example, "Success of the Intermediate System of Prison Discipline," *JPDP* 13 (1858): 16–26; "Irish Convict Prisons," *JPDP* 15 (1860): 36–39.

39. Barnes, *Story of Punishment*, 550–51.

40. Wines, *Punishment and Reformation*, 199–201.

41. "Irish Convict System," *JPDP* 23 (1868): 56–84; Z. R. Brockway, "The Elmira Principle. Address Made to the Toronto Prison Congress by Mr. Z. R. Brockway Superintendent of the State Reformatory at Elmira, New York on the Practical Working of the 'Intermediate Sentence' " (n.p., 1888), 1 Frank B. Sanborn, "The Elmira Reformatory," in Barrows, *Reformatory System*, 28; Eriksson, *Reformers*, 98–106.

42. Blake McKelvey, *American Prisons: A History of Good Intentions* (Montclair, N.J., 1977), 70; Alice Telt Tyler, *Freedom's Ferment* (New York, 1944), 265–85; Charles Loring Brace, *The Dangerous Classes of New York and 20 Years' Work among Them* (New York, 1872), 32–80.

43. Sanborn, "Elmira Reformatory," 28–29, 33; Wines, *Punishment and Reformation*, 192–93; Z. R. Brockway, "The Ideal of a True Prison System for a State. A Paper Read Before the National Congress on Penitentiary and Reformatory Discipline at Cincinnati, on October 12, 1870," 1–12. See also Right Hon. Sir Walter Crofton, "The Treatment of Prisoners," in *Prisons and Reformatories at Home and Abroad. Being the Transactions of the International Penitentiary Congress Held in London July 3–13, 1872*, ed. Edwin Pears (London, 1872), 629–35.

44. Quoted in Wines, *Punishment and Reformation*, 196.

45. Ibid., 192–97; Eriksson, *Reformers*, 98–106.

46. Brockway, "Ideal of a True Prison System," 1–12; Wines, *Punishment and Reformation*, 219; Z. R. Brockway, "Prisoners and Their Reformation," in Wines, *Report on the International Penitentiary Congress*, 182–84.

47. Brockway, "Elmira Principle," 1–7; Sanborn, "Elmira Reformatory," 32. On the history of indeterminate sentencing, see Wines, *Punishment and Reformation*, 208–18; Zebulon R. Brockway, "Character of Reformatory Prisoners," in *Extracts from Peneological Reports and Lectures Written by Members of the Management and Staff of the New York State Reformatory, Elmira, N.Y.*, ed. Fred C. Allen (Elmira, N.Y., 1926), 110–18.

48. Sanborn, "Elmira Reformatory," 28–32; Brockway, "Elmira Principle," 1–7; Brockway, Reformatory System," in *Reformatory System in the United States*, 21–24.

49. Sanborn, "Elmira Reformatory," 38–40; Col. V. M. Masten, *Military Training at the New York State Reformatory* (Elmira, N.Y., 1920), 1–3; Wines, *Punishment and Reformation*, 203.

50. Zebulon Reed Brockway, *Fifty Years of Prison Service. An Autobiography* (New York, 1912), 301; Brockway, "Reformatory System," 25–27; "Experiments in Physical Culture," in Winter, *New York State Reformatory*, 132–44.

51. Brockway, *Fifty Years of Prison Service*, 309.

52. *Annual Report of the Board of Governors of the New York State Reformatory at Elmira, N.Y. for the Year Ending September 30, 1887* (Elmira, N.Y., 1888), 23–29; Sanborn, "Elmira Reformatory," 32–33, 37–38; Brockway, *Fifty Years of Prison Service*, 325; "Results of the Reform System," in Winter, *New York State Reformatory*, 149–69.

53. Wines, *Punishment and Reformation*, 223, 226; Antonio de la Torre, *La Penalidad Social en "Elmira"* (Lima, 1909), 1–36; Georg Stammer, *Strafvollzug und Jugendschutz in Amerika. Eindrücke und Ausblicke einer Gefängnisstudienreise* (Berlin, 1911), 24–28; Alexander Winter, *The New York State Reformatory in Elmira* (London, 1891), 1–6; Shane Leslie, comp., *Sir Evelyn Ruggles-Brise. A Memoir of the Founder of the Borstal* (London, 1938), 122–23.

The Standard of Living of Career Policemen in Victorian England: The Evidence of a Provincial Borough Force

David Taylor
Teesside Polytechnic, Middlesbrough

From the 1840s on, policing became an accessible alternative employment for many, if not all, working men. As the second half of the nineteenth century progressed, a growing number of men made a long-term career of policing. The wider significance of the emergence of a professional police force has been noted on several occasions. Little has been written, however, about the varying experiences of such career policemen and, despite references to regularity of employment, generous wage levels,[1] and real promotion prospects,[2] there has been no serious attempt to assess their material well-being. By examining in detail the experience of the Middlesbrough Borough Force, an attempt will be made to increase our knowledge of these important but neglected questions.[3]

Middlesbrough—that "infant Hercules," to use Gladstone's phrase—was far from being a typical Victorian town. The statistics of population growth demonstrate this clearly. In 1801 there were but four houses and 25 inhabitants; 30 years later the population was a mere 154. The decision to extend the Stockton and Darlington railway and to develop Middlesbrough as a port for the export of coal led to rapid growth. The 1841 census recorded 5,463 people. Ten years later, by which time the importation of pig-iron had led to the opening of the first rolling mills, the total had reached 7,431. The discovery and exploitation of ironore in the nearby Eston hills heralded a further phase of population growth based on the rapid expansion of the iron (and later steel) industry. A near threefold increase brought the town's population to just under 20,000 in 1861, and this was followed by a further doubling of numbers by 1871. The overwhelmingly working-class nature of the town was firmly established in these years as the rapidly expanding, high-wage economy attracted migrants from all parts of Britain. Thereafter,

Table 1
Length of Service of Middlesbrough Police Recruits, 1850s to 1890s (as % of intake)

Decade	Less Than 1 Year	1 to 4 Years	5 to 9 Years	10 to 19 Years	More Than 20 Years	Unknown
1850s	30.2	24.5	10.0	1.9	5.7	28.3
1860s	36.8	20.9	9.2	3.1	6.1	23.9
1870s	25.4	33.6	12.7	4.5	12.7	11.2
1880s	6.6	40.7	8.8	14.3	25.3	4.4
1890s	5.8	26.7	8.1	38.4	18.6	2.3
Average	23.0	28.8	9.9	11.0	13.1	14.2

Source: Constables' Conduct Registers, CB/M/P 29, 30 & 31. This and other material detailed in this chapter is to be found in the Cleveland County Archive.

population growth slackened somewhat, but by 1901 the population was in excess of 90,000 and by 1911 the census returns gave a figure of 104,767. Despite its rapid growth, Middlesbrough remained a compact town with an increasing density of population. Middlesbrough township in 1861 was some 1,080 acres, whereas the civil parish in 1911 was only 2,685 acres.[4]

The creation of the Middlesbrough police force effectively starts with the Improvement Act of 1841 under the provision of which two constables were appointed. More important, however, was the appointment of William Hannan in 1853, who set about expanding the force and improving its efficiency, and the enactment of the County and Borough Police Act of 1856, which acted as a further stimulus to growth. Total numbers rose from fifteen in 1861 to just under sixty (including privately paid constables employed by local firms) in 1871. By the turn of the century the force numbered over one hundred. Thus, the police/population ratio, which stood at 1:1294 in 1861, fell to around 1:900 during the last quarter of the nineteenth century and was further reduced to 1:732 by 1911.[5]

Length of Service and Promotion Prospects

During the second half of the nineteenth century, there was an endless flow of men in and out of the Middlesbrough police force. For many recruits, as elsewhere, policing was a stop-gap, temporary measure to tide them over during slack times in trade. Over the years, however, there was an important change—the emergence of the career policeman. Table 1 summarizes the changes by decade.

Most striking is the high percentage of recruits serving less than five years.[6] Taking the period as a whole, over fifty percent of recruits fell into this category. The figure is probably over sixty percent, as the vast majority of men in the "unknown" category were appointed in the early years and almost certainly did not serve for a year, let alone more than five. There was an appreciable change over time, however, though even in the 1890s just over thirty percent of recruits served less than five years in the force.

The numbers serving for more than five but less than ten years remained roughly constant throughout the period. The number of long-term policemen, defined as those serving ten or more years, increased steadily from the 1870s, and especially from the 1880s. Whereas in the 1850s and 1860s less than one in ten recruits served for more than ten years, by the 1880s this figure had risen to almost one in three and exceeded fifty percent in the 1890s. As time progressed, however, important differences in career profiles emerged.

Of over fifty men recruited in the 1850s, only four went on to serve for more than ten years and only one did not gain promotion. The exception was Robert Wright, who was appointed as a constable at Snowdon & Hopkins, and served a total of fourteen years before resigning without a pension in 1870.[7] The other three were all promoted as far as the rank of inspector while one, Robert Thorpe, went on to become a superintendent. Promotion was fairly rapid. The average length of time it took to become a sergeant was three years and three months, and it took a similar length of time to become an inspector. Thorpe's promotion to superintendent took a further seventeen years.

Little is known of the careers of these men. Charles Bowes served from 1854 to 1876. In 1859 he was recorded as the Drill Sergeant at the Cleveland Academy and in 1864, three years after becoming an inspector, he was appointed collector of the borough rates—a responsibility he bore until his resignation. There is no record of a pension being granted to him, notwithstanding his length of service. John Reed served even longer. Resigning in January 1857 after fourteen months in the force, he rejoined in November of the same year and stayed for the next thirty years. In 1858 he was appointed Inspector of Nuisances and three years later he was promoted to sergeant, becoming an inspector in 1862. He retired on a pension at the age of fifty-six, but died just three years later. By contemporary standards, his had been a long career in an occupation noted for the physical toll it exacted.

The third member of the trio, Robert Thorpe, was the most successful in terms of promotion. Starting at the age of twenty-five as a third-class constable in 1857, he became a sergeant in 1861 and an inspector three years later. Promotion to superintendent did not come until 1881. His career continued until 1890, when—aged forty-eight and having served for twenty-three years—he died on duty.

The early career policeman in Middlesbrough enjoyed rapid promotion to positions of undoubted status. As the force expanded, particularly following the 1856 act, such successes became less common. A total of 163 men were recruited in the 1860s, but the number of career policemen remained low. Some fifteen men served for ten years or more. Of these thirteen, just under eighty-seven percent became sergeants, taking on average five years to gain this first promotion. Only seven were promoted to the rank of inspector. Once again the rate of progress was slower than in the previous decade. It now took on average seven years and seven months from being promoted sergeant. There was one notable and exceptional success. William Ashe, having joined as a third-class constable, worked his way through the ranks to become a chief inspector and finally chief constable.[8]

The career policemen of the 1860s can be divided into three categories. First, there are the seven, noted above, who achieved double promotion, thereby reaching the rank of inspector. William Atkinson is a good example. He joined the Middlesbrough force as a third-class constable in 1866, aged twenty-nine, having had eight years' experience of policing elsewhere. In 1872 he was made a sergeant, but it was not until 1883 that he was promoted to the rank of inspector. Thirteen years later, at the age of sixty-five, he left the force on a pension of two-thirds pay. By any standard his was a long and successful career.[9]

The second category comprises those who reached but did not move beyond the rank of sergeant. The career of Thomas Black illustrates well the experience of the men in this group. He joined the force in 1869, age thirty-three, as a third-class constable with no record of previous police experience. Promotion to sergeant came in 1875, but he remained at this rank, although moving up to the first class, for his last eleven years in the force. For others the period was longer. James Metcalf was a sergeant for nineteen years, but received no pay increase for the last thirteen, while Thomas Jobson remained at the same wage rate for the last sixteen years of a twenty-four-year career as a sergeant. Although such men could look forward to a pension when they retired, the lack of further progress could be a source of frustration.[10]

The sense of frustration was even greater for those in the third category, who remained as constables. This was revealed in the disciplinary records of the men concerned. Thus, for example, Robert Gatenby, having joined the force as a third-class constable at the age of twenty-nine in 1866, progressed to the first-class rank and was awarded a Merit Badge in 1874 for arresting a criminal on a stabbing charge. Thereafter, things began to go wrong. He lost his Merit Badge and saw his pay cut for being drunk on duty at the parliamentary election of February 1874. The financial loss was made good within eighteen months, but Gatenby never gained promotion. Ten years later, still on the same grade, matters finally came to a head. In March 1884 he was reduced to the third class and lost a further forty-four days' pay for being drunk on duty. Four months later he was ordered to resign, having assaulted a complainant. Despite this inglorious end to an eighteen-year career, the Watch Committee, interestingly, allowed him a gratuity of £20. This reflected the growing awareness on the part of its members that there was a problem created by long-serving men who, for

Chief Constable William Ashe with the Middlesbrough Police Cricket Club, c. 1890.

whatever reason, did not gain promotion. To ease the sense of grievance felt by these men, it was finally decided to introduce long-service classes, which would offer recognition and an increase in pay.[11]

In comparison with the previous decade, more men, 134, were recruited into the borough police force in the 1870s. Further, a higher proportion (just under nineteen percent or twenty-five men) went on to become long-serving officers. Of these, only ten (or forty percent) became sergeants compared with sixteen (or about eighty percent) for the previous two decades. Not surprisingly, the percentage of men reaching the rank of inspector was lower—twelve percent compared with approximately fifty percent. Six men received no promotion whatsoever, but nine (or thirty-six percent) were promoted to the Long-Service Class.

These figures suggest that, precisely at the time that the police force was being seen as a more attractive long-term proposition, promotion opportunities for longer-serving men were diminishing. This is confirmed by looking at the average time taken to gain promotion. Whereas in the 1860s those promoted to sergeant achieved this in five years, by the 1870s the figure had doubled to ten years. This compares unfavorably with a Home Office estimate of 1878 that it took four to five years for a constable to become a sergeant.[12] For the few—three in total—who were promoted to inspector, the average time taken to achieve this rank after promotion to sergeant was roughly the same as that of their counterparts a decade earlier. Moreover, the period of about eight years was not out of line with the Home Office figure of eight to ten years' additional service.

A good example of the successful few was Frederick Knowlson. He joined as a twenty-one-year-old in 1872, and reached the rank of first-class constable by 1876. Promotion to sergeant came five years later. In another two years he was promoted to first-class detective sergeant, and followed this with promotion to inspector in 1885. In 1894 he was promoted to superintendent, at which rank he remained until he retired in 1898 after twenty-six years of service.[13]

A similar career profile was exhibited by William Nunn. As a twenty-year-old he was appointed to the fourth class in 1875. By 1880 he had reached first class and three years later was promoted sergeant. In 1890 he became an inspector and remained so until his retirement in 1902.[14]

Of those in the intermediate category of single promotion, a typical example is Hugh Neill. As a thirty-four-year-old with over nine years' previous police service, he was appointed as a second-class constable in 1872. It was not until 1883 that he gained promotion and, despite serving for a another eleven years, he proceeded no farther up the hierarchy. A variation on this theme can be found in the experience of Thomas Raisbeck. Appointed a third-class constable in 1871, having only two years' previous police experience, he was promoted to sergeant in 1874 at the age of twenty-seven.

Thereafter, his promotion hopes diminished. Twenty years later he was still holding the same rank. In this year, however, his long service was recognized, as he was promoted to the service class. A final example in this category is William Brown. Appointed in 1876, he was already thirty years of age. Despite two-and-one-half years in the North Riding Constabulary and a further five years with the York City Police, he was appointed only as a third-class constable. By 1880 he had risen to first class. No further movement was to come until 1894, when he was promoted to the service class. Four years later, after twenty-two years, he was promoted to sergeant.[15]

There was no promotion for the majority of long-term men recruited in the 1870s. John Perry joined in 1872 and became a first-class constable in 1878. For the next fifteen years he remained an ordinary constable. Anthony Bosomworth fared only slightly better. In 1894, nineteen years after he had been appointed, he was promoted to the long-service class as a reward for long service and a good disciplinary record.[16] Not all long-servers were like this. George Dixon was a case in point. Having risen to the rank of first-class constable in 1875, four years after appointment, he made no further progress despite being rewarded for the arrest of two shop-breakers in 1882. Problems set in after ten years with no promotion. In June 1885 he was cautioned for neglecting to work his beat properly and reprimanded for drinking in *The Bridge* while on duty. In March 1886 he was found guilty of two similar offenses and was reduced to third class with the loss of two shillings (10p) pay per week. Five months later he was found to be absent from his beat. For this he was further demoted, his pay reduced to twenty-five shillings and eight pence (£1.28), and he was given a final warning. This appears to have had some effect in that he worked himself back to second-class constable by early 1889. However, in May of that year he was found drunk while in uniform and dismissed. Here was a good example of a man in his forties finding the frustrations and strains of the job too much after fifteen years in service.[17]

Even fewer men were recruited in the 1880s, reflecting the more stable force that was coming into being. Of ninety-one men recruited, thirty-four served for ten years or more. The proportion gaining promotion to higher ranks remained largely unchanged from the previous decade. Thus, forty-four present of these men went on to become sergeants, but taking on average eleven years and eleven months to gain promotion. This figure, however, obscures an important division. On the one hand were those men, eight in total, who became sergeants *after* promotion to the long-service class. On the other hand were those, totaling seven, who were promoted before they gained long-service status. For the former it took fifteen years on average to become a sergeant; for the latter nine years. From this cohort, five men went on to become inspectors, an increase in both absolute and relative terms; two achieved the rank of chief inspector, and one went on

Sergeant Thomas Raisbeck.

to become a superintendent. Interestingly, of these five, three had taken the long route to becoming a sergeant. Less gloriously, two—one from each category—were later demoted to the rank of ordinary constable.

Nineteen men recruited in the 1880s, however, failed to progress beyond the rank of constable. Eighty percent of them, however, gained long-service status and fifty percent reached the third class. Of the three who failed to achieve this status two died while in service. This compares favorably with the previous decade when, of the fifteen men who did not gain promotion beyond the rank of first-class constable, only eight gained long-service status.

The most successful man recruited in the 1880s was John Stones. A local man from Hutton Rudby, he first served with the Durham County Constabulary, but after a year he joined the Middlesbrough Borough Force in 1889 at the age of twenty. He became a first-class constable in 1892 and five years later was promoted to the first service class. In the same year he became a sergeant. In 1900 he was promoted to detective inspector, becoming a chief inspector in 1905 and detective superintendent in 1909.[18] A more typical success story was that of Robert Hall. Having served a probationary period in 1881, he was appointed at the bottom of the ladder as a fifth-class constable. By late 1885 he had risen to first-class constable and gained promotion to the rank of sergeant in 1890. Eight years later he became an inspector and remained in that post for a further seven years until retirement at the age of forty-seven, because of ill health, after twenty-five years' service.[19]

Another man to reach the rank of inspector was William Milestone. He joined the borough force in 1888 with four years' experience with the North Riding Constabulary. Initially, his progress was unspectacular. Having reached the rank of first-class constable in 1891, he remained at that level until 1897 when he was promoted to the long-service class. In December 1899 his career took off. He was promoted to sergeant and in just over three years he became an inspector. A similar, indeed somewhat more successful, career was followed by Robert Grey. Like Milestone he reached the rank of inspector. Further promotion came when he was made chief inspector in 1902. It appeared as if he would go to the very top, for in the same year he received a £50 gratuity from the Watch Committee for his services during the enforced absence, due to illness, of the chief constable, William Ashe. His career, however, finished in sad but spectacular fashion in December when he was dismissed after being convicted of larceny.[20]

Of those who only reached the rank of sergeant, Anthony Robinson is a good example. Born in Barnard Castle, he joined the force as a sixth-class constable in 1883. He worked his way up to first-class, and almost fourteen years after his appointment he was promoted to the long-service class and almost immediately thereafter to the rank of sergeant. A similar career pattern was followed by John Booth.[21]

The analysis of this decade is completed by looking at the long-term

Table 2
Rank and Age Structure of the Middlesbrough Borough Police Force, 1882 and 1889

	1882			1889		
Rank	No.	% of Total	Av. Age	No.	% of Total	Av. Age
Chief Constable	1			1		
Supt.	1			1		
Inspect.	5			4		
Senior Officers	7	11.3	45.6	6	8.3	47.0
Sergeants	10	16.1	39.1	9	12.5	46.6
PC 1st.	25		35.9	41		36.5
2nd.	7		34.0	5		32.2
3rd.	7		30.4	7		27.0
4th.	3		25.0	2		25.5
5th.	2		21.5	1		21.0
6th.	1		67.0	1		40.0
All PCs	45	72.6	34.1	57	79.2	34.4
Totals	62		36.2	72		36.9

Source: Nominal Roll of the Police Force of the County Borough of Middlesbrough, Sept. 1882 and May 1889, Printed Council Minutes, 25 July 1882, CB/M/C, 1/42, 169–70 & 28 May 1889, CB/M/C, 1/49, 234–5.

constable for whom even a sergeant's stripes remained elusive. One such person was Thomas Atkinson. Joining at the age of twenty in 1882, he was still in uniform at the outbreak of the Great War. He reached the rank of first-class constable after five years, but had to wait another nine before being promoted to the first long-service rank. Five years later in 1902 he went up to the second service class and three years later to the third.[22]

The impact of these changes can be seen in a different light by considering the overall structure of the force (see Table 2).

The maturity of the force can be seen in the fact that in 1882 all but one of the sergeants had served for ten years or more, while in 1889 all but two had at least fifteen years' experience. Even more striking, over eighty percent of first-class constables in 1882 had more than five years' experience, twenty-five percent more than ten, and eight percent over fifteen. In 1889 the corresponding percentage figures were seventy-eight, thirty-seven, and twenty-two.

There was, however, a reverse side to the coin. For the career policeman this greater maturity of the force meant relatively fewer promotion opportunities—a situation that was to worsen in the 1890s. Overall recruitment, at eighty-six, was lower than for any decade since the 1850s. Fifty (i.e., fifty-eight percent) served for at least ten years, the highest figure to date. For these men promotion opportunities were more limited than ever. Only fourteen of the fifty became sergeants, and this on average after more than twelve years; only two reached the rank of inspector. On the other hand,

Chief Constable Henry Riches with his Officers, c. 1913.

by way of compensation, every one of the fifty reached the first service class; thirty-eight the second; at least eighteen the third; and ten men were promoted to a special long-service class.

Robert Hird was one of the two men to rise to the rank of inspector. Born in Birkenhead, he served first with the Hartlepool police but after two years, at the age of twenty-three, joined the borough force as a fifth-class constable. In less than three years he had risen to the first class. He was promoted to sergeant in 1902. Within six months he had become an inspector and remained in that post until his retirement in 1914.[23] Almost identical was the career of Matthew Hodgson. Born in Castle Eden, he also served for just under two years in the Hartlepool Borough Force, before being appointed to the fourth class in 1890 when just over twenty-one years old. In two-and-a-half years he reached the first class and was promoted to the merit class in 1896. Two years later he was promoted to the service class, where he was to remain for five years. Promotion to detective sergeant in 1903 was followed by promotion to inspector in 1907. Ironically, it was after achieving this promotion that he was severely warned for drinking in *The Wellington* and neglect of duty.[24]

More modest success was exemplified by George Brett who joined the force in 1893 at age twenty-nine, having moved from his hometown of Alton, Staffordshire. A first-class constable in 1896 and promoted to the service class in 1901, he finally became a sergeant in 1904. He remained in that post until 1912, when his career was terminated by ill health: He was declared unfit for duty as the result of "accidentally inhaling a bad smell when assisting to bring a decomposed body from out of a boiler."[25]

William Seymour was more fortunate. One of the few Middlesbrough-born men to be recruited to the force, his career started in 1893 after eight years in the Royal Artillery. He became a first-class constable in 1896 and eighteen months later took over as drill instructor for an extra shilling (5p) a week. He was promoted to the first service class and became a sergeant two years later in 1903. In both cases, these were worthy men who received promotion after several years of solid service in the force. This policy, however, is no better exemplified than in the case of George Hudson. During his career as a constable he was twice commended (the second time for the arrest of a suspected murderer), and was finally awarded a merit badge "as a reward for general good conduct, zeal and activity displayed in the discharge of his duty."[26] Six months later he was made a sergeant.

Francis was the second Hudson brother from Pickering to join the borough force. He joined two years later than George and appears to have been equally diligent, although somewhat less successful. He was typical of a substantial minority of men who never made the rank of sergeant. A first-class constable by 1896, he moved through the three service classes in 1901, 1905, and 1909. His career had looked as promising as his brother's following the arrest of a burglar at a pawnbroker's on the corner of Station

Road and Boundary Road for which he was highly commended. Unfortunately, in the following year he was severely reprimanded for assaulting William Venables in Craggs Street. He blotted his copy book further in 1910 when he was found to be "too familiar with bookmakers and their touts"[27] while on duty in Stockton Street. This probably ended his hopes of becoming a sergeant, but three years later he was promoted to the new long-service class with merit. The problems of Francis Hudson were not unique. Although one must not overstate the size of the problem, there are signs of frustration among these men that are reflected in their disciplinary records.

The most striking example is John Gladstone Tate. A County Durham man from Bishop Auckland, he joined the force at the age of twenty-eight. Initially there were no problems. By 1898 he had become a first-class constable. Two years later troubles began. He was reduced to the third class for being drunk on duty. Within six months he was back at the top of the constable's scale, but in 1904 he was demoted for being drunk on parade. Clearly the man had potential, for by 1905 he had been specially promoted to the service class. In 1909, however, he was found to be drunk on duty again and was demoted to the third class—a reduction in wages of four shillings (20p) per week. By now the Watch Committee was unhappy about his suitability, but it was not until late in 1912 that he was dismissed. After the fourth offense, drunk on duty again, there was no coming back.[28] Tate had a problem with drink (and was not the only policeman to be in this position),[29] but it would be misleading to see his misdemeanors solely in these terms. Along with several others he found the pressure of work as a constable, and the difficulties in gaining promotion in the early twentieth century, increasingly irksome, if not downright intolerable.

From this survey of the evidence it is clear that as the number of career policemen increased, in both relative and absolute terms, the career opportunities open to these men diminished. Table 3 summarizes the changing situation with regard to long-term policemen, defined as those serving ten or more years.

Such then were the career paths followed by Middlesbrough's long-term policemen. But what were the rewards for their service? How did they compare with other occupations in Middlesbrough?

Wage Rates and Real Wages

When Isaac Wilson, long-time chairman of the Middlesbrough Watch Committee, in his evidence to the 1875 Select Committee on Police Superannuation Funds agreed that police recruitment was "simply a matter of wages,"[30] he oversimplified the situation. Nonetheless, he put his finger on a matter of central importance. A perusal of the Watch Committee Minute Books reveals numerous petitions and appeals from individuals and groups

Table 3
Long-Term Policemen and Career Prospects, Middlesbrough Borough Force, 1850s to 1890s

	Long-term Policemen		Sergeant		Inspector (& above)		Long-service Only		No Promotion	
	(1)	(2)	(3)	(4)	(5)	(6)	(7)	(8)	(9)	(10)
	No.	% All	No.	% (1)	No.	% (1)	No.	% (1)	No.	% (1)
1850s	4	7.6	3	75.0	3	75.0	0	0.0	1	25.0
1860s	15	9.2	13	86.7	7	46.7	0.	0.0	2	13.3
1870s	25	18.7	10	40.0	3	12.0	9	36.0	6	24.0
1880s	34	37.4	15	44.1	5	14.7	16	47.1*	3	8.8
1890s	50	58.1	14	28.0	2	4.0	36	72.0*	0	0.0

* The % figures for *all* men in the long-service category are 67.7 and 100.0, respectively.
Source: As Table 1.

(notably, sergeants, unpromoted first-class policemen) for an increase in wages. Tables 4 and 5 detail actual wage rates for selected years for the Middlesbrough Police Force and certain local industries.

Although very little is known about the occupational backgrounds of recruits to the Middlesbrough force, it is unlikely that there were any significant differences from other urban forces. In other words, the bulk of men would have been drawn from the ranks of the rural and urban unskilled with a minority from the skilled trades.[31] This being the case, it can be seen from the wage figures that policing offered an attractive occupation for unskilled men who could improve their weekly income by six or seven shillings—a figure equivalent to a pay raise of between thirty-three and fifty percent. Moreover, police work was regular throughout the year. Regularity of employment also made policing attractive to more skilled men whose trades were subject to both seasonal and cyclical fluctuations. Against this would have to be set the long hours (and rigorous discipline) associated with policing, but on balance the advantages outweighed the disadvantages.

A closer examination, however, is called for. Detailed pay scales are not available for the earliest years of the force, but by the early 1870s the situation was as follows. Constables could expect to be paid twenty-one shillings (£1.05) per week when on probation, and twenty-two shillings (£1.10) on appointment. Shilling (5p) increments were then paid, assuming no blemishes on the disciplinary record, at the end of six months, one year, two years, and five years. Thus, five years after appointment a first-class constable would receive twenty-six shillings (£1.30). This was also exactly the same as a fitter, turner, or patternmaker would receive in the town's engineering industry, but less than boilermakers, who could expect to receive in the region of one pound and ten shillings to one pound eleven shillings and sixpence (£1.50–£1.58). At the same time, sergeants were paid from twenty-seven to thirty shillings (£1.35 to £1.50), the shilling increment being

James Scott, Robert Spark, and James Salt, Middlesbrough, 1878–1904.

Table 4
Wage Rates (sh/week) in Middlesbrough Police Force, 1871–1912 (Index: 1899 = 100)

Year	1857	1871	1876	1880	1889	1907	1912
Constable							
On Appointment	18	22	26	25/8	25/8	27	27
Index	70	87	97	100	100	110	113
First Class	21	26	29	30	30	30	30
Index	70	86	101	100	100	100	100
3rd. Service Class	-	-	30*	-	-	33	34
Index						110	113
Sergeant							
On Appointment	23	27	31	31	31	34	35
Index	74	87	100	100	100	110	113
1st. Class	25	30	35	35	35	36	37/6
Index	71	86	100	100	100	103	107
3rd. Service Class	-	-	37*	-	-	38/6	42
Index						110	120

* Merit Class

Source: Borough of Middlesbrough, Minutes of Watch, Police and Lighting Committee, 6 Aug. 1857, CB/M/C 2/100, 111 and 7 Mar. 1872, CB/M/C 2/101, 341. Printed Council Minutes, 2 Mar. 1877, CB/M/C 1/129, 25, 23 Mar. 1880, CB/M/C 1/40, 212–13, and 26 Mar. 1889, CB/M/C 1/49, 234–35. Constables' Conduct Register, CB/M/P 31 inside front cover. Other figures recalculated from A. A. Hall, "Working Class Living Standards in Middlesbrough and Teesside, 1870–1914," (unpublished Ph.D. diss., Teesside Polytechnic, 1979).

paid at two-year intervals. Inspectors started at thirty-three shillings (£1.65) and rose to a maximum weekly wage of thirty-eight shillings (£1.90).[32]

The boom of the early 1870s put pressure on the Watch Committee to raise levels of pay in order to keep men. In his evidence to the Select Committee on Police Superannuation Funds, Isaac Wilson noted that "in these years trade was very brisk in our district, the wages were exceedingly high, and as we were obliged to advance our wages by degrees, we perhaps, hardly kept pace with the rise outside, and the men left us."[33]

By the end of the decade the weekly rates for constables were raised from twenty-six to thirty shillings (£1.30 to £1.50); for sergeants from thirty-one to thirty-five shillings (£1.55 to £1.75); inspectors received a minimun of one hundred pounds and two shillings (£100.10) per annum, rising to £135. Comparable rates for engineers and boilermakers were twenty-nine shillings (£1.45) and one pound eleven shillings and sixpence (£1.58) per week, respectively. In the Cleveland blastfurnaces, wages could be as high as forty-six shillings (£2.13) for keepers, thirty-four shillings (£1.70) for masons, and thirty shillings (£1.50) for fitters, smiths, joiners, and metal carriers. On the other hand, coke fillers, weighmen, and keeper's helpers would be likely to earn about twenty-one shillings (£1.05), while ordinary laborers would be lucky to earn more than nineteen shillings (95p) a week.[34]

Comparisons were also made with other forces. Among the northeastern

Table 5
Wage Rates (sh/week) in Selected Industries, Middlesbrough 1871–1913

Year	1871	1876	1880	1889	1907	1913
	(Index 1899 = 100)					
Blastfurnace						
Keepers	-	42/6	40	-	60	-
Chargers	-	33	30	-	42	-
Labourers	-	19	18/6	-	19	-
Puddlers (sh/ton)	9/5	8/3	7/5	6/7	9/1	8/8
Index	142	125	112	100	105	105
Building Trades						
60 hrs/week	-	41/3	37/6	37/6	46/3	-
48 hrs/week	-	33	30	30	37	-
Index	-	110	100	100	123	-
Woodworking Trades						
60 hrs/week	-	35	35	35	42/6	-
48 hrs/week	-	28	28	28	34	-
Index	-	100	100	100	100	121
Engineering Trades	25/9	32	31/6	31/9	35/9	36/9
Index	81	101	99	100	113	116
Boilermakers	33/9	36/3	32/9	36	37	38/9
Index	94	101	91	100	103	108
Agricultural Labourer						
1. Stockton	15/4	-	18	19	20(1901)	-
Index	81	-	95	100	105	-
2. North Riding	13/6	-	16/6	15/6	-	-
Index	87	-	106	100	-	-

Source: As for Table 4.

forces in 1880, only Durham City paid a first-class constable more (the difference was sixpence [2.5p] a week); only South Shields, which was markedly out of line with other forces in this regard, paid a first-class sergeant more; and at the highest level, no other force paid their inspectors as much as Middlesbrough.[35] It is not surprising to find that several men had started their police careers in other local forces only to move to Middlesbrough.

Questions of pay could not be divorced from questions of promotion. For many men it was the prospect of being trapped at the top of a scale that was irksome. This problem had been discerned as early as the 1860s. In 1864 a merit class had been created "in consequence of the great number of changes which have taken place in the force of late... to stimulate men to exertions [and] to reward officers deserving of promotion instead of keep [*sic*] them so long in the lower classes as to create in them a desire to leave for other employment."[36]

The creation of a merit class eased the situation for a while, but matters became more serious in the 1880s, coming to a head in 1890 when the Watch Committee received a petition from its long-serving policemen requesting the establishment of a service class that was beyond that of first class. Eventually this was agreed. Details of rates for the 1890s have not survived, but in the early twentieth century the position was as follows. The scale for constables, after six months' probation, ran from twenty-seven shillings (£1.35) for the fourth class to thirty shillings (£1.50) for the first class. Promotion to the first class would normally take three-and-a-half years after appointment on probation. Seven years after appointment on probation there was promotion to the first service class, which brought an additional shilling (5p) per week. Promotion to the second and third service classes came after further five-year intervals. In other words, a constable not gaining promotion, and with a clean disciplinary record, could reach the third service class with a weekly wage of thirty-three shillings (£1.65) after seventeen years. A similar system applied to the sergeants. Their pay range was from thirty-three shillings (£1.65) as a temporary appointee to thirty-six shillings (£1.80) as a first-class sergeant. This would normally take three-and-a-half years (including six months as an acting sergeant). With four years first-class service would come promotion to the first service class and five years later to the second service class. At this point—twelve years after appointment as a full sergeant—a man would earn thirty-eight shillings and sixpence (£1.93) a week.[37]

Earnings in other local industries at this time put the police rates in context. Engineers could expect to earn thirty-five shillings and nine pence (£1.79), and boilermakers thirty-two shillings and three pence (£1.61) a week. In the blastfurnaces weekly earnings varied considerably. At the top were keepers who earned £3, metal carriers who earned fifty shillings (£2.50), and chargers and mine fillers who received forty-two shillings (£2.10). In the intermediate category were slaggers earning thirty-seven shillings (£1.85), keeper's helpers and enginemen earning thirty-five shillings (£1.75), and coke fillers earning thirty-one shillings and sixpence (£1.58). Among the lowest paid were weighmen, who received twenty-four shillings and sixpence (£1.23), and laborers, who received only nineteen shillings (95p).[38] Compared with unskilled laborers, policemen were well paid. But for the long-serving career policemen, comparisons drawn with other groups were not always favorable.

The policeman did enjoy two major benefits in comparison with other workers. First, his employment was not subject to the fluctuations of trade and all of the problems which that entailed. Second, even before the right to a pension was enshrined in law, he was likely to receive some consideration at the end of his career. A superannuation fund had been established in 1862, and even in the early years very few men received nothing at all. Having said that, the pension was dependent upon the vote of the Watch Committee (something that its long-time chairman Isaac Wilson, for one, opposed), and was a source of contention among the men in the force. Nonetheless, the very fact of a pension was not to be dismissed lightly. By

1875 the pension fund, which was made up of contributions from the men, fines for misconduct of the constables, allowances for serving summonses and executing warrants, penalties imposed in cases of assault on the police, and a share of the penalties imposed in the prosecution of drunkenness, and licensed victuallers and beer sellers, stood at just over £4500. In the early 1860s total payments averaged around £200 per annum, rising to around £500 per annum by the end of the decade.[39] Unfortunately, it is not possible to say precisely how much individuals received. The most notable advance, however, came with the Police Act of 1890, which allowed for a maximum pension of two-thirds of annual pay for a man who had completed over twenty-five years' approved service.

Turning finally to comparisons with other forces, there are figures relating to the year 1914 that set the Middlesbrough experience in a wider context. In contrast to the earlier situation, the relative position of constables in Middlesbrough had declined. In particular there were clear discrepancies for longer-serving men. A constable with ten years' service in the borough force received thirty-two shillings (£1.60). Only Sunderland, in the north-east, paid as little. His counterpart in Newcastle received thirty-four shillings (£1.70) after only nine years. The real problem, however, came from the longest-serving constables. In Middlesbrough, pay after fifteen years was thirty-three shillings (£1.65), the lowest of all northern boroughs and cities. In Sunderland, Gateshead, and South Shields the figure was thirty-five shillings (£1.75) and in Newcastle thirty-seven shillings (£1.85). For constables with over twenty years' service, the Middlesbrough figure of thirty-four shillings (£1.70) lagged behind the thirty-eight shillings (£1.90) paid in Newcastle and the thirty-six shillings (£1.80) paid in Gateshead and Sunderland. Only South Shields had an equal figure. In the light of these comparisons the Watch Committee ordered a two shilling (10p) per week raise for both categories to be effective from April 1914.[40] Sergeants were similarly underpaid. After six years' service in Sunderland, Gateshead, and South Shields a sergeant earned forty-one shillings (£2.05), in Newcastle forty-six shillings (£2.30), but in Middlesbrough only thirty-nine shillings (£1.95). An increase to forty-one shillings (£2.05) after seven years was agreed to by the Watch Committee.

Wage data alone give only a partial picture. To complete the analysis it is necessary to incorporate changes in the cost of living in Middlesbrough during the period. As Table 6 reveals, policing became a more attractive proposition relatively speaking in the last quarter of the nineteenth century in comparison with puddling, the building trades, and boilermaking, although less so with the engineering trades. By the early twentieth century, however, with the exception of boilermaking, the other trades and industries enjoyed a greater increase in real wages than the police force.

In light of the earlier observations about the variety of police careers, the figures given above should be seen as no more than a crude indicator of

Middlesbrough Police Force Inspection, 1913.

Table 6
Comparative Real Wages in Middlesbrough, 1871–1913, 1889 = 100

Year	1871	1876	1880	1889	1907	1913
Puddlers	121	110	100	100	138	128
Building Trades	-	97	90	100	123	-
Agricultural Labourers						
1. Stockton	69	-	85	100	105	-
2. North Riding	74	-	95	100	-	-
Woodworking Trades	-	88	90	100	121	-
Engineering Trades	69	89	82	100	113	113
Boilermakers	80	89	82	100	103	105
PC on Appointment	74	85	90	100	110	110
PC First Class	73	89	90	100	100	97
PC Third Service	-	-	-	-	110	110
Sergeant on Appointment	74	88	90	100	110	110
Sergeant First Class	73	88	90	100	103	104
Sergeant Third Service	-	-	-	-	110	116

Source: As for Table 4, and text therein.

Table 7
Growth Rates (% p.a.) of Real Earnings for Three Career Categories in Middlesbrough Police Force

	Two Promotions	One Promotion	No Promotion
1850s/60s	2.1 - 2.6	2.1	-
1870s	2.4 - 3.6	1.4 - 1.8	1.4
1880s	3.5	1.5 - 1.7	0.6
1890s	2.5 - 3.5	1.4 - 1.8	0.3 - 0.7

Source: Earnings data taken from Constables' Conduct Registers, CB/M/P, 29, 30 & 31; cost of living data from Hall, "Working Class Living Standards."

change. An alternative approach is to calculate real earnings figures for representative individuals for the three broad categories (i.e., 0, 1, and 2 promotions) identified above. Table 7 shows the range of such experiences.

Two points deserve to be made. First, for successful men, promoted to or beyond the rank of sergeant, the rewards were somewhat less in the early years when promotion opportunities were greatest, and somewhat more in the 1890s when promotion prospects were less favorable. In other words, while the proportion of successful men fell over time their material rewards increased. Second, for the growing number of men who never achieved promotion (and that number increased in absolute and relative terms), the rewards clearly diminished over the years. Thus, as gaining a first promotion became more difficult, at the same time the financial rewards for these men were less of a compensation than they had been earlier.

A comparison with other local industries completes the analysis. Table 8

Table 8
Growth Rates (% p.a.) in Real Earnings in Three Middlesbrough Industries

	Blastfurnaces	Puddling	Engineering
1870s	-	-1.4 to 0.4	1.0 to 1.4
1880s	0.9 to 1.1	0.9 to 1.4	0.6 to 1.4
1890s	0.1 to 0.7	0.3 to 1.9	0.0 to 0.2

Source: Calculated from Hall, "Working Class Living Standards," for twenty to twenty-five working years' experience.

Table 9
Middlesbrough Long-Term Policemen: Reasons for Leaving Force (as % of total per decade)

Decade	Total	Pension	Resig.	Resig. (ill)	Died on Duty	Dismissed	Serving 1914
1850s	4	50	25	0	25	0	0
1860s	15	80	7	7	0	7	0
1870s	25	72	4	4	16	4	0
1880s	34	50	0	6	21	9	15
1890s	50	6	8	6	6	2	72
Total	128	39	6	6	12	5	28

Source: As Table 1.

contains the relevant information. Comparing the figures in the last two tables, it can be seen that in terms of real earnings policing was an attractive alternative for most of the period, with the important exception of those men who joined the force in the 1890s and failed to win promotion. This is not to say that there were no problems regarding pay. Overall, the question of pay remained a regular source of dissatisfaction within the force, and of conflict between the police and the Watch Committee. Middlesbrough's reputation as a high wage area added to the pressures. Relations were at times strained, although discontent was always contained.[41] Protest and petitions from below always emphasized the arduous nature of the job, the loyalty of the force, and the better pay elsewhere. Nevertheless, one must not overlook the benefits that the police enjoyed. For the long-term policeman these benefits probably outweighed the disadvantages. There is no evidence of large-scale resignations by these men, as Table 9 shows.

Finally, it would be wrong to see things simply in material terms. The second half of the nineteenth century saw a number of important qualitative changes relating to conditions of work. Changing public attitudes and improved conditions had an important part to play in the development of the Middlesbrough Police Force.[42] In the final analysis, however, a combination of rising real earnings, relative security of employment, and the prospect of a pension played an important part in satisfying the majority. This satisfaction laid the foundations for the creation of a disciplined and efficient police force in the country's most rapidly growing town.

Notes

I would like to thank Malcolm Chase (Leeds University), Richard Lewis (Teesside Polytechnic), and Thelma Taylor for their helpful comments on an earlier draft of this chapter.

1. See, for example, W. J. Lowe, "The Lancashire Constabulary, 1845–70," *Criminal Justice History* 4 (1983): 41–62, who refers to "good pay and generous benefits" at 59.
2. F. McKichan, "Constabulary Duties," *History Today* 30 (Sept. 1980): 38–43, uses this phrase at 43.
3. The analysis and argument developed in this chapter are based on a detailed consideration of the Constables' Conduct Registers for Middlesbrough, Cleveland County Archive, CB/M/P 29, 30 & 31. Individual records, some of which are quoted in this chapter, are to be found in alphabetical order in these registers.
4. The best short introduction remains Asa Briggs, *Victorian Cities*, chap. 6: "Middlesbrough: The Growth of a New Community." For a more detailed study of the social impact of economic change after 1870, see A. A. Hall, "Working Class Living Standards in Middlesbrough and Teesside, 1870–1914" (unpublished Ph.D. diss., Teesside Polytechnic, 1979).
5. The County and Borough Police Act of 1856 can be seen as the culmination of a series of pieces of legislation dating from the Metropolitan Police Act of 1829, the Municipal Corporations Act of 1835, and the Rural Constabulary Act of 1839. The 1856 act made the new police obligatory for all local authorities.
6. Several individual records for the 1850s and 1860s are incomplete. It is unlikely, however, that these men served for any length of time, as their names would occur in the fuller records from the 1870s on.
7. It was not uncommon for local firms to pay the wage bill of a police officer who, although listed as a member of the public force, would operate on the premises of his employer. This practice of private payment was most prevalent, in absolute and relative terms, in the 1860s and 1870s as the following figures show:

Year	Private-Paid Policemen	% of Total Force
1865	14	38
1870	14	36
1875	13	25
1880	5	9
1885	5	7
1890	7	9
1895	4	5
1899	8	8
1905	8	7
1910	8	6

8. Ashe's career took off in 1874 when he arrested a defaulting borough official in Melbourne, Australia, after a six-month pursuit. See my "The Antipodean Arrest:

Or How to Be a Successful Policeman in Nineteenth-Century Middlesbrough," *Bulletin of the Cleveland and Teesside Local History Society* (1990).

9. Constables' Conduct Registers, CB/M/P 29, 30 & 31. Atkinson's brother, Nathaniel, had joined the Middlesbrough police force in January 1866, but having failed to gain promotion, he resigned after nine years' service in April 1875.

10. Ibid. Black left the force with a weekly pension of £1–1–6(£1–12.5) in June 1894 at the age of fifty-eight. Metcalf retired at the age of fifty-seven on a pension of £1 per week in January 1900. Unlike Black, who lived for a further 12 years, Metcalf died 15 months later. Jobson left the force with a pension of £1–3–4 (£1–17) in December 1892 at the age of fifty-nine. It is not known when he died.

11. Ibid. Gatenby's troubles started when he was in his late thirties, but he was not asked to resign until he was forty-seven.

12. Quoted in T. A. Critchley, *A History of the Police in England and Wales, 900–1966* (London, 1967), 155.

13. Constables' Conduct Records, CB/M/P 29, 30 & 31. Knowlson was able to retire at the age of forty-seven with a pension of £100 per annum.

14. Ibid. Nunn retired at the same age as Knowlson, but his pension was only £1–9–0 (£1–45) per week.

15. Ibid. All three men retired in their fifties—Neill at fifty-six, Raisbeck at fifty-two, and Brown at fifty-eight. Their pensions were, respectively, £1–2–8 (£1–13), £1–4–8 (£1–23), and £1–14–0 (£1–70) per week. Raisbeck was one of several men to be assaulted by Irishmen during his career.

16. Ibid. Bosomworth was fifty-two when he left the force with a pension of 19/ (90p) per week. Perry was less fortunate, dying in service at the age of forty-four.

17. Ibid. Dixon was forty-two when he received his first reprimand, and his career ended four years later.

18. Ibid. Stone was still in the force after the Great War when in his fifties.

19. Ibid. Hall was forty-seven and received a pension of £1–3–11 (£1–20) per week.

20. Ibid. Milestone, despite four years' pervious police service, started as a constable in the fourth class. He was still in the force at the outbreak of the Great War at age fifty-three. Grey was sentenced to six months' imprisonment for two thefts of £1–1–0 and £1–5–0 from prisoners. There had been further charges but these were dropped.

21. Ibid. Robinson and Booth were both forty-seven when they left the force. The former received a pension of £68–14–0 (£68–70) per annum, the latter £64–7–1 (£64–35).

22. Ibid. Atkinson, despite joining at the age of twenty, was still a constable in his fifties.

23. Ibid. Hird, like other successful figures, retired at the relatively early age of forty-seven.

24. Ibid. Hodgson was thirty-eight when he became an inspector in 1907, and was still in the force at the outbreak of the Great War.

25. The corpse was said to be in an advanced state of decay, but the precise relationship with Brett's ill health is not made clear (Printed Council Minutes, 25 Apr. 1912, CB/M/C1/72, 630).

26. Constables' Conduct Registers, CB/M/P 29, 30 & 31. Seymour was age thirty-six when he was made a sergeant, Hudson forty.

27. Ibid. Two other constables, Summersgill and Miller, were similarly cautioned.

28. Ibid. Tate joined the force at the age of twenty-eight. His first six years' service were unblemished. From his mid-thirties on he had an obvious drinking problem. The Watch Committee, not for the first time, showed considerable leniency—enquiring into his health on two occasions before finally dismissing him for his fourth offense.

29. It is well known that drunkenness was a major cause for dismissal from the police force. The problem seems to have been most acute in the early stages of a constable's career. It would be wrong, however, to suggest that longer-serving men were free from such troubles. At least 10 percent of the Middlesbrough career policemen had one drinking offense, 5 percent had two or more. Perhaps the most interesting case is that of Robert Spark who served for a total of eighteen years. Although reaching the rank of sergeant, he clearly had a drinking problem and was demoted to the rank of ordinary constable. The Watch Committee, however, persevered with the man. Notwithstanding several long absences from work due to alcoholic poisoning. Eventually, he was dismissed at the age of thirty-four, but was granted a pension of 9/6d. (47.5p) a week.

30. Select Committee on Superannuation Funds. *Parliamentary Papers* (1875), 13, Q.3234.

31. See Carolyn Steedman, *Policing the Victorian Community* (London, 1984), especially pt. 2, chap. 2; and Lowe, "Lancashire Constabulary."

32. Borough of Middlesbrough: Minutes of Watch, Police and Lighting Committee, 7 Dec. 1871, CB/M/C 2/101, 338; Hall, "Working Class Living Standards," Table 5.

33. Select Committee on Superannuation Funds, *Parliamentary Papers* (1875), 13, Q.3234.

34. Borough of Middlesbrough: Printed Council Minutes, 25 Mar. 1879, CB/M/C, 1/39 (1879–80), 129; Hall, "Working Class Living Standards."

35. Borough of Middlesbrough: Printed Council Minutes, 25 Mar. 1979, CB/M/C, 1/39 (1879–80), 139.

36. Borough of Middlesbrough: Minutes of Watch, Police and Lighting Committee, 8 Feb. 1864, CB/M/C 2/101, 123.

37. Police Conduct Register, CB/M/P 31, attached to the inside cover.

38. Hall, "Working Class Living Standards."

39. Select Committee on Superannuation Funds, *Parliamentary Papers* (1875), 13, Q.3249, Q.3265, Q.3271.

40. Borough of Middlesbrough: Printed Council Minutes, 2 Mar. 1914, CB/M/C 1/74 (1913–14), 508–9.

41. Although there was discontent, reflected in attempts to create a union after the Great War, it does not appear to be the case in Middlesbrough that the immediate prewar years were particularly fraught with unrest. I am grateful to Tom Bainbridge of Coulby Newham for this and other information relating to his father's experience of the local police force in the early twentieth century.

42. I am currently working on this aspect of the Middlesbrough police experience, and hope to have the findings assessed in the near future.

A Portrait of a Novice Constable in the London Metropolitan Police, c. 1900

Haia Shpayer-Makov
University of Haifa

The Constable in the London Landscape

By the end of the nineteenth century, the policeman had become an integral element of the London landscape. Distinguished by his uniform and stature from others who frequented London's streets, he was seen everywhere and at all hours carrying out his duties. His diverse tasks made him part of the daily life of Londoners. His role and performance were the subjects of intensive debates in Parliament, government circles, and the press, reflecting his growing social importance. Visitors to London found it natural to refer to his presence in their written impressions, usually positively.[1] As a result, the policeman enjoyed a new prominence in literature, often appearing in novels and short stories. The presence and role of the policeman were not uniformly appreciated and he was a controversial figure throughout the century, but the services he offered came to be considered essential to city life.[2] Outside the anarchist movement there were few who called for the abolition of the police after 1900.

This chapter focuses on the London constable around 1900, when the structure and character of the Metropolitan Police force had already been set. It initially examines his social role and the diverse tasks that made him a common and important figure in the London landscape, and describes some of the difficulties he encountered in his job. The distinctive role of police officers in the largest metropolis in the world raises the question of just what sort of men were attracted to police work, and at the same time regarded by the authorities as suitable candidates. The bulk of the chapter is then devoted to answering this question. Based largely on the surviving service records of policemen, the chapter constructs a socioeconomic profile of a recruit to the Metropolitan Police at the turn of the century. This profile is compared with that of metropolitan policemen earlier in the century. The changing standards of selection of recruits are thus brought to the forefront of historical analysis.

What sort of tasks did routine policing involve? The mandate to prevent crime and regulate public order obliged the policeman to seize suspected criminals, attend police courts, disperse "political mobs" and striking workers, be acquainted with every street, thoroughfare, courtyard, and house in his beat, and be concerned with the security of their inhabitants.[3] He was authorized to arrest suspicious persons, inspect public houses, beer-shops, lodging-houses, and street stalls, look after beggars and tramps, and charge disorderly persons obstructing thoroughfares or causing breaches of the peace. The policeman was also busy arbitrating the moral behavior of the population, preventing the solicitation of prostitutes, and seizing obscene prints and publications. The policeman was thus responsible for regulating life in London's streets and for enforcing established social norms. In addition, the policeman was asked to provide various municipal and welfare services. He had to report whether street lamps were properly lighted, check the nuisance of smoky chimneys and street noises, seize stray dogs, stop runaway horses, rescue drowning people, and carry accident victims to the hospital, report dangerous houses or structures, and watch the outbreak of fires and assist in their extinction before the arrival of the fire brigade. These essential services benefited the entire population and rendered the policeman more acceptable even within working-class communities where hostile attitudes toward the police were common.[4] James Monro, a former commissioner of the Metropolitan Police, elaborated on the role of the London policeman:

> Few crossings in crowded thoroughfares can be got over by the nervous and the timid without an appeal for the courteous help of the policeman; no marriage party in the West End is complete without the attendance of Scotland yard to quietly look after the safety of costly wedding gifts; the labourer in Whitechapel depends upon the early call of the man on beat to rouse him for his work; the police bands often cheer the spirits of unfashionable audiences in the East End, and the police minstrels are cordially welcomed at concerts for charitable purposes. Many a homeless wanderer has to thank the watchful patrol for guiding her to a "refuge" for the night, and it is no uncommon sight to see a child, lost in the streets, trotting contentedly by the side of a burly guardian of the peace in a custody as kindly as it is secure.[5]

No doubt Monro idealized the policeman's role. Yet his description indicates the kind of services that won for the police the appreciation of people across the social spectrum.

New duties were added all the time. Among the more important ones was the regulation of traffic in the metropolis. In this capacity the policeman not only supervised the traffic in the streets, but also ascertained the fitness of public vehicles and licensed the drivers and conductors. He also managed a lost property office and responded to "innumerable questions asked by the army of tourists and strangers found in London every day of the year."[6] More than other government employees, the policeman came into daily contact with the public, and as a symbol of authority became an agent for the transmission of consensual values.

As a general rule, the police officer patrolling the streets was expected to perform his ordinary duties alone and not call any other constable to his aid. During this time he had to "decide instantly, and on his own responsibility," and "to act promptly and decisively, with but little time for reflection."[7] Hence much of law enforcement and maintenance of order was left to the policeman's discretion. He was the first to decide what behavior was tolerable and what was unacceptable and required punishment. Fulfilling a variety of functions—many of which would eventually be taken from him—and serving as the common interpreter of the legal code, the policeman wielded considerable powers over the policed population and played a significant role in shaping life in London.

To be a policeman was not an easy task. The police officer was "not simply the strong and capable citizen patrolling the streets [and] permitted to exercise his powers" as seemed good to him, but rather a member of an organized and severely disciplined force, subject not only to the general orders and regulations in the instruction book, but also "to the orders of his immediate superiors with whom he comes in contact while on duty, whether he approves or not of the commands which they may give."[8] And the Metropolitan Police in the nineteenth century were known for the strict discipline imposed on the rank and file. The autonomy of the policeman was also limited by the need to work strictly within the constraints of the law and be a model "of restraint and politeness," so as to project a neutral image and minimize friction with the public.[9] To be accepted by the public was highly important for the London police, and the patrolman, maintaining constant contact with the public, had to bear the major responsibility for accomplishing the task. The policeman's position was further complicated by the fact that he was rarely called on to deal with elite crime, but was principally limited to controlling and regulating working-class communities of which he was a part. He was asked to serve the interests of the established classes and impose their concepts of morality and work on the laboring population. The difficulties were also physical. Patrol work, carried out by the majority of police officers, required exceptional physical fitness and frequently resulted in bodily harm. Steering between the various constraints and performing police duties efficiently, thus involved difficulties that kept potential candidates at arm's length.

The territory within which the London policeman had to operate created additional difficulties. The London patrolled by the Metropolitan Police covered close to 700 square miles, and its population was over 6.5 million at the beginning of the century, growing at a rate that had changed the city dramatically in a relatively short time. More than 100,000 persons had been added to the metropolitan area every year in the last two decades of the nineteenth century. London was the most densely populated city in the world, embracing accumulated wealth alongside chronic destitution. In addition to acting as local police for the capital of the empire and its vicinity, the Metropolitan Police force had to protect the royal family and other state officials, keep order in state functions, watch government dockyards, carry out the extradition of criminals, provide detective and emergency services to provincial forces, and fulfill other purposes of imperial and national importance. Controlling this vast, crowded, and complex area demanded more diverse skills from the London policeman than in any other force. It also required an ever-increasing number of policemen to meet the demands of a fast-growing population. Between 1890 and 1910 the Metropolitan Police force had grown from 15,264 to 19,418 officers. It represented over twenty-five percent of the total number of policemen in Britain.[10]

The Selection of Policemen

Despite the difficulties and relatively poor pay, applicants outnumbered vacancies almost continuously throughout the period, and the police administration was able to exclude unwanted men and choose the more suitable ones. The shaping of the policeman's character and code of behavior was to take place while in service through instruction, strict discipline, drilling, and experience. But on the assumption that the character of the labor force had an important bearing on police performance and relations with the public, the authorities were careful to sift the sort of people who in their opinion were more likely to become efficient and committed policemen. As a result, the selection was guided by strict written regulations and unwritten codes of acceptance, even though at certain times they had no choice but to accept men below the prescribed standards. In the late 1860s, for instance, only about twenty percent of the applicants were eventually sworn in as police constables.[11] Whom did the authorities select and what were the criteria of selection? The hitherto unutilized service records covering the years 1889 to 1909 contain detailed background information of all recruits to the force and can thus provide us with the data needed to conduct such research.[12]

From the inception of the Metropolitan Police in 1829, appointments generally depended on merit and not on connections or patronage.[13] In the early days the commissioners often got referrals from powerful aristocrats, but even then candidates had to meet the formal criteria. In order to ensure that the applicant was of irreproachable character, he had to provide the authorities with a certificate of character. Only upon the satisfactory completion of the inquiry of the persons who had recommended the applicant was he invited to Scotland Yard to be examined. The policy of recruitment by competitive examination adopted by the police prefigured what was to become a standard procedure in the selection of civil servants generally a few decades later. Police work was open to men who were tall, strong, healthy, and could read and write plainly—characteristics easily detectable by the examining officers.[14] The recruiting team was also faced with the more difficult task of choosing "the cool, smart, self-reliant, penetrating, temperate, forbearing men, who can take order and yet exert their own faculties, and who have an honest character of their own while up to other men's tricks."[15] Whether they managed to recruit such men was open to debate. The qualities of the English policeman were celebrated by many Englishmen and foreigners, the London officers enjoying the bulk of the praise. An American observer commented that "the commanding figure of the London policeman, standing serene, potent, and dignified amidst the crush in the congested thoroughfares, is a very impressive sight."[16] He seemed to "personify the majesty of the law with a superlative degree of suppressed emotion." The London policeman was also depicted as "a big chunk of a man, solid, impassive, unemotional, and thoroughly British" and as "the worthy representative of a free people."[17]

Other commentators were less complimentary, and accused the police of arbitrariness, lack of moderation, and even corruption.[18] Certainly the service records of policemen can provide no guideline in this respect. Neither do they include information on the educational experience of recruits nor about their fathers' occupations, their character references, or medical history. Yet they contain invaluable information on other characteristics of the respondents, which reveals the type of men enlisted by the London police and provides answers to questions such as these: How old were the recruits? What were their physical qualities? Were they family men and how many children did they have? Where did they come from and were they recruited from the local population? What was their occupational background and social origin? What skill did they bring with them, and did they experience social mobility when they entered the force? Who among them had worked in the public sector and for how long? Answers to such questions will highlight the character of the Metropolitan Police force between 1889 and 1909—a period of important changes, both economic and legal, for the police forces in Britain as a whole as well as for the general public. The social composition of the Metropolitan Police force was also undergoing changes. Treating the whole period as one single unit, although essential for the understanding of the police workforce, therefore obscures the dynamics of this force and the persistent trends that characterized it. To enable us to make a meaningful evaluation of the changes in the social structure of the workforce we have examined the way certain trends in our data were modified over the period studied. The results give an accurate picture of the background of a typical recruit. Our sample totaled one-fifth of the annual

Table 1

Age of recruits	percentages
below 20	0.9
20	15.2
21	24.7
22	15.9
23	11.0
24	10.4
25	9.1
26	7.1
27	3.2
above 27	2.5

intake every second year, examining altogether 2,252 officers. The total intake during the period was over 23,000 officers.

Age

From the information available in the constabulary service records, it is evident that the authorities generally recruited men within the limits of the written entry regulations and only occasionally bent the rules. Selection criteria had changed somewhat during the course of the century, becoming generally stricter with time. When the force was first established, entry was limited to people between the ages of eighteen and thirty-five. At the end of the century only men aged twenty to twenty-seven were asked to apply. Men below this age were not "considered fully grown and hardened for the work," and men above this limit were considered too old to start a police career.[19] As can be seen in Table 1, 96.6 percent of the recruits fell within the prescribed limits. Those below the required minimum age were judged to possess physical capabilities that would soon make them fit for police service. The great majority of the men over age twenty-seven were ex-servicemen (ninety-three percent), particularly noncommissioned officers with good testimonials.[20] Most other recruits preferred to enlist almost as soon as it was possible to do so, even though police service was open to recruits up to the age of twenty-seven. Almost forty-one percent of the recruits joined by the time they were twenty-one, and another thirty-seven percent by the time they were twenty-four. The average age of recruits was getting lower as the century progressed, from twenty-six in 1833 to twenty-four in 1850, to twenty-two years and seven months in our own period.[21]

Physique

The required physical qualifications were well above those of the average working man, and they too were progressively more restrictive. If upon the inception of the force the recruit was supposed to be at least five feet seven inches in height, at the turn of the century the figure rose to five feet nine inches. Selection according to height was premised on recognition that the physical stature of individual officers contributed to the effectiveness of policing. According to the sample, the average policeman was 5 feet 10.08 inches in height, and only five percent failed to come up to the minimum standard. The shortest recruit was 5 feet 7.50 inches, while the tallest was 6 feet 10.75 inches. So as to be capable of sustained physical exertion, the policeman was required to have a strong constitution and be free from any bodily complaint. His weight and chest measurements were regarded as an expression of his physical fitness. The sample shows that the average recruit was eleven stones 11.15 pounds in weight and his chest measurement was 35.7 inches. Six percent of the recruits weighed more than thirteen stones, and ten percent had a chest measurement greater than thirty-seven inches. The former head of the New York police depicting the London policeman as "rather tall, stout, but not fat and . . . well proportioned," bore witness to the success of the recruiting team in this respect.[22]

Family Background

The police authorities recognized an advantage in recruiting family men because they tended to be stable workers and more "steady in their conduct."[23] Although in the first few decades of police existence recruits were allowed to have three children, at the end of the century entry was restricted to men with two children. It was probably thought unwise to burden young policemen with the maintenance of several children at the beginning of their careers when wages were hardly sufficient to meet the expenses of a small family. Pressure for a pay raise could thus be abated. Because of the relative youth of recruits only about fifteen percent were married when they entered the service. Obviously, even fewer (nine percent) had any children. About 6.5 percent had one child and the rest had two children.

Geographical Origin

The only restriction regarding geographical origin was that recruits had to be British citizens. Accordingly, less than one percent were born abroad, most of them in British colonies such as Canada, India, Malta, Bermuda, and Burma. The great majority of those born overseas (seventy-four percent) were residents of London when applying for admission to the force. The others lived in various parts of England. Of all other recruits, 2.2 percent were born in Ireland, 2.4 percent in Wales, 3.9 percent in Scotland, and the rest in England (see Table 2).

The smaller proportion of Irish compared to the proportion of Scots was the reverse of their relative strength in the early days of the force. While in the sample period the proportion of Scottish recruits was double their proportion in the force in the late 1860s, the proportion of Irish recruits tended to drop during the course of the nineteenth century.[24] When the force was first established it contained sixteen percent Irishmen.[25] This figure declined to about eight percent in the late 1860s, although the proportion of Irishmen in the force was still the largest of the non-English groups. Around 1890 the proportion of native Irish recruits slumped to half a percent, while native Scots were represented by 5.1 percent and Welsh by 2.8 percent. Yet by the middle of the 1900s the Irish contingent had grown to constitute nearly four percent of the recruits, while the Scottish contingent declined to 3.5 percent and that of the Welsh to two percent. It is interesting that at this point the authorities decided that the number of Irish recruits was "sufficient," and while special recruiting teams were sent to Scotland and various parts of England, orders were given not to include Ireland in the scheme.[26] The traveling costs involved in sending a recruiting team probably constituted an important reason. But it also seems that the Irish, although mostly coming from rural areas, were not regarded as prize candidates. Conversely, believing that the Scots possessed a higher level of education and better physique, greater efforts were made to attract them into the Metropolitan Police.[27] This order of priorities may have had some influence before.[28] No doubt the economic circumstances of Irish society accounted for the fluctuations in the flow of Irish recruits. The downward trend during the nineteenth century reflected the drying up of the Irish reservoir consequent upon the hungry 1840s and the massive immigration resulting therewith.[29] Yet the attitude of the police authorities to recruitment in Ireland suggests that the changing proportions of Irish and Scottish constables in the force may have also reflected official policy.

In conformity with the general fear that London had an adverse influence on its inhabitants, senior officers of the Metropolitan Police aimed at recruiting men from outside London.[30] To have a large proportion of Londoners in the force was believed to be a liability. The Londoner was considered "a very bad policeman," principally because he was "too volatile and conceited to submit himself to discipline," and because he was less robust.[31] In addition, the authorities preferred men with no local connections in order to ensure the impartiality of the labor force.[32] Yet despite the prevailing preferences, throughout the period local lads constituted a significant share of the new policemen. Admittedly, as can be seen in Table 2, only twenty-eight percent of the recruits were born in London, but close to fifty percent had resided in the metropolis before joining the local police. The proportions only worsened with time. Less and less strangers to the community were accepted into the police. Between the early 1890s and late 1900s, the proportion of native Londoners in the force almost doubled, and the proportion of London residents increased by ten percent. We have already seen that the flow of native Scots and Welsh had been curbed. The same was true of the different English regions and most of the English counties. The Irish aside, only the Londoners had increased their representation.

Furthermore, while provincial men were generally preferred to Londoners, it was rural Britain in particular that was regarded as the best source of recruits. Nonetheless, the Metropolitan Police labor force was increasingly drawn from the vast reservoir of the urban working class.[33] Combining Londoners (by birth, residence, or place of employment) with recruits from provincial cities shows the percentage of recruits with some urban experience—either through birth, residence, or employment—to be sixty-four percent. Examining the three types of settlement—London, provincial cities, and rural Britain—over time reveals that while the proportion of Londoners had risen from the early 1890s to the late 1900s (from forty-eight percent to fifty-eight percent), there was a slump in the proportion of recruits from rural areas (forty-one percent to thirty-three percent), and only a slight drop in provincial recruits from urban settlements (eleven percent to nine percent). Considering that the proportion of city men among the recruits did not change dramatically over the sample years, it was rural Britain that slowed its outflow of recruits.

There were different regional responses to the Metropolitan Police's search for recruits. People came from all parts of Britain. Yet a distinct pattern is discernible. Whether examining the place of birth or residence of recruits, it is clear that the movement of employees into the Metropolitan Police was essentially based on short-distance migration. The majority of non-Londoners were born or resided in areas close to London, their number generally declining the farther one was from the metropolis.[34] A significant proportion (about fifteen percent) were born in the extra-Metropolitan Home Counties (about eleven percent were residents of these counties when applying). A similar percentage (about fourteen percent) were natives of other parts of the southeast: 1.2 percent were born in Bedfordshire, 1.5 percent in Berkshire, 1.6 percent in Buckinghamshire, 4.3 percent in Hampshire, 2.4 percent in Oxfordshire, and 2.9 percent in Sussex. The southeast as a whole was thus the main field of recruitment. As Table 2 shows, next came the southwest and then East Anglia. The area north of these regions made a low contribution to the composition of the force, the far north of England providing even fewer recruits. An examination of the place of residence of recruits reveals the same trend.

The entry examinations had taken place in London. Surely the long distance—therefore absence from work—and the traveling costs proved a deterrent to potential candidates living far away, especially in view of the high rate of rejections. But no less important was the high wage level current in the Midlands and even more so in the north and northwest of England, which reduced the incentive to enter the arduous and highly disciplined police service in the metropolis. Even agricultural workers, the lowest paid stratum of workers who had benefited from the relatively high wage rates in the north, had a lower motivation to join the London police than their counterparts in heavily rural and depressed areas such as the southwest, East Anglia, and parts of the southeast. Thus in addition to distance, wages in the counties or regions of origin proved an important factor in determining whether workers sought employment in the Metropolitan Police. Places where earnings did not compare favorably with earnings in London sent a far greater proportion of recruits than places over which London did not possess such superiority. Therefore, counties with large industrial pockets like Lancashire, Yorkshire, Cheshire, Staffordshire, Durham, and Northumberland, contributed a tiny proportion of their population. Northern men who insisted on police employment could turn to local police forces, some of which were paying the London rates and more. Indeed, an examination of the personnel files of the Lancashire constabulary between 1854 and 1870 shows that the majority of officers had come from nearby areas.[35] Despite the distance, Scots tended to be attracted to and accepted into the Metropolitan Police in higher proportions than workers who came from areas closer to London in the north.

Former Occupations

Since entry into police ranks was possible only at a relatively mature age, to be a police officer was never the recruit's first job. All applicants had worked somewhere else before they approached the Metropolitan Police. Moreover, apart from former police officers, all recruits had experienced occupational mobility. Police work demanded no special skill or work experience. Consequently, a wide diversity of skills and trades converged to create the police labor force in London. The information about their previous occupation and employment gives us an important insight into the economic and social origins of recruits.

All recruits had entered the base of police hierarchy where pay was low and work was hard. Men of some means, economic opportunities, and high

Table 2

Region of birth of recruits	percentage
Overseas	0.8
Channel Islands	0.1
Ireland	2.2
Scotland	3.9
Wales	2.4
London	28.1
South East	29.1
South West	13.1
East Anglia	9.4
East Midlands	4.4
West Midlands	2.9
Yorkshire	1.1
North West	1.5
North	0.9

expectations preferred not to look for a solution to their employment difficulties in the Metropolitan Police, and the ranks—except for a few top positions—were drawn exclusively from the working and lower middle class, the first being predominant. Only eight percent had engaged in non-manual work before joining the Metropolitan Police, a low proportion that was, however, eight times the proportion recorded in 1872.[36] That the non-manual component in the force was growing with time is clear from a comparison between the group recruited around 1890 (seven percent) and the one joining in the late 1900s (ten percent). Of all recruits in the sample, three percent were clerks and 3.7 percent small dealers. The percentage of clerks in our period, however, rose by nearly 300 percent (from 1.6 percent to 4.6 percent), and that of small dealers by fifty percent (from 3.1 percent to 4.7 percent). The more acute the struggle of white-collar workers to achieve respectability and mobility, the more they tended to take advantage of the security and promotion opportunities offered by the police.[37] Small businessmen too were in a precarious situation at the end of the century, and therefore grew more keen with time to enter police service. Although they could still benefit from the widening of consumer markets, they were at the same time threatened by "the concentration of capital, the advance of large-scale production, and the rise of cartels and monopolies."[38]

A division of the labor force according to levels of skill confirms the impression that few recruits had a propertied or professional background.[39] As Table 3 reveals, people classified as belonging to social class (1) were not to be found in the police ranks.[40] A small percentage belonged to class (2), out of whom seventy percent were farmers. Considering that in 1901 classes (1) and (2) formed seventeen percent of all males over fifteen in England and Wales, the upper strata of the working population were greatly underrepresented in the London force.[41] Class (3) constituted the largest category. If we separate the clerks and small retailers from the skilled workers, however, we find that those commonly defined as lower middle class constituted about six percent of the force, while the skilled workers formed almost thirty-four percent—still the largest skill category. The division between the semi-skilled and unskilled workers exaggerates the size of the unskilled grouping, since many agricultural workers (here categorized as semi-skilled) recorded themselves simply as laborers, and were thus classified as unskilled workers.[42] But even if we classify all laborers from rural areas as semi-skilled (now constituting nearly forty of the total recruits), the proportion of the remaining unskilled recruits among the entrants (now eighteen percent) was still much higher than among the adult male population at large (11.4 percent).[43] Also, the proportion of semi-skilled workers among the recruits (including laborers from rural areas) was higher than in the general male population, while the proportion of skilled workers was just slightly lower than their proportion in the occupied male population. Apparently, the Metropolitan Police labor force did not reflect the wider social structure, the higher levels being underrepresented while the lower strata of the working population were overrepresented.

Members of the low-paid strata of the working class had compelling reasons to be attracted to police service in the metropolis. Here they enjoyed terms of employment superior to those in most workplaces likely to engage them. The typical unskilled worker in the late Victorian and Edwardian periods "would be very fortunate to have regular work, and was more likely to be taken on casually and irregularly, by the hour."[44] The Metropolitan Police provided job security, hence regular income, to employees consistently following the organization's codes of behavior. Wage-rates were higher than those current in the unskilled market and were supplemented with social

Table 3

Skill of recruits	percentage
(1) Large scale employers and the major professions	Å
(2) Small manufacturers, minor professions, retailers and farmers	2.6
(3) Clerks, small retailers artisans and skilled workers	40.4
(4) Semi-skilled workers	30.5
(5) Unskilled workers	26.5

benefits denied to most other workers. Police work endowed the unskilled with an occupational identity, and, demanding no skill, it was easier for non-skilled laborers to enter this employment than to join the established crafts. By becoming policemen, the unskilled had left no craft to which they felt a particular attachment, and moreover experienced a rise in their social and occupational status. Indeed, police service provided the least skilled sections of the population with the opportunity to transcend the boundaries between casual labor and the employed population and to join the ranks of the respectable working class. The semi-skilled workers, who like the non-skilled laborers possessed no financial reserves, could also only now enjoy security of employment and its beneficial implications. All this explains why the force was dominated by the non-skilled and semi-skilled, who between them made up over half of the total influx.

A closer look at the trades and occupations of recruits reveals that artisans were not heavily represented in the police labor force. The sample contains only one bookbinder, glass cutter, glassblower, lacemaker, and rugweaver, three cabinet makers, four compositors, four shipwrights, and seven each wheelwrights, shoemakers, and tailors (out of 2,252 men).[45] A wide range of occupations were excluded. There were no watchmakers, weavers, spinners, and hardly any other craftsmen identifiable with the textile industry. More dominant among the traditional handicraft occupations were thirty-six butchers (1.6 percent of the total recruits), twenty-seven bakers (1.2 percent), twenty-five blacksmiths (1.1 percent), and members of occupations linked to the building industry, such as forty-six carpenters (2 percent), fourteen masons (0.6 percent), and thirty-three bricklayers (1.5 percent); but they too were present in declining proportions.[46] Obviously, the nature of industrialization after 1830 and the growth of semi-skilled occupations, rapid urbanization, and the rise of bureaucracies caused certain trades to contract and generated a greater variety of occupations, which were then represented in the police labor force. Perhaps the low pay and high vulnerability to unemployment characteristic of some of these trades, like those connected with building, and the poor compensation received in trades such as bakery, explain the greater willingness of these craftsmen to become policemen.[47] It appears that the same rule applied in the case of jobs connected with the new industries, which usually offered higher pay but also embraced depressed workers who were more eager to join the police. Miners and colliers, for instance, who were among the more fortunate workers, contributed only twenty-eight men to the sample (1.2 percent), and engineers contributed only twenty men (0.9 percent). The best-paid workers in the country, such as engine drivers, welders, tool makers, caulkers, patternmakers, and riveters, were hardly represented at all.[48] This is not surprising, since whereas the upper stratum of the working class in London at the end of the century (17 percent of the labor force) was earning above 40s a week, policemen started with 24s.[49] Virtually no stationmasters and only very few inspectors, foremen, or other people of managerial positions were to be found among the recruits. True, the average age of recruitment being low, the recruits hardly had time to become master craftsmen or to be promoted to a high position within their trade whatever it might be. But it is also likely that police service did not attract workers who were enjoying upward career mobility. Thus unless circumstances like irregularity of employment, lack of prospects, and deterioration in working conditions forced workers to apply to the police, they would tend to stick to their trades.

The more conspicuous occupations among the new industries were in the railways (8.6 percent) and other forms of transport (106 men comprising 4.7 percent), many of which bordered between the skilled and semi-skilled categories or were even placed lower down the scale.[50] Indeed, a more detailed breakdown of the group of railwaymen reveals that seventy percent were either unskilled or semi-skilled workers, for whom joining the police often meant a rise in their earnings as well as their social status without the loss of social benefits provided by the railway companies. One hundred sixteen men (5.2 percent) were porters (many in the railway companies), and 122 (5.4 percent) had formerly been engaged in personal service—a declining employment for males in the country—whether as grooms (65 men), footmen (24), servants (22), valets (6), chauffeurs (2), cooks (2), or butlers (1) (with gardeners and gamekeepers, their percentage would be much higher). The single most common occupation was general laboring, forming almost twenty percent of the entire intake. If we reduce the number of laborers who came from rural areas who may have been agricultural workers, their proportion declines to twelve percent. With this addition the percentage of agricultural laborers (farm servants and farm laborers formerly constituting 2 percent) had increased to ten percent. This figure may exaggerate the percentage of agricultural laborers in the force, but it probably brings us closer to a correct estimation.[51] Agricultural laborers, earning on average less than 14s a week during most of the 1890s, obviously gained in terms of both wages and working conditions when they joined the Metropolitan Police.[52] Another essentially agricultural occupation that sent many men to the Metropolitan Police was gardening (5.6 percent).

Although industrial workers predominated in the force, the most sought after policeman was one with a rural background. The emphasis on the merits of recruits with rural origins was actually built into police ideology of the whole pre-war period, and was intimately bound up with the reservations about London and cities in general. Particularly the presence of agricultural laborers was felt to be essential. It was believed that the habits of work and behavior such workers had acquired in the countryside made them both robust and easily amenable to discipline—attributes most valued in a police constable.[53] Unlike the city man, the agricultural laborer was expected to cause no trouble and to do what he was told, having come humbly intending "to acquire knowledge."[54] His tendency to be a stable worker was also considered a great advantage.[55] The rift from agricultural employment throughout the nineteenth century supplied police ranks with these "ideal" recruits in both London and the provinces.

The desire of the authorities to recruit landed men had been satisfactorily met almost until the end of the century. The changes in the structure of rural society, which resulted in the depletion of the agricultural labor force, frustrated this desire. The presence of farm laborers and farm servants was declining both relatively and absolutely. The fall in the number of general laborers was probably related to the same trend, which was also manifested in a sharp cut in the recruitment of rural craftsmen. The slump seems to have gained momentum at the turn of the century, when the percentage of farm laborers (including laborers from rural areas) was declining from 18.3 percent (in 1897) to 5.3 percent (in 1909). The almost unending supply of rural recruits had been drying up, and the force correspondingly shifted toward a heavier concentration on urban workers, particularly from London. But if the Metropolitan Police had been losing their favorable recruits, they were gaining in other respects. The ranks were being filled with men from the upper strata of the wider workforce—both skilled and white-collar workers—who were better able to meet the demands of an increasingly professional and specialized police. The declining proportion of the unskilled and semi-skilled workers was modernizing the social base of the workforce. A sample of the social composition of the Metropolitan Police in the 1970s shows that policemen from non-manual backgrounds formed as much as a third of all the officers, while the semi-skilled and unskilled combined together constituted a lower proportion.[56]

Public Service Record

Naturally, some of the people who applied to join the police had a public service record. In fact, forty percent had been thus engaged, the great majority (almost 30 percent of the total recruits) coming from military establishments. It is true that most public employers provided security of employment and various social benefits denied by most other employers.[57] But the employees who nonetheless had decided to leave their public work while still enjoying regular income and some form of social security, and who were willing to endure the discipline and regimentation characteristic of police work, might well have thought of police employment as a viable alternative. Police life had a lot in common with the public sectors from which recruits had arrived. All were large-scale and uniformed organizations, where the labor force was subjected to a military or quasi-military supervision and worked within a strict framework of procedural rules, but enjoyed economic protection. These similarities might have induced men with public service experience to join, expecting to pick up the new skill with relative ease. As a policeman in London, the ex-serviceman was "not exiled from home and friends," and could "marry and settle comfortably in his native land" in a civilian environment.[58] Police service also often implied a rise in earnings and a certain social mobility for army personnel.

The fact that former employees of military or semi-military establishments saw the police as a natural workplace raises an important question concerning the impact of such experience on the social composition of the Metropolitan Police force. The professional police forces in Britain were established against a background of widespread distaste for continental police forces which were modeled after military organizations, and of fear that such police would be incompatible with British liberties. Influenced by this current of thought, the authorities aimed at avoiding a military image and emphasized the civilian role of policing. Hope was expressed that the policeman would not solely appear as the agent of the government, "exercising powers derived from that fact, but as a citizen, representing the rest of the community" whose power rested "on the support, both moral and physical, of his fellow citizens."[59] Accordingly, the police "were to be unarmed, except for a wooden baton which each man would carry in the tail pocket of a dark-blue and unobtrusive civilian coat."[60] Carrying truncheons rather than "guns or cutlasses and the choice of a blue collar for the uniforms" were ways of disassociating "the new police from the military."[61]

This emphasis on the civilian character of the police did not prevent Robert Peel, the Home Secretary who was the driving force behind the foundation of the Metropolitan Police, from purposely setting up the force along military lines.[62] The force resembled a military establishment in its internal structure, rigid discipline, uniform, and daily drill. Like the army, the police objected to unionism inside the force, and in a paternalistic way claimed to represent the interests of the force better than any of its representatives. In fact, the police had replaced the army when they took over the tasks of civilian control. Moreover, in line with the tradition set by Robert Peel, who insisted that one of the two commissioners should have military experience, many of the appointed senior officers—including the majority of the Commissioners of the Metropolitan Police in the period—were military men.[63] To what extent was the rank and file recruited from the armed forces? This is a crucial question since it can be argued that recruits with a military background could inculcate military values among the labor force, which might be manifested in the relationship between the police and those they were trying to control.

Evidently the majority of police constables had no record of public service work nor of a military past. Less than a third had worked in a military context, and only about twenty-two percent were full-time members of the armed forces; 16.6 percent of all recruits came from the army, 4.1 percent from the navy, and 1.6 percent from the marines. About seven percent had served in the civilian army—most of them in the Volunteer Force (5.6 percent), and only one percent in the militia. Volunteers trained in their spare time, but otherwise worked in a totally civilian atmosphere subject to the various social, cultural, and ideological influences current among the British working class of the time. Of the remaining eleven percent, about four percent had previous police experience—of whom less than one percent had been employed by the Metropolitan Police. Three percent had worked for the railway companies (8.6 percent if we include railwaymen who did not report themselves as former public employees), and 2.2 percent for the general post office. A few had worked for public employers such as the Royal Arsenals, the docks, and the fire brigade.[64]

But most of those who did serve in the regular army had spent a good deal of their formative and impressionable years in a military environment. Around fifty percent of the soldiers and marines had joined the services up to the age of seventeen; recruitment to the navy occurred even earlier. Sixty percent of all ex-navy men had enlisted before the age of sixteen. Although most ex-servicemen had left the regular army on completion of the minimum period of service—like their counterparts who had not joined the police—

they still served a significant period of time prior to their enlistment to the police. Sixty-five percent of the ex-soldiers served six years and over, fifty percent of the policemen with naval experience had served seven years and over (twenty-five percent served nine years and over), and about fifty percent of the ex-marines had served five years and over. This is not to say that army experience inevitably created a military type of person. Enlistment in the armed forces was above all a consequence of economic circumstances, and therefore did not necessarily lead the soldier to identify with a military way of life. We find proof of this in the fact that even after a few years of army service the great majority of ex-soldiers did not write their trade down as soldiers, but recorded their previous trade with which they must have felt a greater identity. Having joined the navy earlier in life, the majority of ex-navy men did define themselves as seamen. Yet whatever the case, spending an extensive period of time in a highly rigid organization was bound to leave some imprint on ex-servicemen.

As shown in Figure 1, the period under review was to see a growing enlistment of public employees, constituting on average over fifty percent of police recruits by the late 1900s. The rise in the twentieth century should mainly be attributed to the termination of the Boer War, to the various structural changes initiated in the armed forces, and to the growing attractiveness of police work for public employees. There was a consistent rise in the proportion of recruits from the navy (fivefold from around 1890 to the end of our period), marines (almost twentyfold), and Volunteers (almost tenfold). Also railway and post office workers now tended to enlist in greater numbers (twofold and more than eightfold, respectively). The tendency was reversed in the case of former policemen whose proportion was cut drastically over the period, with a sharp rise in 1903 (almost 11 percent of the recruits) and a slump thereafter. The share of ex-army recruits was erratic, particularly around the Boer War.

Since the constabulary records provided details about both the date of departure from the armed forces and the entry date into the police, it is possible to say with certainty that most ex-servicemen tended to see police service as their natural choice of employment and moved directly from the army to the police. Examining soldiers, sailors, and marines separately, we find that the majority in each group (59 percent, 78 percent, and 66 percent, respectively) made the Metropolitan Police its first choice of employment.

But were the authorities eager to employ ex-servicemen and public employees in general? Initially they favored recruits from the army. Since the whole police hierarchy had to be manned, the supervisory ranks were also taken from the army—in fact from the non-commissioned officers known for their ability to enforce discipline.[65] A police order of 1845 stated that a certain proportion of the recruits "must be military veterans."[66] In subsequent years, however, ex-soldiers were no longer considered desirable, neither in the Metropolitan Police nor in the provincial forces.[67] In the late

Figure 1
The Pattern of Change in the Movement of Recruits from Public Service to the Metropolitan Police

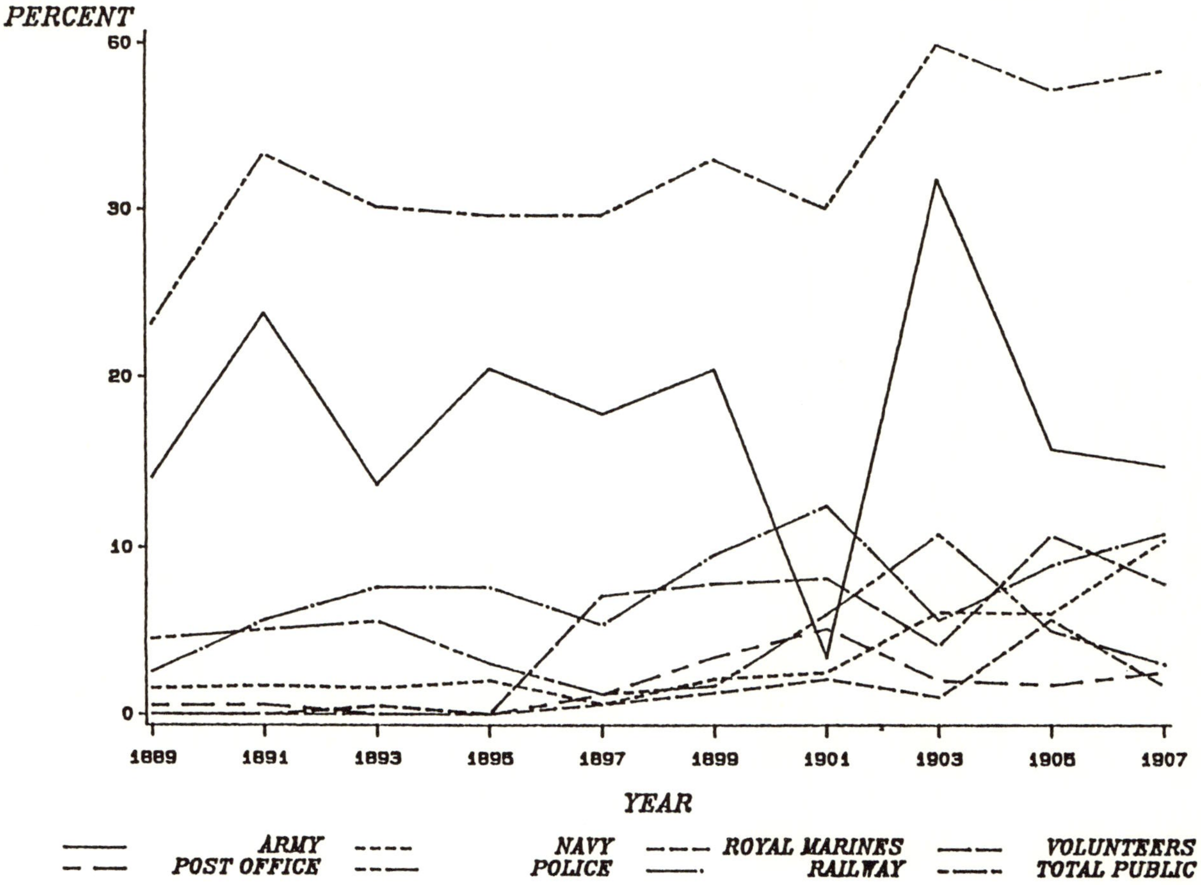

1860s only nine percent of the Metropolitan force was drawn from the army.[68] The reduction of the age limit in the Metropolitan Police to twenty-seven years had further diminished the number of discharged soldiers joining in the mid–1880s.[69] The proportions fluctuated at the turn of the century, but showed a sizable rise in the aftermath of the Boer War.

How can we account for this negative attitude toward soldiers? It was believed that the "training of a soldier does not fit him for discharging many of the most important duties of a policeman."[70] The reasons given were that:

> the whole teaching of a soldier is directed to suppressing his individuality—in the police such individuality is carefully developed; the sentry on his post remains blind to all that goes on around him, except as it concerns the limited range of the post, which he cannot leave—the constable on his beat has to keep his eyes open every moment, note what is passing, and interfere, in the interests of the public, at his discretion; military duty is necessarily unbending—police work is as necessarily elastic.[71]

No doubt the policy makers were also influenced by the general feeling in the country that soldiers were "intemperate" and had "irregular habits."[72] The establishment of an army reserve system later in the century rendered ex-servicemen even less popular. Senior police officers disliked the divided allegiance involved in being both an army reservist and a policeman, a position particularly inconvenient during a war or other emergencies when "trusted and reliable officers" would have to be removed from police ranks and called up to do army service.[73] This fear was justified during the Boer War when the reservists were withdrawn from police duty at a time when their services were "most required in preserving order at home," and when it was "impossible to fill their places." Particularly worrying was the Royal Warrant of February 1900, which provided for the re-enlistment of ex-soldiers for home service. The police administrators were well aware that policemen with previous army service would be glad "to exchange the cares and responsibilities of police duties for the comparative idleness attending Army Service at Home depots."[74] Army reserve men were also known for their lack of discipline.[75] The evidence about the attitude of police officials toward soldiers suggests that they were not troubled by the influence of recruits from a military background on the character or image of the force. What informed their judgment was the suitability of the recruit for police service as they defined it.

Nonetheless, despite deeply-held reservations about the value of ex-soldiers for police work, the regular army was a readily-available source of supply and provided some necessary functions. Non-commissioned officers were needed to impose discipline, and drill policemen and cavalry men joined the mounted branch and performed essential tasks in the country and outlying districts where horses were used for patrol duty.[76] Also, the police administration, like other governmental agencies, was at times pressured by the Secretary of State for War to secure employment for discharged soldiers.[77] As a result, the authorities were occasionally willing to relax the rules concerning the age limit and accept soldiers above twenty-seven years of age. In addition to ex-soldiers, former employees of the Metropolitan Police were likewise unwelcome. Reappointment was certified only under exceptional circumstances.[78]

Conversely, sailors were highly favored by the policymakers. They were considered responsible, good tempered, and used "to endure hardship patiently, and . . . cheerfully."[79] Besides, the Thames River Police, which formed part of the Metropolitan Police force, had a special need for people who could swim and take care of boats. Taking the City Police's preferences as an additional guide, railway porters were also regarded as desirable recruits. The main reasons were their "sound physique" and training "under the inspection of sharp superintendents."[80] In addition, their manners were said to "have been ameliorated by the expectation of tips and softened by well-remunerated attentions to the fair sex." As can be seen, these principles—physical fitness, deference, responsibility, and good character—seem to have guided the Metropolitan Police administration in their search for good constables above all other criteria. Apparently, the past experience of recruits counted to the extent to which it enabled the police to reeducate the new officers and enforce police standards on them.

Summary—The Typical Recruit

Our data cannot throw light on the extent to which the authorities managed to recruit serious, responsible, and self-restrained officers who were polite, impartial, and unprovocative in their contact with the public. With the aid of the service records of Metropolitan policemen at the turn of the century, however, it is possible to assess the success of the authorities in recruiting men with the required qualifications. Obviously the composition of the workforce reflected the employment opportunities in the general labor market. Largely due to the surfeit of candidates, police preferences counted to a considerable extent. Indeed, the registers suggest that the police were successful in many respects. The typical recruit to the Metropolitan Police was, as intended, relatively young but sufficiently old to have experienced life as an adult. He was generally single and childless and well developed physically. In line with police preferences, the typical recruit was by no means a military man, although a significant proportion of the police workforce had served in military or semimilitary frameworks—a proportion that grew after the Boer War.

The picture that emerges also shows that the most likely recruit came from the pool of manual labor and tended to belong to the lesser ranks of the working class—to those bordering on the poverty line. But early in the twentieth century this pattern began to change as the presence of recruits with a nonmanual past became more pronounced. There is no evidence to suggest that the entry of growing numbers of workers with nonmanual backgrounds to the Metropolitan Police was the effect of deliberate policy. Rather, it seems as though the pressures of the labor market on clerks and small-scale entrepreneurs, together with the growing attractiveness of police service for the upper levels of the labor force, account for this trend. After the promulgation of the Police Act of 1890, all veteran policemen were provided with old age pensions in addition to existing benefits, which guaranteed income in case of sickness or accident. The poor wage rates, which declined in real terms in the face of price rises early in the century, caused great discontent among the police labor force and probably deterred certain workers from applying. But the economic and social security offered by the police seemed to have outweighed the disadvantages for a growing number of skilled and educated workers.

The authorities were not unaware of the need for better educated officers. The fact that at the beginning of the century training schools were set up to broaden the education, first of detectives and then of recruits to the uniformed police, suggests the importance attached to the subject. Yet it seems as though the police relied on training-on-the-job and did not put too much emphasis on the level of education prior to recruitment. For the few top positions above superintendent, the authorities preferred "gentlemen of good social standing" who were appointed from outside the force.[81] But for the rest, the vast reservoir of manual labor proved sufficient. The lack of any reference to educational background in the recruit's entry register is a clear indication of this attitude. Presumably a recruit was not asked to state the level of his education since a basic knowledge of reading and writing—which he most probably possessed due to the 1870 Education Act—was what was required of him as a new entrant. The low wages paid by the police further shows that they were not particularly interested in reaching the upper grades of the working class or the lower middle class, whose level of education was likely to be higher.[82] This policy of keeping costs to a minimum and paying low wages at the expense of recruiting a better class of men was not new, but extended back to the early days of the force.[83]

While exhibiting no particular interest in recruiting non-manual workers, the authorities pursued a policy that brought the opposite results. As we have seen, the typical recruit was increasingly urban in origin, despite police preferences for rural recruits and for agricultural laborers in particular. To fill the dwindling ranks of agricultural recruits, the London police took the initiative in the period preceding the First World War, and in addition to recruiting men in London, sent a recruiting team to agricultural areas far away from the metropolis.[84] Going out to the countryside in search of agricultural workers marks the degree of preference for physique and docility over skill and education.[85] The Metropolitan Police were quick to adopt new technologies and advanced scientific procedures to combat crime and maintain order, such as the telegraph, the telephone, Bertillon's system of anthropometrical identification, and classification by fingerprints.[86] But their recruitment policy showed no similar tendency to adapt to the requirements of a modern organization. Evidently, this lack of innovative spirit had a negative impact on the effectiveness of the labor force. The Royal Commission's inquiry into the duties of the Metropolitan Police (1906–8) revealed that lack of sufficient education made the men "hate" writing out reports, and as a result "many a good Constable would 'look the other way' rather than intervene in a case in which he would have to make out a report."[87]

Still, despite police preferences for rural recruits, the ranks were filled with Londoners, many of whom were white-collar workers. Inadvertently, this trend was strengthening the professional character of the London police. The urbanite white-collar and skilled workers were no doubt better equipped to perform the increasingly more various and complex police duties in the bustling metropolis, and could more adequately answer the growing technical and administrative needs of an urban police force at the beginning of the twentieth century. Being used to life in London, they were intimately acquainted with urban policing and with the geographical environment they were supposed to control. They were familiar with local people and the local dialect, and could thus perhaps better understand the ruling norms and practices of the policed population.

Their experience of the metropolis and occupational backgrounds endowed them with the intuition and alertness necessary to deal with the heavy traffic of London and the modern means of communication adopted by the police. Their relatively higher levels of literacy made it easier for them to cope with the mounting demand for reports and bureaucratic control. The growing introduction of specialized jobs into police service, like detective work in the Criminal Investigation Department or its subsidiary the Special Branch, demanded professional skills and more sophisticated backgrounds. Middle-class crime involving embezzlement, forgery, and fraud necessitated qualified personnel with the knowledge of the business and financial world. Indeed, many former clerks soon found themselves working in the Criminal Investigation Department, where "considerable knowledge of the world, good education, good address, tact, and temper" were essential requirements.[88]

Londoners may have been less obedient and ready to be molded than rural workers, as senior police officers had believed. Metropolitan policemen, many of whom had experienced life in London before joining the police, expressed their dissatisfaction with conditions of service in bold ways—through strikes (in 1890, 1918, and 1919), complaints to the press, and attempts to set up a police union. But on the whole the authorities did not have at their command a problematic and a particularly disobedient labor force. Police employees generally followed orders, and fulfilled the tasks of controlling the working population and imposing middle-class values and codes of behavior on them with hardly any overt objection. To be sure, there were class-conscious officers who believed that there was one law for the poor and another for the rich, and that they, as policemen, were the tools of this system.[89] But continued identification with working-class beliefs and values, and familiarity with local people, did not prevent them from defending the status quo and the class system, with brute force if necessary.[90] In the years preceding the First World War, Metropolitan Police officers were often dispatched to locations of industrial unrest where they charged into crowds and attacked pickets.[91] It can be concluded that the urban origin of a growing proportion of the labor force not only proved no obstacle to diligent and loyal policing, but also served to heighten the professional character of the force. A study of the profile of a recruit to the Metropolitan Police at the turn of the century reveals certain characteristics of an important workforce, and bears witness to the interaction between police recruiting strategies and the pressures of the labor market.

Notes

1. See p. 134.
2. For middle-class attitudes toward the police in the early and mid-Victorian period, see Wilbur R. Miller, *Cops and Bobbies* (Chicago and London, 1977), 105–11. For working-class views, see ibid., 120–28; and Clive Emsley, *Policing and Its Context* (New York, 1983), 157–59.
3. "The Police of London," *Quarterly Review* 129 (July 1870): 101–6, 122; "The Policeman's Diary," *All the Year Round* (5 Jan. 1889): 6–11.
4. Raphael Samuel, *East End Underworld. Chapters in the Life of Arthur Harding* (London, 1981), 188–90.
5. James Monro, "The London Police," *North American Review* 151 (408) (1891): 618.
6. William McAdoo, "The London Police from a New York Point of View," *Century Magazine* 78 (Sept. 1909): 50.
7. "Report of the Royal Commission upon the Duties of the Metropolitan Police," *Police Review* (3 July 1908): 321.
8. Ibid.
9. Miller, *Cops and Bobbies*, 38.
10. At the beginning of the twentieth century, the total strength of police forces in England and Wales was 43,384 men, in Scotland 5,114, and in Ireland 12,398 (*Police Review* [10 May 1901]: 218).
11. "Police of London," 97.
12. The service records on which the following analysis is based are available in the Public Record Office (PRO), London, MEPO 4/361–477.
13. PRO, MEPO 2/38, letter by Robert Peel, 10 Dec. 1829.

14. PRO, MEPO 4/36, 8.

15. *Once a Week* (2 June 1860): 523.

16. McAdoo, "London Police," 649–50.

17. Ibid., 650; "The French and English Police Systems," *Cornhill Magazine* 44 (Oct. 1881): 421.

18. For criticism of police performance in our period of study, see testimonies to the Royal Commission on the duties of the Metropolitan Police (1906–8), *Police Review* (27 July 1906): 352, (19 Oct. 1906): 502, (26 Oct. 1906): 508, (2 Nov. 1906): 519, and (9 Aug. 1907): 380; Ex-Inspector John Syme's allegations in *Police Review* (23 Sept. 1910): 425–53, (30 Sept. 1910): 458–59, and (7 Oct. 1910): 470–71. For the divergent opinions on police behavior during disturbances and strikes, see Donald C. Richter, *Riotous Victorians* (Athens, 1981), 15–16, 146; Jane Morgan, *Conflict and Order* (Oxford, 1987), 162–67; T. A. Critchley, *A History of Police in England and Wales* (Montclair, N.J., 1972), 178.

19. *Once a Week* (2 June 1860): 523. There were doubts about the physical capabilities of youngsters in the army as well, although the army continued to enlist men under the age of twenty (Alan Ramsay Skelley, *The Victorian Army at Home* [London, 1977], 257).

20. Charles Warren, "The Police of the Metropolis," *Murray's Magazine* 4 (Nov. 1888): 592.

21. PRO, MEPO 2/26.

22. McAdoo, "London Police," 650.

23. *Report from the Select Committee of Enquiry on the Metropolitan Police* (1834), 16:34. See also *Police Review* (3 July 1908): 319.

24. "Police of London," 98. This was also true in the army (Skelley, *Victorian Army*, 284–85).

25. Report from the *Select Committee of Enquiry on the Metropolitan Police* (1834), 16:34.

26. PRO, MEPO 2/8123, draft letter by the Commissioner to the Home Office, 23 Aug. 1906.

27. PRO, MEPO 2/8124, Eric Thesiger to Commissioner of Police, n.d. (1909?).

28. See Ruth Paley, "An Imperfect, Inadequate and Wretched System'? Policing London Before Peel," *Criminal Justice History* 10 (1989): 116.

29. Colin Holmes, *John Bull's Island. Immigration and British Society, 1871–1971* (London, 1988), 21.

30. London is defined in the broad sense of Greater London, which was coterminous with the Metropolitan Police District.

31. "The Police and the Thieves," *Quarterly Review* 99 (June 1856): 170; Charles Tempest Clarkson and J. Hall Richardson, *Police!* (New York, 1984, orig. ed. 1889), 88; *Police Review* (21 Aug. 1893): 399.

32. Miller, *Cops and Bobbies*, 25–26.

33. Citymen are defined as those who were born, lived, or worked in towns or cities outside London with populations in excess of 20,000. The remaining provincials are described as rural workers, that is, as workers with no record of urban living. This division obviously reduces the number of country-born men, while it defines men who lived in small towns as rural workers. But despite the difficulties of defining rural and urban districts, these provide a valuable framework for discussion.

34. This calculation is based on a study of the place of residence and takes into account the size of population in the different regions.

35. W. J. Lowe, "The Lancashire Constabulary, 1845–1870: The Social and Occupational Function of a Victorian Police Force," *Criminal Justice History* 4 (1983): 46.

36. See John Powell Martin and Gail Wilson, *The Police: A Study in Manpower* (London, 1969), 13. Policemen are not classified as nonmanual here.

37. Gregory Anderson, *Victorian Clerks* (Manchester, 1976), 52.

38. *The Lower Middle Class in Britain 1870–1914*, ed. Geoffrey Crossick (London, 1977), 15.

39. People described their calling inaccurately and left out important information, such as whether they were self-employed, which would have helped to classify them in social terms. Because of the difficulties involved in classifying the various occupations according to skill, percentages must be regarded as approximations. The method of social stratification used here is recommended by W. A. Armstrong, "The Use of Information about Occupation," in *Nineteenth Century Society*, ed. E. A. Wrigley (Cambridge, 1972), 191–310.

40. There was one recruit who defined himself as an architect, but there is no reason to believe he belonged to skill (1) in social and economic terms.

41. J. A. Banks, "The Social Structure of Nineteenth Century England as Seen Through the Census," in *The Census and Social Structure*, ed. Richard Lawton (London, 1978), 197.

42. In any case, by that time an accurate division between the semiskilled and unskilled was difficult to establish as the differences had been leveled off by technical progress (Zygmunt Bauman, *Between Class and Elite* [Manchester, 1960], 144).

43. Banks, "Social Structure," 197.

44. Paul Thompson, *The Edwardians* (London, 1984), 173.

45. By comparison, the force in 1832 was composed of 6.2 percent shoemakers and 1.6 percent tailors. (J. L. Thomas, "Recruits for the Police Service," *Police Journal* 19 [July–Sept. 1946]: 293).

46. Compared to 4.2 percent butchers, 3.4 percent bakers, 1.7 percent blacksmiths, 4.4 percent carpenters, and 2.4 percent bricklayers in the early days of the force (ibid.).

47. Some applicants may have also upgraded themselves to a skilled level although they were unapprenticed and in fact semi-skilled.

48. E. J. Hobsbawm, *Labouring Men* (London, 1976), 288.

49. Ibid., 285.

50. The percentage of railway workers was higher than the one mentioned here since men with trades intimately connected with the railways did not always register themselves as having worked there.

51. On the other hand, laborers resident in London are considered industrial workers although they may have been agricultural laborers in the past; thus the proportion of industrial laborers is somewhat inflated.

52. B. R. Mitchell, *British Historical Statistics* (Cambridge, 1988), 163.

53. *Police Review* (21 Aug. 1893): 399; Raymond B. Fosdick, *European Police Systems* (New York, 1915), 201.

54. Ibid.

55. Fosdick, *European Police*, 201; *Police Review* (26 Apr. 1895): 200.

56. Robert Reiner, *The Blue Coated Worker* (Cambridge, 1978), 150. Unlike our study, these findings are based on fathers' occupations and the classification of policemen as non-manual.

57. Railwaymen who did not report themselves as working for a public service were not counted as such.

58. *Leisure Hour* (7 Jan. 1858): 14.

59. *Report of the Committee on the Police Service of England, Wales and Scotland* (Desborough Committee) (1919), 27:712.

60. Charles Reith, *British Police and the Democratic Ideal* (London, 1943), 36.

61. Richter, *Riotous Victorians*, 5.

62. See Mike Brogden, Tony Jefferson, and Sandra Walklate, *Introducing Policework* (London, 1988), 3.

63. Stanley H. Palmer, *Police and Protest in England and Ireland* (Cambridge, 1988), 294; Clarkson and Richardson, *Police!* 83.

64. Some recruits had worked in two public services. Hence these figures do not add up to 100 percent.

65. John Moylan, *Scotland Yard and the Metropolitan Police* (London and New York, 1934), 35; Palmer, *Police and Protest*, 300.

66. Palmer, *Police and Protest*, 300.

67. Carolyn Steedman, *Policing the Victorian Community* (London, 1984), 70.

68. "Police of London," 98.

69. Warren, "Police of the Metropolis," 592.

70. Monro, "London Police," 621.

71. Ibid.

72. *Police Review* (4 Mar. 1898): 100.

73. PRO, MEPO 2/8821, memo by the commissioner, 18 Nov. 1901.

74. Ibid.

75. Clarkson and Richardson, *Police!* 92.

76. "Our Police System," *Dark Blue* 2 (Feb. 1872): 696.

77. *Police Review* (14 Jan. 1898): 22.

78. *Police Review* (13 Mar. 1893): 122.

79. *Police Review* (26 Apr. 1895): 200–201.

80. Alex Innes Shand, "The City of London Police," *Blackwood's* Magazine 140 (Nov. 1886): 601.

81. Clarkson and Richardson, *Police!* 92.

82. The situation can be compared with the recruitment policy of the San Francisco police, which aimed at reaching high-status applicants and skilled men, and were ready to pay good wages to achieve their aim (Philip J. Ethington, "Vigilantes and the Police: The Creation of a Professional Police Bureaucracy in San Francisco, 1847–1900," *Journal of Social History* 21 [Winter 1987]: 217).

83. Reith, *British Police*, 38.

84. For detailed reports about provincial recruitment, see PRO, MEPO 2/8123 and 8124.

85. This preference was also exhibited by the Toronto Police, which was modeled after the Metropolitan Police (M. Greg Marquis, "Working Men in Uniform: The Early Twentieth-Century Toronto Police," *Histoire-Sociale/Social History* 20 [Nov. 1987]: 265).

86. Richard Bach Jensen, "Police Reform and Social Reform: Italy from the Crisis of the 1890s to the Giolittian Era," *Criminal Justice History* 10 (1989): 183.

87. *Police Review* (9 Aug. 1907): 380.

88. Clarkson and Richardson, *Police!* 263.

89. Carolyn Steedman, *The Radical Soldier's Tale. John Pearman, 1819–1908* (London, 1988), 60.

90. Clarkson and Richardson, *Police!* 205; Critchley, *History of Police*, 165.

91. Morgan, *Conflict and Order*, 157.

A Social History of Theft in Depression and Wartime: The Police Occurrence Books for Hamilton, Ontario, 1934–42

John Weaver
McMaster University, Hamilton

At 1:10 on the afternoon of 22 June 1934, on a west-end Hamilton street, three men sprang from an automobile and intercepted a pair of couriers conveying a leather bag with $4,705.95 belonging to the Tuckett Tobacco Company. One of the holdup men brandished a nickel-plated revolver.[1] The heist was one of several armed robberies in the city that summer; others occurred in a bank, a lunch counter, and two drug stores. With the exception of the bank robbery, the sums taken were under $100. On 3 August a young girl sent by her mother to buy 25 cents worth of meat at the corner grocery returned home in tears. Two older girls, aged ten or twelve, had snatched the quarter.[2] These incidents at extremes on a scale of thefts pose commonplace problems in criminology: What is a crime? Who is a criminal? Indeed, the incidents put a fine point on these questions because the occurrences were reported by the public. Indeed, the report about the quarter denoted a popular perception rather than an institutional determination of what was a theft.

The episodes had little in common apart from the fact that they had been reported in detail to the police during the same summer, and hence appear in a most interesting set of local records.[3] The victims in these incidents had no hesitation in calling on the authorities to deal with the loss of valuables, regardless of the sums involved. This belief in the efficacy of having the police assist with a great variety of problems was widespread, at least in this city. Tending to lost children, sheltering the homeless, assisting with the distribution of relief, subduing the fury of domestic disputes, and maintaining the ambulance service had all been functions performed by the municipal police until after World War I, when policing yielded many social service functions to newly established professions. As late as 1924, the police sheltered and fed some 5,000 people. The Hamilton police long had been appealed to for assistance.[4]

Occurrence Reports and Long-Term Trends

If the reporting of crime by the public appears to be fairly comprehensive, then not only are the resulting records a valuable source, but the acts of reporting are noteworthy in themselves because they temper class-based interpretations about the criminal justice system. The practice of keeping records on the public's reports of incidents began in Hamilton with an 1879 order from the police commission. "All reports of Criminal occurrences made to any member of the Police force must as soon after they are received be reported to the Sergt Major at the police office City Hall to be entered in a book kept for that purpose."[5] The bookkeeping may have lapsed, because the police commission issued another order in 1895: "the Chief should in future cause all reports to be entered in a book kept for that purpose."[6] Thus occurrence books survive for some months in the late 1920s and for various periods through the mid–1940s.

There are grounds for believing that the Hamilton reports of theft must have encompassed a substantial portion of actual crime, despite the problematic nature of reporting noted in criminological studies. One common criticism of occurrence reports as a measure of crime has been the observation that patrolmen and communications officers have filtered out many minor incidents.[7] Yet the Hamilton set contained plenty of seemingly trivial episodes. It also might be argued that victims in certain instances would be too embarrassed by the circumstances of thefts to report them. Some citizens fleeced in compromising situations, however, were candid and their reports enliven the narrative portions of this chapter.

Many of the reporting victims were blue-collar and petty bourgeois residents. Their reporting of crime to the police implies that they accepted the institution as an aid to them regardless of whether the police might have been seen as an instrument of a capitalist elite. Conflict theorists have maintained that the law and its instruments have been created primarily by the ruling classes to serve their interests. Abundant events in the history of criminal justice and policing can be adduced to support conflict theory.[8] Indeed, the Hamilton police force had its roots in social turmoil and labor protest in the 1840s and 1850s.[9] It did pay special notice to the protection of the property of an elite.[10] Nevertheless, recruitment of constables from the working class and the maintenance for decades of social service functions had modified its root character. By the early 1900s, the police force was close to its public.[11]

The willingness of Hamilton residents to report occurrences of both a major and a relatively minor nature translated into the official recording of some 3,900 incidents during twelve months from May 1934 to May 1935.

Table 1
The Criminal Justice Information Sieve: The Case of Hamilton

Record type	Information	How established	Designation
Occurrence books	all reports	telephone; reports to police on beat; complaints to police magistrate	A
Theft occurrence books	thefts extracted from A		B
Occurrences in annual reports	data summary of items in A	counted up from occurrence books	C
Theft occurrences in annual reports	thefts extracted from C	calculated by researcher	D
"Offenses"	thefts drawn from A	police determined	E
Thefts investigated	reported in annual report	police determined	F

This is equivalent to about one incident for every seven or eight households—a level of reporting that provides quite a different impression of crime in the city than one based on statistics generated by the courts. A well-known problem faced by all historical inquiries into crime is that the most accessible sources—the outcomes of court proceedings—represent only an unknown fraction of incidents. Records closest to incidents—initial reports of complaints brought forward to the authorities—rarely have been discovered, although some criminologists undertaking contemporary studies have had access to such reports.[12]

Tables 1–3 provide an abbreviated account of the records maintained by the Hamilton police that dealt with theft. The police kept two sets of occurrence books. In one, all public reports were recorded as they came in. The overwhelming majority were thefts, although assaults, missing persons, and other incidents were written down. Theft occurrences then were extracted and recorded in a separate set. Unhappily, either set of occurrence books for a complete year is too scarce to have made possible any systematic check on the quality of the data labeled as occurrences in annual reports from 1905 to 1946, and again from 1962 to 1970. The occurrences in some books were numbered consecutively for a calendar year so that the survival of entries at the end of a year was sufficient to establish that the reports

Table 2
The Merits, Availability, and Shortcomings of the Records

Record	Merits	Availability	Shortcoming
A	closest to incident and reflects public perception	rare	no time series and data do not equal the data for occurrences in C
B	close to incident	rare	same as above
C	slight remove from A and time series analysis feasible	1905 to 1946 when police report only offenses	not exactly in agreement with A
D	based on B and time series is possible	1905 to 1946	same as for C
E	based on B and time series possible	1922 to present	criteria for selection is not clear; offenses equalled 90-99% of occurrences in annual report
F	none	1905-1950	

Table 3
The Funnel of Theft Cases in Hamilton, 1934–35 and 1942

Stage	Record	Per Cent Cases
Theft detected	A, B, C or D	100
Offenses established	E	95
Investigations	F	20
Convictions	A	5

seem to be fairly accurate. The running totals and the theft occurrences recorded in the annual reports vary only slightly. It is important to stress that this conclusion was based on only four years in the 1930s and 1940s.

Even if we had great confidence in the figures presented in the annual reports, their meaning in a time-series analysis would be clouded, for both they and the occurrence books may capture changes in public attitudes to reporting. For example, data from the annual reports show a steady rise in the occurrences of theft. When controlled for population, there were six to nine reports per 1,000 in the period from 1900 to 1920, nine to fifteen in the 1920s, fifteen to nineteen in the 1930s, and about twenty during the 1940s (Figure 1). Does this mean an increase in theft, a greater tendency of the public to report incidents, or both? How important had reporting become due to the likely growth of property insurance? By 1937, the Hamilton police made appeals through the newspapers to report "anything of a suspicious nature."[13] In sum, the reporting of a theft was a phenomenon subject to many considerations, and several factors made it more likely that citizens would report a theft in the 1930s than in the 1900s.

Of course, there are also data about theft based on court records. Often, such court-generated statistics have been used by historians to fabricate a crime index. In the case of Hamilton, the court records, newspaper coverage of police affairs, and the annual reports of the department permit the reconstruction of a time series on charges laid that extends from the 1850s to the 1970s. That series will not be discussed here in its entirety. Rather we will consider only trends from 1900 to 1950 in order to show one serious problem with claiming that such a series represents an index of crime. While the rate of reporting of occurrences was shown to have risen, the rate of charges laid per 1,000 residents stayed fairly stable at three or four. If anything, it declined slightly (Figure 1). The question of what the two trends depict—the well-known "index question"—has no exact answer, but the contradictory trends in two series of data for the same time and jurisdiction can weaken the integrity of time-series analysis.[14]

There is one question that does not require great trust in either occurrence or court data as indexes of theft. What proportion of reports led to the laying of charges? Conceding that the statistics are problematic, it is still noteworthy that from the 1920s on only around twenty percent of the reports led to charges (Figure 1). The data also show the charges to have been almost constant in terms of the size of the force (Figure 2). That is, to nobody's surprise, theft investigations—and thus charges laid—seem to have been more a function of resources than of reports.

For the years 1900–50, conviction rates in the annual reports were not cited by crime. Consequently, for Hamilton there is no short and simple route to seeing how reports on thefts were pared down to investigations and investigations into convictions. It would be safe to say, however, that no more than five percent of theft occurrences led to convictions.[15] The Hamilton police chiefs had the annoying practice of mixing all manner of offenses in the conviction statistics, including by-law infractions. By this device, the police may have been burying distressing information. In fairness to the police, though, the trifling quality of many thefts and the lack of clues precluded earnest investigation.

A further matter muddies the waters. A very significant proportion of occurrences (Table 4) included an element of doubt as to whether missing articles had been stolen or lost. When an article has been left behind through carelessness and taken by another party, then we might ask whether that

Figure 1
Thefts: Reports and Charges Laid
Hamilton, 1900–50

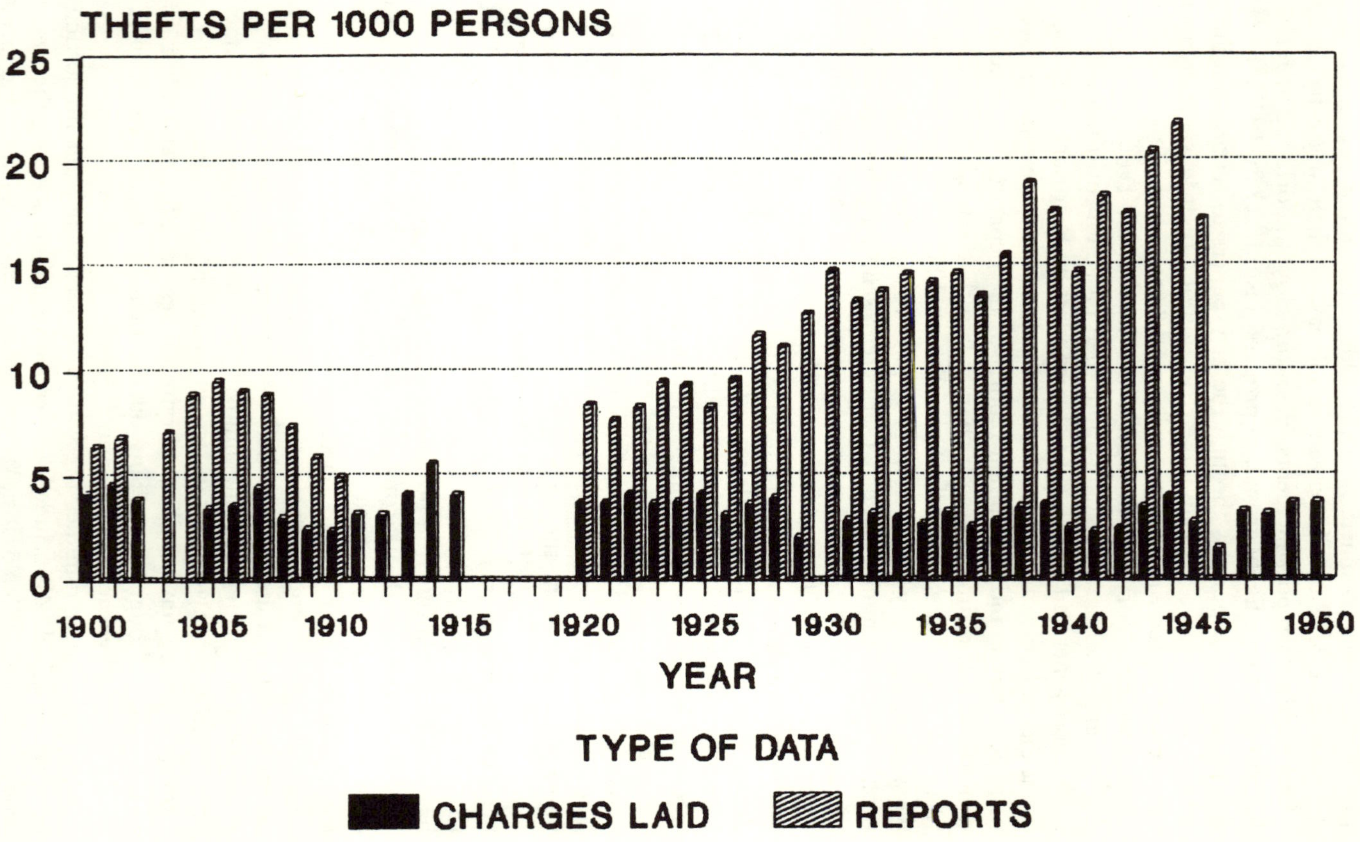

Figure 2
Charges Laid Per Constable
Hamilton, 1900–50

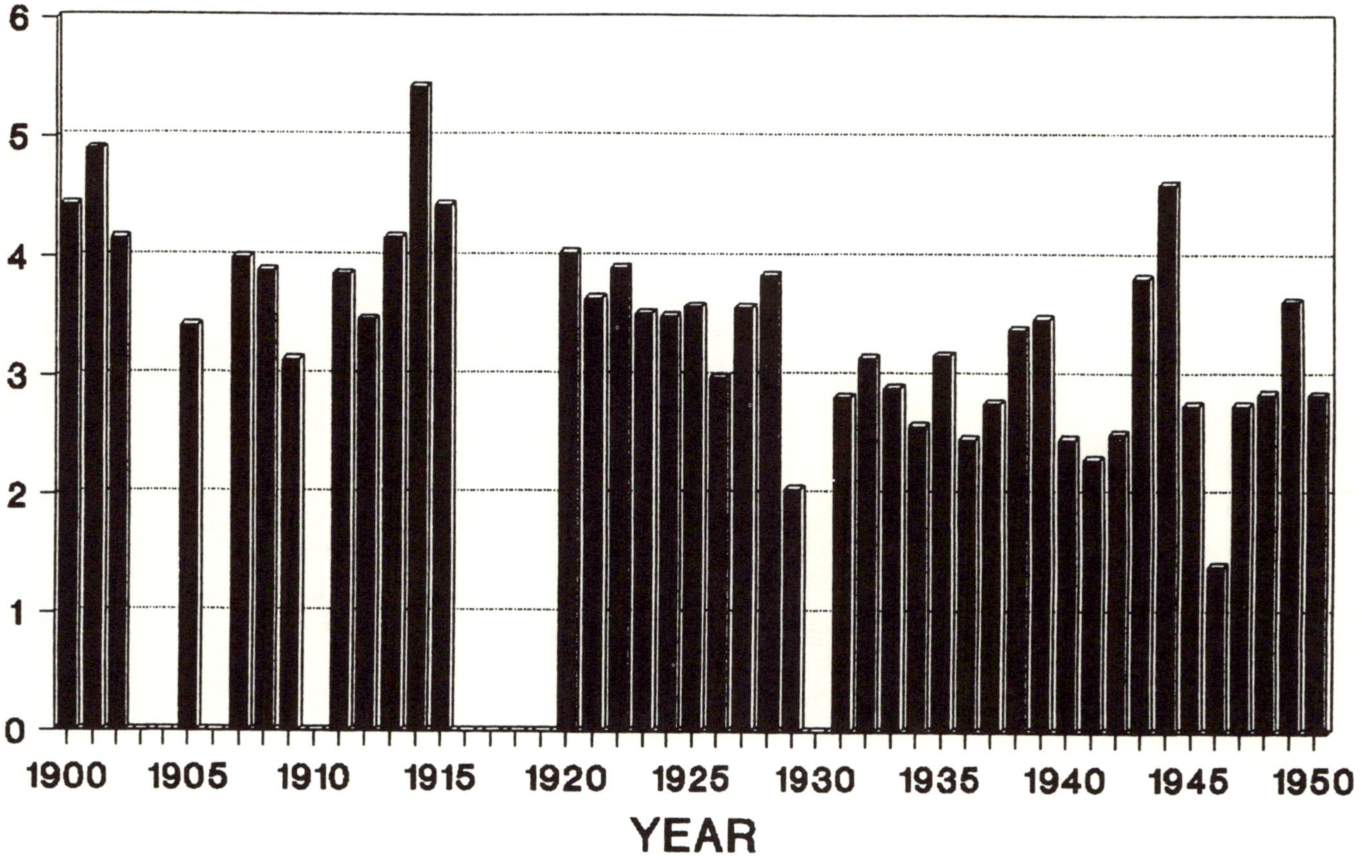

Table 4
Major Groupings of Reported Occurrences

Classification of Occurrence	Percent in 1934-5	Percent in 1942
Stealing small items	45.3%	51.0%
Housebreaking	15.4	8.5
Lost and presumed stolen	12.1	20.7
Burglary	4.1	7.4
Attempted shopbreaking	1.8	-
Attempted housebreaking	1.5	-
Armed robbery*	0.8	0.3
Fifteen other headings	19.0	19.1

*Armed robbery was not a frequent crime, but is presented here for contrast.

theft is of a different order than one where the thief—unassisted by negligence—achieves the transfer of the article. Perhaps the issue can confirm credibility for offense data (Table 1) as a valid basis for an index for crime. This claim reintroduces a methodological problem or even a philosophical issue that will recur several times in this chapter. If what the public considered a theft is of consequence, then the police-generated records about offense, and the court-generated ones about prosecutions, are a tainted source and must be dealt with cautiously, leaving the historian unsatisfied and wrestling with ways of expressing probability. The following account should also leave a basis for questioning whether or not many of the incidents reported to the police in Hamilton warrent the designation of "crime." Occurrence records, which a priori could have been thought to clarify levels of *real* crime, surely complicate rather than resolve formidable grey areas of criminal justice history.

Patterns of Theft and Changing Social Conditions

Every data set has limitations, for questions posed by researchers inevitably reach beyond the parameters imposed by sources. The most annoying limitation of the Hamilton occurrence books is their restricted time span; no time-series analysis is possible using them alone, and yet such analysis is the bread and butter of historical work with criminal justice data. Nevertheless, other things can be accomplished. By adding several variables to those in the occurrence books, it has been possible to delve into the social contexts of theft in two different eras and, indeed, into the grey areas of how to define theft. Moreover, minor but revealing differences in the patterns of theft and in the tone of the reports underline the shortcomings of summary data ordinarily used in criminal justice history. Fortunately for this chapter, the chief constable in 1931 had insisted on an improvement in the quality of the reports on which the occurrence books were based. Among other things, he insisted on theft reports specifying the item taken.[16]

To make the inquiry manageable, every tenth case of theft was drawn to compile a sample, and notes were kept on the more richly detailed typical and atypical cases. The sample made it feasible to use city directories to establish the occupations of the victims, and to assign the address of the crime to one of twenty-nine planning districts of about thirty square blocks each. Entered by longhand into notebooks, the occurrence reports did not adhere to a form. From the content of the reports, it is certain that the vast majority of reports came from victims.[17] The fairly terse accounts included the occasional aside. Virtually all contained the following information: the name of the victim, the address of the complainant, the article stolen, a description of the place from whence the article had been taken, the value of the article, whether the suspect could be indentified or described, and a marginal notation—often in red—about the recovery of the missing article and arrests. The coding process required interpretation of some entries that were understandably vague about whether articles were missing or really stolen.

Studies of other cities during the depression have reached no agreement about the impact of economic collapse on crime rates.[18] Problematic though they are, annual-report data on theft occurrences in Hamilton seem to confirm that the onset of the depression could have been accompanied by a rise in thefts. The pattern is weak, however, as demonstrated in Figure 1, and qualitative evidence contradictory. In the 1932 report, the chief claimed that despite "the exceptional crisis through which we have been passing... there has been no serious increase in crime."[19] In the 1934 and 1936 reports, he commented on unusually large numbers of breaking and entering incidents. And in 1936, he went so far as to claim it was an "epidemic... all over the country."[20] But a similar assertion was made in 1944.[21] In sum, neither the data—somewhat suspect in any case—nor the qualitative evidence make a firm case for theft rising during the depression. What is more, a notable rise in occurrences truly came with the return of prosperity and the booming wartime economy.[22] With this interesting reversal of an assumption of an association between depression and theft in mind, we can turn to a detailed study of 1934–35 and 1942.

By looking at potential motives and opportunities for theft in two periods, no compelling argument can be found for the notion that a theft rate would increase in a period of economic distress, because opportunity is a significant variable and scarcity is a slippery concept. It is possible to see the merit of these caveats from data originating in the occurrence books. The unique

Table 5
Value of Items Reported Stolen

Value	1934-5	1942
$		
0	45.0%	38.4%
1-5	23.9	12.6
6-10	9.2	10.4
11-100	19.1	37.2
101-1499	1.8	1.2
1500 plus	1.0	0.2
mean	$43.	$60.
mean omitting 1500 plus	$14.	$14.

conditions of a depression and a wartime prosperity produced subtle differences in thefts as opportunity and scarcity shifted. Similarities derived from the data, however, stand out initially and significantly. Motives and opportunities—in so far as we can tell—remained fairly consistent throughout the mass of thefts in the two periods. Given certain prevailing traits in the data for the two eras, it seems difficult to accept that crude rates of reported theft—consisting largely of minor items taken on impulse—could be tied to depression conditions. But changing socio-economic conditions could affect marginally a list of items taken and the context—the place and related events—of these thefts. Annual rates alone, therefore, are not the ideal way to study relations between crime and socioeconomic conditions.

Both the consistency and the variability in what was taken provide insight into human frailty across changing social circumstances. Similarity will be considered first. The pettiness of most thefts is striking (Table 5). Once the handful of major holdups are removed from the samples (for they were large enough to skew the mean), the mean value of stolen articles is $14 for both 1934–35 and 1942. With almost a quarter of all reported thefts in the 1934–35 sample valued from $1 to $5 and another forty-five percent having a value of less than 50 cents or no reported value at all (both coded as 0, for values were coded to the nearest dollar), the minor incident involving children that introduced this chapter seems closer to the norm than the armed robbery. Small losses—small at least to the distant observer—filled page after page in both periods, and can help to explain why some reports were not treated as offenses and why few complaints led to police investigations. In the case of many thefts, impulse and opportunity fashioned the deed and the articles taken were commonplace, trivial perhaps to all but the victims.

The circumstances of most thefts imply the youth and inexperience of those committing the acts. Sophistication was rare, opportunity critical. Unlocked cars beckoned to be entered, and the police chief chided careless auto operators in 1936 for encouraging "persons criminally inclined to commit crime."[23] Open windows in the summer were a temptation, as were farmers' trucks parked on side streets on market day.[24] Particulars were unique and with the seasons came slight variations, but many thefts had common traits. What happened to Andrew Comfort[25] was both singular and commonplace. Andrew did not use an ice box in the winter, but put food in a box on the back step. On the night of 15 December 1934, he lost a roast of pork and a glass pie plate. He suspected children who lived in the neighborhood.[26] His casualness had allowed an impulsive act.

The combination of opportunity, youth, and a low level of planning or skill may be an enduring trait of the bulk of urban theft.[27] In their study of residential burglary in Toronto in the early 1970s, Irvin Waller and Norman Okihiro found that about forty percent of entries were through unlocked doors.[28] Even in the depression, many people displayed trust and left low-value articles exposed to young, sticky fingers. Those with more to lose, as we shall witness, may have practiced greater vigilance.

In some cases it seems probable that thefts were the result of more deliberation, even though the takings were slight. Some small thefts even hint at a *modus operandi*—an intentional and premeditated carrying out of many similar actions to yield a significant total of small sums. Purse snatchers who lurked behind their victims in cinemas, and the person or persons unknown who took purses from the autos of widows visiting grave sites, may have had slim pickings on each occasion but a healthy sum over a few weeks.[29] The party who broke into eight gasoline stations across the city in two nights in May 1942 by breaking glass in the front door got small sums in several and none in others, but for two nights' effort garnered about a week's pay.[30] There certainly were calculating criminals. Their presence leaps out from occurrence book pages when a chain of like offenses happened during the same night. The four houses on Cedar Avenue entered the same way on 18 July 1942 comprised a truly exceptional act, but there were other less dramatic examples of deliberate crimes.[31] Sometimes an arrest led to a confession of a string of concentrated break-ins. Some of the sharp rise in these incidents in 1934 as reported by the chief had been committed by Steve Chesick, who was charged with fourteen counts of housebreaking and two of auto theft.[32]

In addition to the "professional" criminals who picked pockets or broke into houses, there were a few short-change artists and safecrackers who turned up in the reports. Beginning in the 1930s, the latter appear to have been driven off the main streets and into smaller out-of-the-way establishments. Larger industries had guards, and downtown stores had begun to place their safes near front doors where they could be seen by police and passers-by. There were risks to breaking into shops near where retailers lived. With what the chief of detectives described as "an effective display of butcher knives and choppers," the Lapcewich brothers—corner grocers residing above their store—sent two would-be thieves to the hospital in November 1935. The brothers had been shot during the confrontation.[33] And there were other reports of citizen pursuit. Out-of-the-way places—coal yards, auto wreckers, lumber yards, and warehouses—proved less nettlesome.[34] In terms of the overall makeup of thefts in the sample years, there is no satisfactory way of determining which thefts were planned (Tables 4–6). Having read most of the reports, it seems that the majority of burglaries were unplotted and directed against residences.[35]

An Assortment of Motives

In addition to the complexity and elusiveness of fixing the level of spontaneity involved in crimes, there is the related matter of motives. Despite the self-evident challenge of dealing with these topics, the reports help us see an improvised side to theft. Irrational "motives" stood behind many thefts. They were not all driven by necessity, alone or even primarily. Risk taking, envy, impulsive gratification, and vengeance accounted for some thefts. The owner of a gas station broken into on the night of 23 December 1935 believed it was "spite work."[36] Doubtless the theft of hundreds of bicycles a year (perhaps as many as 500 in 1934–35 and 900 in 1942) included some coveted for parts and resale, but how many were stolen irrationally when an opportunity arose for a thrill or to inflict discomfort?

If we count bicycles and other small articles found around schools and playgrounds, irrational and impulsive conduct of children could have accounted for far more property crime than the perceived needs of adults. The prevalence of bicycle thefts prompted the introduction of licensing in 1945.[37] Beyond the list of selected articles in Table 6, the complete data string out modest items appearing two or three times in the sample: apples, bread, candy, radiator caps, hubcaps, skates, sleighs, and suitcases. The very small value of stolen articles is a reminder that the majority of thieves, if they really had planned to offset economic distress, likely came up disappointed. Both disappointment and stupidity are not to be dismissed, and they are compatible with the proposition that what many thieves had done was quite irrational and truly "juvenile." The prominence of money and purses among the stolen articles in both periods reinforces the assumption that most thieves acted apart from any crime ring or without any elaborate scheming. Cash has the obvious quality of being immediately negotiable. It did not require the service of a "fence" or other buyer.[38]

Not all small thefts were done for a thrill or on impulse. Perceived need,

Table 6
Leading Articles Reported as Stolen

	1934-5		1942	
Item	n	%	n	%
Items common to both eras				
Bicycles	52	12.6	95	21.5
Money	36	9.3	33	7.6
Purses	35	9.0	29	6.7
Depression items				
License plate	16	4.1	3	0.7
Jewelry	15	3.9	3	0.7
Coats	11	2.8	6	1.4
Milk	8	2.1	1	0.2
Clothing	5	1.3	-	-
Lingerie	5	1.3	-	-
Cigarettes	4	1.0	-	-
Shoes	3	0.8	-	-
Plumbing	1	0.3	-	-
Wartime items				
Tires	8	2.1	25	5.7
Gas ration bks	-	-	11	2.5
Gasoline	2	0.5	5	1.1
Billfold	1	0.3	51	11.7
Keys	5	1.3	11	2.5

even protest, and the host of motives arising from social frustration can be read into a few differences between the articles stolen in the depression and the war years. A graph of occurrences or offenses per 1,000 or 100,000 residents—the routine measures of criminal justice history—could fluctuate but remain silent about precisely what was taken. This silence has forced conjecture about motives and opportunity. Short of interviewing thieves, conjecture will remain in historical analysis, but here with information about stolen articles we draw closer to the nexus of crime and socioeconomic conditions. Thefts are not only points on a graph, but victims, places, and items. Articles of clothing and food were more prominent among the missing articles in 1934–35. So too were cigarettes, a low-cost pleasure item. There were more break-ins, jewelry stolen, and armed robberies (Tables 4 and 6). The latter came complete with the not-too-original order "stick 'em up"![39] The depression may not have affected the volume of crimes against property in Hamilton; rather, its impact may have been expressed on the margins of what was being taken and how.

The occurrence data—as helpful as they are in dealing with item and context—are not free from problems. It is true that people apparently reported a great deal of small crime. Yet the sunny-weather theft of milk—a plausible indicator of distress visible in the depression data—illustrates that the data are flawed. Thus, in addition to data, remarks recorded in the occurrence reports provide crucial evidence on the contrast between depression and wartime. Dairies sometimes received complaints, for some customers assumed negligence by a deliveryman or waited until a second or third incident before calling a police station. A driver for City Dairies reported on 4 July 1934 that milk was being stolen "routinely every morning in the vicinity of Roxborough, Frederick, Robins, Wexford, etc." This was a working-class area and the driver suspected juveniles. Family need is probable, for it is hard to imagine that youths pilfered milk for thrills at 6:00 A.M.[40] A few days earlier, Pete Domitro finally became annoyed enough to report having had "milk stolen off rear steps for about two weeks."[41] Edgar Smith complained on 6 December 1935 that milk had been stolen from him "almost every morning."[42] A similar delayed report had come in on 16 April 1935 from a driver for Hills Bakery; he complained about "rolls" being "stolen almost every morning from the Brass Rail Restaurant" where he left them on the doorstep.[43] When reporting the theft of two baskets of apples on 9 April 1935, grocer Art Black mentioned losses during the preceding weeks.[44] In the depression, the theft of small food items spoke of need and opportunity; the aggregate data on investigations and convictions could never have disclosed this, and even the coding of occurrences obscured the full dimensions of the phenomenon.

It is in the seemingly petty details of thefts or in the chief constable's daily orders to the men or in his annual reports that depression circumstances are revealed. For example, there were thefts of backyard poultry and reports about these were not postponed. What is particularly interesting about them is the fact that the complaints came from the central city during the depression. Chicken coops seem to have been pervasive even in the urban core in 1930s. The stripping of clothes lines also brought immediate reports.[45] Just after dark on 23 March 1935, Mrs. R. Potter saw a man "who looked like a foreigner" enter her backyard and attempt to steal clothes from her line. "He succeeded in getting a bath towell [*sic*]."[46] Another type of theft was notable during the depression when, in Hamilton, a number of houses were left vacant by tenants or defaulting buyers. Their plumbing drew thieves who sold to scrap dealers.[47] But the most telling piece of evidence about hardship in this industrial city was the chief's order of 11 July 1935: "Men on the beats and also those in the Patrol Cars are to pay particular attention to garbage pickers etc. who are around the city at nights. No doubt some of these men are stealing, frequently garden hose, childrens' tricycles, etc."[48]

Finally, the depression precipitated suspicions that would make their way into occurrence reports but never could have surfaced in criminal justice proceedings. Tramps and beggars asked for little as they went from house to house requesting work or a meal. But a few aroused fear. "A tough looking fellow" came to the home of the manager of the Eaton's department store and asked the price of a bed. The wife offered to call the Salvation Army. The man rejected this and went away, stopping to talk to a couple in a car before proceeding to knock on other doors. He may have been trying to "cadge" silver from the couple, but the manager interpreted the episode as evidence of a burglary gang.[49] Fragments of hardship can be gleaned from the depression era reports and they, perhaps more than any highly distilled criminal justice data, document the relationships of theft—and fear of theft—to an economic collapse.

A comparison of wartime and depression data underscores the importance of opportunity and changing elements of scarcity. The war created new forms of scarcity and a distinct set of valuable items that turned up often among public reports of theft: gasoline ration books, gasoline, and auto tires.[50] In the 1930s, an open car tempted the theft of a car blanket or possibly a radio, but in 1942 the object of attention was the ration book. It would be very difficult to prove that "professional" criminals were involved in these wartime thefts; however, rationing was a situation tailor-made for professional crime. When thieves broke into the Imperial Service Station on 28 August, they reaped a bonanza of 1,212 ration coupons.[51] Thieves siphoned off gasoline from trucks at cartage company yards.[52] Deliberate and well-engineered were some tire thefts. Imagine the shock to William Weir when he went out to start his 1937 Pontiac on the morning of 20 November 1942. Overnight, parties unknown had jacked up his car, stolen all four tires, tubes, and wheels; thieves then had lowered the Pontiac onto bricks.[53] The problem of tire thefts, one of national proportions, forced a federal order in council banning the sale of used tires that had illegible serial numbers.[54]

The Scene of the Crime

The data from the coded occurrences highlight the change and the continuity in articles stolen. Before demonstrating that there is much more social history to be garnered from unquantifiable asides in the reports themselves, it is worthwhile scanning the data for what had not changed. In the two periods, the playground and the house remained the principal settings for stealing. Indeed, continuity went deeper. In both periods, the five leading places remained the same, with only a minor switch in ranking (Table 7). The five major articles included some slight changes, but they all remained similar in the sense of being portable and commonplace (Table 6). If any practical lesson can be derived from the data, it would be the timeless one that prevention was the only sensible way of minimizing loss of small articles. The police recovery rate was, as we will elaborate, low. What the locations and the articles suggest—and this seems supported by the presence of many wives as complainants—is that a great deal of reported theft occurred be-

Table 7
Most Frequently Cited Places for Occurrences

	1934-5		1942	
Place	**n**	**%**	**n**	**%**
Common locales				
Playground	97	24.9	122	28.0
Auto	31	8.0	23	5.3
Yard	28	7.2	30	6.9
Garage	15	3.9	17	3.9
Porch	10	2.6	7	1.6
School	9	2.3	9	2.1
Depression locales				
House	60	15.4	38	8.7
Apartment	10	2.6	4	0.9
Vacant house	3	0.8	-	-
Clothesline	3	0.8	2	0.5
Bank	2	0.5	-	-
Railyard	2	0.5	-	-
Wartime locales				
Movie Theatre	3	0.8	9	2.1
Restaurant	2	0.5	9	2.1
Hotel	-	-	7	1.6
Steel Co. works	4	1.0	12	2.8
Nat'nal St'l Car	-	-	7	1.6
Westinghouse	-	-	7	1.6
Dominion F'ndry	-	-	5	1.1
Greening Wire	-	-	4	0.9
Inter. Harvester	1	0.3	3	0.7
Park	1	0.3	7	1.6
Factory yd	2	0.5	5	1.1
Rented room	-	-	6	1.4
Constr'tion site	-	-	2	0.5
Labour barrack	-	-	2	0.5

cause of front doors left unlocked when householders were in yards, out shopping, or away from vestibules where coats and purses lay vulnerable.

Losses from residences in 1942 were low relative to 1934–35, and the reason may have been that more people went out more often. Just below the high-risk locations so common to both eras, a few others turned up with greater frequency in 1942. Restaurants, movie theaters, and hotels surfaced more routinely because Hamiltonians had the money and the leisure for commercial socializing. The morality squad stepped up its activities, "visiting restaurants, dance halls, etc."—not to deal with theft but "averting tragedy to Hamilton homes."[55] Moral strictures, it seems certain, had been relaxed and young people with money stepped out. When they did they also carried tempting billfolds and purses which, from the tenor of reports, a number handled as carelessly as they allegedly managed their chastity. One might have assumed that the depression year would have contained more incidents of stolen money, especially if hypotheses of rational theft and of depression privation as a trigger to some thefts were being proposed. The hitch with these propositions is that even if some of those with a desperate need thought of stealing cash, it was not found often dangling temptingly close at hand.

But in the setting of a heavy-industry city in the midst of full employment, boddle lay about, and young men who had earned some of it put themselves in jeopardy during quests for "a good time." The number of reports of "missing" billfolds in 1942 is astonishing (Table 6). Hamilton had recovered its vigorous night life, attracting factory workers, soldiers, and "lonesome" travelers in town on business. On the night of 25 January 1942, Domenic Kovacs had been drinking heavily at the Grand Hotel. Two new bar chums asked him for a ride. Once in the parking lot, the pair stole his money and a watch.[56] His story was oft repeated with slight variations. On the night of 14 April, Mike Costain linked up with three strangers while drinking at the Grand Hotel—the same place where Kovacs had come to grief. The quartet left together for "a place where they met some women." Later the men robbed him.[57] The mix of women and substantial quantities of alcohol contrasts with depression privation. Harry Baker from St. Catharines settled into the King George Hotel on 30 May 1942 with Evelyn—a woman who "came to his room." Harry procured two bottles of whiskey and—not surprisingly—became intoxicated. Evelyn did not. Harry lost a wallet and a watch.[58] Earlier that year, at the upscale Connaught Hotel, Philip Pidgeon of Montreal invited a woman to his room where he had laid in a bottle of wine and a dozen bottles of beer. In the morning, the bottles were empty, the woman was gone, and so were a watch and lighter.[59]

Of course it was not only men who found that risks accompanied prosperity, independence, and fleeting pleasures. An unidentified married woman brought home an airman for a week and he left with some of her jewelry.[60] Mrs. Amelia Williams, whose husband was overseas, hosted a party on the night of 1 March 1942. One of the guests left with $70 from her purse.[61] Young ladies fell victim to a purse-snatching scam at Westminster Hall, often the site of war-time dances. In early October, a group of four girls turned over their purses to "some chap who told them to check their purses." Exactly one month later, at the same hall, Gertrude Nelson had her purse stolen from the checkroom.[62] Roland's Restaurant, the site for many dances, was another risky spot, as Ellen Donegale found out at an air force dance on 11 April when money and rings were taken from her purse. A few weeks earlier, two people had reported having had their pockets picked there.[63]

In the 1942 sample, the reported thefts of money, billfolds, and purses amounted to 113; in other words, there easily could have been 1,100 such incidents or about three a day. In contrast, in the depression sample over seventy cases had appeared, or around 700 for the year and less than two a day. The forty percent difference far exceeded the city's population growth.

Domenic Kovaks and others like him, flush as never before, found themselves in the company of strangers drawn to employment opportunities. Interesting as an aside about the contrast between depression and wartime society, the contents of wallets and purses were somewhat different. Victims in the latter era not only reported money as a missing valuable, but also their national service registration cards, medical discharge cards, and their work passes to war industries. What was at once both a fairly affluent and freewheeling society was also a regulated one. What remarkable and swift transformations had overtaken this community!

Similar to prior explosive growth periods in the city's history, the war brought into combination unattached young men, people from outside the city, ample drink, and money. The occurrence reports of the depression commented on suspicious people, but they seldom went further in their descriptions because the city's national or ethnic homogeneity was not upset in the depression by newcomers. On the contrary, Hamilton lost people through migration. In 1942, strangers meant "foreigners" and—indicative of the country's "two solitudes"—the French Canadian industrial workers who flocked to Hamilton. Ethnic stereotyping in the reports now became pronounced. A shop-breaker who had highly polished black shoes, nice clothes, a pasty complexion, and black hair combed straight back "looked like an Italian."[64] How well a suspect spoke English or whether he spoke with a French Canadian accent was noted, for the city had become polyglot.[65]

The sudden fusion of strangers may have been remarkably tame and peaceful. Laboring brothers possibly associated freely and generously; they certainly did at taverns. However, the occurrence reports—an admittedly biased source for commenting on brotherhood—imply that the anonymity of strangers encouraged criminal acts. The happy hangouts where strangers bent elbows were high-risk places. Besides the night spots, the very accommodations provided for war-time workers proved insecure. Fred Maychark returned to his rooming house late one Saturday night to find his trunk forced open and a loss of $70 and three new shirts.[66] The Army Trades School staff house was the scene of many thefts; so was Bud Fischer's Hotel, which housed factory workers.[67] Rooming houses were risky locales (Table 7), and workplaces were not immune. Stephen Golitza, for example, had his locker broken into at the steel company and there were other cases here and at Dominion Foundries.[68]

Something else distinguishes the wartime pattern of opportunity—always a very important factor in theft—from that of the depression. In 1934–35, corporations, though often enough stolen from, were not remarkably prominent. But they figured quite prominently in 1942, when almost one in five thefts was reported as taking place at a major establishment (Table 7). Patriotic zeal, it seems, did not have a universal and constant grip on the minds of war-industry workers, as tools, tool boxes, building materials, scrap metal, and gasoline were reported missing. It might have been thought that industries would have been major targets of theft in the depression. Once again, however, the crucial factor was opportunity. War industries generated more possibilities than the depressed factories of the 1930s. During the depression, meat packers, furriers, trucking companies, wholesalers, and railway express offices were tempting targets, except that managers put in special requests to the police for protection at vulnerable times and places.[69] The frantic pace of the wartime city—the comings and goings from plants—precluded diligent scrutiny. In wartime England, according to Edward Smithies' study, the situation was much the same: In the dockyards and factories, virtually everything moveable was in danger of being stolen.[70]

The Victims of Theft

Social scientists since the 1940s often have reported on the existence of comparatively high crime regions within cities, and also on the congruence between these locations and poor housing and poverty. Plausible explanations abound: better preventive steps in wealthier areas, a weaker attachment to property in poor areas, a portion of the city's population with no future reward within existing social relations, less privacy and security in poor housing stock, and disrupted and disorderly lives. The ecological approach, of course, may call attention to high-risk areas, but it does not explain why certain individuals in such areas become criminals.

The ecological observations apply to Hamilton where in 1934–35, forty-nine percent of the reported incidents took place in five central districts (Table 8). All five contained a disproportionate share of the city's tenements and run-down shelter. By contrast, the middle-class suburbs in the west end, represented by four planning areas, accounted for a scant two percent of reports. The contrast in reports by type of neighborhood is important on many counts. It is worth stressing again that citizens, not the police, are the originators of most of these reports. Citizens in poorer parts of the city actively reported losses to the police; they trusted the police and saw them as potentially helpful. What is tragic about the thefts reported from poor areas is that the poor could have comprised a disproportionately large share of the victims of theft in the depression. This assumption, however, commits the ecological fallacy. Location is no proof of social attributes. Thus coding occupations proved a valuable though imperfect route to proving the victimization of the poor. Moreover, the real value to the spatial analysis is that it once again raises the theme of opportunity. The five central districts contained a substantial set of the city's retail streets, hotels, parking areas, and schools.

The proposition that the poor were victimized—that theft was not a Robin Hood endeavor during the depression—gets additional support from a consideration of complainants' situations. Such information was not easily se-

Table 8
Occurrences Reported by City Planning Districts Grouped by Generalized Social Attributes

		1934-5	1942	
Attributes	**N of Districts**	**% of Reports**	**N**	**%**
High percent tenants, tenaments, and deteriorating houses	5	49	8	45
Predominantly working class	6-9	15-20	6-9	15-20
Middle class and working class mix	8-11	13-18	10-13	12-17
Predominantly middle class	4	2	4	3

cured. Terse police reports almost never said anything about the state of the victim's circumstances. The single exception was Mrs. Waincott, who lived in a fairly poor area of the city; she reported that her milk had been stolen the previous two mornings, and volunteered the information that "she is on City Relief."[71] To get some insight into the circumstances of the victims, city directory information was coded (Table 9).

Consider first the set of cases with missing information. Roughly fifteen percent of the people who reported a theft to the police in 1934–35 could not be found in the appropriate city directories, although they had given the police a city address. Perhaps they had moved or lived as boarders or relatives in households where they had not been listed separately. While not firm evidence for impoverished circumstances, the want of a directory listing during the depression is suggestive of a lack of security and independence. Another four percent who were listed cited no occupation in the city directory. It is difficult to say what this meant (retirement, unemployment, or wish for privacy?) Similarly, it is not clear what interpretation to place on finding the surname at the address but not the complainant's name (a child or an adult relative?). And, finally, what can we make of those who gave no address to the police? They constituted a much larger group in 1934–35 than in 1942. Can we assume that many were without a fixed address? In spite of many unanswerable questions, it is not rash to propose that most reporting victims led a precarious existence in hard times.

Table 9
City Director Label for Complainant

	1934-5		1942	
Label	**n**	**%**	**n**	**%**
Out of town	17	4.4	22	5.1
No occupation listed	15	3.9	14	3.2
Not found in directory	58	14.9	76	17.5
Family name at address	10	2.6	44	10.1
No address in report	41	10.5	18	4.2
Corporations	47	12.1	98	22.5
White collar	40	10.3	26	6.0
Shop keepers	26	6.7	24	5.5
Skilled and semi-skilled	40	10.3	41	9.4
Unskilled labour	33	8.5	24	5.5
Others (soldiers)	0	0.0	5	1.1
Widows	11	2.8	6	1.4
Wives	33	8.5	30	6.9
Teachers	11	2.8	5	1.1
Students	7	1.8	2	2.5

Thus, from the foregoing speculations, about twenty percent of the victims may be designated poor by virtue of missing information; and to this we can add half of the shop-keepers (full labels reveal them to be very petty operators: barbers, confectionists, news agents, tobacconists, grocers), half the skilled and semi-skilled laborers, half the widows, and all of the laborers. By such a fair estimate, around forty percent of the victims were poor by definition of occupation, without taking into account that many skilled laborers in the building trades and industry were hard hit by the depression. If we were to ask the question of who the probable well-to-do individual victims were, then it is likely that the tally would constitute only around fifteen percent of the complainants—and that is a high estimate because white-collar occupations included clerks and stenographers. It seems safe to say that half the reported thefts in the depression were committed against fairly poor folk. The fact that so many *reported* losses transpired around houses and apartments during the 1930s, rather than in places of recreation and work, suggests too that crime in the lean years struck hard at those least able to sustain the losses.

There are three other clusters of victims. One of the most numerous set of complainants (8.5 percent) consisted of wives—the householders who noted missing articles or were at home when someone was seen dashing off a porch. Teachers and students produced a school cluster of around five percent. Next came the out-of-town victims (4.4 percent). Does their surprising presence stem from a vulnerability common to all travelers? Hotel rooms and restaurants are not as secure as a house and, as Cecil Fleming discovered, not every house is a home. Cecil drove in from RR#2 Hamilton on the evening of 2 September 1934, looking for a good time. Around 11:00 P.M. he picked up a woman and went to a nearby house where they spent the night. He left at 7:00 A.M. and soon discovered that he was missing $120. He did not press charges.[72] Hotels figured prominently not only as places in which thefts occurred, but also around which crimes developed. Toronto salesman Melville Potash stopped for the night of 5 December 1935 at the Commercial Hotel. Sometime between 9:00 and 11:00, five dresses were stolen from his car.[73] It does not seem improbable that serious thieves watched hotels and nearby parking spots, and that the carelessness of victims created opportunities for impulse thieves. These are propositions supported too by contemporary research.[74]

Overall, the list of parties reporting crimes is heterogeneous, containing a good number of householders, petty bourgeois proprietors, and working men. Additionally, there is the substantial number of reports of relatively small values. The fact that perhaps 1,450 people called the police to complain about the loss of items with no reported value or with values less than $5 says something about their circumstances and their trust in the police. Given the paltry pickings, it is probable that the relatively poor were notably victimized—and probably by the other individuals who also were fairly poor.

Regrettably, the occurrence books say nothing about the suspects that would permit a description of their social status. The term "juvenile" does turn up from time to time. In any case, the reported incidents rarely provided clues on identity to the police (Table 7). Victims could supply a suspect, a description, or evidence in anywhere from twelve to twenty percent of the cases. That is, the police had the foundation for an investigation in just about the same number of cases as they reported investigating in their annual reports.

In about twenty percent of the reported cases it seemed that the case had been complicated by the likelihood of the article having been lost or missing prior to being "stolen." The trail here had to have been weak. In over sixty percent of the cases, the party reporting provided no description or other help for the police.[75]

One lesson to be learned from anthropologists and historians working in the centuries before the modern era is that insights about the commonplace must be extracted from whatever slender and even indirect sources survive. Casually mentioned contexts for medieval or early modern crime and death have provided glimpses into work, family, and play, although the occasions for the asides often were tragic. To a degree, occurrence books can perform a similar function.

Children rode everywhere on their bicycles, dropping them at the edge of playgrounds, forgetting coats at school, and occasionally having both items taken by others. Housewives went about routine chores with doors unlocked. Unless made to reconsider by the startling appearance of tramps or thieves, few doubted they lived in a safe world. We can imagine widows walking from their cars to a graveside and people in the midst of new-found wartime prosperity going out to a restaurant and a movie. There was much trust in this urban society as well as neighborhood convenience. Corner grocery stores and home delivery were prevalent. Early morning summer sounds, now lost, can be heard again: the urban roosters crowing and the clink of milk bottles. We can visualize farmers' produce trucks crowding streets around the century-old market square. Something of the texture of urban life can be rediscovered in laconic reports by police constables who, more than anyone else, dealt with urban society.

As fascinating as authentic vignettes of life might be, as lively as they are when set alongside data, they cannot furnish a methodical account of city life; the glimpses can be only that. Perhaps modern history, with abundant material, is not compelled to burden every happening with significance. If so, and I doubt it, the principal contributions of this chapter to historical enquiry would likely be methodological ones set squarely, if mischievously, in the midst of criminal justice literature.

Accounts of crime and criminal justice from the past often have been confined out of necessity to working with prosecution and conviction data; that is, they have been forced to manipulate data from truncated sources. Therefore, the first conclusion is an obvious one. Having now had a peek into the type of records that come far closer to a full account of incidents, the notorious deficiencies of court and jail records as gauges of crime over time are reconfirmed. Second, the status of occurrence data in annual reports, and of the original occurrences from which they are derived, depends on what guess we are willing to venture about the consistency of incident reporting over time. For the 1930s and 1940s, there appear to have been high levels of public reporting. But had it been so in the 1920s or the 1900s? Time-series analysis must be treated warily due to the likelihood of differences in public reactions. Third, as the occurrence books themselves disclosed, the changing attributes of opportunity and scarcity are neither simple nor to be extracted readily from aggregate data. Depression and war created circumstances that could not have been prepared out of a priori consideration. Correlations of occurrences with economic indicators, therefore, cannot adequately supply connections between crime and *Zeitgeist*. Finally, details about the minor articles taken or missing ought to rattle any trust in the capacity of crude summary occurrence data cited in the annual reports

Table 10
Data Indicating Potential for a Police Investigation

	1934-5	1942
Suspect identified	1.5%	4.1%
Suspect described	14.4	8.5
Police have evidence	2.1	1.1
Item could be lost	19.0	23.9
No description or evidence	63.0	62.4

to provide material for a crime index. Indeed, the original reports force us to ask what is theft. Answers to that question trail off into a conundrum.

It is commonplace in studies of the history of crime and criminal justice to emphasize that moral order matters are the ones that demonstrate that an uncertain number of offenses are generated by policy and police responses to it. To a degree the same pertained for theft where there had to be latitude for police discretion—especially given the number of reports. Some cases were surely disposed of as borderline crimes. The catechism of the Church of England's Book of Common Prayer lists duties to neighbors. My duty to my neighbor, it instructs at one point, is "to keep my hands from picking and stealing." The division into two deeds has merit. Picking, detaching and removing with the fingers, describes much of what the citizens of Hamilton reported: Articles were set down, possibly neglected, and picked by unseen others. Stealing has a deliberate and serious ring. That the police should exercise discretion and not investigate many episodes of picking is understandable.

But what were the police to do about reports of these very petty losses that indicated a public trust in them? For some Hamilton mothers in the great depression, a child's loss of a quarter was a meaningful incident. It is improbable that the misery depicted in Vittorio de Sica's *Bicycle Thief* was equaled in any of the hundreds of Hamilton households that had bicycles picked or stolen in 1934–35 or in 1942, but can we afford to be dismissive when the victims were not? And is it correct to assume that adults did not ride bicycles to work in urban Canada? Alex Dzwolkic, who worked at Dominion Glass Works, and Sgt. MacGuinn, the caretaker of the Armouries, certainly would have disputed the point as victims in 1942.[76] We can assume little. We are left wondering if police officers who determined what was a "real" crime or what deserved investigation were perplexed too. Did they agonize over their ineffectual standing as crime solvers? Did they find it distressing or curious that they could do so little while the public expected so much?

The leads and puzzles presented by the occurrence books in Hamilton may stimulate a search for comparable records in other centers. When more are found and used we may get answers to criminal-justice history questions. But we will also have a number of precious documented glimpses into common lives. The latter may not be typical, but they will be compelling and human. And that perhaps is typical enough.

Notes

The research for this chapter was supported by the Social Sciences and Humanities Research Council of Canada. It is part of a project that examines crime and criminal justice in Hamilton from the 1840s to the 1950s. The author acknowledges the assistance of Michael Martin, Robert Perrins, and Josh Spinner, who assisted with the research for this chapter.

1. Hamilton Public Library (HPL), RG 10 Police Department, Occurrence Books, 22 June 1934. All further citations for these books will be OB and the date.
2. OB, 3 Aug. 1934.
3. On 1 Jan. 1991, freedom of information and privacy legislation in the Province of Ontario extended to municipal records; one consequence was to make it almost impossible in the near future for further research to be done on records used in this chapter.
4. The duties of the Hamilton police as detailed in the police commission's minute books are well summarized by the phrase "aid business," employed by Clive Emsley, *Policing and Its Context, 1750–1870* (London, 1983), 4. The police commission minute books available at the Hamilton Public Library cover the years 1872–1913.
5. HPL, Police Commission Minutebook, 21 June 1879.
6. Minutebook, 5 Nov. 1895.
7. Robert J. Silverman and James J. Teevan, Jr., *Crime in Canadian Society* (Toronto, 1980), 65.
8. Ibid., 6–7.
9. John Weaver, "Crime, Public Order, and Repression: The Gore District in Upheaval, 1832–1851," *Ontario History* (Sept. 1986): 175–207.
10. There are several examples of services for the middle class and the elite. The police maintained a special vacant house patrol in the depression for families away at summer homes. During the many major strikes of 1946, the force attempted and failed to clear picket lines for the entry of men and material, especially at the Steel Company of Canada. There are indications that the force did not relish this last function, and the annual report for 1946 noted that the labor disputes had received more attention from the police and publicity about the police than they deserved when compared to the death toll from auto accidents, which had climbed to about twenty a year.
11. I have hypothesized a high degree of reporting, but a 1976 U.S. study estimated that only 53 percent of personal robberies were reported to police. See Charles H. McCaghy, *Crime in American Society* (New York, 1980), 138. Considering the degree of community support for the Hamilton police forces is one of the aims of the larger study.
12. Irvin Waller and Norman Okihiro, "Residential Burglary in Toronto," in *Crime in Canadian Society*, 307–16.
13. HPL, Hamilton Police Department, *Annual Report for the Year 1937*, 2.
14. For an early (1937) examination of this issue, see Thorsten Sellin, *Research Memorandum on Crime in the Depression* (New York, 1972), 31–62.

15. This is based on the marginal notes in red ink, which denoted an arrest in the case reported.

16. HPL Chiefs' Order Books, Orderbook 1926–35, 3 Dec. 1931.

17. One American study done in the mid–1960s estimated that eighty-six percent of crimes reported to the police are citizen-discovered, the remaining fourteen percent are police-discovered (*Crime in Canadian Society*, 64).

18. For an excellent review of the literature on the depression and crime, see James Huzel, "The Incidence of Crime in Vancouver during the Great Depression," *B.C. Studies* (Spring–Summer 1986): 361–81. Huzel has faith in the serial data for Vancouver, and employs it with economic indicators to achieve sophisticated evidence for a rise in theft during the initial years of the depression. For an old but valuable account of the methodological problems arising from assorted studies of crime and the depression, see Sellin, *Research Memorandum on Crime in the Depression*, 31–62.

19. *Annual Report for the Year 1932*, 2.

20. *Annual Report for the Year 1936*, 7.

21. *Annual Report for the Year 1944*, 8.

22. In his study of wartime crime in England, Edward Smithies noted that "the war saw a marked quickening in pace" of crime (*Crime in Wartime: A Social History of Crime in World War II* [London, 1982], 2).

23. *Annual Report for the Year 1936*, 8.

24. OB, 17 Nov. 1934; 19 Aug. 1935.

25. All names have been changed.

26. OB, 15 Dec. 1935.

27. British and Scandinavian studies conducted from the 1960s to the 1980s have arrived at similar conclusions. Juvenile burglars may be responsible for about half of the burglaries (Mike Maguire and Trevor Bennett, *Burglary in a Dwelling: The Offence, the Offender, and the Victim* [London, 1982], 24–25; George Rengert and John Wasilchick, *Suburban Burglary: A Time and a Place for Everything* [Springfield, 1985], 77).

28. "Residential Burglary in Toronto," *Crime in Canadian Society*, 39–40; *Burglary in a Dwelling*, 166.

29. OB, 31 Aug. 1935.

30. OB, 4–5 May 1942.

31. OB, 18 July 1942.

32. *Annual Report for the Year 1934*, 23.

33. *Annual Report for the Year 1935*, 27.

34. OB, 1 Dec. 1934. The report listed Family Packers, Dominion Metal, and the CPR express office as requesting special attention; Loblaws, a grocery chain store, reported that it had moved its safe to the front of the store. For the reports on more remote places, see OB, 18 June 1934; 3 Sept. 1934.

35. The residential nature of burglary has been noted in contemporary studies done in the United States (*Crime in American Society*, 148–49).

36. OB, 23 Dec. 1935.

37. *Annual Report for the Year 1945*, 7.

38. This observation is commonplace in criminological studies. See *Burglary in a Dwelling*, 18.

39. OB, 27 Mar. 1935.

40. OB, 4 July 1935.
41. OB, 30 June 1935.
42. OB, 6 Dec. 1935.
43. OB, 16 Apr. 1935.
44. OB, 9 Apr. 1935.
45. OB, 14 and 15 June 1934. The same lady had shirts and socks taken two days in a row.
46. OB, 23 Mar. 1935.
47. OB, 26 Mar. 1935.
48. Chief's Order Book, 1926–35, 11 July 1935.
49. OB, 17 Apr. 1935.
50. "Theft of automobile tires and gasoline ration books has given this Department considerable trouble during the past year" (*Annual Report for the Year 1924*, 29).
51. OB, 28 Aug. 1942.
52. OB, 28 Mar., 1942.
53. OB, 29 Nov. 1942.
54. This was recorded in OB, 23 Feb. 1942.
55. *Annual Report for the Year 1944*, 18.
56. OB, 25 Jan. 1942.
57. OB, 14 Apr. 1942.
58. OB, 30 May 1942.
59. OB, 24 Feb. 1942.
60. OB, 5 Jan. 1942.
61. OB, 1 Mar. 1942.
62. OB, 4 Oct. 1942; 4 Nov. 1942.
63. OB, 2 Mar. 1942; 11 Apr. 1942.
64. OB, 6 Mar. 1942.
65. OB, 14 and 21 Feb. 1942.
66. OB, 22 Nov. 1942.
67. OB, 10 and 20 Dec.; 10 May 1942.
68. OB, 18 July 1942.
69. Chief's Order Book, 1926–35, 31 Jan. 1931.
70. Smithies, *Crime in Wartime*, 34.
71. OB, 5 June 1935.
72. OB, 11 Sept. 1934.
73. OB, 5 Dec. 1935.
74. The opportunity-based crimes associated with licensed hotels have been remarked on by Peter A. Engstad, who used 1968 data for Edmonton ("Environmental Opportunities and the Ecology of Crimes," *Crime in Canadian Society*, 203–19).
75. A study of recovery of property stolen in burglaries in the Thames Valley in 1975 showed that only twelve percent of victims saw any of the lost property again (*Burglary in a Dwelling*, 18). Canadian researchers Waller and Okihiro, in "Residential Burglary," and Engstead and Evans, in *Crime in Canadian Society*, 144, "were beginning to suggest that the investigation of burglary should be given lower priority . . . partly because efforts to solve cases were not proving cost effective."
76. OB, 29 Nov.; 8 Dec. 1942.

The Death Penalty under Socialism, 1917–90: China, the Soviet Union, Cuba, and the German Democratic Republic

Andrew Scobell
Columbia University, New York

Introduction

The death penalty is employed by most socialist legal systems.[1] Its use as of 1990 ranged from extensive and vigorous in the People's Republic of China, to limited in the Union of Soviet Socialist Republics (USSR) and the Republic of Cuba, to complete abolition in the German Democratic Republic (GDR). One expert has labeled the death penalty a "hallmark of socialist legality."[2] Is the death penalty in accordance with socialist principles? What rationales are given for its use and how is it employed? What place does the death penalty have in socialist criminal justice systems?

This chapter examines the institution of the death penalty in China and Cuba as well as the now defunct East Germany and the Soviet Union. These four countries have been selected because they represent a cross-section of socialist countries: The Soviet Union is the oldest socialist state with perhaps the most tortuous experience with the death penalty; China employs capital punishment more extensively than any other country in the world today; Cuba represents an orthodox Marxist-Leninist state; East Germany abolished the death penalty in 1987.

Before proceeding, it is important to delineate the parameters of this chapter and to define terms. Socialist countries are those that espouse socialism in their constitutions, namely, public ownership of the bulk of the means of production and a dominant or leading role for the Communist party.[3] Socialist criminal justice systems are those operated by socialist states.[4] The death penalty is defined as the penalty of death codified in the legal codes or statutes of a state for specified acts deemed criminal. The term "capital punishment" in this chapter refers to its imposition through an institutionalized process within the framework of a criminal justice system. The condemned considered here must be formally charged with a capital crime, appear in court, be found guilty, and be formally sentenced to death, usually by the presiding officer of the court.[5] This chapter will not examine "extrajudicial killings" such as deliberate executions carried out by security forces outside the legal framework.[6]

Marx and Engels on the Death Penalty

The death penalty is as old as civilization itself. While socialism clearly did not invent or even reinvent capital punishment, it has had to confront this issue as baggage inherited from feudalism and capitalism. Indeed, the death penalty was employed in all four criminal justice systems of the governments toppled by the communist movements under study.[7] Further, the obvious point must be stressed: the death penalty is not unique to socialist systems. Capital punishment is in fact employed by many governments of differing political persuasions in the world today.[8]

Not surprisingly, socialists tend to view capital punishment in terms of class struggle. Karl Marx saw the death penalty as an instrument of oppression used by the bourgeoisie against the proletariat. He believed that the death penalty was incompatible with civilized society: "It would be very difficult, if not altogether impossible, to establish any principle upon which the justice or expediency of capital punishment could be founded in a society glorying in its civilization."[9] Marx insisted that the only justification for punishment that recognized "human dignity" was Kantian: that punishment was the "right" of the criminal. Even this grand logic should not obscure the fact, said Marx, that punishment always boils down to retribution—an eye for an eye. After all, he wrote, "Punishment is nothing but a means of society to defend itself against the infraction of its vital conditions."[10]

While little thought was given as to the need for the existence of a criminal justice system after a revolution, Marxist theoreticians readily acknowledged the usefulness of terror in furthering their goals. And it was "as an instrument of terror... that executions came to be principally justified."[11] Marx remarked that the "one way" to speed along the transition to socialism was the use of "revolutionary terror." Friedrich Engels also commented that a "revolutionary government... must maintain this rule by means of terror which its arms inspire in the reactionaries."[12] By 1917, according to one scholar, socialist thinking on the death penalty and related issues could be summarized in four basic points. First, crime would gradually wither away after the revolution. Second, criminals were "victims of circumstances." Third, they "should be treated and rehabilitated, not chastised." Fourth, while capital punishment might be useful, it was "fundamentally undesirable."[13]

The Death Penalty in the Soviet Union

Vladimir Ilyich Lenin and the Bolsheviks generally were "ambivalent" about capital punishment and adopted largely a "utilitarian approach" to the issue. In 1901, Lenin reportedly insisted that the "preventive significance of punishment depends entirely not upon its severity but upon its inevitability." Just prior to the October Revolution, Lenin argued all that would be needed to secure the revolution was the arrest of "50–100 magnates and bigwigs of banking capital . . . for a few weeks." Even in November, Lenin expressed the hope that "such terror as was used by the French revolutionaries who guillotined unarmed people" could be avoided in Russia. Lenin also noted its usefulness as a class weapon, however, observing: "No revolutionary government can do without capital punishment, and that the whole question is only against what class a particular government will direct [it]."[14] The Bolsheviks also exploited for propaganda value the reimposition of the death penalty by the provisional government of Alexander Kerensky. The Bolshevik newspaper *Molot* argued that capital punishment was reintroduced "with the view of exterminating the soldiers, workers, and peasants."[15]

The first formal decree issued by the Congress of Soviets after the October Revolution abolished the death penalty. Lenin, who was not present at the session, was furious when he heard the news. According to Leon Trotsky, Lenin exclaimed: "This is madness. How can we accomplish a revolution without shooting?" The death penalty was reinstituted in June 1918 on the grounds that it was necessary to counter the White terror.[16] The first death sentence meted out by a Soviet court was that same month and the condemned was Admiral Mikhaiovich Shchastny of the Baltic fleet. He was found guilty of treason and counter-revolutionary activities.[17] Then in mid-July Tsar Nicholas II and his family were executed in Ekaterinburg on the orders of the Ural Soviet Presidium and with Lenin's approval. The killings were apparently prompted by fears that the monarch would be captured by advancing Czech troops and would become a rallying point for anti-Bolshevik forces. Unlike the case of Shchastny, however, these executions (which were devoid of legal formalities) are best viewed as "extrajudicial killings." Those killed included not only the tsar and his immediate family, but also his household servants and personal physician.[18] These killings signaled the start of a bloody "Red Terror" declared by the Bolshevik government, which officially lasted some six months. According to one scholar, the most intense period of the crackdown on opponents only lasted several weeks, but during this time thousands were probably killed in "mass reprisals."[19]

Since the 1919 criminal code the formal goals of the Soviet criminal justice system have been special prevention, general prevention, and reeducation.[20] The goal of punishment, according to the 1919 code, was reform (Article 8) and any penalty "must be expedient, and at the same time completely free of signs of torture and must not cause useless and unnecessary suffering to the criminal" (Article 26).[21]

In Soviet literature, retention of the death penalty has often been defended as an "exceptional measure of punishment." Soviet legal experts have consistently stressed that the death penalty is a special measure.[22] Article 9 of the Principles of 1919 stated: the offender "can be adapted to the given social order or if he does not submit to adaptation, he can be isolated or, in extreme cases he may be physically destroyed."[23]

Capital punishment was reabolished in January 1920 after the military situation had improved significantly and the White Russian commander Alexander Kolchak had fallen into Soviet hands. The wording of the decree abolishing capital punishment, however, was vague in its scope. The measure was abolished "at present' and "with respect to enemies of Soviet authority." Thus, the measure could be interpreted as being temporary and applicable only to political offenders. The ban on capital punishment, however, did not apply to areas under martial law, and most Soviet-controlled areas were classified as such. Under these circumstances it was not surprising that such "piecemeal restoration" ultimately culminated in a full restoration of capital punishment in May 1920.[24] The death penalty was codified in the Basic Fundamentals of Criminal Legislation of the USSR issued by decree by the Central Executive Committee of the USSR in 1924. This punishment was employed "temporarily . . . pending its complete abolition."[25]

During the Soviet Union's first decade, use of the death penalty declined significantly. According to Ger. P. Van den Berg, the annual number of death sentences was "very high" during the New Economic Policy, but by the late 1920s had fallen to the lowest number since 1917. The figures he cites, which refer only to the Russian Republic, range from 750 to 886 per year in the early and mid-1920s to 300 death sentences in 1928.[26]

The Stalin Years

Under Joseph Stalin the number of death sentences grew steadily, especially with the onset of war with Germany in 1941. In October 1941 a decree permitted the shooting on sight of spies and provocateurs.[27] According to Hazard, this order was invoked only for a limited time in the Moscow region when the German army approached within 100 kilometers of the capital. In June 1942 another decree made the theft of socialist property a capital crime, and some offenders were executed.[28] The one noticeable exception to the use of capital punishment was of course the period from 1947 to 1950 when it was temporarily abolished and replaced by a twenty-five-year sentence in correctional labor camps.[29]

The attention paid to due process and the rights of the individual were at their nadir at the height of Stalin's purges. A December 1934 decree ordered that in "terrorist" cases, investigation was limited to ten days and the accused could be formally indicted only twenty-four hours prior to trial. The defendant in such cases had no right to defense counsel or appeal and, "sentence to the highest degree of punishment must be carried out immediately after the passing of the sentence." This decree was not formally revoked until April 1956.[30] According to one Soviet jurist, at the height of Stalin's purges, "the most stubborn lawyers ended up behind bars together with their clients."[31]

In 1947 the death penalty was abolished for peacetime offenses, officially to bow to the "wishes of trade unions and office-workers and other authoritative organizations expressing the opinions of broad social circles," in recognition of the tremendous sacrifice of the Soviet people in the Second World War. When the death penalty was reintroduced three years later, it was ostensibly "back by popular demand"—from workers and peasants.[32]

But the number of death sentences meted out by Soviet courts—not to mention the number of actual judicial executions carried out—in the early years of the USSR were certainly limited compared to those of Stalin's purges. One can only estimate the number of executions that occurred during this period. In his 1968 work *The Great Terror*, Robert Conquest estimated that there were at least half a million "legal" executions, and about an equal number of executions were later carried out in prison camps.[33] With more open discussion and research on the period now permissible in Russia, not surprisingly, more evidence is coming to light that permits a more accurate assessment of the devastation wrought by the purges. It was in light of this new evidence, that in 1989 Conquest revised his assessment upwards to more than one million persons executed after sentencing by various tribunals.[34] In February 1990 the KGB released a report stating that according to its records, 786,000 people had been executed between 1930 and 1953 for counter-revolutionary crimes or crimes against the state.[35] Despite the three-year period 1947–50 when the death penalty was abolished, Stalin's era was certainly one of lethal excesses.

From Khrushchev to Chernenko

The 1958 Fundamental Principles of Criminal Legislation of the USSR and Union Republics state that the code shall "determine which socially dangerous acts are criminal and shall establish the punishments which are applicable to persons who have committed crimes" (Article 1).[36] The purpose of the punishment is not only to serve as a "chastisement" for a criminal act, but also to contribute to the "reform and re-education of convicted persons in the spirit of an honorable attitude toward labor, strict execution of the laws, respect for the rules of socialist community life, and also prevention of the commission of new crimes both by the convicted persons and by other persons" (Article 20).

A Soviet legal scholar writing in 1961 in an article entitled "The Humanism of Soviet law" stressed "limited" use of the death penalty: "[T]here are crimes which already by reasons of their character do not merit any sort of condescension, and in such cases, humaneness must be shown first of all to society, to him who has suffered from the crime."[37] The oldest rationale for its use, that it is a special weapon employed against "class enemies," became largely obsolete and inconsistent as the bulk of capital crimes shifted from political crimes to those against the person.[38]

The rationale for the increased use of the death penalty in the 1960s given by a high level party functionary was not an increase in serious crime, "but rather the implacability of the Soviet people to all elements that bring shame on Soviet society and mar Soviet life."[39] Members of the public who attended trials in the early 1960s reportedly "expressed their approval" when death sentences were meted out to criminals.[40] Amnesty International noted that this was also true of media reports of verdicts in the 1970s. Further, at least one judge cited "public demand" as a rationale for meting out capital punishment.[41]

During 1961 and 1962 four economic crimes became capital offenses (instituted by decrees as part of an official campaign against corruption). These offenses were the theft of large amounts of state property; manufacturing or trafficking in counterfeit money or securities; speculation in foreign exchange valuables; and receiving bribes in "aggravated circumstances."[42] And during the 1960s and 1970s amendments to the Fundamental Principles of Criminal Legislation doubled the number of capital crimes. Throughout both these decades and into the 1980s, the circumstances in which the death penalty could be imposed for various crimes also increased.[43]

Only a small number of cases seemed to have been commuted. The two known to Amnesty International in the 1970s were evidently successful because of international involvement. A Georgian who had become a Canadian citizen returned to the Soviet Union and was arrested and sentenced to death for war crimes. His sentence was commuted after strong lobbying by the Canadian government. The death sentence of a Soviet Jew for economic crimes was also commuted after international pressure was brought to bear.[44] Since Nikita Khrushchev, the time elapsed between the sentence and date of execution has varied widely—from about a week to as long as eighteen months. The sailors allegedly executed in 1975 for mutiny aboard a Soviet naval vessel were reportedly executed shortly after their court martial (see below). War criminals have also been executed very swiftly. Meanwhile, one economic criminal was sentenced in 1975 and then executed about a year-and-a-half later.[45]

There have, however, been miscarriages of justice in more recent decades too. Some persons found guilty of capital crimes and given death sentences have later been exonerated. They were found to be the victims of either overzealousness or outright fabrication on the part of the police and the judiciary. Fortunately, in most of the known cases, the condemned escaped execution. The most notorious examples of improper death sentences are the Mogilev affair of 1972 and the Vitebsk case of the mid-1980s.[46]

In Khrushchev's time, the number of death sentences was significant but much lower than under Stalin. According to statistics for one area, in about one-third of all cases of premeditated murder, the offender received the death penalty. Out of the 267 murderers convicted in Rostov for the period 1961–63, eighty-eight were sentenced to be shot. If these statistics were representative of the entire country, then some 2,200 murderers received death sentences each year.[47] The number of capital offenses grew as did the number of people executed for economic crimes with the advent of a campaign against economic crime waged during the early 1960s. Amnesty International estimates that "about 250 people" were executed in the period 1961–64 for economic crimes. The numbers for economic crimes declined thereafter but continued to be high in the central Asian republics of Armenia, Georgia, and Azerbaijan at least through the first decade of Leonid Brezhnev's reign.[48]

During the mid–1970s "approximately 30" death sentences were meted out each year. The bulk of the death sentences for the period 1974–76, some forty-four percent, were for war crimes committed during World War II. The second largest group of condemned were murderers: They comprised some one-third of all capital cases.[49] According to Berg, no offender convicted of rape was sentenced to death by the Moscow City Court between 1965 and 1975, and only a small number received death sentences following this period.[50] Between 1974 and 1976, seventeen persons convicted of nonviolent economic crimes were sentenced to death, comprising twenty-eight percent of all death sentences during the period.[51] Despite the significant proportion of death sentences handed out for economic crimes, most defendants convicted of official and economic crimes during Brezhnev's time were dealt with leniently—most received fines.[52]

At least one person in the mid-1970s was executed for a state crime: spying for a foreign government. There were also reports of the execution of sailors in 1975. The military men were apparently found guilty of an unsuccessful mutiny aboard the Soviet warship *Stovozhevoi* while it was cruising the Baltic Sea.[53] More recently, Soviet officials have openly admitted that the incident occurred. While all the details are still not clear, it appears that at least Captain Valery Sablin was sentenced to death and subsequently executed.[54]

By way of comparison, the death penalty was used more frequently in the Soviet Union during the 1960s and 1970s than it was by Eastern European governments during the same period. One expert has concluded that not only was its use by other Soviet bloc countries "insignificant," but that generally the Soviet criminal justice system relied on "harsh penalties" much more than its East European neighbors.[55]

Gorbachev

As of 1990 legislation provided for eighteen capital crimes in peacetime. The following crimes against the state were capital: treason; espionage; terrorism against the state; plotting to commit serious state crimes; terrorism committed against foreign diplomats; sabotage; serious acts against another "working people's state"; banditism; disrupting corrective labor institution; resisting a military superior; and hijacking (if it involved loss of life or grave bodily harm).[56] Crimes against the person comprised three of the total: aggravated rape and intentional homicide in aggravated circumstances; and "infringement on the life" of a policeman in aggravated circumstances.[57]

In the Soviet Union, the death penalty traditionally is carried out by shooting except for war criminals who are hanged. All criminal cases—except those involving espionage and crimes committed against military, KGB, or prison personnel—are heard in civilian courts. Soviet desire for proper legal procedure can be gauged from comments by a Moscow newspaper columnist on the 1989 Salman Rushdie affair. He wrote:

> It should be noted that the opinion of the spiritual head of Iran who does not hold any official post, is not the same as a sentence carried out. Rather it is the emotional reaction of a man whose religious sensibilities have been insulted. No death sentence has been passed on S. Rushdie in Iran. Under Muslim law only a court of the Shari'ah can impose certain sentences.[58]

In capital cases, a defense lawyer is required by Article 22 of the 1958 Fundamental Principles of Criminal Legislation. Of course all lawyers worked for the state Ministry of Justice and were unlikely to defend their clients too aggressively. However, times may be changing. In February 1989 Soviet lawyers took a major step toward asserting their independence when they formed the first "self-governing bar association."[59] Anecdotal evidence suggests that lawyers may be proving more activist. For example, a defense lawyer adopted a high profile in the highly publicized 1988 trial of nine former Uzbekistan police officials (including Yuri Churbanov, son-in-law of the late Leonid Brezhnev) held in Moscow for corruption. The lawyer complained bitterly to the judge that his clients could not receive a fair trial because the men had already been found guilty by the media.[60]

Capital crimes must be heard in an intermediate court (city, regional, or territorial) or above. Since the republics of Lithuania, Latvia, Estonia, Moldavia, and Armenia have no intermediate courts, capital cases are tried in the supreme courts of these respective republics.[61] This is important because this denies a defendant found guilty and sentenced to death in any of these republics of the right to appeal the sentence since, according to Article 44 of the Fundamental Principles of Criminal Procedure, rulings of the supreme courts are not "subject to appeal." In at least one capital case the defendant was tried by the USSR Supreme Court and had no recourse to appeal. Akhmed Akhmedov, an Azerbijiani, was sentenced to death for murder and inciting ethnic violence against Armenians. His sentence was "not subject to appeal or protest in any process of revision" because the case was tried by the highest court in the land.[62]

Capital cases are tried by a three-man collegial panel of a judge and two people's assessors in the language of the republic, region area or locale, or "majority of the people in the locality." A majority decision (i.e., two out of three) is insufficient to pass a sentence of death.[63] The judge is likely to be the only member of the panel with significant legal training as the assessors are laymen who are selected to serve for a prescribed period of time each year.

There are two possible methods of appeal. The condemned has seven days in which to appeal the sentence to the Supreme Court of the Republic (except in the above-mentioned five republics, where the supreme courts function as the court of first instance). A procurator or court chairman can also appeal the case through judicial review.[64] A pardon is also a possibility, but it is vaguely described. According to the 1977 state constitution, the Presidium of the USSR Supreme Soviet may pardon a criminal or commute a death sentence to imprisonment (Article 121), but the individual must reportedly petition for this. If any of the above processes are successful the defendant receives a twenty-year prison term.[65] At least two death sentences were commuted in the 1980s. A student in Kazakhstan who was condemned to die for the December 1986 murder of a policeman had his sentence commuted by the Presidium of the Supreme Soviet in 1988. Later the same year, a regional party first secretary from Uzbekistan who was sentenced to death for accepting large bribes had his sentence commuted to fifteen years in prison.[66]

An important element of Mikhail Gorbachev's sweeping reforms is overhaul of the Soviet legal system. Significant penal reform seems to be an integral part of this.[67] Part and parcel of this reform is a major revision of death penalty measures. The current draft criminal code dramatically decreased the number of capital offenses: It recommends only six capital crimes in peace "time, and virtually all are acts of violence. These offenses are treason, espionage, terrorism, subversion, premeditated murder "with aggravating circumstances," and the rape of a minor.[68] No longer are there to be any economic crimes that carry the death penalty. Further, a substantial number of violent acts that are labeled "especially grave crimes" will no longer be capital offenses and will carry only a maximum of fifteen years' imprisonment. This includes the crimes of Nazi or war criminals.[69]

The draft limits capital punishment to males between the ages of eighteen and sixty. Perhaps the most significant changes are the abolition of the death penalty for women and elderly males.[70] This special treatment for women appears to reflect pervasive sexism in Soviet society and the sexual discrimination codified in Soviet law.[71] These proposed limitations also mirror the reforms made in the criminal code of 1903 sponsored by Tsar Nicholas II and demonstrate the strong humanistic trends in Russian culture.[72] The proposed criminal code also has a statute of limitations on capital crimes. If approved in its current form, the draft provisions would prohibit the death penalty for crimes committed more than fifteen years before criminal proceedings are instituted.[73]

In its introduction to the text of the new draft criminal code made public in December 1988, *Izvestiya* asserted that the legislation should play an integral role in the "stepping up of the struggle against crime and the elimination of the factors that give rise to it."[74] The newspaper continued:

> While severe measures of punishment should be applied to persons who commit crimes that represent a danger to society, who have previous convictions, and who stubbornly refuse to engage in an honest working life, wider use must be made of the opportunities offered by the law to give punishments not involving deprivation of liberty in cases of persons guilty of committing less dangerous crimes and capable of being corrected without isolation from society.

The draft Article 2 states that the criminal code should promote both the "prevention of crimes and the education of citizens." Article 3 further states that the code should be "based on the rule of law, democracy, inescapability of liability, equality of citizens before the law, personal and culpable liability, justice, and humanism."

In keeping with this spirit, the Soviet government decided on an early release for the young West German pilot of a small private plane that violated Soviet air space in 1987. Mathias Rust was convicted of illegally entering Soviet territory and "malicious hooliganism" after he flew unannounced into Soviet air space and landed his aircraft in Moscow's Red Square. He was sentenced to four years in prison, but was released after serving little more than one year. An official of the Soviet Prosecutor's Office explained: "We took this humanitarian step because Rust has fully realized his guilt. We commit acts of mercy toward our convicts provided they repent."[75]

Recently many Soviet legal scholars have acknowledged that the death penalty does not seem to be a deterrent to crime.[76] As one legal expert noted in 1989: "[T]he death penalty for grave cases of bribery in the USSR, for example, has been in existence since 5 May 1961, but the number of such crimes trebled between 1977 and 1987 alone."[77] The following month, Chairman Yevgeniy Alekseyevich Smolentsev of the Supreme Court of the Soviet Union in a discussion of penal reform, insisted that the element of deterrence could not be discarded. He said: "One should not fail to take account also of the fact that the possibility of the application of such a measure [i.e., capital punishment] has a certain deterring and restraining influence on criminal elements and thereby furthers the general prevention of premeditated murders."[78]

Recent available evidence suggests that most Soviet citizens favor the death penalty. Since 1987 capital punishment has become an acceptable topic of public debate and the issue has been widely discussed. According to Fyodor Bulatsky, chairman of the Public Commission on Humanitarian Cooperation and Human Rights and a People's Deputy, the "majority" of Soviet people "favour the use of capital punishment in retaliation for certain crimes like manslaughter" (i.e., violent crimes).[79] Most letters to the editor of *Moscow News* on the subject of the death penalty favor its continued use.[80] A survey of letters appearing in the Soviet press during 1987 by Radio Liberty analyst Valerii Konovalov on the death penalty also demonstrated a majority in favor of retaining the measure. Konovalov notes one letter from a worker in Novosibirsk claimed that all seventy-nine of the fellow factory workers he polled were against abolishing capital punishment.[81]

Many in the intellectual community, however, favor limiting use of the death penalty, and abolishing it as a penalty for economic crimes—if not abolishing it completely. This reflects in part a desire to ensure that the mass executions that took their toll on the ranks of Soviet intellectuals in Stalin's day are never repeated. Bulatsky states that the "use of capital punishment for political crimes once started can be very difficult to rein in."[82]

This desire among the Soviet intelligentsia also reflects the traditional cultural and intellectual identification of the Russian elite with Western Europe.[83] One of the most recent and highly publicized expressions of this sentiment is Gorbachev's desire for the Soviet Union to be part of a "common European home."[84] This influence can be seen in a letter to the editor of *Izvestiya* that urged the USSR to "follow the example of civilized Europe" and abolish capital punishment.[85] Soviet jurists reportedly also favor abolishing the death penalty for economic crimes and limiting its application to violent crimes.[86] One law student writing in 1987 argued that while "common sense" dictated abolition of the death penalty for all but a few "especially grave crimes," he personally believed "socialist humanism requires that it be abolished altogether."[87] Two legal scholars also argued for total abolition. They insisted that the separation of the death penalty from all other punishments in the Soviet criminal code represented "hypocrisy" rather than "emphasizing the exclusive nature of the penalty."[88]

Gorbachev apparently strongly favors restricting use of the death penalty. The Soviet leader singled out reform of capital punishment regulations for special mention during his address to the United Nations General Assembly in New York in December 1988.[89] Gorbachev's ideas about thoroughgoing reform of the criminal justice system almost certainly have their origins in his unusual educational background. While other party leaders of his generation studied engineering or agriculture, Gorbachev earned a law degree at Moscow University.[90] His personal convictions about restricting the use of capital punishment are likely reinforced by a desire to garnish support among the Soviet intellectual community and by a wish for the Soviet Union to be seen as the equal of advanced Western societies.

Soviet media coverage continues to play up public approval for the death penalty, but this is more subtly expressed than in the Chinese press (see below). A 1988 account in *Pravda* of the conclusion of an unsuccessful aircraft hijacking runs in this vein. Four hijackers who originally seized a bus full of school children in the town of Ordzhonikidze in North Caucasus negotiated with Soviet authorities and exchanged the children for an aircraft. They then ordered the crew to fly to Israel, where the hijackers surrendered to the local authorities who sent them back to the Soviet Union. Commenting on their arrival back in the USSR, as the four hapless hijackers were hustled off the plane and into waiting police vehicles, the journalist recorded that someone in the crowd of observers shouted "scum!" While the writer observed that a court would "decide their fate," an aircraft crew member noted, these criminals "will not escape retribution."[91]

The Supreme Court Chairman Smolentsev buttressed his claim that the death penalty was a deterrent with the argument that, whether valid or not, what was important was that the Soviet people believed this: "a majority of citizens" had made it plain that they felt capital punishment deterred crime.[92]

Under Gorbachev the number of executions in the Soviet Union seems to have fallen to an all-time low. Glasnost permitted far more open discussion of Soviet crime and punishment and official figures on both were eventually published. In January 1991 the Justice Ministry reported that there were 770 executions in 1985, 344 in 1987, and 276 in 1989.[93] There had been "a two to three-fold drop" in executions, according to Chairman Vladimir Terebilov of the Soviet Supreme Court in March 1989.[94] One researcher found that of sixty-one death sentences issued by Soviet courts in 1987, seventy-five percent (forty-six of sixty-one) were for crimes of violence such as murder, rape of a minor, and attempted hijacking. The remainder of the condemned were almost equally divided between war criminals and economic offenders.[95] More than half of the death sentences known to Amnesty International in the period from 1985 to May 1988 were for war crimes or murder. These figures do not include reports of dozens of Soviet soldiers shot for insubordination in Afghanistan.[96]

More recently, the overwhelming majority of death sentences appear to have been meted out for murder. Of nine sentences the author collected from a random survey of Soviet media reports, seven were meted out to murderers.[97] The remainder comprised one war criminal who was convicted in August 1988 of complicity with the Germans in the Ukraine during 1942–43, and a bookkeeper from Central Asia who was found guilty of embezzling millions of rubles in state funds.[98] Noteworthy is the fact that at least since the mid–1970s no women have received death sentences,[99] and at least if the draft criminal code is adopted, this de facto situation will become de jure.

The Death Penalty in China

Like Lenin, Mao Zedong saw capital punishment mainly as a tool to be used against counter-revolutionaries, and stressed that it should be used cautiously and in a limited fashion.[100] Nevertheless, during the early years of the PRC, hundreds of thousands of "enemies of the people" were executed—700,000 according to an unofficial version of Mao's 1957 speech, "Problems Relating to the Correct Handling of Contradictions among the People."[101] After this initial rush, the number declined substantially, and from the mid–1950s until the mid–1960s estimates of the number of executions range from one hundred to several thousand annually.[102]

In the chaotic decade of the Cultural Revolution (1966–76) one expert has estimated 500,000 were killed as a direct result of rampant violence and persecution.[103] Most of these people, however, were not found guilty of capital offenses through proper legal procedure, and many of these deaths were the result of mob violence as well as suicide or physical abuse by Red Guards. One of the most famous victims of this period was Zhang Zhixin. A loyal Communist Party member and a dedicated mother, Zhang was accused of counter-revolutionary crimes in 1969 and languished in prison until her execution in April 1975. She was posthumously rehabilitated and became a symbol of all those who had been wronged during the Cultural Revolution.[104]

According to one legal scholar, Mao's approach to the death penalty was cautious and magnanimous and could be summed up by three main points. First, "While most criminals do not have to be executed, the death penalty cannot be abolished nor can a general amnesty be granted." Second, it is important to distinguish different types of offenders: Different penalties should be meted out to "principal offenders" (*zhijie yuantou*) than to "accomplices" (*pubian yuantou*). Third, do not execute all those guilty of capital crimes, "but rather adopt the approach of 'sentencing to death, suspending the sentence, subjecting them to reform through labor and observing the consequences.' "[105] The scholar claimed that Mao considered the most important purpose of the legal system was to achieve the "greatest benefit for the greatest number of people." Thus, "[t]he people's benefit is our highest law."[106] The death penalty has been viewed by the Chinese Communist Party (CCP)—as it has by the Communist Party of the Soviet Union—as a temporary measure. As a 1957 Chinese legal text book explained: "We are retaining the death penalty while in the process of gradually abolishing it, and we are reducing the scope of the application of the death penalty to a minimum."[107]

In Mao's China particularly, there was constant reference to the fact that executing dangerous or serious criminals meets with strong public approval. Mao commented in the early 1950s that some criminals must be executed "so as to assuage the people's anger."[108] A 1957 handbook for cadres involved in the criminal justice system recommended that the death penalty be used in instances where "death alone" could "satisfy the people's anger."[109] An American lawyer commenting on the penal system in China during the 1970s seems justified in saying that "the sentence in China is set according to community passion . . . and the indignation of the masses."[110]

The Deng Era

The number of capital crimes has grown steadily since the promulgation of the first penal codes in 1979. Prior to these codes, a broad range of crimes were capital, essentially mirroring the current gamut of capital offenses contained in the 1979 law and subsequent amendments.[111] As of 1990 the number of capital offenses stood at forty-eight, including ten military offenses. The Criminal Code of 1979, which became effective 1 January 1980, originally contained twenty-one capital offenses, but twenty-seven additional offenses were added through subsequent legislation.[112] Fourteen are counter-revolutionary offenses.[113] If these crimes are "especially odious" or "serious," they carry the death penalty (CrLaw Article 103). Among the crimes considered counter-revolutionary are scheming to "subvert the government or dismember the state" (Article 92), arranging an "armed mass rebellion" (Article 95), and hijacking (Article 100).

Capital crimes that "endanger public security" include arson and breaching dikes (CrLaw Article 106). There are two offenses against the person that are capital crimes: "intentional murder" (*guyi sharen*) (Article 132) and rape if the victim is not yet fourteen years old or if the case is "serious" (Article 139). In 1983 the Standing Committee of the National People's Congress (NPC) approved legislation adding seven more capital offenses. Among these were gang fighting, pimping, and teaching "criminal methods."[114] In May 1989, revealing "state secrets" became a capital crime—and the definition of what constitutes a state secret is very broad.[115]

Over the decade of reform China's leaders have repeatedly expressed serious concern about the prevalence of corruption. In the early days of the post-Mao reforms China's paramount leader Deng Xiaoping warned that crimes such as "corruption, embezzlement, speculation and profiteering" were increasing.[116] Ten years later, President Ren Jianxin of the Supreme People's Court (SPC), told the NPC that economic crime was "rampant."[117] Despite this persistent concern, only one economic crime was designated as a capital offense in the 1979 Criminal Code: "especially serious" corruption involving state personnel (Article 155).

As part of its campaign against corruption, however, the government soon increased the number of capital economic crimes. In March 1982, a

Renmin Ribao editorial declared: "The government and Party have always advocated using capital punishment as little as possible but the shocking incidence of economic crimes has reached such proportions that they must be seriously punished. A small number of extremely serious criminals must be punished by means of the ultimate penalty in order to serve as a warning to others."[118] That same month the Standing Committee of the NPC approved capital punishment in "serious" cases of smuggling, speculation, habitual theft or swindling, drug trafficking, bribery, and the theft or unlawful export of "precious cultural relics."[119] A month later, in April, Deng told the politburo that the country had to be prepared for a protracted battle against economic crimes. To combat this scourge the death penalty would be necessary in "particularly grave" instances of corruption.[120]

In January 1988 the Standing Committee of the sixth NPC passed legislation making three more economic crimes capital offenses. Smugglers of drugs, precious metals, rare animals or their products, or goods valued at more than RMB 500,000 can now be sentenced to death. Armed defense of contraband is also a capital crime.[121] The death sentence can now be meted out to embezzlers, thieves, swindlers, or receivers of bribes of RMB 50,000 or more.[122] And effective January 1982, members of all branches of the People's Liberation Army (PLA) can receive the death penalty for crimes such as passing military secrets to the enemy or foreigners, spreading rumors that undermine military morale, desertion, or robbing and harming civilians.[123]

The goal of "criminal punishment" in China is explicitly stated in the Criminal Law of 1979: "to defend the system of the dictatorship of the proletariat [i.e., rule by the Communist party]," protect the property (both collective and individual) and rights of the people, "and to safeguard the smooth progress of the cause of socialist revolution and socialist construction."[124] Chinese communists see the goals of punishing criminals as being three-fold: to "punish and reform" the criminal (also known as "special prevention"), to deter and educate would-be criminals, and to deter and educate the entire people (collectively known as "general prevention").[125] According to Article 1 of the Criminal Law, in administering criminal justice, China should follow "the policy of combining punishment with leniency."

Deng Xiaoping spoke directly about the death penalty in 1986. He said: "the death penalty cannot be abolished, and some criminals must be sentenced to death." Rather than focusing on counter-revolutionaries as Mao had done, Deng singled out habitual criminals who "refuse" to repent. These individuals "must be executed, but of course we have to be very careful in such matters." Execution, insisted Deng, is an "indispensable means" through which to educate the masses.[126] Chinese officials and spokesmen continue to emphasize what while the death penalty could not be abolished, it was only used in an "extremely small" number of cases.[127]

In post-Mao China the burden of proof lies with the accused. According to Article 28 of the 1979 Criminal Procedure Law, it is the defendant who must prove his innocence or lack of criminal responsibility. A study by one group of scholars found defendants succeeded in having the charges against them dismissed in only some two percent of all criminal cases.[128]

A person charged with a capital crime faces an uphill battle to avoid a guilty verdict and a death sentence. The chances of having a fair trial have improved slightly in Deng's China over what they were in Mao's day. Since 1980 class background is legally not supposed to be taken into account and the criminal law is "equally applicable to all citizens" (CrPL Article 4). Furthermore, a defendant now has the right to be represented by a lawyer or layman (CrPL Articles 26 and 27). But defense lawyers are expected to set the interests of the "socialist cause and the people" above those of their clients.[129] Typically defense attorneys "play a passive role" in the Chinese courtroom."[130] The effectiveness of lawyers in capital cases can be seen from the outcome of a recent case involving eight men accused of rioting in Beijing in June 1989. All were convicted and sentenced to death. Only one lawyer was able to save his client from execution: he successfully convinced the court that his client was mentally retarded.[131]

The process of criminal appeal is becoming an integral part of the post-Mao legal system. While more and more defendants are appealing their convictions and sentences, very few have their convictions overturned or their sentences reduced. Defendants were acquitted in only twenty-one of the almost 7,500 criminal appeals heard by the Intermediate Court of the Beijing municipality.[132] Only one condemned individual is known to have successfully appealed his case all the way to the SPC.[133]

Courts of the second instance have violated Article 127 of the Criminal Procedure Law and increased the severity of sentences. In 1984, the High People's Court of Yunnan Province decided that a life sentence for a murderer who broke up a love triangle was not severe enough and imposed a sentence of death.[134] According to Amnesty International, the State President has never exercised his power to pardon convicted criminals.[135] In 1983 the time permitted for a condemned criminal to appeal the death sentence was cut from the ten days allowed by Article 131 of the Criminal Procedure Law to just three days.[136]

According to Article 15 of the 1979 Criminal Procedure Law, an intermediate court is the court of first instance in cases involving a capital crime. The case is tried by a collegiate panel of one judge and two people's assessors, but on an appeal between three and five judges preside (CrPL Article 105). Article 125 stipulates that the verdict should be rendered within two months of the defendant being formally charged. Article 13 of the Criminal Procedure Law was amended in June 1981 to allow "when necessary" the high people's court of a province, autonomous region, or municipality to approve death sentences instead of the SPC.[137]

Most criminal cases involving capital crimes seem to be resolved within six months and, in many instances, in ninety days or less.[138] The process of arrest, trial, conviction, pronouncement of a death sentence, and execution can be exceedingly swift. In at least one case two men were executed just six days after being apprehended.[139] However, in another instance a capital punishment trial dragged on for four years.[140] The criminal justice process can also be quite secretive. The family of a Hong Kong man accused of masterminding a robbery in neighboring Guangdong Province was never informed of his trial dates or the guilty verdict. The man's wife learned of her husband's death sentence on the television news only after he had been executed.[141] In addition, some sources have alleged that cities and provinces were issued arrest and execution quotas by Beijing. The CCP Central Committee or even Deng Xiaoping himself may have issued such a directive as part of a 1983 crackdown on crime.[142]

Chinese authorities have also subjected condemned criminals to degrading treatment prior to their executions. Open trucks often transport the condemned through the streets of their former neighborhoods for family and friends to see.[143] Signs hang about their necks listing their crimes and capital sentences. According to Article 45 of the Criminal Law, execution is by shooting and this is usually done by a single bullet to the back of the head. Although by law execution is not to be a public spectacle, public-sentencing rallies are permitted by Article 155 of the Criminal Procedure Law and such rallies are quite common. Despite the letter of the law, public executions have taken place; some executions have also been shown on state-run television.[144] Recently, degrading treatment of the condemned has extended beyond death. The organs of executed Chinese have been removed for transplant operations without the permission of either the condemned or of their families. The practice reportedly has included kidney transplants in mainland hospitals for wealthy overseas Chinese who pay with foreign currency.[145]

The majority of death sentences over the past decade have been given out as punishment for crimes of violence. In 1988 the president of the SPC claimed that at least 90 percent of death sentences and sentences of life imprisonment were meted out to violent criminals.[146] Two researchers concluded that the majority of offenders executed during 1978 and 1979 were rapists and murderers.[147] Of more than 250 criminals executed in 1983 some eighty percent were found to be violent criminals.[148] According to the U.S. Department of State, the "great majority" of persons executed in post-Mao China were found guilty of "serious nonpolitical crimes."[149] Those political dissidents that are executed seem to be those convicted of violent crimes of treason. People have been executed for the following "counterrevolutionary" crimes: stealing firearms and explosives, hijacking, and spying for a foreign government.[150] Only eight percent of political cases result in the execution of the perpetrator.[151] Only thirteen percent of all crimes seem to be political in nature.[152]

Few economic offenders are sentenced to death. Less than 10 percent of all executed criminals are convicted of economic crime,[153] although perhaps half of all crime in China can be classified as economic.[154] Procurator General Liu Fuzhi of the Supreme People's Procuratorate reported that only 1.25 percent of those convicted of corruption and bribe taking in 1988 were sentenced to death.[155] During the 1980s, however, there appears to have been a significant rise in the number of economic criminals executed in China.[156]

Ordinary Chinese citizens are more likely to face execution than members of the CCP or their families. While Party members make up less than four percent of the total population, they account for as much as thirty percent of criminal cases.[157] A graphic demonstration of the inequities within the system was visible in the outcomes of two cases reported by the same newspaper.[158] A department store employee received a one-year suspended prison term for repeated instances of flagrant corruption. At about the same time a self-employed man was executed after being convicted of dismantling and selling railway tracks. The major reason for vastly different treatment of the culprits in the two cases seemed to be that the former was a CCP member while the latter was not. In one study, members of the CCP comprised just 3.2 percent of the total number of death sentences meted out (6 of 187), but accounted for thirty-one percent of the criminals (587 of 1,869).[159] The few well-connected figures that are executed receive great publicity in an effort to demonstrate that no one is above the law. Such is the case with the execution of Marshal Zhu De's grandson for rape and other crimes in 1983.[160] Meanwhile, the chief culprit in the Hainan Island speculation racket, the most infamous case of corruption in Deng's China, received only a life sentence.[161] If he had not been a senior CCP official, he most likely would have been executed.

Many of the criminals executed in the 1980s were under thirty years old.[162] The wave of juvenile crime is of great concern to Chinese authorities. In July 1988 SPC President Ren Jianxin announced that half of all criminal cases involved culprits younger than twenty-five years old.[163] More recently it appears that the proportion of juvenile crime committed by females has risen dramatically. Whereas in the early 1960s the ratio of male to female offenders was 100:1, it is now reportedly 10:1.[164] Although the vast majority of executions have been for what would generally be viewed as serious crimes, some petty criminals have also received capital punishment. In 1987 a man who snatched a tourist's purse in a city park was sentenced to death.[165] Other Chinese have been executed for dealing in forged residence permits,[166] hosting "dancing and sex parties,"[167] running a brothel, and showing pornographic films.[168]

The number of executions in post-Mao China is the highest since the early years of the People's Republic. Between 1978 and 1987, this writer estimates that at least 10,000 and perhaps as many as 20,000 people were executed in China.[169] The number of annual executions also seems to have increased significantly over this period. At least 2,900 executions occurred between 1978 and 1982, while over the following four years 7,000 and possibly even 14,000 persons were executed.[170] In a special global report on capital punishment issued in 1989, Amnesty International estimated that as many as 30,000 Chinese may have been executed between 1983 and 1987.[171]

Following the suppression of the student-led pro-democracy movement in China in 1989, there have been allegations of numerous executions being carried out in secret. These claims should be viewed with caution since Chinese leaders would have little to gain from such additional brutality.[172] Not publicizing such killings would carry no deterrent value—a major rationale for executions in the PRC. There is little doubt that martial law enforcement troops in Beijing shot hundreds of civilians on the weekend of 3–4 June 1989.[173] Certainly China's leaders have acted repressively: thousands have been arrested, among whom many have probably been tortured and some may have died from abuse suffered while in detention.[174] Since the bloody suppression of the Beijing demonstrations in early June, however, China's leaders have made great efforts to promote a more conciliatory image to the people. Nevertheless, the government has not shied away from continued executions. This is consistent with the pattern of use of capital punishment during the Deng decade and not a response tailored to deal with those involved in the 1989 demonstrations.

Deng reportedly ordered that the death penalty be used only in the most serious cases of unrest.[175] Out of the hundreds of thousands of Chinese who participated in the protests, only a small minority have been charged in criminal offenses; most were given prison terms. Only forty-odd individuals are known to have been executed for offenses directly related to the protests.[176] All of the death sentences were meted out for acts of violence. A typical case involves two workers and an unemployed man who were convicted of setting railway carriages aflame and preventing firemen from battling the blaze on 6 June 1989 in Shanghai. Six other rioters were given prison terms for their parts in the same incident.[177] Twenty-six of the twenty-seven people convicted of rioting and looting in Changsha, Hunan Province, on 22 April 1989 were sentenced to prison terms. One worker received a suspended death sentence for assaulting a policeman.[178] To date all of those executed have been workers, peasants, or unemployed youths.[179] No students are known to have been executed and the authorities have taken great pains to point this out.[180] Nonetheless, this writer believes that it is no exaggeration to state that the government of Deng Xiaoping "may be the most efficient and effective Chinese government in centuries at implementing capital punishment within an institutionalized legal framework."[181]

Despite remaining adamant about the death penalty, the Chinese government has demonstrated heightened sensitivity to foreign criticism of its use. While there is no evidence that foreign condemnation has curbed the use of the death penalty or halted any executions, there are indications that the PRC has been stung by these criticisms. One example of this is a 1984 article in *Renmin Ribao*: While "foreign bourgeois 'humanitarians' " claimed that China's use of the death penalty was " 'inhumane,' " was it " 'humane,' " asked the article, "to let murderers "continue to kill good people?"[182] A further example of this is the attention given to the death penalty in a selection of papers published in 1985 by the Chinese Legal Studies Society. Only twenty-two papers out of the 113 presented to a conference on Mao and legal theory the previous year were selected for inclusion in the edited volume. Two of the twenty-two were devoted to explaining China's use of the death penalty.[183]

Indeed, a major reason given by one of the authors for dealing with the subject of the death penalty was in order to respond to foreign criticism. According to Guo Daohui:

> Overseas some people also do not well comprehend, and some people with ulterior motives unceasingly attack, our country's institution of the death penalty. They say that this type of serious punishment for criminal elements is "inhuman and brutal", "violates the United Nations Declaration of Human Rights", openly express "strong protest" and demand abolition. . . . To these kinds of misinterpretations and slanders, it is also necessary to furnish serious and principled answers.[184]

It is conventional wisdom that Chinese citizens favor capital punishment.[185] While no opinion polls have been carried out in the PRC on the subject, polls in the adjacent British colony of Hong Kong demonstrate overwhelming support for the death penalty, at least for the violent crimes of rape and murder.[186] It is crystal clear, however, that the Chinese desire a strong government that maintains law and order and promptly and forcefully metes out severe punishment to lawbreakers.[187] In 1988 one non-communist intellectual urged Chinese courts to make examples of officials convicted of serious wrongdoing. He argued that "it is sometimes necessary to decapitate somebody in order to vent the people's anger."[188]

The Suspended Death Sentence

A distinguishing feature of China's death penalty regulations, which merits special attention, is the "death sentence suspended for two years" (*sixing huanqi ernian zhixing*) (CrL Article 43). This punishment seems to be uniquely Chinese, with a history dating back to imperial times.[189] According to one mainland legal scholar, the suspended death sentence was instituted in early 1951 to specifically deal with counter-revolutionaries, and was codified the following year in central government regulations.[190]

The suspended death sentence seems to be tantamount to life imprisonment. The punishment emphasizes the seriousness of the offense while at the same time demonstrating the court's benevolence. Rarely does an execution seem to be carried out at the end of the two-year assessment period.[191] All statements by PRC officials and scholars stress that few of those given suspended sentences are ultimately executed. One scholar writing in 1984 stated it is only a "very small number" (*hen shao*); he insists that "not more than one or two out of every ten" are eventually executed.[192] An editorial in the *Beijing Review* also claims the "majority" of suspended death sentences "are later resentenced to life or fixed term imprisonment."[193] This writer was able to find only one instance in which suspended sentences were carried out. Two ethnic Tibetan convicts, who were reportedly already serving suspended death sentences at the time of their second offense, were executed in May 1990. The two convicted murderers were discovered plotting a "mass prison escape"—an offense that is punishable by death.[194] The death sentence suspended for two years may be as widely used as the immediate death sentence.[195] A review of Chinese court documents over one six-month period uncovered similar totals: 198 executions and 214 suspended death sentences.[196]

According to Article 44 of the Criminal Law, only adults eighteen years and older can be executed. Sixteen- and seventeen-year-olds can receive suspended death sentences, however, if the crime is "particularly grave." Under a suspended death sentence, a prisoner's attitude and performance are supposed to be assessed at the end of two years. If, in the judgment of a collegiate panel, a prisoner has "truly repented" (*queyou huigai*), the death sentence can be commuted to a term of life imprisonment. If the panel concludes the prisoner has demonstrated "meritorious service" (*ligong*)—for example, turning police informant—the sentence can be reduced to fifteen or twenty years in prison. The SPC must approve any decision to actually execute a suspended death sentence (CrL Article 46 and CrPL Article 153).

For an execution to occur, the panel must have "verified evidence" (*chazheng shushi*) that the convict "resisted reform in an odious manner" (*kongju gaizao qingjie elie*) (CrL Article 46 and CrPL Article 153). The wording of the article suggests that resistance, as long as it is not too flagrant, will be tolerated or even ignored.[197] Perhaps the clearest indication of this point was the commutation of the suspended death sentence imposed on Mao's widow, Jiang Qing, at the end of the two-year observation period. Jiang and former Vice Premier Zhang Chunqiao are perhaps the best known recipients of suspended death sentences. In January 1981 Jiang, Zhang, and eight others were found guilty of plotting to "subvert the government and overthrow the people's democratic dictatorship."[198] One of Jiang's biographers, Ross Terrill, believes the 1983 decision of the collegiate panel got Beijing "off the hook of having to execute Mrs. Mao."[99] Yet, China's leaders were never really "on the hook." All that was legally required of the panel in order to recommend Jiang's suspended death sentence be commuted was for it to conclude that she had not resisted reform in an "odious manner." There was no pressure on the panel to either claim Jiang had repented or to cover up evidence of resistance to reform.

While the suspended death sentence is touted by Chinese officials and legal scholars as an outstanding example of humanitarianism,[200] there are indications that in practice its application is anything but humane. Although, as has been suggested above, suspended death sentences are rarely implemented, the procedure followed by authorities in arriving at commutation is less than clear. In at least some cases the condemned prisoner seems to exist in a state of limbo, not only during the two-year observation period, but in the period following this as well. The evaluation at the end of two years may or may not be conclusive, and consideration of the death sentence can be postponed indefinitely. Thus the sentence of death may loom over a prisoner for many years.[201]

On the other hand, at least some prisoners have earned successive reductions in sentences. One convict in Shenyang who was originally sentenced to death with a two-year suspension was given four separate reductions of sentence (*jianxing*)—the largest single reduction was five years. But even in this case, there is no mention of when the official decision was made to commute the death sentence, indicating that the process of dealing with suspended death sentences is more haphazard in practice than it is supposed to be.[202]

The Death Penalty in Cuba

Shortly after seizing power in Cuba in 1959, Fidel Castro's government introduced Law No. 425, which formally introduced the death penalty into post-Batista Cuba. The decree qualified Article 25 of the 1940 Constitution, which had abolished the death penalty. Issued on 14 January 1959, the measure allowed the new regime to use the death penalty against those who opposed the revolution. The decree stated:

> An exception is made [i.e., capital punishment is permitted] in the cases of the armed forces, the repressive organizations of the dictatorship, the auxiliary groups organized by it and of spies for crimes of a military nature or crimes committed with the purpose of or intention of restoring or defending the regime put down on 31st December 1958, and those persons guilty of treason or subversion of the institutional order or of espionage on behalf of the enemy in the course of war with a foreign power.[203]

Additional Legislation in 1960 increased the number of capital crimes, and these were codified in the Code of Social Defense of 1973. These offenses were retained in the 1979 Penal Code. The Penal Code of 1987—the most recent codification effort—eliminated five capital crimes, including robbery committed "with violence against property" or committed "with violence or intimidation against persons."[204] Currently twenty-one civilian offenses carry the death penalty. These are contained in the 1987 Penal Code which took effect 30 April 1988.[205] These include five "Crimes Against External State Security" and an equal number of offenses against "internal state security." The former consist of acts against the "independence or territorial integrity of the state," the "promotion of armed action against Cuba," "armed service against the state," aiding the enemy, and espionage. The latter comprises rebellion, sedition, usurping political or military authority, sabotage, and terrorism.

Furthermore, five crimes "against peace and international law" carry the death penalty: "hostile acts against a foreign state," genocide, piracy, mercenary activity, and the "crime of apartheid." This last offense appears to be vaguely defined and may be intended to garnish the support of black Cubans who have endured a long history of racial discrimination. Having this offense on the books also cannot but help Cuba's image in Africa, where Havana has been active and vocal in opposing the government of South Africa. Three other offenses are also considered capital if they are committed with the intent to commit any of the above-mentioned fifteen crimes. The three crimes against the person are: murder, rape when the victim is less than twelve years of age or if serious injury or illness results, and "pederasty with violence" if the victim is younger than fourteen years old or serious injury or illness results. This last crime appears to be a reflection of the strong machismo element in Cuban culture and its intolerance of homosexuality.[206] The death penalty can also be meted out for nineteen offenses committed by soldiers under the Military Offenses Law of 1979. Most, but not all, of these military crimes are applicable only in time of war.[207]

According to the head of the National Revolutionary Police (NRP), the 1987 Criminal Code represented an "efficient tool" with which to manage the criminal justice system.[208] The stated objective of the prison system is "re-education." This comprises three components: "socially useful work," political or ideological education, and the rewarding of good behavior and observance of the rules.[209] The death penalty "can only be applied by the court in the most serious cases of crimes for which it is established," according to the 1987 Penal Code. Execution is by firing squad. Only those twenty years and older can receive a death sentence. Women cannot be condemned to death if they are pregnant either at the time the crime was committed or when the sentence is pronounced.[210]

Although the accused has the right to a lawyer, one is often not provided until the trial hearing. The bulk of political cases are allegedly decided not by the courts but by the Department of State Security (DSS) or secret police. At the hearing the *fiscal*, or prosecutor, presents evidence the government has collected in the case and makes a recommendation on how to proceed in the case.[211] Thus often during the course of the preliminary investigation and pretrial detention, the defendant is without counsel. The accused or his family can approach a lawyer himself, or one will be assigned for him. Consistent with practice in the Soviet Union and China, defense lawyers in Cuba are in a "weak position."[212] It has also been reported that some lawyers have been jailed for defending political prisoners, and in November 1985 one jailed lawyer apparently died in the hospital "under unexplained circumstances."[213] They are often restricted to appealing for clemency. Their limited role is due in part to the fact that private practice was outlawed in 1974, and virtually all lawyers must be affiliated with "lawyer's collectives." Despite this, official instructions issued to court personnel in January 1987 stipulate that defense lawyers be given all courtesies and assistance to carry out their work.[214] These instructions apparently apply only to prisoners held by the NRP and not to those detained by the DSS.[215]

A capital case is heard by a collegiate panel of judges. The panels do seem to exercise some degree of independence; they have rejected sentencing recommendations from the prosecutor. The prosecutor in a highly publicized 1989 case asked the judges to mete out the death penalty to seven of fourteen soldiers on trial, but the panel of judges only passed capital sentences on four of the defendants.[216] According to Amnesty International, some prisoners have not received "written confirmation of their sentences" when their death sentence had been commuted on appeal. Further, relatives were often not allowed to visit the condemned. In some cases they were not informed of the date or place of an execution; some relatives were not told where the body had been buried.[217]

When a sentence of death is handed out, it is automatically appealed to the Supreme People's Court (SPC). The case must then be reviewed by the Council of State, which acts on the recommendation of the Ministry of Justice. The council has the power to grant clemency by commuting the sentence to a maximum of thirty years in prison.[218] In the case of the four military officers sentenced to death on 7 June 1989 by a special military tribunal, the sentences were automatically appealed to the Military Affairs Court of the SPC. The following day the high court confirmed the sentences. On the afternoon of 9 June the twenty-nine members of the State Council convened for the sole purpose of reviewing the facts of the case. Reportedly in a "unanimous decision" the body decided not to commute the death sentences. Castro declared that he was satisfied that the case had been decided with "exceptional fairness."[219]

Cuba's Minister of Justice Juan Escalona Reguera told Amnesty International in March 1988 that a total of 237 persons had been sentenced to death by Cuban courts since 1959. Of these, 216 had been actually executed, while the remainder had their sentences commuted. The minister insisted that the vast majority of these death sentences had been meted out in 1959.[220] Most of those executed were reportedly violent criminals.[221] All four of those on death row in Boniato Prison met by the Amnesty International delegation in 1988 were convicted of violent crimes.[222] None of those executed have been women.[223] According to the human rights organization, there has been "a considerable drop in the use of the death penalty since the early 1980s,"[224] and no one was executed in 1988.[225]

The most significant use of the death penalty in Cuba in recent years was the sentence and execution of four senior military officers in 1989. The four—Arnaldo Ochoa Sanchez, Jorge Martinez Valdes, Antonio de la Guardia Font, and Amado Padron Trujillo—were reportedly executed by firing squad under spotlights at four o'clock on the morning of 13 July.[226] Ten others were sentenced to prison terms ranging from ten to thirty years. All four of the condemned were accused of a multitude of criminal offenses, including drug trafficking, treason, and immoral conduct. The most serious charge—the only one that carried the death penalty—was that the men had carried out "hostile acts against a foreign state," essentially the most convenient charge on which to justify the executions. Most of the emphasis during the trial was on their betrayal of the trust of the Cuban people—especially the troops under their command—and the damage they had done to Cuba's international reputation. This aspect was put in very personal and emotional terms, with the prosecutor noting that the alleged ringleader General Ochoa had "betrayed Fidel."[227] There is evidence to suggest that the case was much more than an "ordinary" trial. The wholesale effort at character assassination is characteristic of a political show trial.[228] The trial may have been the outcome of a high stakes power struggle: Ochoa and his brother officers sought nothing less than the ouster of Castro and his brother Defense Minister Raul Castro.[229] The significance of this case lies in the fact that the condemned were purged regime elite. While certainly communist leaders have not hesitated to employ capital punishment to dispose of rivals,[230] they have largely refrained from using this measure in recent decades.

Cubans also feel strongly that the authorities should get tough on crime. Of 149 people surveyed in November 1988, fifty-six percent felt that the crime rate had increased since May when the new Criminal Code came into effect.[231] Thus, while the views of Cuban people cited by the authorities and official media on the harsh 1989 sentences on fourteen senior military men for treason and drug trafficking may not be true, accurate, or even representative of Cuban society, these opinions are quite plausible.

The authorities played up apparent public pressure for severe punishment and public approval of the outcome of the case. The prosecutor in his summary argument to the court stated: "Those men who fought in Angola ... have been betrayed by [General and prime scapegoat] Ochoa, and they are asking for justice."[232] Cuban radio reported a letter, sent to Castro by a brigade of Cubans serving in Nicaragua, expressing "indignation " over the "stain" on the "sacred name of the fatherland" by the Ochoa clique and insisting on "exemplary punishment."[233] Castro remarked to the State

Council on the outcome of the case, as reported on Havana television, that he was "obligated to be severe" on the sentence out of respect for the Cuba "internationalists" (i.e., soldiers and technicians working abroad) whom Ochoa had betrayed.[234] In radio interviews a Ministry of Interior worker, a doctor, and a student all claimed they approved of the sentences.[235]

The Death Penalty in East Germany

Before *the* abolition in East Germany in 1987, the death penalty could be imposed for offenses including murder under certain circumstances, aggression against the state, genocide, war crimes, treason, espionage, sabotage, and nine military offenses.[236] For at least seven years prior to its complete abolition, East Germany ceased to pass death sentences. Even before de facto abolition, use of capital punishment was very limited. In fact, between 1973 and 1976 it appears that only five persons were executed. Three of these were for murder and the others for genocide and espionage, respectively.[237]

This figure for executions does not include deaths of individuals shot while trying to cross illegally into West Germany. Amnesty International estimates deaths in this manner to number "less than 10" annually.[238] The strict and severe enforcement of border regulations by the government continued until the mid-1980s. The government announced in 1985 that all "automatic shooting devices" along its borders had been dismantled and declared its intention to remove all minefields. The government also reportedly revised its standing orders for border guards to shoot on sight any individuals attempting to flee the country. About the same time that the death penalty was abolished, border guards were given instructions to shoot only in cases of desertion of if they were attacked.[239]

According to the resolution that abolished capital punishment passed by the State Council in July 1987, "the criminal law serves to protect socialism, its citizens and their rights, and promotes the reform of the criminals to respect legality and act responsibly in society: it is not revenge or state retaliation against offenders."[240] The East German government's official reason for abolishing the death penalty was that it was no longer necessary. Its use was "based on the historical need to prosecute Nazi and war criminals, crimes against peace, humanity and human rights, as well as the most serious crimes against the sovereignty of the GDR and against the lives of its citizens." The resolution continued:

> As a result of the successful development of socialist society . . . [a] stable political, economic and social basis, which guarantees a high level of public order and security . . . the crime rate has gone down, so that today the GDR has one of the lowest crime rates in the world. The majority of crimes committed in the GDR are less serious. For years crimes of killing and other dangerous offenses involving violence here have been only a small proportion of all crimes.[241]

A crucial factor in the GDR government decision was the drop-off in the trials of former Nazis for crimes committed under Hitler. Significantly, the third paragraph of the resolution rationalizing the abolition of the death penalty states: "The GDR has fulfilled its national and international responsibility for the consistent punishment of Nazi and war crimes and the eradication of fascism and militarism." Interestingly, the extensive use of the death penalty in Hitler's Germany has been cited by a GDR legal scholar as further indication of the evil nature of that regime.[242] An added incentive to abolish the death penalty was that it would be favorably received by the Western world—a sign that the human rights situation was improving in East Germany—and would help the GDR to gain economic concessions from the West.

Analysis

The above case studies have shown that the institution of the death penalty has its own distinctive characteristics in each country. In the Soviet Union, a strong tradition of Russian humanitarianism has tempered the use of the death penalty at certain junctures in its history. In the case of the PRC, the death sentence suspended for two years seems to be a uniquely Chinese feature. In Cuba, the capital crime of pederasty appears to reflect the particularly strong sense of revulsion Cuban society has toward homosexuality. In the GDR, capital punishment has been viewed largely as a means to deal severely with the crimes of the Nazi past.

Nevertheless, these case studies also seem to possess certain common characteristics that suggest a core of attributes peculiar to the way socialist governments approach the subject of capital punishment. The four governments:

1. insist that the death penalty is a temporary measure
2. remain theoretically committed to the abolition of the death penalty
3. stress that capital punishment be used in a limited number of cases
4. insist capital punishment is to be used only for those who commit the most serious or terrible crimes
5. officially rationalize the death penalty on the grounds of its deterrent or educative value and to protect society, but in the final analysis most seem to justify its use to appease the public
6. generally, over time, tend to use the death penalty less and less, with the exception of a temporary rise—often during a period of economic liberalization

Socialist state constitutions and criminal codes tend to emphasize the inherent goodness of man and express confidence in the ability of the socialist system to mold a new socialist man. Socialist legal systems stress that criminals can be made to see the error of their ways. Thus punishment should serve to reform and educate the offender. The existence of crime and social deviance are blamed on lingering pernicious capitalist, bourgeois, feudal, or counter-revolutionary influences. Once these negative forces are stamped out, socialists reason, then virtually all crime will disappear.[243]

In the Soviet Union, China, and Cuba the rationale most often cited for use of the death penalty is that of deterrence. Its deterrent value, however, has not been convincingly documented or statistically demonstrated anywhere in the communist world. In fact complete statistics on crime and punishment are not made public in many communist countries. Neither China nor Cuba publishes statistics on the use of the death penalty.[244] The PRC does issue general statistics on crime and punishment, but condemned criminals are included together with all criminals sentenced to five or more years in prison.[245] In 1989 a Lithuanian legal scholar stated: "Scientific investigation results deny that the application of the death penalty decreases the incidence of crime." If this was the official rationale for its use, he said, then capital punishment ought to be abolished.[246]

Beneath the deterrence rationale lurks a less scientific argument for the continued use of the death penalty: retribution, or satisfaction of the general public's sense of justice. Governments seem to rely on public support for the death penalty to rationalize its use. That the majority of citizens in socialist states seem to favor the use of the death penalty is rarely examined in Western surveys of capital punishment in these countries.[247] While segments of a society, particularly intellectuals, may favor abolition of the death penalty, a majority of citizens appears to favor capital punishment for violent crimes such as murder.

The Evolution of Socialist Criminal Justice Systems

The preceding overview of the death penalty in four socialist legal systems suggests a general pattern of evolutionary change. The following is a tentative outline that may or may not be unique to socialism, and may be common to many revolutionary regimes.[248]

Stage One—The Terror Stage. This period begins with the seizure of power by the Communist party. The "revolution" is finally followed almost immediately by a concerted crackdown on selected opposition figures. This often includes mass roundups and arrests of elites from the old regime for "reeducation" or "reform" in prison camps, as well as numerous—although not completely indiscriminate—summary executions.[249] The emphasis at this stage is on counter-revolutionaries, reactionaries, or war criminals. The revolutionaries are intent on strengthening their hold on power by destroying their most serious enemies, intimidating opponents, and gaining support from the general population.

Stage Two—Routinization or Codification of Repression. A formalized court system is established and the criminal justice system becomes somewhat routinized. A specialized bureaucracy develops with its own institutional framework and standard operating procedures. A criminal code is promulgated or a set of codified regulations is distributed within the system (these may or may not be publicly disseminated).[250] Although the death penalty is included in the criminal code or regulations, generally its use significantly declines, especially for political crimes. The use of capital punishment for violent crimes, however, gradually increases.

Stage Three—Readjustment. After a decade or so of operation, the existing criminal code governing the criminal justice process undergoes significant revision. Revision often seems to occur after a new paramount leader assumes power.[251] A readjustment appears to parallel a period of economic liberalization. Reforms in the economy often are accompanied by a rise in corruption, and the leadership amends existing regulations to criminalize what it views as harmful economic activities. This can include an increase in the number of capital crimes, especially economic offenses.

Stage Four—Reform. The leadership launches a serious concerted effort to radically reform the criminal justice system. There may be efforts to decriminalize many offenses and provide leniency for first-time offenders. Maximum prison terms are often shortened, and a major effort is made to decrease the prison population. This has already occurred in Cuba and seems to be presently underway in the Soviet Union.[252] It is by no means clear whether East Germany had reached this stage in 1987. While the GDR did abolish the death penalty, the government remained extremely repressive.[253] At the same time, there may be public debate and pressure for greater attention to human rights. This appears to be a reflection of a natural awakening of social consciousness as well as the impact of Western notions of universal human rights. There are often calls, particularly from intellectual circles, for restrictions on the death penalty or for its complete abolition—especially for nonviolent crimes. Some segments of society may begin to view the death penalty as a barbaric and uncivilized measure that is incompatible with socialist legality and values.[254]

Stage Five—Pressures for Harsh Measures. In the Soviet Union and Cuba, which have both reached Stage Four, it is generally acknowledged that the crime rate has risen dramatically. As the criminal justice system is liberalizing and becoming more lenient, public pressures are growing for a renewed crackdown on crime. There will likely be demands for harsher penalties, including increased use of the death penalty. These pressures are fueled by dramatic incidents such as the killings of policemen in 1989 in both the Soviet Union and Cuba. In February 1989, two Soviet policemen were gunned down by criminals in the city of Gorky.[255] The following month a Cuban policeman was stabbed to death in a Havana street while trying to protect a woman from an assailant.[256] In China too the crime rate seems to have risen dramatically, and Chinese policemen have also been killed in the line of duty.[257] China, however, seems to have skipped Stage Four.

Generational change in leadership seems critical to this process of evolution. Those socialist legal systems that do not conform to the above pattern of evolution have often stagnated under the rule of an older generation of leaders. Thus, the extended rule of Castro in Cuba, and Mao and then Deng in China, may help explain why the natural evolution of the criminal justice system in both countries has been retarded or disrupted. New leaders do make a difference.[258] A rise in educational levels among the population may soften public support for the death penalty. Generally, the higher the level of education, the more likely it seems a person is to oppose capital punishment.[259] Certainly the distinctive culture of each country also plays an important role in the overall evolution of a criminal justice system—just as each culture helped shape the institution of the death penalty in the four case studies examined above.

Conclusion

The death penalty holds an interesting niche in socialist criminal law. It confronts socialist governments with a dilemma. The overriding principle of socialist criminal justice is reform of the offender. Most socialist governments argue that use of the death penalty is a temporary necessity that will eventually be abolished. At least two governments (the Soviet Union and Nicaragua) have abolished the death penalty shortly after seizing power.

While there has been no headlong rush among socialist countries to follow East Germany's example, there is a clearly discernible trend among some states toward limiting the use of the death penalty. These countries include Mongolia, Yugoslavia, and, most recently, Albania.[260] Cambodia abolished the death penalty under Article 35 of its new 1989 constitution. The new Romanian government abolished capital punishment in December 1989—although not until after it had executed deposed leader Nicholae Ceausescu and his wife after a perfunctory trial.[261] The new draft constitution of Mozambique made public in January 1990 contains an article abolishing the death penalty.[262]

Mao said: "Once a head is chopped off... it can't be restored."[263] Certainly the death penalty is a final solution offering no opportunity for reform of the condemned. Socialist governments thus tend to emphasize the educational role of capital punishment—its deterrent value. This correlates with Harold Berman's thinking on the subject of socialist legal systems. In an effort to find something truly socialist, he concluded that a "distinctive feature of Soviet law is its educational role."[264]

Is the death penalty socialist? Judging by the statements of Marx and Lenin and subsequent socialist leaders and theoreticians, the death penalty is not socialist. Rather, it is a necessary evil to be employed temporarily by a revolutionary government against dangerous and recalcitrant enemies of socialism or the revolution. This writer argues that the use of the death penalty in contemporary socialist criminal justice systems is *not* consistent with socialist values and the government's own professed goals. This is particularly so in the case of China. Most of those executed are common criminals, not counter-revolutionaries. Significant numbers of nonviolent criminals and petty offenders are executed, which also seems to run counter to socialist theory. In practice, socialist states view economic crime with particular seriousness. Indeed, Hazard considers the concept of economic crime to be a "major hallmark" of socialist legality.[265] In the Soviet Union and China certain economic crimes are capital offenses, but this is not the case in Cuba.[266]

If actual usage is not in accordance with socialist principles, then why is the death penalty used? It is employed because governments find it useful. It is a means of ridding society of some dangerous, troublesome, and/or antisocial elements. The death penalty is also a means of legitimizing the regime. The act of execution—as well as the process by which the accused are apprehended and sentenced—demonstrates graphically that the state apparatus is committed to, and capable of, keeping social order and providing a safe environment for its people. Furthermore, most public opinion surveys in countries around the world reveal that a clear majority of people favor the death penalty, particularly for violent criminals. The functioning of the criminal justice system provides the general populace with proof that justice is done, and thus enhances the credibility and status of a government in the eyes of the people. The appeals process in the criminal justice system is, as one scholar has noted, "particularly well suited to legitimizing the central authority and its policies."[267]

In the short term, chances for a reduction and/or greater uniformity in the application of the death penalty appear to be good in the Soviet Union. In Cuba, however, this step will probably have to await the death or overthrow of Castro. In China, the short-run prospects for a let up in the use of capital punishment are bleak—barring an unforeseen breakthrough such as the dramatic one recently achieved in South Africa.[268]

This writer believes that ultimately the death penalty will be abolished by all governments—including socialist ones. There appears to be a trend discernible today toward gradual abolition of capital punishment by a growing number of countries around the globe. Best thought of as a process rather than as an outcome, abolition generally seems to follow a clear and unmistakable pattern. First, the number of executions declines markedly, until they dwindle to a mere handful annually. Second, the death penalty is abolished de facto, initially through commutations and pardons, and then through discontinued use by the courts. Capital punishment then finally is abolished in law. This is essentially the course taken by East Germany.[269]

The glaring exception to this global trend appears to be China. Yet, in time, even the world's most populous state may eventually undergo the abolition process. An important indication of how long this process should take will come in 1997, when Beijing resumes sovereignty over Hong Kong. The territory, currently under British control, has had de facto abolition since 1966. About a dozen death sentences are meted out annually in local courts, but all are commuted to life imprisonment by the territory's British governor. Whether executions will resume in Hong Kong after 1997 following a thirty-year hiatus remains an unanswered question.[270] Beijing's attitude will be crucial in determining the death penalty's future in the territory. The fate of capital punishment in Hong Kong will also be a useful litmus test of the strength of the Chinese government's resolve for further sustained and vigorous use of this penalty in China as a whole.

In conclusion, while the eventual abolition of capital punishment appears inevitable, socialist governments seem destined to struggle with the issue for the foreseeable future. Perhaps the death penalty is best viewed as a hallmark of the contradictions evident in socialist criminal justice systems.

Notes

An earlier version of this chapter was presented to the "Seminar on Law in the Communist World" at the Columbia University School of Law, New York City, May 1990. I wish to thank R. Randle Edwards, John N. Hazard, Michele Bulatovic, Irene Liu, and fellow students in the seminar for their advice and comments.

1. Socialist governments that retained the death penalty in their criminal justice systems as of 1 Jan. 1990 included Albania, Angola, Bulgaria, Czechoslovakia, China, Cuba, Ethiopia, Hungary, Laos, Mongolia, Mozambique, North Korea, Poland, the Soviet Union, Vietnam, and Yugoslavia.

2. Leon Lipson, "Execution: Hallmark of 'Socialist Legality'," *Problems of Communism* [hereafter *PofC*] 11 (5) (Sept.–Oct. 1962): 21–26. Lipson also notes that capital punishment is inconsistent with socialist criminal justice theory.

3. The author recognizes that the definition of a socialist state is the subject of much debate. For more on this subject, see Stephen White, "What Is a Communist System?" *Studies in Comparative Communism* 16 (4) (Winter 1983): 247–63.

4. John N. Hazard, *Communists and Their Law: A Search for the Common Core of the Legal Systems of Marxian Socialist States* (Chicago, 1969), 8. All four countries that are the focus of this chapter are included in Hazard's list. There is, of course, far from unanimous agreement as to whether communist legal systems actually qualify as a distinct form. See, for example, Harold J. Berman, "What Makes 'Socialist Law' Socialist?" *PofC* 20 (5) (Sept.–Oct. 1971): 24–30.

5. The extent to which the trial is fair, merely a formality, and/or the outcome is predetermined is not at issue. Rather, there must be some effort to conform to a semblance of legal procedure. The degree of fairness with which the death penalty is administered will, however, be assessed later in this chapter. The distinction I am making is perhaps best captured by William Adams, "Capital Punishment and the Russian Revolution" (Ph.D. diss., Columbia University, 1968), 317–19.

6. Extrajudicial killings are defined as "deliberate killings of prisoners as well as killings of people who, while not in detention, are singled out for execution as a result of a policy at any level of government to eliminate specific individuals, or

groups or categories of individuals." See Amnesty International, (AI) *People's Republic of China: Preliminary Findings on Killings of Unarmed Civilians, Arbitrary Arrests and Summary Executions Since July 3, 1989* (New York, Aug. 1989), 7.

7. In the cases of Russia and Cuba, however, the situation was not clearcut. In the former, the provisional government that overthrew the Romanovs in March 1917 abolished the death penalty almost immediately, but then reintroduced it in July in an effort to turn around the rapidly deteriorating military situation in the war with Germany. The decree covered offenses by soldiers "at the front." In the latter, the capital punishment regulations in effect were temporary. The Cuban Constitution of 1940 had abolished the death penalty, but the government of Fulgencio Batista suspended the document in the 1950s. On Russia, see Adams, "Capital Punishment," 251, 280. On Cuba, see AI, "Cuba: Recent Developments Affecting the Situation of Political Prisoners and the Use of the Death Penaty" [*sic*] AI Index: AMR 25/04/88 (New York, Sept. 1988), 4.

8. For a survey of the use of the death penalty in countries around the world, see AI, *When the State Kills*... (New York, 1989).

9. Marx, "Capital Punishment," *New York Daily Tribune*, 18 Feb. 1853, cited in *Marx and Engels: Basic Writings on Politics and Philosophy* (Garden City, 1959), 487.

10. Ibid., 488.

11. Adams, "Capital Punishment," 222.

12. Ibid., 222–23.

13. Ibid., 247.

14. Ibid., 413, 427, 219, 312, 330, 314.

15. Cited in ibid., 300–301.

16. Cited in ibid., 321–22; Lipson, "Execution," n. 2 at 21.

17. Adams, "Capital Punishment," 342–46. The ruling was a surprise to many since at no point in the trial had a death sentence been mentioned as a possible punishment. The prosecutor merely urged the court to find Shchastny "guilty in full measure." There was also debate on the legal status of the death penalty. On the confusion, see ibid., 346–49.

18. Richard Pipes, *The Russian Revolution* (New York, 1990), chap. 17; Edvard Radzinsky, "Who Killed the Romanovs?" *New York Times* [hereinafter *NYT*], 20 July 1991, 19.

19. Adams, "Capital Punishment," 362–67.

20. The emphasis, however, has shifted among these aims, often to the neglect of the other one or two. "Revenge" has also been an important aim of the Soviet criminal justice system. See F. J. Feldbrugge, *Soviet Criminal Law: General Part* (Leyden, Holland, 1964), 199–200.

21. Cited in R. W. Makepeace, *Marxist Ideology and Soviet Criminal Law* (London, 1980), 104. These goals are consistent with those stated in the 1958 criminal code.

22. Adams, "Capital Punishment," 392; Lipson, "Execution," 23.

23. Quoted in Adams, "Capital Punishment," 413.

24. Ibid., 378–91.

25. Lipson, "Execution," 22.

26. Ger P. Van Den Berg, *The Soviet System of Justice: Figures and Policy* (Dordrecht, 1985), 87.

27. Makepeace, *Marxist Ideology*, 196.

28. Hazard, "Soviet Wartime Legislation," *Russian Review* (1942), cited in Makepeace, *Marxist Ideology*, 197–98.

29. Ibid., 204.

30. Cited in ibid., 142, 239.

31. Michael Dobbs, " 'You May Someday Have the Right to an Attorney, Comrade'," *Washington Post* [hereinafter *WP*] 26 Feb. 1989, A32.

32. The government also claimed it was necessary to counter foreign efforts to undermine the Soviet state (Lipson, "Execution," 22).

33. Robert Conquest, *The Great Terror: Stalin's Purges of the Thirties* (New York, 1968), 527–29.

34. Conquest, "Unearthing the Great Terror," *Orbis* 33 (2) (Spring 1989): 239–46. The bulk of this piece consists of a translation of an article that appeared in *Izvestiya* giving new revelations about killings near Minsk.

35. "Soviets Put Executions by Stalin at 786,000," *NYT*, 14 Feb. 1990, A10.

36. As cited in William E. Butler, *The Soviet Legal System: Selected Contemporary Legislation and Documents* (New York, 1978), 661–84. The Fundamental Principles of Criminal Procedure can also be found here.

37. Quoted in Lipson, "Execution," 26.

38. Adams, "Capital Punishment," 437.

39. Quoted in Harry Willets, "The Wages of Economic Sin," *PofC* 11 (5) (Sept.–Oct. 1961): 28.

40. Ibid.

41. AI, *The Death Penalty* (London, 1979), 138–39.

42. Lipson, "Execution," 24.

43. AI, *Death Penalty*, 131–33; "USSR: The Death Penalty Debate" EUR 46/40/87 (London, Nov. 1987), 1–3.

44. AI, *Death Penalty*, 137–38.

45. Ibid., 138.

46. See Valerii Konovalov, "Cases of Erroneous Passing of the Death Sentence in the Soviet Union," *Radio Liberty Research Bulletin* [hereinafter *RLRB*], 1 July 1987 (RL 248/87); and Valerii Konovalov, "The Mogilev Affair," *RLRB*, 11 Nov. 1987 (RL 446/87).

47. Berg, *Soviet System*, 109, and Table 119 at 310.

48. AI, *Death Penalty*, 132.

49. Ibid., 137.

50. Berg, *Soviet System*, 72.

51. AI, *Death Penalty*, 137.

52. Berg, *Soviet System*, 60–66, 72–73.

53. AI, *Death Penalty*, 137.

54. That this incident occurred was acknowledged several years ago, but the Soviets recently confirmed the matter to U.S. author Tom Clancy in early 1990. See a letter to the editor, "Hunt for Red October," *NYT*, 26 Mar. 1990, A16; and Jack Anderson and Dale Van Atta, " 'Red October' based on a real incident," *Patriot-News* (Harrisburg, Pa.), 26 Mar. 1990, A7. Clancy's best-seller, *The Hunt for Red October*, is based on this incident.

55. Berg, *Soviet System*, 102.

56. The last offense was added by a Jan. 1973 decree. See ibid., 267.

57. AI, "USSR," app.

58. Moscow *Argumenty I Fakty*, 4–10 Mar. 1989, cited in Foreign Broadcast Information Service, *Daily Report: Soviet Union* [hereinafter FBIS-SOV], 8 Mar. 1989, 18–19.

59. Dobbs, "You May Someday Have the Right to an Attorney."

60. Felicity Barringer, "At Moscow Trial, Some Unlikely Court Theatrics," *NYT*, 6 Sept. 1988, A5. The "theatrics" were "worthy of an American trial lawyer."

61. AI, *Death Penalty*, 133, 135.

62. Tass International Service, 17 Dec. 1988, cited in FBIS-SOV, 19 Dec. 1988, 30.

63. AI, *Death Penalty*, 134.

64. Ibid., 134, 135.

65. Ibid., 136.

66. See Paris AFP in English, 2 Aug. 1988, cited in FBIS-SOV, 2 Aug. 1988, 47–48; Moscow Tass, 10 Nov. 1988, cited in FBIS-SOV, 14 Nov. 1988, 77; AI, *When the State Kills*, 224.

67. Mikhail Gorbachev, *Perestroika: New Thinking for Our Country and the World* (New York, 1987), 109.

68. *Izvestiya*, 17 Dec. 1988, cited in FBIS-SOV, 18 Dec. 1988, 29.

69. Julia Wishnevsky, "Draft Principles of Soviet Criminal Legislation Published," *Radio Liberty Report on the USSR* 1(2) (13 Jan. 1989): 2.

70. *Izvestiya*, 17 Dec. 1988, cited in FBIS-SOV, 18 Dec. 1988, 29.

71. For a comprehensive and up-to-date look at the inferior status of women in Soviet law, see Laurie Essig, "Perestroika and the Woman's Question," paper presented to the "Seminar on Law in the Communist World" at Columbia University School of Law, Apr. 1990.

72. Adams, "Capital Punishment," 59. Makepeace states: "Russia has a very long history of hostility to the death penalty, dating back to the . . . eleventh century" (*Marxist Ideology*, 78).

73. Wishnevsky, "Draft Principles," 2.

74. *Izvestiya*, 17 Dec. 1988, excerpts cited in FBIS-SOV, 18 Dec. 1988, 28–30.

75. Moscow *Izvestiya*, 4 Aug. 1988, cited in FBIS-SOV, 5 Aug. 1988, 26–27.

76. Hazard, *Communists and Their Law*, 448.

77. Sofia Kelina, "Returning to the Theme: Death Penalty: What Has Changed in Two Years," *Moscow News Weekly* (in English) [hereinafter *MNW*], 9–16 July 1989, 15.

78. Moscow domestic service, 12 June 1989, cited in FBIS-SOV, 20 June 1989, 73.

79. He believes the Soviet public was much like the public in Western countries in this regard. " 'MN' Interview: Chinese Variant: Causes and Results," *MNW*, 9–16 July 1989, 6. Interestingly, the comments were made in reference to the use of the death penalty by the Chinese government in the aftermath of 4 June 1989.

80. A growing minority, however, reportedly favor its complete abolition. Sofia Kelina LLD, "Death Penalty: What Has Changed in Two Years," in ibid., 15.

81. Valerii Konovalov, "The Death Penalty in the USSR, 1987," *RLRB*, 25 Jan. 1988 (RL 41/88), 2.

82. " 'MN' Interview."

83. For a survey of the history of Western influence on Russia and its impact,

see Donald W. Treadgold, *The West in Russia and China*, vol. 1, *Russia, 1472–1917* (New York, 1973).

84. Gorbachev, *Perestroika*, 194–95. Gorbachev also refers to Russia's historic ties with Europe at 191.

85. See letters to the editor commenting on the new draft Fundamentals of Criminal Legislation made public in December 1988. *Izvestiya*, 13 Jan. 1989, cited in FBIS-SOV, 27 Jan. 1989, 72, 73, quote from 73; Konovalov, "Death Penalty in the USSR, 1987," 2.

86. Konovalov, "Death Penalty in the USSR, 1987," 3.

87. Yu. Kudryavtsev, *Nedelya*, 19–25 Oct. 1987, cited in *Current Digest of the Soviet Press* [hereinafter *CDSP*] 39 (42) (1987): 6.

88. Moscow *Izvestiya*, 25 Jan. 1989, cited in FBIS-SOV, 26 Jan. 1989, 67–68.

89. *Pravda*, 8 Dec. 1988, cited in FBIS-SOV, 8 Dec. 1988, 17.

90. Jerry Hough, *Russia and the West: Gorbachev and the Politics of Reform*, 2d ed. (New York, 1990), 29–30. At least one Soviet legal expert, Arkady Vaksberg, has cautioned against attaching too much significance to the influence of Gorbachev's legal training on his political outlook. Lecture given by Vaksberg at the Wilson Center of the Smithsonian Institution, Washington, D.C., 11 Apr. 1989.

91. *Pravda*, 5 Dec. 1988, cited in FBIS-SOV, 6 Dec. 1988, 110–11. For more on the hijacking, see Moscow Tass [in English], 2 Dec. 1988, cited in FBIS-SOV, 2 Dec. 1989, 38–39.

92. Moscow domestic service, 12 June 1989, cited in FBIS-SOV, 20 June 1989, 73.

93. Execution statistics were "declassified" and full disclosure was promised. See Moscow *Izvestiya*, 17 Jan. 1991, cited in *CDSP* 43 (3) (1991): 30. In 1989 Soviet authorities published crime statistics for the first time. See Moscow *Izvetiya*, 15 Feb. 1989, cited in FBIS-SOV, 1 Mar. 1989, 76–77.

94. He did not specify an exact time period or give any hard data. Moscow Tass International Service, 1 Mar. 1989, cited in FBIS-SOV, 2 Mar. 1989, 79.

95. Konovalov, "Death Penalty in the USSR, 1987," 1.

96. AI, *When the State Kills*, 224, 225.

97. In the two most serious cases, two pairs of partners in crime received death sentences. In the first case a police officer and a former CPSU member with a university education were convicted of murder, attempted murder, and extortion in Donetsk. See Moscow *Izvestiya*, 23 June 1988, cited in FBIS-SOV, 29 June 1988, 83–84. The second case concerned two men convicted of murder, robbery, and "malicious hooliganism" stemming from ethnic unrest in the Republic of Uzbekistan. See *Izvestiya*, cited in *CDSP* 41 (44) (1989): 27–28. Two cases appear directly related to growing ethnic strife in Central Asia. The first case is that of a Kazahk student, mentioned earlier, whose death sentence for the murder of a policeman was commuted by the Presidium of the Supreme Soviet in mid–1988. Another interethnic case concerns an Azerbaijani convicted for murder and inciting mob violence against Armenians in the city of Sumgait in February 1988. See *WP*, 20 Nov. 1988, A31. In another case the ringleader of a criminal gang—a sixth-year medical student—was sentenced to death for several murders and numerous robberies. The gang's arsenal included grenade launchers and a machine gun. See *Izvestiya*, 20 Nov. 1989, cited in *CDSP* 41 (47) (1989): 30–31.

98. Moscow Tass in English, 8 Aug. 1988, cited in FBIS-SOV, 9 Aug. 1988, 52; "Book-keeper to Die," *Financial Times* (London), 15 Dec. 1988, 2.

99. AI, *Death Penalty*, 137; Konovalov, "Death Penalty in the USSR, 1987," 1.

100. "Strike Surely, Accurately and Relentlessly in Suppressing Counter-revolutionaries," *Selected Works of Mao Tse-tung*, 5 vols. (Beijing, 1969–77) [hereinafter *SWMTT*], 5:53–56.

101. See *The Secret Speeches of Chairman Mao: From the Hundred Flowers to the Great Leap Forward*, ed. Roderick MacFarquhar, Timothy Cheek, and Eugene Wu (Cambridge, Mass., 1989), 142. Zhou Enlai reported that 830,000 people were "destroyed" in the years up until 1954. See Edgar Snow, *The Other Side of the River*, cited in Jerome Alan Cohen, *The Criminal Process in the People's Republic of China, 1949–1963: An Introduction* (Cambridge, 1968), 543–44.

102. Shao-chuan Leng, *Justice in Communist China: A Survey of the Judicial System of the Chinese People's Republic* (New York, 1967), 166–67; Stephen B. Davis, "The Death Penalty and Legal Reform in the PRC," *Journal of Chinese Law* 1 (2) (Fall 1987): 310.

103. Harry Harding, "The Chinese State in Crisis," in *The Cambridge History of Modern China*, vol. 15, *Revolutions within the Chinese Revolution, 1966–1979*, ed. Roderick MacFarquhar and John K. Fairbank (Cambridge University Press, forthcoming).

104. See Roger Garside, *Coming Alive: China after Mao* (New York, 1981), 278–84; AI, *China: Violations of Human Rights: Prisoners of Conscience and the Death Penalty in the People's Republic of China* (London, 1984), 74–75. Officials have also acknowledged at least one other execution of an innocent victim on trumped-up charges. See ibid., 75.

105. Guo Daohu, *"Lun juyou zhongguo tese sixing zhidu"* [The distinguishing features of China's institution of the death penalty], in *Mao Zedong sixiang faxue lilun lunwenxuan* [Selected papers on Mao Zedong thought concerning legal theory] (Falü chubanshe, Dec. 1985), 133–34.

106. Ibid., 146.

107. Teaching and Research Office for Criminal Law of the Central Political-Legal Cadre's School, ed., *Zhonghua Renmin Gongheguo xingfa zongze jiangyi* [Lectures on the general principles of criminal law of the People's Republic of China], cited in Cohen, *Criminal Process*, 538.

108. See Mao, "Strike Surely, Accurately and Relentlessly"; and "Combat Bureaucracy, Commandism and Violations of the Law and Discipline," both in *SWMTT*, 5: 5, 56, 86.

109. "Lectures," 538, 535. For examples of this rationale from the early 1980s, see *Beijing Ribao*, 19 July 1981, cited in FBIS, *Daily Report: China* [hereinafter FBIS-CHI], 29 July 1981, R/2; and "Crime and Justice," *China Reconstructs*, Aug. 1984, 39.

110. Cited in Davis, "Death Penalty," 327. Davis also concludes that public support for capital punishment is a significant factor in its continued use.

111. See Cohen, *Criminal Process*, 535–36.

112. For a more complete list of capital crimes as of 1987, see Andrew Scobell, "Strung Up Or Shot Down?: The Death Penalty in Hong Kong and China and

Implications for Post–1997," *Case Western Reserve Journal of International Law* 20 (1) (Winter 1988): 150–54.

113. A counter-revolutionary crime is defined in Article 103 of the Criminal Law as one committed with the intention of "overthrowing the political power of the dictatorship of the proletariat and the socialist system."

114. "Decision on the Severe Punishment of Criminal Elements Who Seriously Endanger Public Security," cited in *The Criminal Law*, 241–45.

115. The law apparently applies literally just to the act of making information public—not giving the information to a foreign government—about virtually any sphere of activity in China. See Xinhua, 5–6 Sept. 1988, cited in FBIS-CHI, 6 Sept. 1988, 31–33.

116. "Uphold the Four Cardinal Principles" (30 Mar. 1979), in *Selected Works of Deng Xiaoping (1975–1982)* (Beijing, 1984) [hereinafter *SWDXP*], 176.

117. *Renmin Ribao* [hereinafter *RMRB*], 9 Apr. 1989, cited in FBIS-CHI, 2 May 1989, 84. There is no precise definition of what constitutes an "economic crime" either in Chinese law, or in the literature on the subject. This allows the authorities much latitude in dealing with cases labeled as such. The broad definition of economic crime includes infractions such as bribery and embezzlement, and normally involves economic losses to the state. See Deborah E. Townsend, "The Concept of Law in Post-Mao China: A Case Study of Economic Crime," *Stanford Journal of International Law* 24 (1) (Fall 1987): 239–42. For some definitions of what constitutes economic crime, see "Act of the PRC for Punishment of Corruption," promulgated in April 1952, cited in Cohen, *Criminal Process*, 308–11; "Decision of the CCP Central Committee and the State Council on dealing blows at serious criminal activities in the economic field," cited in FBIS-CHI, 14 Apr. 1982, K/1–K/9.

118. 10 Mar. 1982, cited in AI, *China*, 57.

119. "Decision of the Standing Committee of the National People's Congress Regarding the Severe Punishment of Criminals Who Seriously Undermine the Economy," 8 Mar. 1982, cited in *The Criminal Law*, 229–40.

120. "Combat Economic Crime," 10 April 1982, in *SWDXP*, 381.

121. Xinhua, 21 Jan. 1988, cited in FBIS-CHI, 22 Jan. 1988, 9.

122. "Supplementary Regulations on Punishment for Crimes of Corruption and Bribery," cited in FBIS-CHI, 2 Feb. 1988, 14–16.

123. "Provisional Regulations of the PRC on Punishing Servicemen Who Commit Offenses Against Their Duties," cited in AI, *China*, 57.

124. Criminal Law, Article 2. This code appears, along with the Criminal Procedure Law and several amendments, conveniently in both Chinese and English in *The Criminal Law*.

125. "Lectures," 81.

126. "Talk at a Meeting of the Standing Committee of the Political Bureau of the Central Committee (17 Jan. 1986)," in Deng Xiaoping, *Fundamental Issues in Present Day China* (Beijing, 1987), 137–38.

127. See, for example, An Zhiguo, "On Capital Punishment," an editorial in *Beijing Review* [hereinafter *BR*], 7 Nov. 1983, 4.

128. John F. Copper, Franz Michael, and Yuan-li Wu, *Human Rights in Post-Mao China* (Boulder, 1985), 109, 111, Table 5.

129. "Provisional Act on Lawyers of the People's Republic of China," cited in

Shao-chuan Leng and Hungdah Chiu, *Criminal Justice in Post-Mao China: Analysis and Documents* (Albany, 1985), 272.

130. Ibid., 95.

131. Xinhua, 24 June 1989, cited in FBIS-CHI, 26 June 1989, 44; AI, *Preliminary Findings*, 45.

132. See Margaret Y. K. Woo, "The Right to a Criminal Appeal in the People's Republic of China," *Yale Journal of International Law* 14 (1) (1989): 134–36, and n. 126. The right of appeal is given in Article 129, CrPL.

133. AI, *China*, 66–67.

134. Cited in Woo, "Right to a Criminal Appeal," 138. The defendant was convicted of murdering his lover's husband.

135. AI, *China*, 71. The president receives his power to pardon convicted criminals in Article 80, 1982 PRC Constitution.

136. "Decision of the Standing Committee of the National People's Congress Regarding the Procedure for Rapidly Adjudicating Cases Involving Criminal Elements Who Seriously Endanger Public Security," cited in *The Criminal Law*, 246–47.

137. "Decision of the Standing Committee of the National People's Congress Regarding the Question of Approval of Cases Involving Death Sentences," cited in ibid., 217–19.

138. Copper et al., *Human Rights*, 109–13, esp. Table 6.

139. AI, *China*, 69.

140. The culprit, an embezzler, committed the offenses between August 1984 and February 1985. He was sentenced to death and executed in October 1989 after a four-year trial. See Beijing Xinhua, 26 Oct. 1989, cited in FBIS-CHI, 30 Oct. 1989, 67.

141. "Wife first heard of execution 'on TV'," *South China Morning Post* [hereinafter *SCMP*] (Hong Kong), 28 May 1986, 10.

142. Davis, "Death Penalty," 319; Leng and Chiu, *Criminal Justice*, 137; Radio October Storm (clandestine broadcast), 12 Jan. 1984, cited in FBIS-CHI, 20 Jan. 1984, K/18–K/19.

143. For an eyewitness account, see "A Glimpse of China's Hidden Face of Fear in the Killing Fields," *SCMP*, 19 July 1987, 9. This humiliation of the condemned is also noted by AI. See *Amnesty International Report 1987* (London, 1987), 227–28.

144. For examples, see Michael Weisskopf, "China Says Crime Cut; Executions Up," *WP*, 21 Jan. 1984, A1, A20; "A Glimpse of China's Hidden Face"; and AI, *China*, 73–74. The June 1989 executions of three Shanghai men were reportedly carried out in public. See *NYT*, 22 June 1989, A1, A10.

145. Executioners allegedly give their full cooperation—going so far as to shoot the condemned in the heart instead of the head if the eyes are the desired organs for transplantation. See Jon Swain, "Executed Chinese Used as Organ Donors," *Sunday Observer* (London), 24 June 1990, 24.

146. "Anti-Crime Drive Brings Results," *BR*, 18–24 Apr. 1988, 11.

147. Leng and Chiu, *Criminal Justice*, 137.

148. "Recent Wave of Executions in Red China," *Inside China Mainland* (Nov. 1983): 11–14.

149. U.S. Department of State (USDOS), *Country Reports on Human Rights Practices for 1985* (Washington, D.C., Feb. 1986) [hereinafter *CRHRP 1985*], 738.

150. Leng and Chiu, *Criminal Justice*, 146.

151. Copper et al., *Human Rights*, app., Table 8 at 115.

152. Ibid., app., Tables 1 and 2 at 106–7. The President of the SPC claimed political offenses constitute less than one percent of total crime (FBIS-CHI, 27 June 1983, K/3).

153. Ibid., Table 8 at 115; and "Recent Wave of Executions."

154. Copper et al., *Human Rights*, Tables 1 and 2 at 106–7.

155. *RMRB*, 9 Apr. 1989, cited in FBIS-CHI, 2 May 1989, 75. Liu told the NPC in March 1989 that only 74 of 5,911 offenders sentenced were given "punishment greater than life imprisonment." Presumably this figure includes some death sentences suspended for two years.

156. Davis, "Death Penalty," 320.

157. See Copper et al., *Human Rights*, 117; and app., Table 8 at 115–16.

158. *SCMP*, 1 May 1988, cited in FBIS-CHI, 4 May 1988, 34–35.

159. If suspended death sentences are included, the percentage of CCP members remains almost the same (3.8 percent or 9 of 235). See Copper et al., *Human Rights*, app., at 113–17, Table 8 at 115–16.

160. See Leng and Chiu, *Criminal Justice*, 108; *Hsin Pao*, 30 Nov. 1983, cited in FBIS-CHI, 1 Dec. 1983, W/3–W/4.

161. The racket was also extensive and involved numerous work units on Hainan Island. See Zhongguo Tongxunshi, 28 May 1986, cited in FBIS-CHI, 30 May 1986, W/7; and Harry Harding, *China's Second Revolution: Reform after Mao* (Washington, D.C., 1987), 150.

162. Leng and Chiu, *Criminal Justice*, 141–42; AI, *China*, 59–61.

163. "Crackdown on Crime Stressed," *BR*, 8–14 Aug. 1988, 6–7. See also "Young Delinquents Cause Concern," in ibid., 11 May 1988, 8–9.

164. See article by a Hong Kong journalist after a visit to a Nanjing prison. Hong Kong *Ta Kung Pao*, 6 Nov. 1989, cited in FBIS-CHI, 15 Nov. 1989, 58–60.

165. "*Taibao Luo Peiliang Taiyuan Zaoyu Jishi*" [The true account of Taiwan compatriot Luo Peiliang's Taiyuan encounter], *RMRB* overseas edition, 11 Dec. 1987, 4.

166. Public notice of execution in Kunming, Yunnan, Oct. 1983.

167. *Amnesty International Report 1986* (London, 1986), 218–19.

168. Ibid., *1988* (London, 1988), 156.

169. This estimate is derived from figures obtained from the following sources. See SPC work report, which gives the number of death sentences appealed to the court over a five-year period, cited by Xinhua and cited in FBIS-CHI, 27 June 1983, K/7. USDOS, *Country Reports on Human Rights Practices for 1986* (Washington, D.C., 1987), 684.

170. Ibid. (The first figure is from the SPC work report, the others are from the U.S. Department of State.)

171. AI, *When the State Kills*, 122–23.

172. This, of course, is not to say that these reports should be completely discounted. On the rumors, see *Ming Pao*, 15 June 1989, cited in FBIS-CHI, 15 June 1989, 16; Sheryl WuDunn, "China Said to Continue Arrests Quietly," *NYT*, 17 July 1989, A3; AI, *Preliminary Findings*, 46. For a critical assessment of the foreign

press coverage of the government suppression of 1989 student movement, see 'Tiananmen: What Did Happen?" *Asiaweek* (Hong Kong), 22–29 Dec. 1989, 30–33. A major criticism is the inflated and inaccurate casualty figures bandied about by the Hong Kong and Western press. Of course, the absence of official figures for death sentences and executions invites such speculation.

173. For an examination of these "extrajudicial" killings, see AI, *Preliminary Findings*.

174. On estimates on the numbers of arrests, allegations of torture, and deaths of detainees, see ibid., 27–38; WuDunn, "China Said to Continue Arrests Quietly."

175. *Wen Hui Po* (Hong Kong), 28 June 1989, cited in FBIS-CHI, 28 June 1989, 11–12.

176. See AI, *Preliminary Findings*, 45–46. Lowell Dittmer cited a figure of "around 26" executions. See Dittmer, "China in 1989: The Year of Incomplete Reform," *Asian Survey* 30 (1) (Jan. 1990): 34.

177. Beijing Xinhua Hong Kong service, 25 Aug. 1989, cited in FBIS-CHI, 30 Aug. 1989, 43–44.

178. Hunan provincial service, 22 June 1989, cited in FBIS-CHI, 23 June 1989, 28. For examples of other rioters who received prison terms, see Beijing domestic service, 16 Aug. 1989, cited in FBIS-CHI, 17 Aug. 1989, 48–49; Beijing Zhongguo Xinwenshi, 9 Oct. 1989, cited in FBIS-CHI, 11 Oct. 1989, 57.

179. See also Beijing domestic service, 17 June 1989, cited in FBIS-CHI, 19 June 1989, 25–26; Hong Kong AFP, 2 Nov. 1989, cited in FBIS-CHI, 3 Nov. 1989, 54.

180. Most press reports of the riots that occurred in Chinese cities in the summer of 1989 state that students were not involved. See, for example, Beijing Xinhua Hong Kong service, 25 Aug. 1989, cited in FBIS-CHI, 30 Aug. 1989, 44. Chinese leaders, such as CCP Secretary Jiang Zemin, have emphasized that misguided students who participated in the spring 1989 protests would receive lenient treatment while those who committed violent acts would be swiftly and severely dealt with and could expect "not even one iota of forgiveness." See "Jiang Reiterates Party's Policies," *BR*, 10–16 July 1989, 7.

181. Scobell, "The Death Penalty in Post-Mao China," *China Quarterly* 123 (Sept. 1990): 515.

182. *RMRB*, 18 Jan. 1984, cited in FBIS-CHI, 23 Jan. 1984, K/7.

183. Guo Daohui, "The Distinguishing Features"; Xing Zhong, "*Shilun sihuan zhidu de biyaoxing*" [Examining the necessity of the institution of the suspended death sentence], both in *Mao Zedong sixiang faxue lilun*, 133–47 and 148–55, respectively.

184. Guo, "Distinguishing Features," 133. See also, An Zhiguo, "Truth of Executing Criminals in Tibet," *BR*, 17 Oct. 1983, 5. This editorial tries to counter Western criticism of the execution of six persons in Tibet. The editor insists that all six, including two Tibetans, were not political dissidents, but hardened criminals.

185. R. Randle Edwards, "Civil and Social Rights: Theory and Practice Today," in *Human Rights in Contemporary China*, ed. R. Randle Edwards, Louis Henkin, and Andrew J. Nathan (New York, 1986), 54. See also Nicholas D. Kristof, "Law and Order in China Means More Executions," *NYT*, 15 Jan. 1991, A2.

186. A poll was taken in the mid–1970s of students at the University of Hong Kong. Of the 500 responses, more than 90 percent favored the death penalty for premeditated murder while a majority also favored execution for three other offenses

(rape, armed robbery, and bodily harm). P. B. Harris, "The British Parliament, The University of Hong Kong" (unpublished manuscript, 1975). Other smaller and more impromptu polls show similar findings. See, for example, P. Choy, "Survey Shows What the Public Thinks: 'Death for Killers,' " *Sunday Post-Herald* (Hong Kong), 29 Apr. 1973, 2. A 1990 survey found more than 70 percent of those polled favored retention of the death penalty after 1997, when the territory reverts to Chinese control. See *International Herald Tribune* [hereinafter *IHT*], 6 Nov. 1990, 7. On the peculiar circumstances surrounding the death penalty in Hong Kong, see Scobell, "Strung Up or Shot Down?"

187. A national survey conducted in early 1989 showed that personal safety (i.e., the threat of crime) was a serious concern for urbanites (Xinhua, 10 May 1989, cited in FBIS-CHI, 16 May 1989, 61–62).

188. *Wen Wei Po* (Hong Kong), 4 Apr. 1988, cited in FBIS-CHI, 12 Apr. 1988, 39. The actual method of execution stipulated in Article 45 of the 1979 Criminal Code is by shooting.

189. See, for example, Derk Bodde and Clarence Morris, *Law in Imperial China: Exemplified by 190 Ch'ing Dynasty Cases* (Philadelphia, 1967), 138.

190. Xing, "Examining the Necessity," 148. The author does not note the pre–1949 history of the measure, and credits Mao with the concept.

191. Scobell, "Strung Up or Shot Down?" 159. The warden of the Shanghai Municipal Prison told a group of visiting American legal scholars in 1981 that no prisoners in the institution with suspended death sentences had ever been executed. See Leng and Chiu, *Criminal Justice*, n. 23 at 157. This was apparently the case in Mao's day and, interestingly, also true during the Qing dynasty. See a 1959 statement by Minister of Public Security Luo Ruiqing, and Edgar Snow, *The Other Side of the River*, both cited in Cohen, *Criminal Process*, 539. On the Qing dynasty, see Bodde and Morris, *Law in Imperial China*, 138. For a discussion of the significance of the suspended death sentence, see *RMRB*, 4 Jan. 1980, cited in FBIS-CHI, 22 Jan. 1980, L/11–L/12.

192. Xing, "Examining the Necessity," 155. It is quite likely that this proportion, rather than being based on hard statistical data, merely parrots Mao's words as they are recorded in "Strike Surely, Accurately and Relentlessly," in *SWMTT*, 5: 55. Mao says that only 10–20 percent of all counter-revolutionaries sentenced to death should actually be executed.

193. An Zhiguo, "Notes from the Editors: On Capital Punishment," *BR*, 7 Nov. 1983, 4.

194. "Chinese Execute 2 Tibetan Prisoners," *IHT*, 30 May 1990, 2. For more details of the alleged escape plot itself, see Lhasa television, 18 May 1990, cited in FBIS-CHI, 21 May 1990, 56.

195. See ibid.; Leng and Chiu, *Criminal Justice*, 132; AI, *China*, 64–65. The suspended death sentence was also widely used in Qing China. See Bodde and Morris, *Law in Imperial China*, 138; Wang Hui-tsu, "Seek to Preserve Life," cited in Sybille Van Der Sprenkel, *Legal Institutions in Manchu China: A Sociological Analysis* (London, 1962), 140.

196. Leng and Chiu, *Criminal Justice*, 132.

197. Scobell, "Strung Up or Shot Down?" 159.

198. Jiang and Zhang were also convicted of more than thirty murders and held responsible for the deaths of thousands of others. See *A Great Trial in Chinese*

History: The Trial of the Lin Biao and Jiang Qing Counter-Revolutionary Cliques, Nov. 1980–Jan. 1981 (Beijing, 1981), 205–19. Zhang also had his death sentence commuted to life imprisonment. See the SPC president's work report in FBIS-CHI, 27 June 1983, K/2–K/3.

199. Ross Terill, *The White-Boned Demon: A Biography of Madame Mao Zedong* (New York, 1984), 393.

200. See, for example, an article by the Minister of Public Security in *RMRB*, 28 Sept. 1959, cited in Cohen, *Criminal Process*, 539; and for a more recent claim, see *RMRB*, 4 Jan. 1980, cited in FBIS-CHI, 21 Jan. 1980, L/11–L/12.

201. Communication from Randle Edwards, Columbia University School of Law, Apr. 1990.

202. "*Zhongguo tansuo gaizao fanrende xintujing*" [China explores new avenues for convicts to better themselves], *RMRB* overseas edition, 12 Oct. 1988, 4.

203. Adele G. van der Plas, *Revolution and Criminal Justice: The Cuban Experiment, 1959–1983*, trans. Peter Mason (Dordrecht, Holland, 1987), 11, and n. 16 at 26–27.

204. Cited in AI, "Cuba," app. 2.

205. All twenty-one offenses are listed in ibid.

206. Plas, *Revolution*, 145.

207. AI, "Cuba," 25.

208. Havana Moncada, Jan. 1989, cited in FBIS, *Daily Report: Latin America* [hereinafter FBIS-LAT], 7 Apr. 1989, 6.

209. AI, "Cuba," 14.

210. Cited in AI, "Cuba," 25.

211. Ibid., 3–4, 23.

212. Ibid., 3.

213. USDOS, *CRHRP 1985*, 485.

214. AI, "Cuba," 23.

215. Ibid., 23–24.

216. Havana radio and television, 6 July 1989, cited in FBIS-LAT, 11 July 1989, 3–10.

217. AI, "Cuba," 4; AI, *When the State Kills*, 126.

218. AI, "Cuba," 25; AI, *When the State Kills*, 126.

219. On the appeals process, see Havan International Service, 9 July 1989, and Havana Radio Rebelde, 10 June 1989, both cited in FBIS-LAT, 10 July 1989, 1–2. On Castro's remarks, see Havana Rebelde Television, 12 July 1989, cited in FBIS-LAT, 12 July 1989, 1.

220. AI, "Cuba," 26.

221. *Amnesty International Report 1983* (London, 1984), 130.

222. AI, "Cuba," 26.

223. Ibid.

224. Ibid., 4.

225. AI, *When the State Kills*, 126.

226. Paris AFP, 9 Nov. 1989, cited in FBIS-LAT, 9 Nov. 1989, 4.

227. Prosecutor's closing statement broadcast on Havana radio and television, 6 July 1989, cited in FBIS-LAT, 11 July 1989, 3.

228. See the prosecutor's closing statement broadcast on Havana radio and television, 6 July 1989, cited in FBIS-LAT, 11 July 1989, 3–10.

229. This is the account given by a French journalist and Cuban exile with information from a letter allegedly written by Padron shortly before his arrest. According to this version of events, the four officers were executed for "plotting to overthrow Castro." See Paris AFP, 9 Nov. 1989, cited in FBIS-LAT, 9 Nov. 1989, 4. See also Madrid EFE, 10 July 1989, cited in FBIS-LAT, 11 July 1989, 11. To refute this "imperialist propaganda," the National Cuban Lawyers Union issued a statement insisting that it was not a "political trial," but another example of the "ordinary penal process" at work (Havana television, 7 July 1989, cited in FBIS-LAT, 10 July 1989, 2).

230. Myron Rush, *How Communist States Change Their Rulers* (Ithaca, 1974), 305–9.

231. Madrid EFE, 7 Nov. 1988, cited in FBIS-LAT, 8 Nov. 1988, 6. The 1987 code eliminated certain crimes and generally lowered penalties across the board.

232. Havana radio and television, 6 July 1989, cited in FBIS-LAT, 11 July 1989, 4.

233. Radio Rebelde, 8 July 1989, cited in FBIS-LAT, 10 July 1989, 3.

234. Havana Rebelde television, 12 July 1989, cited in FBIS-LAT, 12 July 1989, 1.

235. Radio Rebelde, 7 July 1989, cited in FBIS-LAT, 10 July 1989, 3.

236. AI, *Death Penalty*, 115–17. For a full listing, see "The Penal Code of the GDR," (1968), cited in *Law and Legislation in the German Democratic Republic* 1–2 (Berlin, 1979).

237. See AI, *When the State Kills*, 74; AI, *Death Penalty*, 116.

238. See ibid., 117.

239. USDOS, *CRHRP 1985*, 980. On the changing of orders to border guards, see *Die Welt* (Bonn), 25 Sept. 1987, cited in FBIS, *Daily Report: Eastern Europe* [hereinafter FBIS-EEU] 29 Sept. 1987, 14. The orders were apparently issued personally by the former East German leader Erich Honecker. See *NYT*, 2 Dec. 1990, 23.

240. "Resolution of the GDR State Council on the Abolition of the Death Penalty" (17 July 1987), ADN International Service, 17 July 1987, cited in FBIS-EEU, 20 July 1987, G5–G6.

241. Ibid.

242. John Lekschas, "Critique of Bourgeois Criminology," in *Socialist Criminology: Theoretical and Methodical Foundations*, ed. Erich Buchholz et al., trans. Ewald Osers (Westmead, Farnborough, Hants., 1974), 115–16.

243. For an overview of Marx and Engels on crime, see Makepeace, *Marxist Ideology*, 29–36.

244. On China and Cuba, see AI, *When the State Kills*, 122, 126. This lack of complete information on death sentences and executions also holds true for the GDR. Researchers can only estimate the number of death sentences and executions based on press reports and occasional public statements and fragmentary data issued by officials. In China information can also be gathered from public notices of execution. These notices are important sources of information. They give details of the defendant and his/her crime. A large scarlet check across the notice indicates that the defendant has been executed. See *Far Eastern Economic Review* (Hong Kong), 16 Feb. 1984, 13–14.

245. See Townsend, "Concept of Law," 248–49. For example, the SPC president reported that 30.8 percent of the 368,790 criminals sentenced during 1988 were given punishments of "death or prison terms of at least five years up to life." See Beijing Xinhua [in English], 29 Mar. 1989, cited in FBIS-CHI, 29 Mar. 1989, 24.

246. The scholar insisted that the critical barrier to abolishing the death penalty was public opinion: "a large segment of society" continued to demand harsh punishments for criminals. See Vytautas Pieliakas, *Tiesa* Vilnius, 1 Feb. 1989 [in Lithuanian], cited in FBIS-SOV, 5 April 1989, 84.

247. Research on the death penalty in socialist countries often has a built-in bias because it is conducted by organizations or individuals that oppose capital punishment in principle. Thus, Amnesty International—a group that advocates complete abolition of the death penalty—while laudably impartial and objective overall, is unlikely to draw attention to evidence that suggests a majority of people in China support capital punishment. Of course, the majority of members of most societies and cultures favor the swift and stern punishment of convicted criminals, including use of the death penalty. In the United States, for example, polls show strong public support for the death penalty. See *The Gallup Report* 280 (Jan. 1989): 27–29.

248. It should be noted, for example, that Fidel Castro's movement initially was not a communist one. A Communist party was not officially established in Castro's Cuba until the mid-1960s.

249. Revolutionary socialist justice, while far from a model of judicial virtue, is hardly mob justice. Thus, for example, in the USSR of 1920 even the "fearsomely powerful" Revolutionary Tribunals executed only 3.4 percent of the defendants brought before them (776 of 26,738), and in 14.8 percent of all cases, the defendants were found innocent (Makepeace, *Marxist Ideology*, Table 3.2 at 81). Similarly, in Cuba in February 1959, 45 members of Batista's air force went on trial for murder and genocide. Although the prosecutor demanded death sentences for 40 of them, the court ruled that the evidence was inconclusive and dismissed all the charges. At Castro's insistence, there was a retrial with new judges in which 43 of the 45 were convicted of various charges and sentenced to prison terms of between 2 and 30 years. None were executed. See Plas, *Revolution*, 12–13.

250. China did not promulgate a formal criminal code for thirty years, but by the early 1960s it possessed an "integrated and well-ordered system" with established procedures and regulations. See Cohen, *Criminal Process*, 18.

251. This occurred in the Soviet Union after Stalin and in China after Mao. In 1958 the USSR Supreme Soviet adopted the Fundamental Principles of Criminal Law, the Fundamental Principles of Criminal Procedure, and the Fundamental Principles of Court Organization. In China, the NPC passed the Criminal Law and Criminal Procedure Law in 1979.

252. On Cuba, see Havana Trabajadores, 3 Feb. 1989, cited in FBIS-LAT, 16 Mar. 1989, 2; Havana Radio Rebelde, 1 June 1989, cited in FBIS-LAT, 7 June 1989, 9; and AI, "Cuba." On the USSR, see Wishnevsky, "Draft Principles"; and a commentary on conditions in labor camps in *Izvestiya*, 13 March 1989, cited in *CDSP* 41 (11) (1989): 22–23.

253. See AI, "German Democratic Republic: Sweeping Laws—Secret Justice" (AI Report, 1989).

254. A nascent movement to limit use of the death penalty may be stirring in

China. In early 1989 some Chinese jurists suggested restricting the scope of capital punishment ("Criminal Law Called to Revise [*sic*]," *BR*, 24–30 Apr. 1989, 11).

255. Moscow *Pravda*, 8 Feb. 1989, cited in FBIS-SOV, 14 Feb. 1989, 72.

256. Havana television, 20 Mar. 1989, cited in FBIS-LAT, 21 Mar. 1989, 30.

257. In one case two policemen—including the local police chief—were shot dead in Guangxi Province in Oct. 1989. See Hong Kong Zhongguo Tongxunshi, 25 Oct. 1989, cited in FBIS-CHI, 3 Nov. 1989, 57.

258. Valerie Bunce, *Do New Leaders Make a Difference?: Executive Succession and Public Policy under Capitalism and Socialism* (Princeton, 1981).

259. Gallup opinion polls in the United States suggest that college graduates are somewhat more likely than ordinary citizens to oppose the death penalty for murder. See, for example, *The Gallup Report* 280 (Jan. 1989): 27–29.

260. On Mongolia and Yugoslavia, see the country reports in AI, *When the State Kills. On Albania, see WP*, 2 Apr. 1990, A1, A16.

261. On Cambodia, see the April 1989 constitution cited by Phnom Penh domestic service, 5 May 1989, cited in FBIS, *Daily Report: East Asia*, 9 May 1989, 39. On Romania, see *NYT*, 9 Jan. 1990, A12.

262. Article 38, Mozambique draft 1990 constitution. See Maputo *Noticias*, 10 Jan. 1990, cited in FBIS, *Daily Report: Sub-Sahara Africa*, 14 Mar. 1990, 59.

263. "On the Ten Major Relationships," (1956) *SWMTT*, 5: 299–300.

264. Berman, "What Makes 'Socialist Law' Socialist?" 30.

265. Hazard, *Communists and Their Law*, 479.

266. In the GDR up until 1987 the crime of "diversion" of state property carried a death sentence (Article 103 of 1968 Penal Code). Diversion is arguably an economic crime.

267. Woo, "Right to a Criminal Appeal," 153.

268. In addition to releasing Nelson Mandela, legalizing the African National Congress, and opening negotiations aimed at dismantling the system of apartheid, the government of President F. W. de Klerk promised a drastic reduction in its use of capital punishment. In Feb. 1990 de Klerk said the death penalty would be limited to only the most "extreme cases." As many as 100 executions have been carried out annually each year in South Africa. See *NYT*, 3 Feb. 1990, 6.

269. AI, *When the State Kills*, 73–75.

270. For a discussion of the major factors that will determine the use of the death penalty in post–1997 Hong Kong, see Scobell, "Strung Up or Shot Down?" 163–67.

Book Review Essay: Criminality upon and beneath the Surface in Victorian England

David Englander
The Open University, Milton Keynes

Thomas Boyle, *Black Swine in the Sewers of Hampstead: Beneath the Surface of Victorian Sensationalism*. New York: Viking, 1990; London: Hodder and Stoughton, 1990. 273 pp. £19.95.

Rob Sindall, *Street Violence in the Nineteenth-Century*. Leicester and London: Leicester University Press, 1990. 168 pp. £27.50.

High-minded, serious, rational, and progressive. Yes, the Victorians were all that. The queen's reign witnessed a sustained rise in living standards, a reduction in drunkenness, and the curbing of coarse, vile, and brutalizing pastimes. The pace of change, though, was not uniform. Historians preoccupied with process trends and outcomes or the imperatives of the literary canon have shown insufficient interest in the demands and sensibilities of a mass reading public and the tasteless texts with which it was so liberally supplied. Such carelessness makes it easy to forget that the age of improvement was also an age of titillation, and that, for all the talk of progress, the Victorians remained a bloodthirsty lot. Take the Empire, for example. Never mind the spiel about civilizing the heathen; half the fun of the white man's burden lay with the massacres, unspeakable slaughter, and scenes dreadful beyond description that were filed by intrepid journalists. Crime was even more pervasive.

Look at the newspapers. Not the gutter press, but the journals taken by the cultivated classes. They are absolutely full of monstrous murders, frightful affrays, singular suicides, and fatal felonies. Column upon column is devoted to woundings, maimings, poisonings, and hair-raising incidents of death and violence. Those who think of the Victorians as tight-lipped prudes will be shocked by how little feelings were spared. Child murder like that of Sarah Ann Crosby, who in 1845 was literally roasted to death over the kitchen fire by a drunken slut of a mother, made particularly fine copy. Arsonists and abortionists were equally newsworthy as, of course, was the minister who appropriated a cadaver from his own churchyard to advance the career of his surgeon son. Crime reporting, though, was by no means confined to the doings of the British. The handiwork of the Heidelberg executioner in dispatching a murderess was, for example, much admired. A silent thrill, we are told, ran through the assembled public as the broad two-handed sword was raised and the head severed from the body with a single blow. "The head was then held up to the gaze of the crowd, while the body sank through a trap door, and the dismal scene closed." Our own preference for the rope was not in one wit diminished by the exotic horrors of Continental contemporaries. The extraordinarily popular chapbooks, ballads, and broadsides of the period—above all, the blood-chilling commentaries of Catnach's "Seven Bards of the Seven Dials"—indicates the taste of the semiliterate masses and a dimension of the Victorian frame of mind that has not so far received the attention it merits.

But if individual acts made for a good read, the statistics of crime made for a nightmare. The country had, it seemed, gone to the dogs. Thieving, violence, and insubordination rose alarmingly in the early years of the queen's reign. So said the statisticians. In 1842, assizes and quarter sessions dealt with 31,309 prosecutions compared with a mere 4,605 prosecutions in 1805. The English, though, were sweet, docile things by comparison with the Irish and the Scots—at least according to Archibald Alison, who in 1844 told readers of *Blackwood's Edinburgh Magazine* that crime had risen 700 percent in England, 800 percent in Ireland, and 3,500 percent in Scotland. How long, he wondered, could civilization withstand such lawlessness and depravity?

The rational middle classes who read his article and its many variants no doubt harbored similar fears. They need not have done so. Modern historians are now agreed that official criminal statistics are suspect. Deficiencies in definition, collection, and presentation are well known, as are the distortions created by legislative and administrative change and by differences in the effectiveness of law enforcement. Then there is the disparity between real and recorded crime. So much went unreported and so much unsolved as to make it impossible to form a true picture of the extent of criminal activity. The conclusion is inescapable. The figures are so flawed that, as a direct measure of criminality, they are well nigh useless. Or are they?

At this point we pause. The one historian to jettison the lot, J. J. Tobias, is an isolated figure within criminal justice history. Most scholars, following in the footsteps of V. A. C. Gatrell, have accepted a qualified view of criminal statistics and argued that within certain imposed limitations they are usable. Understandably so! Without these data, research would be much reduced in scope. Evidence from law-breakers themselves, being hard to come by and difficult to handle, is not likely to supply a satisfactory alternative. Because our subject matter is the lowest of the low, the prospects for a meaningful "history from below" are poor. Apart from gallows confessions and the autobiographies of reformed criminals as narrated to dextrous prison officials, there are a handful of authentic accounts like that of David Haggart, "the Switcher," a petty thief who was eventually sentenced to death; or John Lee, "The Man They Could Not Hang" (although they tried to do so on three occasions); or Arthur Harding, an East End tough who might so easily have been hanged. Harding, however, was exceptional. His life story, as told to Raphael Samuel, indicates what is lost rather than what is recoverable. Most of his kind took their experiences to the grave with them. As they cheated contemporaries in life so they cheat posterity in death.

And so we hesitate, holding fast to criminal statistics as the servant-keeping classes once held on to nanny. Not, however, Rob Sindall, who rejects outright the whole corpus of historical knowledge based on these deficient data. Nay, he goes further. Sindall will have no truck with the compromises—"literary contortions," he calls them—of those who acknowledge the imperfections in criminal statistics but proceed as though the admission had neutralized its own negative import. Crime, he insists, is socially constructed and therefore variable in definition. Criminal statistics are part of the construction process. "The statistics," he tells us, "are therefore a measure, not necessarily of what was happening, but of what people believed was happening.... Their value lies in forming the basis of the picture of crime which powerful influences in nineteenth-century society thought confronted them." Preeminent among those influences were the middle classes and its press. Figures be damned! We must get back to the creators of opinion and the significance of their creations.

Sindall is not alone. Thomas Boyle, too, believes that press coverage of crime represents something significant. *Black Swine in the Sewers of Hampstead* is a lively and interesting study of the development of sensationalism in newspaper journalism, its influence on fiction, and its place in the popular culture of the period. Both volumes began life as doctoral dissertations, but in style and substance they are very different. Sindall, a hard-nosed empiricist who works within the mainstream of criminal justice history, is preoccupied with the perception of street violence and its implications for the police, judiciary, and legislature. Boyle, a literary historian in the "Victorian studies" tradition, seems to be as much concerned with the human condition as the Victorians' engagement with it. Sindall is terse, combative, and workmanlike; Boyle is mannered, indulgent, and distracting. The former writes strictly for the professionals; the latter for the *New York Times Review of Books*. Neither is satisfactory. Both are useful.

With concepts and terminology drawn from the sociology of deviance, Sindall examines the presentation of street violence in British cities from the 1850s to the 1880s, and the ways in which specific scares in London, Liverpool, and Manchester influenced policemen, judges, and politicians. Put briefly, his thesis is that the dangers were much exaggerated and that periodic panics were stirred up by the media in order to boost circulation. How these things came to pass, though, is not very clear. "It would be gratifying to be able to identify a clear guiding rule which editors followed when identifying an initial deviance," we are told, "but it is impossible to do so." "Moral panics were like Topsy—they just grew." Why respectable readers were so susceptible to media scares is equally unclear. The author's prejudices, alas, make it impossible for him to supply a convincing answer. The middle classes as presented here are not even a caricature—just an expression, a trigger for legislators and law-enforcers, rather than a fit subject for serious enquiry.

But if Sindall is not interested in the comfortable classes, Boyle is not interested in anything else. His book is primarily about the mind of the middle classes or, more precisely, about the "mass invasion of crime into the Victorian consciousness." His judgments about the coverage of crime are likewise dissimilar. Whereas Sindall sees sensationalism as a form of trivialization pursued by an irresponsible press, Boyle views crime reporting as a form of social criticism that challenged order and progress, and let loose the senses on a world fastened by the rational and the godly. The controversy, as embodied in the "Sensation" novels of Collins, Braddon, and Dickens was, he shows, about the ways in which our culture grappled with those dark, irrational forces that respectable society tried so desperately to repress or deny.

This book, then, addressed issues that are metaphysical and psychological, and only incidentally criminological in character. Connections can, however, be made. Boyle makes some but misses others. In particular, he fails to examine "crime" as a form of ideology, and so is unable to explain how it became permanently loaded with anxieties about social change and social deterioration. Sindall, too, fails to examine the displacement process that is so central to the moral panics with which he is concerned. His suggestion that the middle classes got a "kick" out of crime because it did not in reality pose a real danger to their person or property strikes me as unconvincing in itself and positively bizarre, when supported by reference to the self-same criminal statistics that were previously deemed to be worthless. Even if crime were nothing more than a form of entertainment, its popularity would still require explanation. At times, too, Sindall writes as though what is not true is not real, or at any rate not significant. Thus we are presented with a contrast between a professional police force concerned with real crime and media-generated myths as though the police and bureaucracy were external agents and not part and parcel of the myth-generating process. He seems unmindful of the role performed by criminal statistics not only in mobilizing fears and allocating resources, but also in legitimating the work of the state and its policemen. *Street Violence in the Nineteenth Century* is also unsatisfactory in presentation. H. M. Hyndman was not the author of *A Commune for Socialism*; the Whitechapel murders did not occur in 1889; *All the Year Round* was not published in 1962; and "Manchunian" is incorrect.

Boyle and Sindall have produced flawed but important books. Both authors are pushing outwards the frontiers of criminal justice history and, like it or not, pressing us toward a greater public involvement with the implications for current practice. This is as it should be. Historians of crime do have an important contribution to make. But if it is to be effective, it must say more than what is wrong with past policies; it must actively work toward the discovery of a new paradigm in which law and order can be located. We may in the process have to acquire new skills and perform new roles. So be it. Those who do not wish to go the distance should not step into the ring.

Book Reviews

Lyman L. Johnson, ed., *The Problem of Order in Changing Societies: Essays on Crime and Policing in Argentina and Uruguay, 1750–1940*. Albuquerque: University of New Mexico Press, 1990. xx & 161 pp. Illustrations, tables, notes, sources, and index. $14.95.

Given the very limited work done to date on Latin American social history and the legion of unanswered questions that remain, one might perhaps question whether the activities of criminals should occupy the attentions, and the apparently increasingly scarce resources, of historians. The six essays in *Problem of Order* offer strong arguments that they should. Because crime is socially defined and less selectively enforced, its study provides insights into structures and relations of power, class, race, and gender as these are manifest in both the law and in the day-to-day "vernacular" (p. x) of streets and courts. Such information is no less important to Latin Americanists than to historians of Europe and North America. Indeed, given the limited range and general disarray of sources available to investigate the lives of nineteenth-century Latin Americans, and the poor in particular, deviants may be almost the only members of large categories of persons about whom we can recover detail.

The editor organized *Problem of Order* chronologically, but he could have done this topically as well. Two of the essays, for example, focus on the experiences of women. Susan Socolow uses criminal cases to look at social values and gender relations in late colonial Buenos Aires and the impacts on these of race and class. Those cases involving women that came before the courts included almost exclusively elite women in the role of victims of interpersonal, and usually sexual crimes, as opposed to economic or political crime. What became of female thieves, or prostitutes, or maids, or poor street venders who cut their rivals over business competition or a man's attentions is unclear. Donna Guy, on the other hand, focuses on poor women, looking at female prostitution in the Buenos Aires of 100 years later. Probably not surprisingly, she finds that laws purportedly enacted to protect poor women served, instead, as vehicles to harass and control them. Brothels and their inhabitants repeatedly fell victim to disputes among a municipal government that licensed and taxed them, police and neighbors who perceived them as foci of public disorder, and doctors and social reformers who hoped to eradicate the social and physical ills they associated with prostitution.

Two essays deal with crime and the definition of criminality in the lives of lower-class males. Richard Slatta and Karla Robinson show that, despite the political and ideological differences that separated the Unitario regime of the 1820s from the Rosas dictatorship of the 1830s and 1840s, the reality of law and law enforcement for poor men in Buenos Aires and Buenos Aires province in these years remained much the same. The state employed harsh vagrancy laws and the threat of forced army service to coerce seasonal labor for the landowning elites from a reluctant and mobile gaucho population. Given such a criminal justice system, it is no surprise that John Chasteen finds Uruguay's gauchos (and this applied to Argentina's as well) seeking immediate redress for real or imagined injuries or affronts with their knives, rather than through recourse to law.

Finally, two of the chapters compare crime in Argentina in the half-century after 1880 to experiences in North America and Europe during these same years. Julia Kirk Blackwelder demonstrates that specific political and cultural patterns are at least as important in understanding patterns of crime as are the general measures of "modernization" on which most theories of criminal history in industrializing societies focus. For example, Buenos Aires' lack of a North American-style political machine interested in patronage resulted in a falling police-population ratio as the city expanded, which, together with a shift of police manpower to the new suburbs to protect middle-class property, meant a decline in arrest rates for discretionary crimes such as disorderly conduct. Contrary to the pattern of North American and European cities, however, violent crimes and crimes against property did not decrease with urbanization and industrialization. Buenos Aires, then, according to the statistics, was becoming a more orderly but not a safer city! Lyman Johnson broadens the scope of this analysis to compare arrest statistics from Buenos Aires, Tucuman, and Santa Fe for the years 1900–1930 to see how these fit with theories derived from North Atlantic history and how they vary over time under the impacts of what he labels "export dependent capitalism." While the figures he discovers often prove "fascinating, but difficult to interpret" (p. 122) or refuse to yield clear trends, they do refute any simplistic linking of crime patterns and urbanization/

industrialization and, together with those of Blackwelder, call into question explanations of changes in crime, law, and law enforcement based only on North American and European experiences.

In all, *The Problem of Order* is compact, well written, well argued, and, to coin a phrase, a "path-breaking" little book. Perhaps only one small caveat is in order. If it certainly was the case that by the 1880s Argentina was among the most thorough and sophisticated collectors of social statistics in Latin America, it is also true that local lore has it that "statistics are the poetry of Argentina." Figures collected and published for and by government agencies (and this of course applies not just to Argentina) generally serve many masters, of which accuracy is often not the most important. In undertaking broad, synthetic essays, several of the authors have no option but to rely on published data; but defects in this material, at least as much as contradictions in Argentina's historical development, may be responsible for some of the difficulties they encounter in attempting to interpret what they find. Given, too, the tremendous power of numbers to convince, the unwary and those unfamiliar with Latin America should be warned of the dangers of taking these too seriously.

David J. McCreery
Georgia State University

Iver Bernstein, *The New York City Draft Riots: Their Significance for American Society and Politics in the Age of the Civil War.* New York: Oxford University Press, 1990. xii & 363 pp. Illustrations, maps, appendixes, notes, bibliographical essay, and index. $29.95.

J. Matthew Gallman, *Mastering Wartime: A Social History of Philadelphia During the Civil War.* Cambridge, England, and New York: Cambridge University Press, 1990. xiv & 354 pp. Illustrations, tables, appendix, bibliographic essay, and index. $49.50.

Neither of these two books was written as a history of crime or social control. Nevertheless each will be interesting to historians in these fields because both monographs discuss issues of the social and political context of disorder and its consequences. J. Matthew Gallman's study of Philadelphia is focused on the city and how its residents as individuals and as members of social groups or classes and institutions coped with the disruptions and demands of the American Civil War. He covers diverse areas including individual reactions to separation and death, what sorts of Philadelphians served in the Union army, how workers coped with inflation and sought to improve their positions, and how wartime demands affected Philadelphia's economy. Gallman skillfully handles both impressionistic and quantitative historical evidence. His discussion of the war's impact on ordinary urban crime and disorder (chap. 7), the police problem of thousands of soldiers passing through on their way to war (chap. 8), and the means by which Philadelphia avoided riots against the 1863 military draft (chap. 7) will be of most interest to readers of *Criminal Justice History*.

Iver Bernstein's book is differently conceived and developed than is Gallman's view of one city's response to all the faces of war. Bernstein uses the episode of New York's draft riots as the pivot for an exploration of the city's social and political conflicts that contributed to the riots and of how the riots in turn shaped new patterns that emerged after the Civil War.

Although Gallman's analysis of ordinary crime and disorder modifies some hypotheses and makes intelligent use of arrest reports to discern changing patterns, this review will focus on the two books' discussion of the draft riots. This provides an opportunity for comparing how diverse groups of people in the two cities responded to an unpopular policy of the national government, the draft.

In the early spring of 1863, the Union was facing a shortage of manpower to carry on the bloody, apparently inconclusive, and increasingly unpopular Civil War. In March 1863, Congress passed the Enrollment Act that established the Union's first federal conscription. The measure was meant to encourage enlistment; conscription was resorted to only when states did not meet their quota of men for federal service. The law also provided for various ways of avoiding military service altogether: Draftees could supply a substitute to serve in their place or pay a commutation fee of $300.

Although conscription provided only ten percent of the Union army's manpower, it represented a very direct, intrusive federal presence in the lives of ordinary citizens. The substitution and commutation provisions seemed to favor the rich who could afford the high fee (many unskilled workers might earn $300 in a year). Many working-class Northerners also resented the war's shift from preservation of the union to freeing the slaves (the Emancipation Proclamation took effect in January 1863). The draft crystallized old social and political animosities of largely Democratic, often foreign-born workers against Republicans who had sought to impose Protestant notions of morality and social order on their neighborhoods. Workers in both Philadelphia and New York protested the inequities of conscription and the change in war aims, but their anger had very different results in the two cities.

New York's officials were unprepared for the five days of rioting that followed the first attempt to draft men on 13 July 1863. In hindsight, it seems that they should have been more alert, as all the signs of an impending conflict were present. Bernstein analyzes the grievances of certain groups of artisans, industrial workers, and day laborers against the city's Republicans, and many workers' long-standing resentment of blacks and of the state-controlled metropolitan police who zealously enforced unpopular liquor and Sunday-closing laws.

Bernstein's most important contribution to understanding the riots themselves is his identification of distinctive stages. In the early part of the week, protest against the draft took the form of a predominantly building-trade artisan and industrial worker "strike" against conscription, which was a calculated effort to stop the draft from going into effect. By mid-week the protest had turned violent, and many of the artisans had repudiated the demonstrations. In this stage the burning of federal draft offices escalated into attacks on the police, prominent Republicans and their homes, as well as the offices of Protestant reform institutions. Industrial wage workers and unskilled laborers now dominated the protest, and the composition of the crowd was more heavily Irish Catholic than earlier. Violence against Republicans soon expanded to a final stage: lynchings of blacks, especially in the waterfront neighborhoods which earlier in 1863 had witnessed a tumultuous longshoremen's strike against employment of low-wage black workers. The lynchings, though, were more vicious than the earlier beatings and ransacking of blacks' houses. Saloons and brothels with black or mixed patrons were also targets of the crowd, which included large numbers of women and young boys. These Irish unskilled men, women, and boys were the diehards who fought the soldiers and police block-by-block in the struggle for control of the streets.

Bernstein argues that an important factor in both the causes and consequences of the draft riots was the division among New York's merchant elite between Democrats and Republicans. Anti-draft protestors had originally hoped that Democratic city officials and the state governor would find some way to prevent the draft from actually taking place in New York. They were unsuccessful, and Democratic newspapers and politicians did their bit to arouse anger against the draft and the Emancipation Proclamation. Republicans shared some of the responsibility because they did not seem to understand how explosive the draft was as a focus for long-standing grievances.

After the riots, Democratic merchants and officials established a municipal fund to provide substitutes or commutation fees for all draftees needing them. They were concerned with conciliating the rioters, and did nothing to aid blacks who had lost their homes or were prevented from going back to work after the riots were over. Many Republicans, on the other hand, favored a drastic solution: martial law for the city and prosecution of Democratic officials whom they viewed as instigating the riots or abetting the violence. Republican merchants viewed the rioters themselves harshly and sympathized with their black victims, organizing charities to help those who had lost their jobs or homes.

In the short term, the Democrats' conciliatory policy won, partly aided by President Abraham Lincoln's understanding that harsh reprisals would only exacerbate disaffection and disorder in New York. The direct beneficiary of conciliation was Boss Tweed and Tammany Hall. Tammany dominated the city until it lost the allegiance of the Democratic elite because its frauds threatened the city's credit and it lost the support of organized building-trades workers resentful of the Hall's ties to building contractors whom the workers were fighting for the eight-hour day. Finally, Tammany was undone by a reprise of the draft riots, the 12 July 1871 Orange riots, in which Irish Catholic crowds attacked a parade of Irish Protestants. The police were unable to prevent the violence; militia troops fired into the crowd, killing several people. Tammany's conciliation, an effort to prevent the Protestants from marching, failed. The balance of power shifted at least temporarily to members of the elite who believed in firm control of the working classes. This summary does not do justice to a subtle and complex argument that dissects the politics of a major urban riot, but should give an idea of how Bernstein is able to develop a multi-level explanation of the causes and consequences of the draft riots.

Gallman's Philadelphia story is briefer and less thoroughly developed because the city did not experience draft riots. The question is obvious: Why not? Philadelphia workers, especially the Irish, were no friendlier to the blacks and just as resentful of the $300 commutation fee as their New York counterparts. One reason Philadelphia avoided violence is that the city was very successful in meeting its quotas by enlistments, encouraged by offering bounties to volunteers. Gallman emphasizes that Philadelphia officials had the New York example before them and could anticipate trouble. Gallman does not discuss Philadelphia workers' attitudes toward the police, but at one point mentions that they were known for their toughness since many were former members of the street gangs that had made the city notorious before the war (p. 191). Philadelphia's leaders successfully deployed police and military force to discourage potential rioters. Soldiers were more available in Philadelphia than in New York, where they had to be called from the Gettysburg battlefield area.

Perhaps as a conciliatory move at the request of leading citizens, Lincoln replaced an unpopular New Englander with General George Cadwallader as commander of the city's military forces. Cadwallader was a Democrat, who in 1844 had put down a nativist riot with a good deal of bloodshed. He was tough but also not obviously the enemy of Irish workers. In contrast, Lincoln made a similar gesture in New York, appointing respected Democrat John A. Dix head of the Union Department of the East, only *after* the draft riots. Gallman mentions that the Democrats were a factor to be reckoned with in Philadelphia, but it seems that they (at least the "peace Democrats" who favored ending the war with slavery intact) were not as powerful as in New York. Philadelphia's main problem of political order was protecting

Democrats or an occasional Southerner who did not support the war effort from being beaten up by angry Republicans.

Gallman does not discuss another element worth considering in making the comparison between Philadelphia and New York. The proportion of immigrants in the Quaker city was less than in New York (one-third compared to nearly one-half in 1860). According to Dennis Clark the Irish in particular were somewhat better off in Philadelphia because of a more diverse economy with more Irish in skilled trades, enough land within the city to prevent New York's tenement overcrowding, and an established earlier Irish immigrant group (see Clark, *The Irish in Philadelphia* [Philadelphia, 1974], 40–58, 74–87). Gallman points out that the leading spokesmen of organized skilled labor criticized the commutation clauses but generally endorsed the need for a draft (p. 221). As we have seen, in New York groups of skilled workers initiated the antidraft protests.

Each of these two differently conceived books has something to offer to historians of crime and criminal justice. Bernstein's is particularly valuable in dissecting the political and social roots and consequences of a major urban riot, with many of his insights and approaches contributing to our understanding of riots in general. Gallman, though this is not his intention, also adds to our knowledge of riots by describing circumstances that contributed to one *not* taking place.

Wilbur R. Miller
State University of New York, Stony Brook

Desmond H. Brown, *The Genesis of the Canadian Criminal Code of 1892*. Toronto: Osgoode Society, 1989. x & 253 pp. $35.00

There can be little argument that the Osgoode Society has done much, since its incorporation in 1979, to improve the state of Canadian legal history. One of its most recent publications, Desmond Brown's *The Genesis of the Canadian Criminal Code of 1892*, is yet another example of the society's ongoing efforts. Although the author notes in his introduction that with the code Canada became "the first self-governing jurisdiction in the British empire to codify its law," his interest does not rest with this "first" per se, but with the broader questions of how and why Canada codified its criminal law. Brown certainly provides considerable insight into the question of the "how," but in the end we are still puzzled by the "why" (p. 3).

There are two broad themes running through Brown's examination of Canadian codification. The first is to contrast the success of the Canadians with the failure of British jurists and parliamentarians to codify the common law. It is clear from Brown's research that the absence of an English criminal code was certainly not for want of either proposed codes or aspiring codifiers. Yet despite numerous parliamentary committees, the examples of codification in the American states, and Sir James Fitzjames Stephen's draft codes of 1878 and 1879, the English Parliament never supported such an initiative. On the other hand, between 1867 and 1892 Canadians managed to compile a consolidation of the disparate pre-Confederation criminal statutes and eventually mold it, and Stephen's draft code, into a Canadian criminal code. This is the unmistakable theme of Canada's throwing-off its old colonial strictures and accomplishing what the mother country could not do. Distinctly nationalistic and whiggish, it fits easily with the interpretations advanced before 1930 by the father of Canadian constitutional history, W.P.M. Kennedy.

The second theme of Brown's book focuses specifically on the process whereby Canadians managed to achieve what England had not. Although he does not overtly employ such a phrase, this theme can be identified as the triumph of new world practicality over the hide-bound ways of England. In very simplistic terms, there was a common sense in the work of Canadian draftsmen who reduced one-sentence Victorian statutes of 700 words to a more succinct and understandable form. This theme is an important one for understanding late nineteenth-century Canadian legal culture. While often appearing to be slaves to English practice and precedence, Canadians were not immune to the more open environment of North America. As evidence Brown writes that by 1867, "all the British North American colonies except Prince Edward Island and British Columbia had accomplished what the chancellors of England from the time of Henry VIII had never been able to achieve; they had managed to consolidate and codify the public statute law of each jurisdiction and to repeal all the law that had preceded it" (p. 91).

The greatest strength of Brown's approach is that he recognizes the politics of codification, an activity that had the appearance of something distinctly legalistic. There are two levels of politics at play in the story he tells. The first relates to the decisions any draftsperson makes in phrasing, shaping, and bringing meaning to the law. Consider the implications of pruning an English statute of 700 words and in the process making the meaning of that enactment intelligible to the average literate person. Suddenly the law becomes understandable; it fails to be the private domain of those learned in the ancient forms and rhetoric of the common law. The second level of politics that Brown highlights occurred in the House of Commons. Canadian codification succeeds in part because unlike their British counterparts, those backing the code in Canada successfully orchestrated the perceptions about, and the presentation of, the code in the House. Sir John Thompson's introduction of the code was accompanied with so little fanfare that the opposition party was convinced that the enactment contained little that was new or innovative. The House had already approved of the code by the time its real innovation was revealed.

Despite the insight provided by his awareness of politics, Brown's book has a number of difficulties. First, of its seven chapters, only two are actually devoted to codification. Chapter 1, for example, entitled "Definitions and Descriptions," is an unnecessarily confused discussion of Jeremy Bentham's idea of what codification entailed. Part of the problem here is one produced by the limitations of language. Given individual inclinations and circumstances, distinctions between what Bentham defined as codification, rationalization, and reduction are in of themselves, defined by usage. After touching upon English, French, German, and Canadian versions of codification, Brown completes his journey by admitting that "there may be as many variants of the concept of 'code' as there are codes themselves" (p. 11). It appears that codification, like beauty, is in the eye of the beholder.

The second weakness of Brown's book is his strained attempt to distill a Canadian legal culture. Beginning in 1749 with the arrival of Colonel Edward Cornwallis in Nova Scotia and concluding with a commentary on the Imperial criminal statutes that had survived confederation in 1867, Brown highlights reception dates, the impact of Loyalists, the Quebec Act of 1774, legal education, and popular resistance to the abolition of the grand jury as forming a backdrop to Canadian codification. The conclusion he draws is that "the legal system of British North America on the eve of Confederation was quite unlike that of England" (p. 57). More specifically,

> the fragmented legal education system, the provincial legal profession, and the insular courts were also unlike their English progenitors, and, to a greater or lesser extent, unlike each other. Moreover, in constitutional terms, Canadians were creatures of rational, written constitutions. Since public and private law had been codified at the provincial level, they did not have to struggle with a random and incomprehensible collection of statutes scattered through the legislative record of a century or more. For all these reasons the Canadian lawyer and parliamentarian saw the legal system from a perspective quite different from that of their English colleagues. (p. 69)

Why this is noteworthy is unclear, since as Brown quotes Lawrence Friedman, any attempt by those first settlers to have reproduced the English system "would have been both miraculous and insane" (p. 39). If it would have been insanity to reproduce England in North America, why are we surprised when we discover that Canadians were "quite different" from Englishmen?

Brown's efforts to define the Canadian legal culture through comparisons with England point to a third difficulty with his approach. Given the efforts of American codifiers such as David Dudley Field in New York as well as similar efforts in Georgia and California before 1867, it would appear sensible to view the Canadian experience as part of a North American phenomenon. Therefore, rather than being portrayed as something wholly anomalous within the context of empire relations and development, the Canadian consolidation and codification should be perceived as consistent with its North American environment. Thus an examination of Canadian codification should focus explicitly on the process of balancing an Imperial heritage with a new world experience.

Finally, although Brown chose to concentrate on the genesis of the code, as opposed to its impact, one wonders what changes the code brought to the daily administration of justice throughout the country. Did the code in fact make the criminal law more understandable and accessible? Brown tells us that Sir John Thompson wanted to "reduce the amorphous and baffling common law to succinct and understandable principles" (p. 148). Did the reduction produce these principles? We really do not know if a justice of the peace in Red Deer, Alberta, was able to administer the criminal law with any more skill in 1920 than had a similar functionary in Berlin, Ontario, in 1885. Thus beyond the assertion that the code made the criminal law more understandable, we do not know what its impact was.

Overall, *The Genesis of the Canadian Criminal Code of 1892* is, in the end, both an insightful and perplexing book. There is little question that the first codification of criminal law in the British Empire was significant, although its importance lays with what such an endeavor says about late nineteenth-century Canadian legal culture. Unfortunately, Brown spends too much time portraying this culture in comparison with Britain, rather than placing it within the North American context. Without a clear picture of what the legal culture of nineteenth-century Canada was, as opposed to what it was not, Brown is unable to provide a sense of how that culture made codification possible. Thus while he gives us an informative description of how Canadians codified their criminal law, the reasons why codification was completed remain unclear.

Jonathan Swainger
University of Northern British Columbia, Terrace

Elaine S. Abelson, *When Ladies Go A-Thieving: Middle-Class Shoplifters in the Victorian Department Store*. New York: Oxford University Press, 1989. ix & 292 pp. Illustrations, notes, and index. $29.95.

In *When Ladies Go A-Thieving*, Elaine S. Abelson focuses on the rise of the department store as a symbol of the developing consumer culture of the late nineteenth and early twentieth centuries. According to Abelson, the new shopping palaces vividly represented society's "discovery of abundance." Where once patrons were expected to enter stores with specified needs and select merchandise neatly hidden from sight, the modern department store catered to different objectives. Through their fountains, wide aisles, and elaborate displays, stores such as Macy's and Bloomingdale's were arranged to tempt women to buy nonessential and costly luxuries. By the early twentieth century, such department stores had transformed shopping from an activity to attain necessities into a middle-class female pastime designed to fill the days and define the rising status of their largely female clientele.

Yet in "tempting" these women, managers of large department stores discovered the negative consequences of nurturing desire. Open displays not only enticed women to purchase items; they also lured them to acquire articles without paying for them. Increasingly, owners expressed concern over shoplifting by their middle-class patrons. Although they hired detectives, installed mirrors, and purchased locked glass counters, the "shrinkage" in stock continued. Shoplifting, in fact, well symbolized the paradox of consumer culture: while enticing their customers into desiring goods they neither needed nor could afford, managers of shops could hardly allow their customers to act irrationally on their desires and pilfer their merchandise.

The shopkeepers' response to this dilemma, Abelson argues, revealed the complex interaction of gender and class in turn-of-the century culture. Although lower-class men and women could easily be branded thieves and be incarcerated for their illegal actions, middle-class, respectable "ladies" could not be treated in such a manner. The managers of department stores strove to create a place of fantasy for their clientele that catered to their every whim; they hardly wished to disrupt the pleasure of buying by accusing their customers of thievery. Nor could they set the words and honor of their working-class shop girls—who were often entrusted with controlling thievery—against the reputation of the wives and daughters of bankers and ministers. Instead, leading experts in merchandising developed "covert" means such as mirrors and floor walkers to dissuade shoplifting, and accepted most losses as part of business.

Similarly, shopkeepers developed class- and gender-based explanations for the existence of thievery among a group of women who seemed able to afford the goods they often hid in the folds of their clothes and umbrellas. Such actions, they declared, were a reflection of the limitations of the "weaker sex." Fragile and unused to heady temptation, they became overcome by the luxuries before them. Although they hardly planned to "steal," they found themselves unable to resist acquiring the desired items. By the late nineteenth century, this explanation received additional support through medical interpretation. Such women, physicians argued, were not simply weak, but were indeed "sick." Rather than being perpetrators of a crime, they were themselves victims. Linking their thievery to a variety of "female problems," physicians proclaimed the women to be suffering from the specific—and newly coined—disease of kleptomania.

Abelson's story is both interesting and well told, although at times a bit repetitious. Through word and illustrations, she depicts the growth of the Victorian department store as a central stage for middle-class women. She clearly demonstrates the concerns and fears of the rising shopowners and experts on merchandising as they implemented antitheft measures and development rationales for what they assumed was a widely shared practice.

Yet in giving greatest attention to the owners and managers of department stores, and relying primarily on their manuals and textbooks, Abelson also limits her study of both shoplifting itself and the middle-class criminal. While arguing that shoplifting was a serious and pervasive problem, she is never able to define the extent of the crime. Relying primarily on estimates from managers, it is impossible to tell if large numbers of women resorted to the practice, or if this was simply the perception of the stores' managers.

Nor is Abelson able to explain the reasons for the development of late nineteenth-century shoplifting. In the course of the book, she suggests three possible reasons for this phenomenon. At times, she seems to agree with the nineteenth-century explanation. Department stores, she argues, presented great temptations for "many women" who gave in to their impulses (p. 56). At other times, she argues that the crime reflected the "twin pressures of money and status" in a developing consumer economy (p. 165). Women, she contends, had little control over money; they were dependent on their husbands to provide them with economic support. At the same time, however, they were expected to obtain the symbols of rising middle-class status. Shoplifting then became a "budget-stretching device" that allowed women to obtain more than they could purchase through their husband-dictated allowances (p. 167). Finally, Abelson suggests that for some, shoplifting may have been "a rational act of defiance to punish others—husbands and families—by punishing themselves," as well as reacting "against their own dependence and economic powerlessness" (p. 171). While each of these explanations may have merit, her book affords little opportunity to test their validity against the experience of the women themselves.

Abelson's examination of the evolving category of kleptomaniac is also limited somewhat by both its brevity and imprecision. Categories such as moral insanity, neurasthenia, and ovarian insanity are often used interchangeably, although they reflected medical beliefs that often did not exist simultaneously. Similarly, it is impossible to know the impact of medical ideas. Although she argues that "Everyone seemed to know about kleptomania" (p. 195), and "many lawyers 'came around' " to this plea (p. 90), we do not learn how often it was cited, if it was accepted by the women themselves, or if it led to conflicts among the medical, legal, and merchandising communities.

Abelson admits that some of these issues were difficult if not impossible to answer. The limitations of sources, the often-adopted pseudonyms of the middle-class criminals, and the tendency for shopkeepers to drop the charges when restitution was made, all restrict in-depth interpretation of the women themselves and the crime they committed. As a result, *When Ladies Go A-Thieving* clearly describes the development of the managers' fears and explanations for shoplifting. It raises interesting—if still unanswered—questions about the middle-class women who entered the Victorian department store and became entrapped in criminal activities.

Carole Haber
University of North Carolina, Charlotte

Terence Morris, *Crime and Criminal Justice Since 1945*. Oxford: Basil Blackwell, 1989. 198 pp. £6.95.

This book offers an overview of crime and criminal justice in post-war Britain. It is designed to be accessible (and useful) to general readers, criminal justice professionals, and students of history and criminology. With an envisaged readership as wide as this, it is perhaps inevitable that some will be disappointed. Overviews are by definition both ambitious and selective. On the positive side, many readers will appreciate Morris's attempt to identify connections between crime and punishment, and the social, economic, and political trends throughout this period, underlining that crime and criminal justice cannot be examined in a social vacuum. In particular, readers from outside the United Kingdom will find his thematic approach and basic chronology useful. The book is broadly divided into two historical periods: 1945–60 and 1960–88. Within this framework the author discusses the topics of crime, policing, the judiciary and magistracy, penal practice, and penal reform.

On the negative side, some readers may have reservations about particular issues selected for in-depth analysis. For example, Morris has chosen to focus very strongly throughout this book on the subject of capital punishment. While many commentators may agree with him that the abolition of the death penalty in 1965 was "the most important theme in post-war penal reform" (p. 78), it is surely not necessary in a book of this scope to include details of parliamentary votes cast on the issue, well into the 1980s. Politically the issue is (forgive the phrase) a dead one. More significant is the fact that forty-eight inmates of British prisons committed suicide in 1989 (twenty-five of whom were remanded in custody at the time). Although the death penalty was and is a very emotive issue, it should not deflect attention from other more pressing problems confronting the criminal justice system in the postwar era.

Morris does examine the roots of the current penal crisis in Britain. He charts the deterioration of the prison estate since the war, and rightly indicates the absurdity of the current (costly!) prison-building program, which will do little to alleviate overcrowding and appalling conditions of containment if new prisons are to be used to accommodate yet more offenders sentenced to imprisonment by the courts. If history teaches us anything, it teaches us that imprisonment is counterproductive: it does not deter offenders or reduce crime. Morris rightly argues that the effects of overcrowded and unsanitary conditions, an undue emphasis on security (even for petty offenders, vagrants, and drunks), longer sentences, and demoralization of prison staff have all contributed to the deepening penal crisis (p. 136). Since the publication of this book, the Strangeways Prison riot has rendered many of these problems dramatically visible.

In his chapter on "Judges and Magistrates 1945–60," Morris relies heavily on discussions of selected (in)famous cases and particularly (in)famous judges. While this discussion does reveal the crustiness, eccentricity, and in some cases incompetence of the judiciary, there are times when his anecdotal and largely biographical approach becomes a little tiresome. Curiously, one of the most astute and appropriate quotes (relating magistrates' lack of formal training), is relegated to a footnote in a later chapter: "I once enquired of a Chairman of the [Magistrates] Association what might be done about those appointed before 1965 but who declined to take up the opportunities for training. His reply was epigrammatic and revealing: 'Where there is death, there is hope' " (p. 123). The public outcry generated by recent outrageous sentencing decisions of certain elderly male judges (particularly where cases involved women) seems to reflect similar sentiments of despair!

Where issues of gender, race, and criminal justice are concerned, this book is unhelpful. Although we are told that in 1985 12.5 percent of men and 17 percent of women in penal institutions were from ethnic minorities, this is written off as attributable to "the individual's socioeconomic status" (p. 139). Although Morris acknowledges that racism within prisons is a "potentially volatile feature," he asserts that "such evidence as there is suggests that discrimination is not widespread" (ibid.). Recent research points to the contrary. In his final chapter, Morris does not do justice to the concerns of what he terms "the left" regarding the treatment of black people within the criminal justice system. Lumping together these concerns with those of "feminist groups," he denies the existence of "oppression" in rather dismissive terms: "The courts seldom rise to the degree of conscious sophistication necessary to decide that this or that offender is a proper case for 'oppression.' Most of the time those who send people to prison do so because they cannot think of anything else to do with them" (p. 167). But sentencers do not have to *intend* to oppress and discriminate for their decisions to have precisely those consequences.

When discussing changes in criminal activity and punishment, Morris gives a sound summary of the principal issues involved. Importantly, he notes that the growth of crime during 1960–88 has to be seen in terms of new opportunity structures for crime. During this period the portability (and marketability) of consumer durables, supermarket shopping, self-service petrol stations, and the availability of cars all made crime more possible and profitable (pp. 97–98). At the same time, he touches on two other crucial themes: the relationships among crime, poverty, and punishment (p. 105) and the increase in "crimes of disorder" (p. 99). In relation to the latter, Morris observes that the "New Policing" that has emerged since the late 1970s is now "more relevant to the maintenance of public order" than to the control of crime (p. 166). Consequently, earlier reservations about police accountability and the adequacy of complaints procedures (p. 65) are now more significant than ever.

The principal aim of this book is to trace the historical roots of contemporary themes in crime and criminal justice. In relation to certain themes (such as judicial and police accountability, penal reform, links among the economy, crime, and punishment), it does this fairly well. But I would see it as a basic introductory text and not, as the publisher suggests, "essential reading."

Dee Cook
University of Keele

Michal R. Belknap, *Federal Law and Southern Order: Racial Violence and Constitutional Conflict in Post-Brown South*. Athens: University of Georgia Press, 1987. ix & 387 pp. Illustrations, bibliographical essay, notes, and index. $35.00.

The reluctance of the federal government to respond forcefully to anti-civil rights violence in the South during the 1950s and 1960s has been a staple of scholarly accounts of the period. Michal R. Belknap, a legal historian at the California Western School of Law, analyzes the constitutional bases for this reluctance and describes how and why federal officials abandoned their cautious interpretation of federalism for a more activist role after the Freedom Summer of 1964. The result is a searing indictment of the Justice Department and of the Eisenhower and Kennedy administrations.

After a brief and effective summary of the legacy of white southern violence against blacks during and since Reconstruction, Belknap discusses the weak response of the Eisenhower administration to the growing resistance and violence in the Deep South. At issue was the administration's interpretation of Section 241 of the U.S. Code, a remnant of Reconstruction-era legislation, which made it a crime to conspire "to deprive others of their rights to due process and equal protection of the laws." Neither Eisenhower nor his Justice Department believed that Section 241 applied to civil rights violations perpetrated by individual citizens in the states, effectively eviscerating that statute. Only when a state officially and openly violated a federal court order (as in Little Rock) did Eisenhower take action.

The Kennedy administration—especially Attorney General Robert F. Kennedy and Burke Marshall, the head of the Justice Department's Civil Rights Division—followed Eisenhower's hands-off-the-South policy, issuing numerous recondite opinions on the concept of dual sovereignty and the limitations of federal power. Belknap does a fine job of analyzing these ideological arguments, but he does not sufficiently expose their disingenuous nature. Nor does he probe the political reasons behind them. Ultimately, the constraints on both the Eisenhower and Kennedy administrations were political, not ideological, and we need to know why the principals in those administrations sought to appease southern leaders at every turn. In Eisenhower's case, prior to 1957 at least, there was some hope that the Republican party could redeem Dixie, particularly after Ike's strong showing in the 1956 presidential election. As for the Kennedy administration, his narrow election victory and the influence of southern congressional leaders on New Frontier legislation extended federal reluctance to intervene in the South.

The reluctance of the Justice Department is especially glaring since even J. Edgar Hoover's FBI came to realize (albeit not until 1964 with its COINTELPRO operation) that white violence in the South was indeed a threat to the region's and the nation's internal security. The major turning point came with the disappearance of the three civil rights workers during the Mississippi Freedom Summer of 1964. The personal pique of President Lyndon B. Johnson also played an important role in shifting government policy to a more activist stance, as did the growing realization among leading Democrats that the nation's ideals as well as the party's strength in the urban Northeast and Midwest required a more confrontational stance against obstructionist southern leaders. It was also becoming apparent that average southern whites were in advance of many of their leaders on civil rights issues. With the assistance of the FBI, the Justice Department filed federal lawsuits under Section 241 against the alleged murderers of the civil rights workers and against the suspects in the murder of a U.S. army officer, Lemuel Penn, murdered as he traveled through Georgia (state prosecutions failed to return convictions). The charges were conspiracy rather than murder since murder was not then a federal crime. In 1966, the U.S. Supreme Court upheld the convictions in the *U.S.* v. *Guest* (the Penn case) and *U.S.* v. *Price* (the Mississippi case), thereby broadening the definition of Section 241. In the process, the Court invited Congress to write a new law specifying clearly the right of federal intervention in cases of anti-civil rights violence (including murder).

Belknap is at his best in describing the ultimate irony of federal intervention. The law, passed as Section 245 in 1968, went unused for more than a decade. What had happened between 1964 and 1968 was that white southerners became disenchanted with the continued violence and began to return convictions in civil rights-related cases. The basic fear, according to the author, was that persistent violence threatened law and order in the South and hurt the region's image at a time when southerners hoped to sustain and increase a new era of economic prosperity. So white southerners, not the federal government, were most responsible for quashing anti-civil rights violence. While Belknap is essentially correct in this assessment, fear of increased federal intervention and the growing political pressure and power of southern blacks played more of a role than the author acknowledges in turning southern opinion against unprovoked violence.

Belknap has researched his subject thoroughly, presents a complex argument with clarity, and makes a significant contribution to the growing body of scholarly analysis on the civil rights era. His book is a fine companion to Kenneth O'Reilly's study of the FBI's involvement in the civil rights movement, Tony Freyer's legal analysis of the Little Rock crisis, Steven F. Lawson's works on the Voting Rights Act, and Hugh David Graham's recent book on the federal government and the 1964 and 1965 Civil Rights Acts.

David R. Goldfield
University of North Carolina, Charlotte

Samuel R. Gross and Robert Mauro, *Death and Discrimination: Racial Disparities in Capital Sentencing*. Boston: Northeastern University Press, 1989. xvi & 268 pp. Tables, appendixes, notes, and index. $30.00.

In *Furman* v. *Georgia* (1972), the U.S. Supreme Court ruled all existing capital punishment laws unconstitutional, concluding that the methods of awarding death sentences were arbitrary and discriminatory. Some observers believed that an end to capital punishment was in sight. In *Gregg* v. *Georgia* (1976), however, the Court approved several new death penalty statutes that had been written to avoid the problems of arbitrariness and discrimination. *Death and Discrimination* is a study of these new laws in operation through 1980; as their title suggests, authors Samuel R. Gross (a law professor) and Robert Mauro (a psychologist) believe that the application of the death penalty continues to discriminate against blacks.

Their book has two main parts. The first reports the results of their large-scale study of capital sentencing in eight states during the period 1976–80. The three states with the most death sentences—Georgia, Florida, and Illinois—receive the most detailed attention. Only a tiny fraction of homicide cases—roughly one in one hundred—result in a death sentence. Gross and Mauor compare cases that produce death sentences with the larger population of homicide cases. They draw their data set from the Supplementary Homicide Reports (SHR) compiled by the FBI. The SHR lists characteristics of every homicide known to the FBI, including information about the offender, the victim, and the setting and circumstances of the crime.

The results of their research (which originally appeared in the *Stanford Law Review* in 1984) reveal the same pattern in all eight states: individuals convicted of killing whites are considerably more likely to receive the death penalty than individuals convicted of killing blacks. This pattern holds even after the introduction of several control variables, including the killer's race, the victim's sex, the location of the homicide (urban/rural), and three measures of aggravated circumstances (whether the killer and victim were strangers; whether the crime involved multiple homicides; and whether the killing occurred during the commission of a felony). When the variables are combined in multiple-regression analysis, the race of the victim continues to have a powerful effect: "the killing of a white victim increased the odds of a death sentence by an estimated factor of 4 in Illinois, about 5 in Florida, and about 7 in Georgia" (p. 69).

Of course, this finding is not what most people have in mind when they talk about discrimination and the death penalty. In general, Gross and Mauor's data do not support the common-sense assumption that black defendants are more likely to receive capital sentences than white defendants; other things being equal, white and black defendants were about equally likely to be sentenced to death under the post-*Furman* laws, but people who killed whites received markedly harsher treatment than those who killed blacks. In other words, the criminal justice system seems to value the lives of white victims more than those of black victims.

The book's second major section discusses the implications of the study's findings for the law of capital punishment. In particular, the authors trace the decisions of the lower federal courts and the Supreme Court in *McCleskey* v. *Kemp*. The *McCleskey* appeal presented evidence from a comparable, but even more detailed study of post-*Furman* capital sentencing in Georgia, which found that the defendant's race had a modest impact on capital sentences, while the victim's race had a far more pronounced effect. The courts rejected the *McCleskey* appeal. Gross and Mauro dissect and criticize the various opinions from the district court, the circuit court, and the Supreme Court. After *McCleskey*, they argue, "de facto racial discrimination in capital sentencing is legal in the United States" (p. 212).

Death and Discrimination presents what may be the best social scientific data and legal scholarship that can be marshaled against the contemporary system of capital punishment. The presentation of the results of the authors' study of capital sentencing in eight states is clear and persuasive; there can be little doubt that killings of white victims more often lead to death sentences. But the implications for social policy are less clear; here, some readers may disagree with the authors' conclusions. While the book has a narrow focus, historians of crime and criminal justice may benefit from the authors' detailed analysis of the issues during the most recent stage in capital punishment's evolution.

Joel Best
Southern Illinois University, Carbondale

Bert Useem and Peter Kimball, *States of Siege: U.S. Prison Riots, 1971–1986*. New York: Oxford University Press, 1989. vi & 278 pp. Illustrations, appendixes, notes, sources, and index. $29.95.

This book is the culmination of an intensive study of nine prison riots, including Attica (New York), Joliet (Illinois), and Santa Fe (New Mexico), in five states between 1970 and 1989. The authors open with a summary chapter on the history of prisons and riots between 1950 and 1975. This is followed with a chapter for each of the major prison riots mentioned above and two chapters covering a number of riots in the prisons of Michigan and West Virginia. The authors rely on the reports of official investigations of the riots as their primary source of information. In addition, extensive interviews with public officials, journalists, quasi-official observers, witnesses, and inmates expand the information found in the reports. As a result, this study emphasizes the details of the events from their preinception phase through their conclusion.

The authors place the prison riots in the context of the larger society and suggest that these are not chaotic, irrational, and isolated events occurring in penal institutions outside the social and political environment. Using the theoretical constructs of the sociology of collective behavior, combined with portions of social disorganization theory, particularly a combination of deprivation and breakdown theory, the authors argue that prison riots are complex and require more than the traditional protest or irrational behavior models to explain their occurrence. Prison riots are not spontaneous or inevitable, nor are they similar across time and region. Riots occur after a long period of development and take on a variety of dynamic characteristics.

According to the authors, riots occur in institutions "with a particular sort of pathology" that "saps the ability of the state" to respond, which in turn convinces the inmates that the "imprisoning conditions are unjust" (p. 218). For these authors riots are neither protests, political events, nor examples of irrational behavior. Each riot has its own characteristics and its own mix of complementary and contradictory elements. They contend, however, that riots occur when the breakdown of the state's ability to respond coincides with a perception by inmates of the state's illegitimacy. The breakdown generally is a result of weakened budgets, operational disorganization, and loss of control by prison administrators. These conditions result in violations of normative and legal standards of prison environments, and prisoners respond to that decay.

Although the authors do an admirable job in reminding us about the influence the external environment has on the prison, this obviously is the most difficult aspect of causality to prove. There is sound evidence to support the authors' conclusion that the urban gangs of the 1980s changed the demographics of the prison population, that the "revolution" in the law surrounding prison issues changed the nature of prison environments and prison administration, and that the fear of disorder resulted in a societal shift to longer sentences. Because the authors used only nine riots in five states and did not study similar prisons in other states that did not have riots, their conclusions cannot be generalized.

Historians will be intrigued by the coverage of the mid-twentieth century. There are ample examples of the shifting ideology regarding rehabilitation and the political conflicts of the 1960s, but the history of prisons and prison riots is sparse. Further, there is no discussion of prisons or prison riots prior to the 1950s, which limits the authors' ability to discuss the impact of social change on riots and weakens their conclusions about the variations they found in the 1970s and 1980s. In fairness to the authors there are a few studies of prison history available, yet that gap does affect the strength of their findings.

These comments, however, should not be construed to mean that this is not a study of important dimensions. This study is a sophisticated analysis of the details of prison riots that focuses on their causes, developments, variation, effect, and policy implications. This detailed analysis is then viewed through the lens of sociological theory around social change and collective behavior. The result is a thoroughly fascinating study of prisons and prison riots. The book will be useful in upper division and graduate courses. Researchers and policymakers will be challenged to think of public policy initiatives in these areas from a new foundation.

John A. Conley
SUNY College, Buffalo, N.Y.

Mick Ryan and Tony Ward, *Privatization and the Penal System: The American Experience and the Debate in Britain*. Milton Keynes: Open University Press, 1989. xiv & 120 pp. £8.99 paperback; £27.50 hardback.

The relationship between ideology and penalty is a subject of immense importance. In recent years the revisionist analyses of Michel Foucault, Michael Ignatieff, and David Garland concerning discourse, knowledge, and power in relation to penalty have led to profound and invigorating debate between revisionists and their critics about the historical direction of Western penal systems. Indeed, on a less theoretical level the subject is one of pressing interest and importance, for it can scarcely be doubted that a dominant ideology or theology will have concrete and swift consequences for the penal apparatus within its grasp. In early eighteenth-century England the ideological surge of justification of property rights at the expense of custom led to savage disposals of minor property infringers. In mid-nineteenth-century England a severe and disciplinary evangelical theology brought in its wake the separate cellular prison, a forcing house of atonement, reflection, and repentance.

Ryan and Ward have written a book which, in my view, is best discussed as a case study of the penetration of penality by ideology. It concerns the subject of privatization and penality in both the United States and Britain. The book consists of five chapters. Chapter 1 reminds us that privatization of penality is only a minute part of the program of privatization urged by the new Right, whose faith is placed in a deregulated free market and a minimal (albeit virile) state. For the service of this private enterprise will compete in a way that is cost-effective and allows maximum effective targeting and flexibility of method to the state. At once therefore we are into that fascinating project, the rewriting of history; for the new ideology must have it that the ancien regime of statist Beveridgean welfarism was doomed to extinction, like the dinosaur, cumbersome, inflexible, set in its ways, entrusted with lethargy, of minute intelligence, and sustained by monopolistic and vested interests.

The second chapter leads the reader through the complexity of North American privatization in the penal system and faces us with the issue of meaning. When we talk of penal privatization, do we mean prisons built and run for profit by private corporations who bill the state for each inmate? Do we merely mean supply of services to state-owned and -run prisons? Do we mean consortia of private companies and voluntary philanthropic groups establishing community-based programs of treatment? Do we mean private exploitation of prison labor for profit? This chapter is rich in detail about private American penal projects and graphically depicts the energy and potency of the privatizing corporations in the prosecution of their crusade.

The rest of the book is about British penality and begins with the question that is fundamental to so much of the history of this century of ideology. How does ideology pass from founding thesis to operational practice? The authors discuss the growth of think tank groups dedicated to the general propagation of privatization, in particular, the Adam Smith Institute set up in Virginia in 1978 and registered as a British Charity in 1981. The steps by which this body edged penal privatization onto the British political agenda through its contacts with the Conservative party are carefully described down to the point at which a Conservative-dominated select committee traveled to the United States to see things firsthand. Overcome with admiration for the Corrections Corporation of America, the report of the Conservative members (the Labour members refused to give assent to the report) unambiguously recommended that "the Home Office should . . . enable private sector companies to tender for the construction and management of custodial institutions" (Fourth Report Home Affairs Committee, p. vii). It might be added that the chair of this committee is now retired and spends his retirement acting out his enthusiasm as new chair of Contract Prisons Plc (U.S.).

At this point this reviewer has to pause in order to consider the ready market American penal ideologies find in Britain. What happens there today, as the authors remark, happens here tomorrow. So in the early 1830s the British government sent William Crawford to study the American prison system; he came back with the preposterous panacea of cellular confinement as a spiritual forcing house. Relics of his report litter the English penal system to this day. Again, at the turn of the nineteenth century exceedingly problematic notions of indeterminate sentences for reformatory purposes were imported (albeit tailored to younger offenders) from the United States after Prison Commission Chairman Sir Evelyn Ruggles-Brise went over to see the Elmira Reformatory scheme for himself. Now, with privatization the one-way traffic has begun again. Why is it always the Americans who must teach us about penal policy? Indeed, I would have thought at the present time that it would have been much more valuable to seek instruction from the European community if British statesmen and civil servants feel they must look elsewhere for inspiration.

In Chapter 4 the authors discuss private interests in the penal system historically in a way that is well enough informed albeit based on widely known printed sources. They are somewhat skeptical of those who warn of the danger of voracious and cruel Hogarthian turnkeys if private prisons return to Britain. Yet they themselves describe things that John Howard, the eighteenth-century prison explorer, would instantly have recognized—that, for example, in 1981 sixteen Colombians suspected of illegal immigration were incarcerated by Donner Incorporated in a single 12 foot by 20 foot cell for two days. Not unnaturally they tried to escape and one of them had to be shot dead for this.

This book should be widely read by penal theorists and practitioners. The book is far from being a one-sided polemic, but is a self-critical and very well informed work in which the authors conclude that there is an ethical problem with administering the hard end of punishment for profit motives. They do accept, however, the notion of partnership between public and private sectors to mount, say, schemes of community-based treatment. I believe they are profoundly right to be deeply worried about private joint stock companies getting hold of the heavy carceral side of the British penal business, yet I am not sure that they have convinced me that they, and I, are on the winning side in this.

Like Ryan and Ward, I believe that the shareholders' wealth will be the major consideration in the minds of the private company's directors. Like them, I also believe that manpower will be a very expensive item and will therefore be reduced in favor of coercive technologies and equipment. Like them, I believe that incarceration becomes tolerable only if human contact is emphasized, and that prison visits, football matches, and pumping iron in the gym are indispensable to prisons. Like them, I believe that privatizers will be exceedingly hard to hold accountable, and that Jeremy Bentham was particularly naive in that part of his propagation of private prisons that related to public accountability. In addition, I myself find it unacceptable that the peculiar prerogative of the monarch and the duty of Parliament in respect of direct care of prisoners should in any way be dissipated. In saying this, I, like Ryan and Ward, reiterate support and enthusiasm for partnership between private and public in all sorts of imaginative schemes and, like them, have no doubt that Foucault and Garland went much too far in their dismissal of penal welfarist interventions.

Those who oppose the private management of prisons are, however, on very weak ground if they merely defend the ancien regime so savaged by the new Left back in the 1960s and by Goffman and Foucault and all those right- and left-wing writers who turned on the old system of state monopolized penal corrections that had prevailed since 1810. The debate has to be developed a good deal further, and Ryan and Ward have done a public service in helping it forward. I have to say that, however, if I were a betting man, my money, despite every instinct in me, would at this moment be on the Corrections Corporation of America Plc and on all those sharp-eyed, smart young securicorps guards who have been so busy staffing prison ferries owned by Sealink, prison hulks for nonwhite suspected illegal immigrants.

Bill Forsythe
Exeter University

Richard O. Curry, ed., *Freedom at Risk: Secrecy, Censorship, and Repression in the 1980s*. Philadelphia: Temple University Press, 1988. xviii & 423 pp. $16.95 (paperback), $37.95 (cloth)

"An announcement about this book [should be sent] to all of the constitutional law professors in America," says Father Robert Drinan in a Temple University Press *Freedom at Risk* advertisement. Drinan's enthusiasm is shared in the same ad by renowned scholar James MacGregor Burns. Burns describes this anthology as a "wide-ranging treatment, both hard hitting and reasoned, of secrecy, censorship, and repression at the hands of the Reagan operatives." It encompasses, Burns concludes, a "stellar roster of experts" who dramatize "the vulnerabilities of the American creed of freedom on many fronts." Drinan's and Burn's praise for this anthology is more than seconded by several faculty members whom Temple University Press quotes as strongly advocating its course adoption. Karl Valois of the University of Connecticut at Torrington reports, for example, that Curry's collection has been "a resounding success" in his American history survey courses. And Joanna Cowden of California State University at Chico advises that any teacher "who wishes to engage the hearts and minds of students and to kindle classroom discourse on contemporary issues should assign this book."

Well aware that *Freedom at Risk* has stimulated such responses—and that it has won awards from the Free Press Association and the Gustavius Myers Center for the Study of Human Rights in the United States—I must respectfully dissent. A massive portion of this volume is written in a Good Guys-Bad Guys style. It is suffused with a liberal bias that serves as a major obstacle to its objectively treating the serious and far-reaching public policy issues it addresses. Some of its chapters are deficient from the perspective of the criteria of acceptable scholarship.

Curry and his contributors focus on a number of freedom of expression and privacy issues that deserve the most careful attention. What impact has the Reagan administration had on the free flow of academic information? What has it done to the Freedom of Information Act? How has it attempted to exclude controversial foreign speakers under the McCarran–Walter Act? Has it and the federal courts made progress in imposing a new law of seditious libel on the American people? Has the Reagan "war on drugs," and the concomitant campaigns of public agencies and private corporations, led to a new era of repression? How has the federal government employed disinformation against the public? To what extent has a politicized Federal Bureau of Investigation posed a serious danger to civil rights and liberties? Is the U.S. government inflicting outright conspiracy trials on those who dare to challenge its policies? Have libel laws been carried so far that they are muzzling the media? What have been the effects of Reagan's efforts to secure a conservative judiciary?

All of these issues suggest strongly that, as always, serious threats exist to American freedom. On many of the questions presented, I would no doubt share the writers' policy suggestions. But I have the strongest reservations about how they reach them.

Of the twenty-five chapters in this volume, there are only four that I would consider first-rate contributions to modern free expression and privacy commentary. These include Thomas I. Emerson's "The State of the First Amendment as We Enter '1984,' " Nat Hentoff's "Presumption of Guilt," Athan Theoharis's "Conservative Politics and Surveillance: The Cold War, the Reagan Administration, and the FBI," and Geoffrey R. Stone's "The Reagan Administration, the First Amendment, and FBI Domestic Security Investigations."

The rest contain so much axe-grinding, or so many assertions without properly cited evidence, or so much unnecessary duplication from one to another, that their direct usefulness in the classroom, without a large amount of supplementary material, would be highly questionable.

In concluding, I mention one more problem. *Freedom at Risk* is surely useful as a sometimes insightful and suggestive, although highly biased, initial probing into the implications for civil rights and liberties of many of the policies and actions of the Reagan administration. But to extend it into the college setting as a text that offers a clear picture of what is currently happening under the Bush administration is indefensible. Far too many of *Freedom at Risk*'s chapters have a time warp quality. They devote numerous pages to policies that might or might not be adopted. They too often leave the reader in the midst of the alleged minute pending details of a controversy. There would thus appear to be no way for an instructor to use them effectively, and fairly, without updating them substantially.

Dennis R. Dorin
University of North Carolina, Charlotte

Index

Contributors

Joel Best is professor of sociology at Southern Illinois University, Carbondale. His recent publications include *Threatened Children: Rhetoric and Concern about Child Victims* and *Images of Issues: Typifying Contemporary Problems* (New York, 1989).

John A. Conley is professor of history and chair of the criminal justice department at the State University of New York College at Buffalo. He has given many scholarly papers on crime and policing in European conferences, and has published widely on the history of prisons and police in the United States.

Dee Cook is lecturer in criminology at the Centre for Criminology, University of Keele, England. She is the recent author of *Rich Law, Poor Law* (Milton Keynes, 1989), a study of social welfare fraud, and is currently researching white-collar crime and business fraud.

Dennis R. Dorin is professor of political science at the University of North Carolina at Charlotte. He has authored more than seventy articles and essays on the judicial process.

David Englander is a lecturer in European humanities studies in the department of history, The Open University, Milton Keynes, England. His major publications include *Landlord and Tenant in Urban Britain 1838–1918* (Oxford, 1983) and *Culture and Belief in Europe 1450–1600* (Oxford, 1990). He has completed a study of public order in Britain during World War I, and is currently writing a reassessment of Charles Booth's *Life and Labour of the People of London.*

Bill Forsythe is a lecturer in social work at Exeter University, England. Having worked for ten years with the British Probation Service at both field and senior levels, his articles on British prison discipline include "A System of Discipline: Exeter Borough Prison 1819–1863," "The Reform of Prisons 1830–1900," and "Penal Discipline, Reformatory Projects and the English Prison Commission 1895–1939."

David R. Goldfield is the Robert Lee Bailey Professor of History at the University of North Carolina at Charlotte. Among his books are *Cotton Fields and Skyscrapers: Southern City and Region* (1982) and *Black, White, and Southern: Race Relations and Southern Culture* (1990). He has written or co-authored several other books in the field of southern history, and serves as a consultant to museums and historical societies in the South.

Carole Haber is associate professor of history at the University of North Carolina at Charlotte. She is the author of *Beyond Sixty-Five: The Dilemma of Old Age in America* (Cambridge, 1983), and—with Brian Gratton—a study of the social history of old age in America that is currently in press.

Eric A. Johnson is professor of history at Central Michigan University, Mount Pleasant. He wrote "Women as Victims and Criminals: Female Homicide and Criminality in Imperial Germany, 1873–1914" *CJH* 6 (1985). He has recently edited *Quantification and Criminal Justice History in International Perspective*, a special volume of *Historical Social Research/Historische Sozialforschung 4* (Cologne, 1990).

David J. McCreery is associate professor of history at Georgia State University. A specialist in Latin American history, he is the author of *Desarollo Economico y Politica National: El Ministerio de Pomento de Guatemala, 1871–1885* (1981).

Wilbur R. Miller is associate professor of history at the State University of New York, Stony Brook. A historian of American policing, he is the author of *Cops and Bobbies: Police Authority in New York and London* (Chicago, 1977), and a forthcoming book, *Revenuers and Moonshiners: Enforcing Federal Liquor Laws in the Mountain South, 1865–1900.*

Douglas M. Peers is assistant professor of history at the University of Calgary, Alberta, Canada. Recent articles on war and finance in late eighteenth- and early nineteenth-century British India have appeared in *International History Review* 11 (1989), *Historical Journal* 33 (1990), *International History Review* 12 (1990), and *Modern Asian Studies* (1991). His current research interests include a comparative study of the types of legal systems employed in the European and Sepoy armies.

Andrew Scobell is a doctoral candidate in the department of political science, Columbia University, New York. His previous work in this area has appeared in articles published recently in *Case Reserve Journal of International Law* (1988), *Asian Survey* (1988), and *China Quarterly* (1990).

Haia Shpayer-Makov, lecturer in history at the University of Haifa, Israel, has written "The Reception of Peter Kropotkin in Britain, 1886–1917," *Albion* (1987); "Anarchism in British Public Opinion, 1880–1914," *Victorian Studies* (1988); and "The Making of a Police Labour Force," *Journal of Social History*. His current research involves the London Metropolitan Police.

Russell C. Smandych is assistant professor of sociology at the University of Manitoba, Winnipeg, Canada. He is the co-author of *Canadian Criminal Justice History: An Annotated Bibliography* (Toronto, 1987), and has published articles on the history of Canadian anti-combines legislation and the Upper Canadian poor law. Current research is the study of comparative criminology, and co-editing a collection of essays on the history of children and youth in Canada.

Jonathan Swainger is currently a lecturer in Canadian history at the Terrace campus of the University of Northern British Columbia. He has written on the business activities of the legal profession in Alberta, and is currently writing articles on the Quebec judiciary, criminal law in central Alberta, and capital crimes in late nineteenth-century British Columbia.

David Taylor is senior lecturer in history at Teesside Polytechnic, Middlesbrough, England. He has recently published "The Antipodean Arrest: Or How to Be a Successful Policeman in Nineteenth-Century Middlesbrough," *Cleveland & Teesside Local History Society Bulletin* (1990); and "Crime and Policing in Early Victorian Middlesbrough, 1835–55," *Journal of Regional and Local Studies* (1991). He is currently continuing a study of crime and policing in nineteenth-century Britain.

Joseph L. Tropea is associate professor of sociology at George Washington University, Washington, D.C. Recent publications include histories of special school populations, nineteenth-century transformations in municipal administration, and comparative organizational work on state institutions. His current research interests include rule regime transformations in the making of capitalist societies and changes in Central Europe.

Robert G. Waite is a Washington, D.C. based historian who specializes in the history of American prisons, and crime and law enforcement in twentieth-century Germany.

John Weaver is professor of history at McMaster University, Hamilton, Ontario, Canada. His work on Hamilton and urban Canadian history includes *Hamilton: An Illustrated History* (1982) and *Shaping the Canadian City: Essays on Urban Politics and Society, 1890–1920* (1983).

Notes on submissions:

The general rule guiding authors and editors is that submissions should follow as closely as possible the formats of the most recent publication. Therefore, the previous volume of *Criminal Justice History* should be consulted for guidance. The basic format used is the University of Chicago Manual of Style.

Editorial correspondence and submissions:

Professor Louis Knafla
Department of History
University of Calgary
Calgary, Alberta
Canada T2N 1N4

Books for review, proposals to review, and reviewer registrations should be sent to the appropriate review editor:

U.S.A. and Canada

Professor Julia Kirk Blackwelder
Department of History
University of North Carolina
Charlotte, NC 28223
U.S.A.

Other areas and transnational:

Professor Clive Emsley
European Centre for Policing
The Open University
Milton Keynes MK7 6AA
England